YALE ROMANTIC STUDIES: 2D SERIES, 21

ᘓ POETIC PATTERNS IN RUTEBEUF: A STUDY

IN NONCOURTLY POETIC MODES
OF THE THIRTEENTH CENTURY:
:BY NANCY FREEMAN REGALADO

YALE UNIVERSITY PRESS, 1970
NEW HAVEN AND LONDON ᘓ

LIBRARY OF CONGRESS CATALOG CARD NUMBER: 70-104620
ISBN: 300-01218-7
DESIGNED BY SALLY SULLIVAN,
SET IN LINOTYPE GRANJON TYPE,
AND PRINTED IN THE UNITED STATES OF AMERICA BY
VAIL-BALLOU PRESS, INC., BINGHAMTON, N. Y.
DISTRIBUTED IN GREAT BRITAIN, EUROPE, ASIA, AND
AFRICA BY YALE UNIVERSITY PRESS LTD., LONDON; IN
CANADA BY McGILL-QUEEN'S UNIVERSITY PRESS, MONTREAL; AND
IN MEXICO BY CENTRO INTERAMERICANO DE LIBROS
ACADÉMICOS, MEXICO CITY.

TO ANTONIO

ACKNOWLEDGMENTS

"Au besoing voit on l'ami" says the medieval proverb, and I owe much to friends who met in various ways my needs while I was writing this book. Professor Howard Garey of Yale offered unstintingly of his patience, time, and knowledge in overseeing the composition of the manuscript. To Professor Daniel Poirion of the University of Grenoble, I owe a special debt, since he launched me into medieval studies and kindly consented to read and offer very helpful suggestions for the revision of the completed manuscript. Professors Henri Peyre, Victor Brombert, and Kenneth Cornell of Yale and Erich Köhler of Heidelberg also read my manuscript and offered valuable comments as well as their warm encouragement. I am particularly grateful to Professor Eugene Vance of the University of Montreal who added many useful commentaries after reading Chapter 4. Conversations with Professors Paul Zumthor of Amsterdam, Robert Lopez of Yale and with fellow students William McNaughton, Robert Somerville, and Stephen Nichols contributed a great deal toward the forming of many ideas expressed here. I am greatly indebted to friends for generous help with readings in Latin, German, and Italian—Arnold Kerson, James McIntosh, Alex Gelley, Jonathan Conant, Joachim Herchenbach, Edgar Pauk—as well as to Yvonne Tucker, Nancy Thompson, and John Coleman who read and commented on parts of my text. All the staff of the Yale library, and particularly Mrs. Margaret Coons of the Interlibrary Loan Department, helped me countless times and with great patience. A sabbatical semester from Wesleyan University was of much help in freeing time for revising my manuscript. Finally I owe much to my mother and my husband's family who helped me at many points along the way. Discussions with my husband led me to new intellectual horizons, enabling me to greatly enlarge the scope of this book and it is with gratitude for such new perspectives that I affectionately dedicate this book to him.

CONTENTS

INTRODUCTION

What we know about Rutebeuf may be quickly said: author of 56 extant pieces written from 1248 to approximately 1277, he was perhaps originally from Champagne, but lived most of his life in Paris. Yet those who have written about Rutebeuf have discovered such a unique and attractive poetic personality within his few dozen poems that they have returned to him again and again.

The most recent edition of Rutebeuf's poetry, by Edmond Faral and Julia Bastin[1] is, in part, the sum of almost half a century of work by Faral on the historical, linguistic, and literary problems posed by Rutebeuf's poetry. Their edition is a masterpiece of scholarly research into the historical setting of each of Rutebeuf's works, as well as a scrupulous edition of the texts according to all the known manuscripts. My indebtedness to their careful dating, to their exact readings of each text, and to the wealth of references they provide to primary sources in thirteenth-century history and literature in their *Introduction, Notices,* and notes is incalculable. Every student of Rutebeuf will find, as I did, that his task is greatly eased by the work of Faral and Bastin and their edition is the indispensable and greater complement to the commentary on Rutebeuf's poetry I offer here.

There is not a large body of criticism of Rutebeuf's poetry, although there are many editions of individual poems. The earliest reference to Rutebeuf appears in Claude Fauchet's "Des anciens poètes françois" (1581); the seventeenth-century Jansenist historian, Le Nain de Tillemont, alludes to Rutebeuf in his *Vie de saint Louis* as a poet "aussi peu honneste que les autres de ce temps-là" (5, 207). Jubinal's edition in 1839 made Rutebeuf's complete works available

---

1. *Oeuvres complètes,* ed. Edmond Faral and Julia Bastin, 2 vols. (Fondation Singer-Polignac, Paris: Editions A. et J. Picard et Cie., 1959–60) hereafter referred to as FB.

to the public for the first time. His edition was followed by Paulin Paris's article on the poet in the *Histoire littéraire* (*20, 719–83*) of 1849, by Adolf Kressner's edition in 1885, and by Léon Clédat's general introduction, *Rutebeuf* (1909). While nineteenth and early twentieth-century criticism of Rutebeuf tended toward a linguistic or historical approach, more recent critics such as Ulrich Leo, Albert Junker, and Edward Billings Ham began to pay more attention to Rutebeuf's poetic technique. Gustave Cohen's Sorbonne production of the *Miracle de Théophile* in 1933 contributed to a renewal of interest in Rutebeuf as dramatist, as did the 1925 edition of the play by Grace Frank. The recent volume *Rutebeuf,* in the collection "Ecrivains d'hier et d'aujourd'hui (24)," by my former Wellesley professor Germaine Lafeuille, provides pictures and background material for the author's time, a choice of lightly modernized texts, bibliography, and a useful introduction to Rutebeuf, superseding Clédat.

The commentaries of many recent critics have been misleading, I feel, in that they try to dig out and identify ideas and sentiments in Rutebeuf's poetry, believing that these express the poet's own convictions. They use modern notions of "sincerity" and "originality" for their appraisal of Rutebeuf's art, which, I believe, can be better studied through its determining links with a particular public and a particular literary tradition. Rutebeuf's is not a work lending itself to any deduction of a coherent ideology; there are so many contradictory points of view that Ham even proposed attributing "Rutebeuf's" works to several authors.[2] Could Rutebeuf, enemy of the Mendicant friars, have supported the Crusades preached by these same monks? Could the moralizing poet who spoke out against the "plaies du monde" be the same who punned on his own weakness for dice? Just what is the mixture of literature and what Leo calls "real reality" in the "personal poetry" of Rutebeuf?

I have discussed the variety of critical suppositions about

2. Ham, Edward B., ed. *Renart le Bestorné,* (April 1947), 39–49; see p. 279, n. 22.

Rutebeuf's "opinions" and the degree of "truth" in each text in connection with his Crusade poems, the University polemic and his poems of misfortune.[3] In every case, the best explanation of the works can only emerge from the identification of Rutebeuf's public and by the works themselves, by the conventions of each genre, its motifs, its characteristic ideas and vocabulary, not from hypotheses about Rutebeuf's possible personal opinions or habits. Since Rutebeuf is a medieval poet deeply rooted in a milieu and an epoch, it is the cultural pattern, what Fustel de Coulanges calls *croyance,* the accumulated assumptions, beliefs, and practices of the age which we must see in order to understand how Rutebeuf wrote, and why he wrote as he did. The poetic patterns in Rutebeuf which I have described in this study are not only the secrets of poetic technique within his work. They are also the web of relations linking the poet to his public, and Rutebeuf's poetry to the artistic conceptions of his time. Patterns are, then, both cultural and formal structures. The poet writes poems within those genres which please his public, and genres are preexisting patterns of theme, form, and vocabulary which assure communication with his public. Such patterns provide models and matter for expression without completely determining what the poet will say.

The notion of patterns of thought or of literary expression in no way contradicts the notion of meaning or art. Patterns indicate the general significance to be attributed to the death of a prince, to avaricious behavior, to love or poverty. They provide a mold, an armature for the expression of particular ideas or feelings: the *complainte* speaks of grief, the *chanson* of love. Yet the vocabulary, the themes, or the larger units of *motif* and *registre* defined by Zumthor in his *Langue et technique poétiques à l'époque romane,*[4] provide only patterns, and the poet must constantly choose how to fill the space laid out for him by literary, intellectual, moral, or theological traditions. But the medieval poet did not seek to be "original" in our modern sense. The search for "origins," for the

3. See Ch. 1, p. 43, n. 77, Ch. 2, p. 72, pp. 77–79, 106; Ch. 5, nn. 1 and 2.
4. (Paris, 1963), Ch. 3.

first texts, created *ex nihilo* and which launch each genre, pursued
by so many critics, misses the true nature of medieval creativity,
which is a perpetual renewal of preexisting structures. The constant
reuse and changing of poetic forms and themes in the middle ages
has been admirably described by C. S. Lewis, in his "Genesis of a
Medieval Book," [5] as an astonishingly vital and adaptable creative
process. Dragonetti, too, in the "Essai d'interprétation" which concludes his vast study of *La Technique poétique des trouvères dans
la chanson courtoise,* emphasizes that far from attempting to escape
his "cultural memory" the medieval poet finds within topics and
tradition the dynamic spark inspiring both the poet and his
public. [6] Poetic patterns are never static nor confining for the medieval poet.

Medieval poetry is, therefore, not a depersonalized art, but an
art in which the personal, the incidental, and the exceptional are
not left to stand alone nor sought out, as in our time, but one in
which the poem reveals a preestablished whole, an inherited pattern into which every incident fits. The particular enters into
literature only as part of some larger pattern, and it is this larger
pattern which explains and justifies the individual person or event.
The poet does not attempt to create a work out of his own life, his
own opinion. The poet's representation of a self can only enter the
poem within certain set contexts, and the opinions he expresses will
probably be those of some group rather than his own. Rutebeuf's
polemical verse, for example, uses terms and themes deriving from
a general satirical tradition to explain particular events within the
University of Paris. The poet does not want to represent his personal convictions in these poems, but rather to incorporate a factional interest into a moral structure agreed on by all.

Although medieval poets wrote within traditional forms, they

5. In his *Studies in Medieval and Renaissance Literature,* ed. Walter Hooper
(Cambridge, England, 1966); see especially pp. 36–40.
6. Bruges, 1960; see pp. 539 ff. I have been greatly helped by similar studies
defining the essential structure of different genres: Per Nykrog's *Les Fabliaux*
(Copenhagen, 1957), and Marcel Batallion's introduction to his edition of *Lazarillo
de Tormes* (Paris, 1958).

did not, in the thirteenth century, exclude the present and the immediate. On the contrary, the present was pushed explicitly into poetry, in part because it could be made to appear sublime, heroic, exemplary, as in Rutebeuf's noble Crusade poems. Those poems gave no hint of dissent or defeat, but painted the Holy Wars as a great adventure, a hero's way to Paradise. In the same way Joinville's portrait of his king eliminated the opaqueness and defects of the man; the king's historical being was structured to form the portrait of a saint. Didactic literature, too, like Rutebeuf's Crusade, University, and estates poems, drew more and more heavily upon *exempla* of current events which gave force and immediacy to the moral topics. Rutebeuf's works must also be seen as sharing the thirteenth-century gift for warming traditional figuration with the breath of vital experience. The ox and the ass, for example, had long been traditional figures of the Nativity; in the thirteenth-century Chartres jubé the animals are present, tasting the hay in the manger, a touch corresponding to no traditional concept, but only to the artist's wish to make his figures credible, natural. Thus, once we have made the effort to replace ourselves in Rutebeuf's time, to see how a poet sets about writing a poem, we can better proceed to see why Rutebeuf chose certain forms and just how he imprinted his individual touch on the patterns.

The matter and form of Rutebeuf's work owes much to his public. Medieval poets wrote within fashionable genres, and professionals wrote saleable works. Holzknecht's contention that medieval authors could not make a living from writing is not borne out by evidence, gathered by Faral, that many *jongleurs* and *ménestrels* survived and even prospered on their earnings.[7] The poet's relation to his public was also far more direct, less mediated, than in our time when books, publishers, printers, and libraries intervene. Even when the medieval poet attempted to influence or

---

7. Karl Julius Holzknecht, *Literary patronage in the Middle Ages* (Philadelphia, 1923) p. 236; Faral, *Les jongleurs en France au Moyen Age* (Paris, 1964), Ch. 5, "Les Revenus des jongleurs," Ch. 6, "Les Corporations et les confréries," and Rutebeuf's own *Charlot le Juif et la peau de lièvre,* vv. 39–69.

to reform his public, he was highly responsive to their tastes and interests.

Who, then, were Rutebeuf's patrons, and what was his public? He is not associated with any one group alone, nor with one court, nor even with any single patron or type of public. Rutebeuf lived, a free agent, in Paris, and wrote for several men and for different groups, adopting, as we will see, the points of view of his different patrons.

Only a description of Rutebeuf's public can explain why Rutebeuf is, in many ways, an exceptional figure in thirteenth-century French literature.[8] He wrote in an extraordinarily large number of genres: two saint's lives, a miracle narrative, a miracle play, a mime, fabliaux, satires, didactic works, and the striking group of poems of misfortune where the poet paints himself as a poor fool. Rutebeuf seems to have touched every genre except precisely those genres most cultivated in his time in the provincial courts and literary centers; he wrote no epics, no romances, no courtly *chansons*. Only four of his works are songs (FB, I, 211), while the works of his great immediate predecessors and contemporaries—Thibaut IV de Champagne, Colin Muset, and Adam de la Halle—are almost entirely lyric. Adam, indeed, was the great musician of his day, "parfais en chanter" according to the *Jeu du pèlerin,* prologue to Adam's *Robin et Marion.*

The typical thirteenth-century public, whether courtly, urban, or monastic, expected all but comic poetry to have an uplifting intent, a moral object, although courtly works were aimed toward refinement of sentiments profoundly different from those approved by the Church, while noncourtly works often hid political propaganda behind moralization. Also almost all thirteenth-century serious poetry, both lyric and non-lyric, borrowed many of its rhetorical concepts and poetic techniques from the Latin tradition of oratorical eloquence, as Dragonetti and Faral have shown.[9] Form was seen as a

8. FB I, 32–64, "L'Auteur," provides detailed information enabling the editors to conjecture what Rutebeuf's origins were, what education he had received, and indicate his place among polemical writers of his time.

9. See Dragonetti's *Technique poétique des trouvères dans la chanson courtoise*

powerful means of persuasion, but Rutebeuf's objects are both more wide-ranging and more immediate than the courtly lover's plea for his lady's favor. Advocate of repentance, of the Crusades, of the secular university masters, of his own pocket, Rutebeuf often resembles the preacher or the lawyer in whom formal expertise exists for polemical or practical ends and not essentially as an end in itself, as for the courtly poet. The important difference between a courtly public and Rutebeuf's heterogeneous urban public lies finally in the poetic ear of each. The courtly milieu provided the poet with a trained public, attuned to formal perfection in a few genres. Rutebeuf's public was as interested in what a poem said as in its form, and appreciated a wide range of topics and viewpoints.

We have only a few more poems attributed to the aristocratic Thibaut de Champagne (1201–1253) than to Rutebeuf, although Thibaut's fame and position more surely guaranteed survival to his works than to those of Rutebeuf, who is not mentioned by any contemporary. But Thibaut deviated from the courtly love matter of his *chansons* and *jeux-partis* only to write a few Crusade songs, some honoring the Virgin, and one religious *serventois* of a moralizing satirical nature against clerical abuse. The tone and style of all his works is elevated in tone except in the somewhat lighter *débats* and *pastourelles*. Of course, Thibaut wrote for a public particularly skilled in courtly forms. Champagne had been a literary center since the latter part of the twelfth century when the great trouvères—Conon de Béthune, Gace Brulé, Chrétien de Troyes—contributed to the enchantment of a few decades there.[10]

While in the twelfth and fourteenth centuries a great many poets lived at courts, in the thirteenth we can name but a few, such as Thibaut, Adenet le Roi, a professional raised at the court of Henri III, Duke of Brabant, and Adam de la Halle who ended his days serving Robert II d'Artois with Charles d'Anjou in the ill-starred kingdom of Naples. The feudal nobles had been impoverished by

---

(Bruges, 1960) and Edmond Faral, *Arts Poétiques du XIIe et du XIIIe siècle* (Paris, 1923).

10. See John F. Benton, "The Court of Champagne as a Literary Center," *Speculum, 36,* No. 4 (October 1961) pp. 551–91.

the Crusades; Guiot de Provins laments in his Bible (1206) the death of eighty-six princely patrons *outremer* (vv. 282–485). The lavishness of the first years of Northern courtly fashion was reduced to a trickle before the mid-thirteenth century and Rutebeuf's time.

The royal court, moreover, which had its principal seat in Paris, had never been a center of literary patronage,[11] and Louis IX, like his predecessors, was not inclined to offer more than courteous tolerance to the "menestrier aus riches homes" whom Joinville tells us came to his table.[12] The king's modest *cote de chamelot* and watered wine proved his indifference to this world, and a debate to pass a joyous hour at Louis' court was more apt to turn on the qualities of a *preudhom* than on whether ladies are best loved for their virtue or their beauty, as at Thibaut's.[13] Joinville's words are confirmed by contemporary popular panegyrics of St. Louis:

> Quant Saint Loïs chanter vouloit,
> De Dieu ou de sa mère chantoit;
> Ne fust chançon nule chantée
> Du siècle; mès de Notre-Dame
> Povoit chanter et homme et femme.[14]

Alphonse de Poitiers, like his brother Louis IX, was a pious and economic ruler, but he was frail and lived mostly in Paris. Princely in his liberality on occasion,[15] he was not courtly in the narrower sense, that is, he was little given to feasts, rich clothing, and expensive leisure-time entertainments of the sort provided by courtly *menestrels*.

Few nobles outside the royal family chose to live in Paris, prefer-

11. See Bezzola, *Les Origines et la formation de la littérature courtoise en Occident (500–1200)*, (Paris, 1944–67) 1ère partie, pp. 301 ff., 3ème partie, 2, 349–65.

12. Joinville, *Vie de saint Louis*, ed. Natalis de Wailly, 2d ed. (Paris, 1874), p. 368.

13. Joinville, *Saint Louis*, ed. Natalis de Wailly, pp. 12, 16–18, 366–68. Thibaut de Champagne, *Oeuvres*, ed. A. Wallensköld (Paris, 1925), *Jeu-parti, 38*, p. 23.

14. Achille Jubinal, *Nouveau Receuil de contes, dits, fabliaux* . . . (Paris, 1839), 2, 201.

15. Joinville, *Saint Louis*, tells how Alphonse would distribute his winnings or the amount of his losses after a game of dice, p. 228. See Runciman's portrait of Alphonse in his *Sicilian Vespers* (Baltimore, 1960), pp. 87–88.

ring, perhaps of necessity, to move from domain to domain, to con-
sume their revenues in kind.[16] Colin Muset (fl. c. 1230–1250?) chose
this wandering aristocratic public for his own, unlike Rutebeuf who
seems to have remained almost all his life in Paris and its environs.
No aristocratic amateur, Colin Muset was a professional who wrote
to please a courtly public, although he sang more willingly of the
bone vie than of *fine amors*. He led a life typical of the travelling
jongleur, wandering from court to castle in Champagne and along
the Lorraine frontier, often fatigued "de chevauchier toz bo[o]us/
Après mauvais prince angoissous" always hoping to find the ideal
patron, "large, qui ne vousist conter." [17]

For the most part, however, poets of mid-thirteenth-century
France turned to cities like Arras or Paris where a nonaristocratic
public provided them with a living. Yet the *Société de jongleurs et
bourgeois* and the *Puy* of Arras, for whom Adam de la Halle
(d. 1286?) first wrote, cultivated the courtly genres assiduously, in
imitation of the aristocratic courts, and only occasionally admitted
a vulgar chuckle in some satirical pieces or in works like Adam's
Jeu de la Feuillée. But Pirenne tells us that Paris did not have a
wealthy leisure class of financiers like those of Arras, to patronize
such a courtly-style society.[18] The Parisian population of the thirteenth century was composed largely of merchants, local tradesmen,
churchmen, students, teachers, and royal administrators, few of
whom had the taste, training, or leisure for the refined courtly
chanson and *jeux-partis*. Didactic, comic and satirical works were
more to their liking as well as works written to flatter new urban
groups like the *Dits des marchéans* by "Phelippot," and the anonymous *Dits des .II. changeors, des boulangers* and *des paintres*.[19]

Although no documents remain proving payment to Rutebeuf by
anyone, the whole group of poems about the University quarrel

16. Henri Pirenne, *Medieval Cities*, trans. F. D. Halsey (New York, 1925), pp.
130–31.

17. *Chansons*, ed. Joseph Bédier (Paris: CFMA, 1938), *14*, vv. 16–17, 4.

18. *Economic and Social History of Medieval Europe* (New York, 1937), 1, 128–29,
152–53.

19. Edited respectively in Montaiglon and Raynaud, eds., *Recueil général des fabliaux* (Paris, 1872–90), 2, 123–29; ibid., *1*, 245–54; Achille Jubinal, ed., *Jongleurs
et trouvères* (Paris, 1835), 138–42; Achille Jubinal, ed., *Nouveau Recueil*, 2, 96–101.

were surely written to please or were commissioned by the faction of secular masters; it seems Rutebeuf obtained political ammunition for his polemical writings from the masters themselves.[20] Guillaume de Saint-Amour himself, leader of the masters of Theology, could not have been Rutebeuf's sole patron, although he is the central figure in the polemic, since the poet continued to write works favoring the University cause long after Guillaume had been exiled from Paris. The University masters could scarcely have been munificent patrons, since they had to take up a collection among themselves in order to pay the way for their delegation to Rome in 1254 (FB, I, 72). Rutebeuf's kindly verses on Parisian students in the *Dit de l'Université* and *Les Plaies du monde* (vv. 37-39, 89-104) are unlike the diatribes of other moralists, and suggest that not only the University masters but the student population furnished pay and public to the poet.

Works like the *Miracle de Théophile, La Voie de Paradis,* and *La Vie de sainte Marie l'Egyptienne* must have also been written to order, (See FB, I, 337; II, 13-16) since the two works which Rutebeuf does explicitly state were written on commission are the same sort of pious yet elegant pieces. His *Miracle du sacristain et de la femme au chevalier* was ordered by a certain Benoit, probably a member of the higher clergy (FB, II, 205-06); his *Vie de sainte Elysabel* was commissioned by Erart de Lézinnes of Champagne, for Isabelle, daughter of Saint Louis, and wife of Thibaut V of Champagne (FB, I, 36 and II, 60).

Other poems explicitly requested money, payment, or protection, like Rutebeuf's epigrammatic *De Brichemer,* his *Complainte* and *Pauvreté Rutebeuf,* and his moralizing *Dit d'Aristote* and *Paix Rutebeuf* as well. Yet of all the "bone gent" Rutebeuf addressed in his Crusade poems and his poems of misfortune, he specifically thanked for his patronage only Alphonse de Poitiers in his *Complainte Rutebeuf* (vv. 158-165) and his *Complainte de comte de Poitiers* (vv. 37-8).

20. See FB *1, Notices* and notes to Section I, "L'Eglise, les ordres mendiants et l'Université."

Rutebeuf's eulogies were perhaps written to elicit payment or at the request of bereaved families. But all of Rutebeuf's eulogies and panegyric pieces, except that for Anceau de l'Isle, are directly connected with the propaganda campaign on behalf of the Crusades and were probably paid for by an ecclesiastical Crusade promoter such as the papal legate Simon, (FB, I, 84–93) or Erart de Lézinnes himself (FB, I, 432) who could also have ordered Rutebeuf's other Crusade poems.[21] To judge by these names and others cited in Rutebeuf's crusade exhortations—Geoffroi de Sergines, Erart de Valery, Robert II d'Artois, Henri II of Champagne, Charles d'Anjou, and Louis IX as well as Louis's sons Philippe and Jean Tristan—Rutebeuf seems to have looked for payment principally to members of the houses of Champagne and France, although mostly in connection with the Crusade effort. Rutebeuf wrote, however, more often of disappointed expectations than of gratitude to his few benefactors.[22]

Finally, Paris itself was the essential and nurturing environment of Rutebeuf's poetry.[23] Unattached to any single group, to any one patron, he was free to hawk his talents where he could in the city, and was thereby freed from the intellectual dictates of court, *puy,* or monastery, free to write for diverse audiences and within many genres. Rutebeuf's varied themes—comedy, politics, piety, and poverty—pleased this vast public for whom courtly love had little appeal.

While a courtly poet would write much the same sort of verse in Arras, Champagne, or Blois, Rutebeuf's poetry is steeped in a Parisian atmosphere. In his *Ordres de Paris,* the poet describes each religious house according to its geographical location within Paris, ironically noting the richly shining rooftops of the new buildings of the Trinity friars, who were dedicated to poverty, the convenient proximity of the austere Carmelite monks to the Béguines (FB, I,

21. See notices to FB, I, "Les Croisades", and Ch. I, 4, esp. n. 82.

22. See *La Pauvreté Rutebeuf,* vv. 13–24, *Voie de Tunes,* St. XVII, *Renart le Bestourné,* vv. 55–63, *De Brichemer.*

23. See my "Two Poets of the Medieval City: Rutebeuf and Villon," *Yale French Studies,* "Paris in Literature", *32* (Oct. 1964), 12–21.

321–22). Rutebeuf describes the increasing powers of the Mendicant friars as an invasion of the city:

> Sont seignor de Paris en France,
> Si ont ja la cité porprise.
> Diex gart Paris de mescheance
> Et la gart de fausse creance,
> Qu'ele n'a garde d'estre prise. (vv. 20–24)

He looks out at the end of the poem to see even the Carthusians drawing close to "la bone vile" (v. 147).

The city itself becomes a theme in the *Ordres de Paris* as in anonymous works like *Les Rues, Les Crieries,* and *Les Moutiers de Paris*,[24] inspired by the same thirteenth-century urban taste for self-portrayal evident in the satirical pieces and plays from Arras. Rutebeuf evokes the excitement of the city streets in his *Dit de l'Université de Paris* where he portrays a peasant's son come to the city to study, but led astray by the tempting delights of Paris:

> Par chacune rue regarde
> Ou voie la bele musarde;
> Partout regarde, partout muze;
> Ses argens faut et sa robe uze;
> Or est tout au recoumancier. (vv. 27–31)

The poor in Rutebeuf's poetry are not the landless second sons of noble families off to seek their fortune, nor the dull-witted *vilains* of the country. The scraps of humanity appearing in Rutebeuf's *Griesche d'hiver* and *d'été* are as typically urban as the three thieves of Arras in Jean Bodel's *Saint Nicolas*. Rutebeuf's *ribauds de Grève* are the unheroic, resourceful spendthrifts of city street-corners, loafers greedily quick to enjoy what they can squeeze from the moment. Paris is the poet's measure of wealth and poverty,

> A Paris sui entre touz biens
> Et n'i a nul qui i soit miens.
> (*Pauvreté Rutebeuf*, vv. 39–40)

24. Barbazon and Méon, *Fabliaux et contes,* 2 (Paris, 1808), 236–92. See also Alfred Franklin, *Les Rues et les cris de Paris* (Paris, 1874).

and new aspects of subjectivity appear not in terms of an inner relation of the poet to himself, but in his relation to a complex city
environment. The city walls are Rutebeuf's vantage point, from
which he looked out to Rome, to Tunis, and beyond the seas to
the Holy Land.

When we see Rutebeuf before his public and compare him to
contemporary poets, he appears one of the most believable and ac-
cessible figures of medieval literature. He is no romantic hero, gal-
lantly suffering, nor is he a radical reformer of the Church as some
critics have wished to paint him, and it is misleading to attempt to
understand him in such modern terms. But his works are a guide
for much of thirteenth-century French poetry, particularly that of
the second half of the century when the provincial courts were tem-
porarily eclipsed, and, for the first time, Paris was the literary as
well as the intellectual center of Europe. Rutebeuf wrote no great
hierarchical constructions like the *Divine Comedy,* no sustained
epic, romance, or *Roman de la Rose.* But his concerns often seem
closer to ours than those of Chrétien de Troyes or Guillaume de
Lorris, who give us rather the pleasure of an unfamiliar, an out-
moded, an enchanted world far from our own.

The freedom from musical constraint, which gave the work of
the courtly trouvères a somewhat rigid elegance, led Rutebeuf to
write works that often seem talky, overlong, and unformed. His
poems scarcely seem composed, but ramble on from subject to subject and contain many *chevilles* or fillers; they often fail to maintain the poetic intensity of the briefer courtly *chanson.* Rutebeuf
does not sing, as do all the earlier trouvères, and it is only in the
modern sense that Rutebeuf may be called lyric, since he often uses
a subjective mode. He speaks, and his characteristic form is the
protean *dit* that, like those amorphous creatures living half in the
sea, half on land, best survived environmental change. For within a
century after Rutebeuf, poetry had almost completely broken its
ties to music. The thematic freedom of the *dit* meant also that all
sorts of moral, historical, and personal speculations, largely excluded from the courtly song, could enter poetry and live on,
even in the stricter spoken forms of the later middle ages, most re-

markably in Deschamps' *ballades*. It is easier to say what Rutebeuf's poetry is not, than what it is: not courtly, not lyric, and not personal either, if one equates personal with a direct poetic transcription of individual experience. Yet it is a work strongly identified by its time, by the place in which it was written, and by the poet who wrote it, since his poetic manner is distinctive, although the man himself is elusive.

Rutebeuf's poems are often laden with rhetorical ornament, yet he leaves his readers with the general impression of an artless, everyday language. Master of all the tricks of the poet's trade that his public might call for, he is master, too, of that final trick that makes us believe there is no magic, no trick, no art at all. We believe what we hear, when we read him, just as we believe in the poet's voice, not as a sum of rhetorical effects, but as his own, his unique creation.

CHAPTER ONE: THE POET AS MORALIST

POPULARIZATION OF MORAL CONCERNS One of the most striking characteristics of the thirteenth century is the widespread vulgarization of moral concerns hitherto restricted to ecclesiastical circles and Latin writings. Vernacular literature had developed its own themes and forms in the eleventh and twelfth centuries, first in the heroic, patriotic epic and in hagiography, then in the portrayal of courtly relationships and society in verse and novel. Although Provençal literature found a secular, satirical vein in the *sirventés,* northern didactic and satirical literature of the twelfth century, on the other hand, was written largely within clerical circles. Even in lighter moments, as in Nivard de Ghent's *Ysengrimus* (ca. 1148), the story of the wolf turned monk, the themes are tonsured to suit clerical interests and tastes. Virtually all the laments on the world's corruption were directed against ecclesiastical abuses, to form, in Yunck's phrase, "the literature of a priestly class." [1]

Tension between reality and ideal was naturally felt first most strongly within the Church. The Church preached a doctrine of indifference to worldly affairs, yet it was forced to deal with money and temporal goods because it had assumed heavy social burdens such as schools, charities, and the administration of the Crusades. The same tension between the ideals of Christianity and the reality of human institutions was soon felt with great strength in the growing urban centers, where the impact of commerce was greatest. Moral anxiety in the lay world arose in part from the lack of concepts available to express human relations based on monetary exchange instead of on the supposed spiritual values of an earlier

---

1. John Adam Yunck, *The Lineage of Lady Meed. The Development of Mediaeval Venality Satire,* Univ. of Notre Dame Publications in Mediaeval Studies, 17 (Notre Dame, Ind., 1963), p. 187.

feudal age.[2] One might more correctly say that only very negative
moralistic terms existed to describe commercial dealings: bankers
who earned interest were usurers; lawyers who requested payment
were said to sell justice. Accusations of greed and envy, the ever
common themes of moral and satirical texts, thus became more
numerous and more shrill. In treatises on moral corruption Avarice
often replaced Pride as the root from which the tree of vices
sprang.[3] Money, then, was seen as disrupting human relationships; [4]
secular interests were judged to be in conflict with the divine goal
of salvation.[5]

Rutebeuf was one of the many vernacular poets to respond to
anxiety over human relations as it was felt in the lay world of the
cities. He shared the eternal moralist's longing for an idealized past
age; he condemned in violent terms a present seen as an age of rapacity and selfish striving:

> Toz fu estez, or est yvers;
> Bons fu, or est d'autre maniere,

2. See Marc Bloch, *Feudal Society, 1*, trans. L. A. Manyon (Chicago, London,
and Toronto, 1961), Pt. IV, "The Ties between Man and Man: Vassalage and the
Fief," 145 ff.

3. See Morton W. Bloomfield, *The Seven Deadly Sins* (East Lansing, Mich.,
1952), pp. xiv and 95.

4. A debate poem called *Du Denier et de la brebis* illustrates how the difference
between a "natural" and a monetary economy appeared to an amateur 13th-century
economist. The lamb says that he provides milk, cheese, meat, and wool; moreover,
he is the image of the Lamb of God. *Dant Denier* responds loftily that he serves
to build roads and bridges and to wage wars; nothing can be bought or sold without him, since he establishes the true worth of goods. He is so beloved that men
would pluck him from a manure heap, while none would save the lamb from a
ditch. "Tu tols à droit, dones à tort," answers the lamb, and the debate ends, unresolved (ed. Achille Jubinal, *Nouveau Recueil, 2*, 264–72). For examples of the
many vernacular poems on money see Yunck, *Lady Meed*, pp. 211–15; Edmond
Faral, *Les Jongleurs en France au moyen âge* (Paris, 1910), p. 215; and C.
Lenient's chapter "Dom Argent," in *La Satire en France au moyen âge* (3d ed.
Paris, 1833), pp. 181–93. Henri Pirenne establishes clearly that although there was
an increased amount of money in circulation, there was never a "natural economy"
in medieval France; see esp. pp. 78 and 138 of his *Economic and Social History of
Medieval Europe*.

5. See Auerbach's study of conflict between the kingdom of God and historical
existence in Dante and as a source of "Christian unrest" characteristic of medieval
and Renaissance European history (*Literary Language and Its Public in Late Latin
Antiquity and in the Middle Ages*, trans. Ralph Manheim [New York, 1965], pp.
306–10, 337–38).

> Quar nule gent n'est més maniere
> De l'autrui porfit porchacier,
> Se son preu n'i cuide chacier.
> Chascuns devient oisel de proie:
> Nus ne vit més se il ne proie.[6]
> (*L'Etat du monde,* vv. 4–10)

Rutebeuf reinterpreted old tales to illustrate the moral he preached to a commercialized society. The monk Gautier de Coincy, for example, had accused his Theophilus of selling his soul to the Devil because of wounded pride.[7] Rutebeuf, a layman, portrayed a Théophile who denies God for money and who is terrified of poverty. Théophile is deeply distressed by the thought of the social humiliation which accompanies poverty:

> N'est riens c'on por avoir ne face:
> Ne pris riens Dieu ne sa manace.
>
> • • •
>
> Quar qui a apris la richece,
> Molt i a dolor et destrece
> Quant l'en chiet en autrui dangier
> Por son boivre et por son mengier:
> Trop i covient gros mos oïr. (vv. 19–20, 63–67)

The moral of Rutebeuf's *Théophile* is, of course, a condemnation of such greed for worldly goods. All the riches in the world are not worth damnation; "Richece, mar te vi!" cries Théophile (v. 427).[8]

---

6. The fundamental and characteristic conservatism of the medieval moralists appears in many other works, as in these verses from *La Mule sanz frain*: ". . . on se doit tenir totes voies/ Plus as viés qu'as noveles voies" (vv. 15–16, *Nouveau Recueil de fabliaux et contes inédits, 1,* ed. Dominique Méon [Paris, 1823], 2).

7. See Gautier's long moralization on *Orgiuelz,* in "Comment Theophilus vint a penitance," vv. 1875–1950 (*Miracles de Nostre Dame, 1,* ed. V. Frederic Koenig [Geneva and Lille, 1955], 162–67). Pride, in contrast with the worldly sin of avarice, was a spiritual sickness to which monks were particularly prone; see Zozimas in Rutebeuf's *Vie de Sainte Marie l'Egyptienne,* a victim of "elaction," who thinks: "Je sui li grains, il sont la paille" (v. 570; see vv. 561–91).

8. In spite of this moralistic condemnation, Rutebeuf very frequently uses financial metaphors to speak of salvation; man "bargains" for heaven in this world. See, for example, *La Mort Rutebeuf:*

The tremendous appeal of the Mendicant orders' reevaluation of poverty must be seen as a profound reaction to this emerging economic structure. Saint Francis rejected both money and property as unnatural, as a constraint on joyous, loving behavior between men, and as an obstacle to the imitation of Christ.[9] The Mendicant renewal of monasticism is but one manifestation of a reforming spirit which swept the early thirteenth century and which is as characteristic of the times as is the rapid economic growth and the rise of powerful secular states. Indeed, all the ecclesiastical reform movements must be seen as a reaction against a commercial spirit, as well as part of the papal effort to hold temporal power in a world rapidly slipping away from the control of the Church.[10]

Vulgarization of the concern for morality must be considered as part of a historical process. Only in this way may one understand

---

Se por moi n'est au Jugement
Cele * ou Diex prit aombrement   * the Virgin
Mau marchié pris au paumoier. (vv. 10–12)

See also *Voie de Tunes,* v. 102, and *Sacristain,* vv. 16–32. In spite of his condemnation of greed, Rutebeuf is evidently influenced by commercial values and uses comparisons which his public would understand. His vocabulary is evidently influenced by commercial values and terminology which his public responded to more than theological abstractions.

9. For discussion of Franciscan poverty and its social context see Hans Baron, "Franciscan Poverty and Civic Wealth as Factors in the Rise of Humanistic Thought," *Speculum, 13,* No. 1 (January 1938), 1–37; M. D. Lambert, *Franciscan Poverty: The Doctrine of the Absolute Poverty of Christ and the Apostles in the Franciscan Order, 1210–1323* (London, 1961). See also Max Scheler, *Ressentiment,* ed. Lewis A. Coser, trans. William W. Holdheim (New York, 1961), pp. 91–93, for an interesting view of voluntary poverty as spiritual richness; and Norman Cohn, *The Pursuit of the Millennium: Revolutionary Messianism* (New York, 1961), pp. 161 ff., for the cult of total poverty among heretical sects. The strength of the Mendicant appeal can be measured by the swiftness with which begging orders spread all over Europe until they were, in Chaucer's words, "as thikke as motes in the sonnebeem" (*Wife of Bath's Tale,* v. 868, in *Canterbury Tales,* ed. A. C. Cawley [London, 1958]).

10. The need to defend Christendom and the reforms of clerical abuses and ignorance went together with the papal attempt to retain temporal power. The major papal moves to retain secular power were: support of the new universities (until these threatened to become autonomous bodies); instruction of the laity; protection of the supranational Mendicant orders, who eventually acted as papal inquisitors and Crusade tax collectors; the Crusades, which were an important base of papal political power, since popes could requisition the financial resources of both national clergy and secular states.

how vernacular lay poets such as Rutebeuf came to tax kings, popes, and prelates with their failings, and how a sense of moral fervor came to burn as hotly in the lay world as it ever did in cathedral or convent.

The Fourth Council of the Lateran (1215) gave an official impulse to the renewed desire of the Church to instruct the lower clergy and laymen in the meaning and practice of Christian doctrine. Pope Innocent III, influenced by the evangelizing of Saint Francis, whose order was recognized by this Council, supported recommendations for regular preaching to the general public in the vernacular.[11]

A trend toward vulgarization existed before the Lateran Council, however. This is apparent if we compare two sermon handbooks, one from the late twelfth century, the *Summa de arte praedicatoria* of Alanus de Insulis,[12] and one from the early thirteenth century, the *Sermones vulgares* of Jacques de Vitry.[13] Alanus attempted to codify authoritative biblical and patristic texts appropriate for sermons to the learned, to princes, and to ecclesiastics. Jacques de Vitry's congregation was much more varied than that of Alanus: 35 of his 75 sermons were addressed to lay groups of merchants, vinedressers, servants, citizens, and burghers.[14] He illustrated moral

11. See Philip Hughes, *The Church in Crisis: A History of the General Councils, 325–1870* (New York, 1961), p. 218; and F. M. Powicke and C. R. Cheney, *Councils and Synods, 1,* Pt. II (Oxford, 1964), 47–49, which gives extensive bibliography on the Fourth Lateran Council. E. J. Arnould studies the effects of the canons of this Council with particular reference to English and Anglo-Norman vernacular didactic works, but also discusses French writings, in his *Manuel des péchés: Etude de littérature religieuse anglo-normande (XIIIe siècle)* (Paris, 1940), esp. pp. 4–42. See also Bloomfield, *Sins,* pp. 91–92.

12. *Patrologia latina,* CCX, gen. ed. J.-P. Migne (Paris, 1855), cols. 109–98.

13. Jean Baptiste Cardinal Pitra, ed. *Analecta novissima spicilegii solesmensis (Altera continuatio),* 2 (1898). Robert Somerville suggests that these sermons were preached before Jacques de Vitry left Flanders to take up his post as Bishop of Acre (1216), since Jacques made reference in them to burghers, communes, and fairs, typical of the Flanders region (unpublished seminar report, Yale University, New Haven, 1965).

14. *The Exempla or Illustrative Stories from the "Sermones Vulgares,"* ed. Thomas Frederick Crane (London, 1890), pp. xlii–iv. J.-Th. Welter has edited "Sermo [LX] ad agricolas et vinitores et alios operarios" in his *L'Exemplum dans la littérature religieuse et didactique du moyen âge* (Paris and Toulouse, 1927), App. I, pp. 457–67. See also A. Lecoy de la Marche, "La Composition des audi-

problems with scenes drawn from daily life and secular literature—
that is, with exempla rather than with learned commentary on
authoritative texts—saying in his prologue: "Relinquishing rare and
cultivated words, we must turn our minds to the edification of the
ignorant and to the instruction of country folk . . . for they are
influenced more by outward examples than by authorities or profound maxims." [15] Jacques de Vitry preached to an increasingly
complex society where distinctions of class and rank were based on
work and wealth as well as on birth; he was popularizing religious
instruction rather than sounding depths of theological intricacy.

THE ESTATES OF THE WORLD   The idea of instructing
the illiterate in the vernacular soon appeared in all sorts of pious
literature.[16] The first vernacular moralists immediately adopted the
conventions of preachers and Latin satirists; they, too, wrote poems
ad status, to the different estates of men, grouping their moral exhortations according to class distinctions and illustrating them with
scenes from daily life.[17]

The idea of organizing moral or satirical criticism of society by

---

toires," in his *La Chaire française au moyen âge, spécialement au XIIIe siècle
d'après les manuscrits contemporains* (Paris, 1886), pp. 205–09. Humbert de
Romans, fifth General Master of the Dominicans (d. 1277), outlined sermons for
100 different social groups in his *De eruditione praedicatorum* (in *Maxima bibliotheca veterum patrum et antiquorum scriptorum,* 25, ed. Margarino de la Bigne
[Lyons, 1677], 421–567).

15. "Relictis enim verbis curiosis et politis, convertere debemus ingenium nostrum
ad edificationem rudium et agrestium eruditionem. . . . Magis enim moventur ex-
terioribus exemplis quam auctoritatibus vel profundis sententiis" (*Exempla,* p. xli n.
All translations from Latin are mine unless otherwise indicated.) This collection
of exempla was soon imitated by many authors of sermon manuals (see Welter,
L'Exemplum).

16. One of the earliest vernacular sermons is in verse, the "Grant mal fist Adam,"
which drew simple moral lessons from the history of mankind from Adam to
Noah. The author ended with an apology for not using the language of the learned:
"Por icels enfanz/ Le fiz en roumanz/ Qui ne sunt letrez;/ Car miex entendrunt/
La lange dunt sunt/ Dès enfance usez" (ed. Achille Jubinal [Paris, 1834], p. 32;
Pfander dates this sermon from the first half of the 12th century, in his *Popular
Sermon of the Medieval Friar in England* [New York, 1937], p. 21).

17. Guichard, lord of Beaulieu, called his scowling review of the ways in which
the "siècle" had declined a *Sermon,* and started off as would a preacher speaking
to a popular audience: "Entendez vers mei les petiz et les granz;/ Un deduit vos dirai,
bel est et avenanz,/ . . ./ Jo lerai le latin, si dirrai en romanz;/ Cil qui ne set

social groups is very ancient.[18] The groups were separated in the early middle ages into the clergy, the nobility, and the third estate. Refinements and subdivisions soon appeared, so that authors wrote about the various clerical rankings and distinguished knights from tournamenters and squires. The increasing complexity of urban society gave rise to subdivisions by trade in the third estate: lawyers, merchants, town officials.[19] The first French estates poem was by a cleric, Etienne de Fougères, Bishop of Rennes, and his *Livre des manières* (1176) drew heavily upon Roman satirists and Latin didactic works.[20] Hugues de Berzé, however, when he preached on the decline of "provoires, chevaliers and laboreours," stated in his *Bible* (first third of the thirteenth century) that his own experience of the world justified his invasion of a moral domain hitherto limited to ecclesiastics:

> Pour ce vueil au siecle moustrer
> Ainsi com je sai sermoner
> Qui ne sui ne clers ne letrés
> Ne je trai autorités,
> Fors de tant que je sai e voi. (vv. 387–91)

---

gramaire ne soit neint dotanz" (no ed., Paris, 1834), p. 9. There are many French estates poems; for examples see: *Li Romans de carité*, *1*, by the Renclus de Moiliens, ed. A.-G. Van Hamel (Paris, 1885); *De Triacle et de venin*, *Dit des Patenotres*, in Achille Jubinal, *Nouveau Recueil*, *1*; Jean de Condé, *Li Dis des estas dou monde* (*Dits et contes*, *2*, ed. A. Scheler [Brussels, 1866], No. XXXVI).

18. See Kerstin Hård af Segerstad, *Quelques Commentaires sur la plus ancienne chanson d'états française*, "Le Livre des manières, d'Etienne de Fougères (Upsala, 1906); Ruth Moll, *The Three Estates in Medieval and Renaissance Literature* (New York, 1933), an exhaustive study of the variations on the theme and its formal devices in Continental and English literature. Examples of Latin estates poems: "Frequenter cogitans de factis hominum," and "Viri fratres, servi Dei" (*Poésies populaires latines du moyen âge*, ed. Edélestand du Méril [Paris, 1847], pp. 128–36, 136–44; *De diversis ordinibus hominum* (*The Latin Poems Commonly Attributed to Walter Mapes*, ed. Thomas Wright [London, 1841], pp. 229–36).

19. See Lecoy de la Marche, "La Société d'après les sermons," *La Chaire française*, pp. 314–492; and L. Bourgain, *La Chaire française au XIIe siècle d'après les manuscrits* (Paris, 1879), for similar criticism of the estates in 12th-century sermons (pp. 271–369).

20. Partially edited with résumé in *La Vie en France au moyen âge . . . d'après les moralistes du temps*, *2*, ed. Ch.-V. Langlois (Paris, 1925), 1–26; see Hård af Segerstad, *Livre des manières*.

This unscholarly layman clearly felt that austere clerics had no monopoly on salvation, and he ended his poem with a defense of his own right to point out moral truths, even though he thoroughly and sinfully enjoyed himself in this world: "Tex ne set conseillier lui/ Qui donne bon conseill autrui" (vv. 871–72).[21]

Rutebeuf, writing two generations later, makes no such effort to justify his lay moralizing. He speaks as one who assumes naturally the right to denounce the world's corruption:

> Rimer me covient de cest monde
> Qui de tout bien se vuide et monde.
> *(Plaies,* vv. 1–2)

Indeed, the themes of Rutebeuf's estates poems, *Les Plaies du monde* and *L'Etat du monde,*[22] remain so close to the monotonous stereotypes of the standard developments of sermons and school exercises[23] that it is clear that by Rutebeuf's day, lay moralizing was already a tradition in vernacular writing. Rutebeuf touches on the usual themes: the avarice of clergy, stinginess of lords, and greed of the third estate, yet seldom in a particularly distinctive way in these

21. *La "Bible" au Seigneur de Berzé,* ed. Félix Lecoy (Paris, 1938). Hugues de Berzé's smiling nature and courtly training shine through the moralist's mask; see, for example, his accommodating view of sins of love (vv. 823–54): not only do those who love pretty, not ugly ladies commit beautiful sins, but such sins have the advantage of being "plus plaisans a remenbrer;/ . . ./ Qui repentir se porrait/ Dou bel pechié, il an aroit/ Cent mil tans de bien que dou lait."

22. The poem *La Vie du monde* can only with difficulty be attributed to Rutebeuf. In addition to the editor's comments (FB *1,* 389–92) I would add the following internal evidence: Stanzas X–XI (S II, sts. XIV, XIX) contain criticism of the papal Crusade fiscal policy and disparage Louis IX's Crusade efforts, but these themes do not appear in the body of Rutebeuf's Crusade poetry (see below, pp. 42–44). Rutebeuf taxes Romans with greed and hypocrisy (see *Dit d'Hypocrisie,* vv. 103–220), yet never mentions simony as does the *Vie du monde* (S I, v. 18; II, v. 22). Although Rutebeuf objects to papal intervention in the University polemic (see below, Chaps. 2 and 3), he nowhere else shows the violent Gallican tendencies of S I, sts. VII and VIII (S II, st. XVIII).

23. Olga Dobiache-Rojdestvensky cites an example of extreme stereotyping of the estates theme in the hands of an untalented scholar-Goliard: "Recessit hoc tempore/ lex a sacerdotibus,/ iustitia a principbus,/ consilium a senioribus,/ charitas a prælatis,/ disciplina a literatis," etc. (*Les Poésies des goliards* [Paris, 1931], pp. 165–66; see p. 161). See Chap. 4, below, on school exercises.

poems.[24] The brief mention of three satirical themes in *L'Etat* that are nowhere else mentioned in his poetry—the lawyers "de lor langues vendeeur" (v. 82), the merchants "qui font maint mauvés serement" (v. 126), and "ces païsanz des vingnes" (v. 144)—reinforce the impression that Rutebeuf is working in imitation of well-formulated patterns without attempting to develop them fully.

Even Rutebeuf's criticism of the nobility is far from being as harsh as Faral would have it (FB, *1*, 377). Perhaps because of his limited experience of courtly themes, Rutebeuf seems to feel an awed reluctance to criticize knights except in the most tentative and schematic way:

> Chevalerie est si grant chose
> Que la tierce plaie n'en ose
> Parler qu'ainsi com par defors;
> Quar tout aussi comme li ors
> Est li mieudres metaus c'on truise,
> Est ce li puis la ou l'en puise
> Tout sens, tout bien et toute honor,
> Si est droiz que je les honor. (*Plaies*, vv. 105-12)

He adds only that knights are not what they used to be, since a "leus blans," symbol of devouring avarice, "a toz mengiez" (v. 118).[25] In *L'Etat du monde* he merely sketches the nobility through brief references to men whom his audience would quickly recognize as models of chivalric courage and generosity:

> Je n'i voi Rollant n'Olivier
> • • •
> Il n'i a més nul Alixandre [26] (vv. 149, 152)

24. Secularization of satirical themes is evident when we note the absence of comment on simony in Rutebeuf's works, although he refers to sale of civil offices (*Etat*, vv. 93–106); see Yunck, *Lady Meed*, p. 190, and pp. 197–99 on Rutebeuf.

25. Wolves often symbolize rapacity; see Adolpf Katzenellenbogen, *Allegories of the Virtues and Vices in Mediaeval Art from Early Christian Times to the Thirteenth Century*, trans. A. J. P. Crick (New York, 1964), p. 61; *Roman de la Rose* by Guillaume de Lorris and Jean de Meun, ed. Ernest Langlois, *3* (Paris, 1921): "Baillif, bedel, prevost, maieur,/ Tuit vivent près que de rapine;/ Li menuz peuples les encline,/ E cil com lou les deveurent" (vv. 11,540–42).

26. Rutebeuf cites Roland as the image of courage in *Dit de Pouille*, v. 24;

and ends with a venerable pun, "Chascuns a son Donet perdu" [27] (v. 158).
When one compares these schematic verses on knights with Rutebeuf's truculent exhortations to lords and princes in his Crusade poems, and his vigorous statement of the virtues of generosity in his *Dit d'Aristote*, the former seem such a timid handling of moralistic criticism that I am inclined to call them early poems of Rutebeuf.[28] Not only does he seem closely bound by his poetic models, but his criticism of the clergy does not even mention the Dominicans and Franciscans. He makes only a vague reference to "gent d'Ordre" as dishonest executors of testaments (*Plaies*, vv. 69–86). If the poems had been written during or after the University polemic (see below, Chaps. 2 and 3), he would surely have alluded to it, as he did in his *Ordres de Paris* and in his *Voie de Paradis* (see below, pp. 96, 173). Nor does Rutebeuf develop in any other poem the idea of rivalry between the Mendicant orders, which he portrays in *L'Etat* with a touch of irony for their interpretation of brotherly love:

> Li uns covenz voudroit de l'autre
> Qu'il fust en un chapiau de fautre
> El plus pereilleus de la mer:
> Ainsi s'entraiment li aver. (vv. 37–40)

What concrete details and images Rutebeuf does add to the estates theme are evocations of an urban setting. He includes the cries of begging friars, "Donez, por Dieu, du pain aus Freres" [29]

Alexander reappears in the *Complainte du comte de Poitiers*, vv. 80–82 (see below, p. 60), in *Ordres de Paris*, v. 118, and the *Dit d'Aristote*.

27. See FB, *1*, 388, note to vv. 157–58, and FB, *1*, 384, note to vv. 21–22; Adolf Tobler cites Rutebeuf, Guillaume de Deguilleville, and Marcabru, in "Long temps a que no fon Donatz," *Vermischte Beiträge zur französischen Grammatik, 2,* (2d ed. Leipzig, 1906), 223–24.

28. The editors' dating of these poems (FB, *1*, 377, 382–83) is tentative, as they themselves say. The themes of clerical avarice and criticism of administrative greed are *topoi* impossible to date in any one period of the poet's career.

29. Compare with verses 75–100 of Guillaume de la Villeneuve's *Les Crieries de Paris au XIIIe siècle* (ed. Alfred Franklin, *Les Rues et les cris de Paris* [Paris, 1874], pp. 157–59).

(*Etat*, v. 33), the "genz menues/ Qui besoingnent parmi ces rues" (*Etat*, vv. 135-36), the students (*Plaies*, vv. 89-104), and the "provost et bailli et maieur," town officials accused of defeathering "toz les costez/ A cels qui sont en lor justise" (*Etat*, vv. 98-99)—all typical figures of city population. A comparison of this cautious treatment of city scenes with the expansive delight in detail of the estates poem which opens the *Tournoiement d'Enfer*[30] shows that Rutebeuf has confined himself to the barest possibilities of the theme. While he says of merchants that they

> . . . jurent que lor denrees
> Sont et bones et esmerees
> Tel foiz que c'est mençonge pure,
> (*Etat*, vv. 127-29)

the author of the *Tournoiement* shows us their skillful deaconing and shameless ballyhoo:

> [Il] font les druz motons pignier
> Tent que il sont dougiez et biauz,
> Puis les vendent por bons aigniaus
> Et jurent saint Pere et saint Pol:
> 'Veez quel cuir, veez quel pol'
> . . .
> Assint esploitent li plusor. (vv. 562-66, 570)

Rutebeuf will learn later to enliven moralizing with bits of dialogue to replace dry generalizations. Thus, in *Renart le Bestourné* (after 1261), an attack on Louis IX's policy of austerity (FB, *1*, 534), the author reveals his criticism through a lively street scene in which several gossips discuss King "Noble":

> Se Nobles savoit que ce monte
> Et les paroles que l'en conte
> Parmi la vile,—
> Dame Raimborc, dame Poufile,

30. Ed. A. Lângfors, in *Romania*, *44* (January-October 1916–17), 511–58.

Qui de lui tienent lor concile,
Ça dis, ça vint,
Et dient c'onques més n'avint
N'onques a franc cuer ne sovint
De tel geu faire! (vv. 37–45)

It seems hard to believe that a poet might expect remuneration from any group exposed to a public tongue-lashing in these lay sermons (FB, *1*, 382); yet evidence that poets expected to be paid for them appears in the *Dit des planètes*,[31] an astrological version of the estates theme. The anonymous poet associates the seven planets with the seven days of the week and seven estates of man:[32] *Lundi*, for example, the moon, represents the "estat de gent religieuse," who bring rains of fresh and tender pity when full of humility, but who are subject to dry spells of vainglory and hypocrisy when humility wanes. Yet, after berating all the clients who could pay— nobles, clerics, merchants, even the poor with their mite—the poet extends a begging hand:

S'il vous samble que je di voir,
Si m'en créez séurement,
Et se vous avez aisement,
Si me faites aucun confort.
Diex vous gart de vilainne mort!

Poets, then, expected payment for moralizing as well as entertaining, and the large number of didactic *dits* surviving from the thirteenth century shows that a considerable public appreciated and paid to hear these edifying tracts.

Vernacular poets did more, however, than reflect the filtering down of moral issues to a popular level. They shared also in the ecclesiastical effort to instruct laymen in religious practices. The relation between poetry and sermons could be direct: poets occasionally composed poems about sermons they had heard, particularly

31. *Nouveau Recueil,* ed. Jubinal, 1, 372–83.
32. See Bloomfield, *Sins,* pp. 233–36, for other works associating sins with estates and planets.

those relating to themes from daily life. A favorite topic of medieval preachers, for example, was the excessively elaborate headgear of women.[33] The *Dit des cornetes* popularized a sermon by the Bishop of Paris against wigs and pointed coifs, showing how the sermon became the talk of the town:

> Se des fames ne nous gardon,
> Ocis serommes.
> Cornes ont por tuer les hommes.
> D'autrui cheveus portent granz sommes
> Desus lor teste.
> L'en doit bien redouter tel beste;
>
> . . .
>
> L'evesque l'a apercéu;
> Si ne s'en puet estre téu,
> Ainz en sermone,
> Et à toz cels .x. jors pardone,
> Qui crieront à tel personne
> 'Hurte belin!' *. . .* Watch out for the ram!
> Genz s'en gabent, n'est pas frivole,
> Parmi la vile.[34]

The gap between sermons and didactic poems was further narrowed by the use of rhythm and rhyme in vernacular sermons.[35]

33. The great Dominican preacher Etienne de Bourbon included five exempla on wigs alone in his *Tractatus de diversis materiis praedicabilibus* (see *Anecdotes historiques, légendes, et apologues tirés du recueil inédit d'Etienne de Bourbon*, ed. A. Lecoy de la Marche [Paris, 1877], Nos. 274, 275, 284, 287, 289). Pierre de Limoges and Henri de Provins both preached at Paris in 1272–73 against the headdresses of Parisian women (Lecoy de la Marche, *Chaire française*, pp. 439–40). No. 186 of the *Tabula exemplorum secundum ordinem alphabeti* reproaches "mulieres que se indecenter hornant et colorant" (ed. J.-Th. Welter [Paris and l'oulouse, 1926], p. 52).

34. Achille Jubinal, ed., *Jongleurs et trouvères* . . . (Paris, 1835), pp. 87–93. Compare with the biting satire against moneylenders, *La Patrenostre a l'userier*, a rhymed version of a sermon preached at Paris by Cardinal Robert de Courçon, papal legate of the early 13th century. (Text edited in Eero Ilvonen, *Parodies de thèmes pieux dans la poésie française du moyen âge* [Helsinki, 1914], pp. 66–77; see Lecoy de la Marche, *Chaire française*, p. 528, on Robert de Courçon).

35. See Bourgain's *Chaire française*, pp. 227–32, and his "Les Sermons latins rimés au moyen âge," *Mémoires de la Société Nationale d'Agriculture, Science et*

Moreover, didactic poems imitate sermon techniques; in both, for example, are found sacred interpretations of profane lyrics. A famous religious gloss of the song "Belle Aaliz mainz s'en leva" is attributed to Etienne de Langton, Archbishop of Canterbury;[36] and a similar vernacular *Moralités sur ces sis vers* explains the religious significance of a frivolous song, "C'est la jus c'on dit ès prés."[37]

ALLEGORY AND THE ROAD TO PARADISE Preaching *ad status* was only part of the joint effort of preachers and didactic poets to awaken the moral conscience of the general population. The same Lateran Council of 1215 which had recommended preaching to the faithful further decreed, in the canon "Omnis utriusque sexus," the annual obligation to confess and take communion at Easter. The necessity for definite instruction of laymen in repentance and confession thus arose, entailing a need for exact and simple definitions of sin and its effects so that every man could be guided toward salvation.[38]

Preachers early made use of allegory in order to describe sin, and often tied allegory in with sermons to different estates. Etienne, Bishop of Tournay (d. 1203), wrote a sermon in which he describes the marriage of the Devil and Malice. The wedding is staged in full allegorical and nuptial detail: the bride is attended by Hate of Neighbor and Disdain for God; the reception is catered by Gluttony and Drunkenness. Their diabolical offspring marry various social

---

Arts d'Angers, Nouvelle période, 22 (1880), 215–31. See also Lecoy de la Marche, *Chaire française,* pp. 279–87; Arnould, *Le Manuel des péchés,* p. 35; and Th.-M. Charland, *Artes praedicandi; Contribution à l'histoire de la rhétorique au moyen âge* (Paris and Ottowa, 1936), p. 154. Although it is true, as Pfander observes, that didactic poetry does not usually use the divisions of theme peculiar to sermons, Rutebeuf imitates this sermon technique in his *Nouvelle Complainte d'outremer* (Pfander, *Popular Sermons,* pp. 16–18; see below, p. 48, note 96.

36. Cited by A. Lecoy de la Marche, *Le Treizième Siècle littéraire et scientifique* (Bruges, 1894), pp. 140–41. Jacques de Vitry uses the same song to describe the coquetry which prevented women from getting to church on time (*Exempla,* p. 114, No. 273).

37. Jubinal, ed., *Nouveau Recueil,* 2, 297–303. Similarly, miracle stories derive their form from the profane fabliaux (see below, p. 245).

38. See Arnould, *Manuel des péchés,* pp. 15–17, and Pfander, *Popular Sermons,* pp. 10–11, for vernacular sermons on sin and confession.

groups: Simony weds the bishops, Hypocrisy the monks, Robbery the princes, and Swindle the merchants, while Lust remains single to enjoy the favors of all. Thus Etienne taxed each group with its most characteristic failing.[39]

The moral force that allegory could exert upon men's imagination is felt in the teachings of Saint Francis. Although his language and images were often popular in flavor,[40] Francis infused the more cultivated tradition of didactic allegory with tremendous expressive power. When he spoke, for example, of his "marriage" to *Madonna Povertà,* he communicated to others, by his figure of speech, his own direct intuition and poignant feeling of the holiness of voluntary poverty. Francis' image of Lady Poverty was not merely a rhetorical device or an ennobling concept; it was an image which fired the imagination of those who heard it and moved them to great acts of renunciation.[41]

When Rutebeuf used allegory to instruct laymen in their religious duties and to lead sinners to confession, he was, then, imitating a well-established didactic tradition.[42] His allegorical *Voie de Paradis* was specifically written for use during Lent and corresponds to special sermons given during this period to prepare hearers for their annual confession and communion (FB, *1, 337*). The *Voie* uses the traditional theme of the pilgrim's dream journey to the other world as a framework for its teaching.[43] The goal of the pilgrimage (Lent) is "la meson de Confesse" (v. 145), and the pilgrim's arrival in the town of *Repentance* coincides with the annual fair—that is, the celebration of Easter (v. 858).

39. Bourgain, *Chaire française,* pp. 220–23. Once again, the same theme recurs in vernacular didactic literature, in the *Mariages des filles au diable* (13th century), in Jubinal, *Nouveau Recueil, 1,* 283–92.

40. See Erich Auerbach, *Mimesis: The Representation of Reality in Western Literature* (New York, 1957), pp. 146–48.

41. See the accounts of the conversion of early Franciscan disciples in Bonaventura's *Vie de saint François d'Assise,* trans. Damien Vorreux (Paris, 1961), pp. 59–60.

42. In the light of my findings in this and succeeding chapters, Bossuat's statement that Rutebeuf "échappe aux tendances didactiques de son temps" is quite unjustifiable (*Le Moyen Age: Histoire de la littérature française, 1* [Paris, 1962], 102).

43. See Bloomfield, *Sins,* passim; and Welter, *L'Exemplum,* p. 92. Auerbach describes Dante's renewal of the theme (*Literary Language,* p. 233).

This special didactic intention may explain the apparent incompleteness of Rutebeuf's *Voie,* for the narrative abruptly breaks off with the arrival at *Confesse.* There is no awakening, no moralizing on the joys of confession, as in works of more general didactic intent. There is no final exhortation to the hearers, and the pilgrim never actually reaches Heaven as did the hero of another *Voie de Paradis* attributed to Raoul de Houdenc, who finally kneels before the Throne of God to hear:

> . . . Raoul, bien l'as fet.
> Pardonné te sont li mesfet
> Dont tu m'avoies coroucié.[44]

Rutebeuf leaves his audience at a morally oriented crossroads where he himself, as the pilgrim, had stopped at the beginning of his *Voie.* His hearers must choose for themselves the *right* road, narrow and difficult, or the left, "larges est, més toz jors estrece" (v. 58), which only seems "delitables et aaisanz" (v. 51), since it ends in Hell's prison.

Unity in the *Voie* is provided by the subjective point of view of the dreamer-pilgrim, identified as "Rutebeuf,"[45] who discovers for himself all the horrors of vice and joys of virtue. Yet Rutebeuf's desire to represent his experience of sin and repentance as a model for all is clear from the beginning.[46] *Pitié,* who welcomes him at his first night's hostel, *Penitance,* sets his task:

> Li preudon me dist: "Biaus amis
> Cil sires Diex qui vous a mis
> El cuer de fere cest voiage
> Vous aidera au mal passage.

44. Vv. 968–70, in Achille Jubinal, ed., *Œuvres complètes de Rutebeuf, trouvère du XIIIe siècle, 3* (2d ed. Paris, 1874–75), 195–234; hereafter referred to as *O.C.;* the *Voie* of Raoul was also edited and translated in Raoul de Houdenc, *Songe de Paradis,* ed. Philéas Lebesgue (Paris, 1908), 99–189.

45. Vv. 26–27; see also below, p. 266.

46. Auerbach describes as uniquely Christian the relationship between the author and his audience, in which we find "an interweaving of accusation and self-accusation" (*Literary Language,* pp. 297–98).

> Aidiez cels que vous troverez,
> Conseilliez cels que vous verrez
> Qui requerront vostre conseil." (vv. 95–101)

A sermon-like note is struck in the prologue as well, where the figure of the sower recalls the parable of the good seed (see later, Chap. 4). The poet reminds his hearers that they must labor and plow their souls in order to reap a "semence devine" (vv. 9–16). The lovely picture of spring, with the rejoicing "vermine," the proud, flower-bedecked earth, and the planting of crops, contributes to the central theme of rebirth and renewal of the soul through the Easter confession.[47]

The moral imperative of the *Voie* is presented as a catechism. When *Pitié* tells Rutebeuf he must avoid *dame Avarisce, dame Envie,* and *Vaine Gloire,* the pilgrim asks, "Ha! Diex, et qui m'enseignera/ Comment je les eschiverai?" (vv. 138–39). *Pitié* thereupon launches into a 727-verse description of the vices and virtues he depicts both as human figures and as houses. In contrast with the pilgrim of Raoul's *Voie,* who actively experiences each vice and virtue as an adversary or ally,[48] Rutebeuf is an armchair tourist. His first abortive trip along the right and left paths (vv. 29–73) is his only active effort; and he completes his voyage uneventfully in the last 38 verses.

Rutebeuf used allegory in his *Voie,* as did other preachers, moralists, and *romanciers,*[49] less to personify abstract ideas than to identify, externalize, and objectively judge inner states and feelings. When

---

47. Dream narratives like Rutebeuf's *Voie* often begin with a description of spring; see, for example, *De la Fole et de la sage* (Jubinal, ed. *Nouveau Recueil, 2,* 73–82) or the *Voie de Paradis* of Baudouin de Condé (*Dits et contes . . . . ,* ed. A. Scheler [Brussels, 1866], No. XVIII). The description of spring is, of course, a topic which serves as prologue in works as varied as courtly love lyrics or late Latin hymns and panegyrics. See Roger Dragonetti, *La Technique poétique des trouvères dans la chanson courtoise,* pp. 163 ff.; and discussion by Ernst Robert Curtius, *European Literature and the Latin Middle Ages,* trans. Willard R. Trask (New York, 1953), pp. 185 ff.

48. In Raoul's *Voie* the pilgrim is attacked by "larrons" (the vices), rescued by Faith and Hope: the narrative is a lively adventure story.

49. See C. S. Lewis, *The Allegory of Love* (New York, 1958), pp. 29–32, for discussion of Chrétien de Troyes' use of allegory to describe inner states of love.

Rutebeuf speaks of *Envie,* for example, he is less interested in the concept than in helping his hearer recognize the feeling within himself. When the didactic poet tells a story of *Envie's* evil and miserable acts, he is not merely stage-managing an ideological puppet show but describing in a vivid and sensible way the necessary relation between inner feelings and human acts.

The description of the virtues and vices as houses into which man enters is a variant of the traditional image of the body itself as a dwelling in which vices and virtues struggle.[50] The old *Psychomachia* of Prudentius, in which the vices and virtues fought on the terrain of "Mansoul," [51] is, then, in Rutebeuf, completely externalized. Man is the spectator of his soul; he is waylaid by his emotions, is helped by his strengths, and dwells in his acts. Man's inner soul is thus understood in a rather fragmented way.

A further disadvantage of such allegorical description of human psychology is that the contradictory yet simultaneous feelings which make up an individual's total state of mind at any one moment are isolated, and each is refined to a simple essence. No allegorical personification, therefore, ever has the depth and complexity of a real person. To counteract the shallow simplicity of allegorical characters, then, the moralists tried to describe them as realistically as possible [52] and to show their interaction by grouping them together. The feelings and moods represented objectively in the personified allegories may also be "experienced" by a human hero, who thus serves to reunite the separate elements of feeling in a single conscience. Yet in Rutebeuf's *Voie* the pilgrim hero has so little direct

50. See v. 337 of *Voie* below, p. 36; and Roberta Douglas Cornelius, *The Figurative Castle. A Study in the Mediaeval Allegory of the Edifice* (Bryn Mawr, 1930), Chap. 2, "The Castle of the Body," and pp. 7–8 on Rutebeuf's *Voie*. See also Aquinas' description of meditation as withdrawal into one's house (*Philosophical Texts,* trans. Thos. Gilby [New York, 1960], pp. 1–2, from Opusc. IX, *Exposition de Hebdomadibus,* Prologue).

51. *Psychomachia,* ed. and trans. H. J. Thomson, in *Prudentius, 1* (Cambridge, Mass., and London, 1949), 274–343.

52. See the valuable study of allegorical characterization by Howard R. Patch, ("Characters in Medieval Literature," *Modern Language Notes, 40,* No. 1 [January 1925], 1–14), in which he points out that the allegories had to "reflect real life in order to point their moral" (p. 5).

contact with the personifications that we cannot fully identify the allegorical vices and virtues as *his* feelings and acts.

We might say that the average medieval moralist does not have a strongly internalized sense of good and evil. Man often appears, as in the *Miracle de Théophile*, as a helpless victim of the vices, sin, and the Devil, or as a wretch who is saved by the miraculous intervention of the virtues, the Virgin, or God.[53] Yet these moralizing works must have been intended to arouse a sense of spiritual self-consciousness and responsibility in the hearer, who was to apply the lessons taught to his own individual experience of sin and repentance.[54]

The moralist's task, therefore, was first to portray clearly to his hearer the nature and effects of the vices and virtues—hence the elaborate descriptions of allegorical figures. Rutebeuf represents the dwellings of both the vices and virtues as being in poor condition. Those of the vices are inherently weak, because their strength is only façade, their promise of refuge, illusion. Pride's house is

> . . . moult orguilleuse;
> Bele est, més ele est pereilleuse,
> Qu'ele chiet par un pou de vant.
> Moult est bien fete par devant,
> Assez miex que n'est par derriere,
> Et s'a escrit en la mesiere;
> 'Ceenz esta Orguez li cointes
> Qu'a toz pechiez est bien acointes.' (vv. 151–58)

53. See Br. Leo Charles Yedlicka, *Expressions of the Linguistic Area of Repentance and Remorse in Old French*, Catholic Univ. Studies in Romance Languages and Literature, XXVII (Washington, D.C., 1945), p. 422. Yedlicka cites the characteristic self-appellations of the repentant sinner, "dolanz, lasse, chaitif," as illustrative of this feeling of helplessness; see, for example, *Théophile*, vv. 384, 392, 396, etc.

54. Compare, for example, the verses ending the *Dit du Buef*, a miracle tale illustrating the value of confession:
> Vous qui avez oy ce biau dit recorder,
> En cest example-ci vous devez remirer
> Aussi de vos péchiez, et de vous confesser.
> (Jubinal, ed., *Nouveau Recueil*, 1, 72)

The houses of the virtues are dilapidated, since no one lives in them;
yet their beauty could be restored if anyone would care for them.
Dame Humilitez looks out through the broken windows of
"Leauté" and "Foi," while *Larguece* languishes at her door: *Avarisce* has enticed men of every social class away from virtue.

> Més Avarisce a enchanté
> Si les chenuz et les ferranz
> Et toz les bachelers erranz
> Et chanoines et moines noirs,
> Que toz est gastes li manoirs. (vv. 638–42)

Rutebeuf occasionally explains the moral meaning of his descriptions, as in the description of *Luxure's* house:

> Nus n'i va ne riant ne baut,
> Tant soit ne garçon ne ribaut,
> Qui corouciez ne s'en reviengne;
> Et ceste reson nous enseigne
> Que nus hon ne s'i doit embatre
> Por solacier ne por esbatre. (vv. 465–70)

Yet he needs not intervene often, since moral and description are
generally identical and self-explanatory in these object lessons.

Rutebeuf purposely makes the vices as sordid as he can to discourage potential sinners. This is a more effective or at least a more
orthodox didactic technique than that of Huon de Meri, who, in
his allegorical *Tournoiement de l'Antechrist,* passes in battle review
the vices clad as splendid "barond'enfer," symbolic shields aglitter
with "faus argent." "Ne n'ot fors chevaliers de pris," says Huon,
showing the vices to be redoubtable enemies in contrast with Rutebeuf's pale and furtive deceivers.[55] Those who frequent *Avarisce,*
for example, in Rutebeuf's *Voie,*

> . . . sont tuit si homme noir,
> Non pas tres noir, més maigre et pale,

55. Ed. P. Tarbé (Reims, 1851), pp. 26, 37.

> Por lor dame qui est trop male.
> Ausi les tient comme en prison.
> Més de ce fet grant mesprison
> Qu'a nului nule bonté n'offre.
> Enmi sa sale, sus un coffre,
> Est assise, mate et penssive;
> Miex samble estre morte que vive. (vv. 204-12)

Envie inhabits a dark valley amid squalor and gloom; *Luxure,* at the very bottom of the descent to perdition, lives

> En une recules obscure.
> Onques nus preudon n'en ot cure
> D'entrer la jus por l'obscurté,
> Qu'il n'i a point de seürté. (vv. 461-64)

Rutebeuf is more interested in describing the nature of sin than in maintaining consistent allegorical personifications which act as characters in a full-fledged "psychodrama." Instead of a complete story, then, we find Rutebeuf developing allegory in several ways to make his moral point. The poet may illustrate sins and virtues by showing them in action. Prudentius, in his *Psychomachia,* dramatized the interplay of emotions and actions through his central image of a battle. Rutebeuf refers briefly to this dynamic conception when *Pitié* describes the fight between *Orguex li outrageus* and *Dame Humilitez:* [56]

> Soventes foiz assaut li * livre.   * *Humilitez*
> Or oiez comment se delivre
> Et escoutez en quel maniere.
> S'ele rist et fet bele chiere.

56. Conflict seems to be one of the fundamental elements in medieval thinking from the disputatious method of Abelard's *sic et non* to the representation of psychology as a *psychomachia,* arising, in part, from the tension we have described between chivalric or Christian values and economic institutions. The idea of a struggle between good and evil, represented by the victory of the Virgin over the Devil in many miracles, lies also behind the medieval legal process of trial by combat; the righteous triumphed because they were supported by God. In poetry this taste for argument appears in the numerous *débats, tensons,* and *jeux-partis.*

> Et fet samblant riens ne li grieve
> Ce c'Orguex contre li se lieve,
> Lors acore de duel et d'ire
> Orguex, si qu'il ne puet mot dire.
> A tant s'en part, ne parle puis,
> Maz et confus ferme son huis. (vv. 543–52)

Pitié's account of this battle would gain in dramatic suspense if we did not feel that we were seeing an action which occurs over and over again and always with the same outcome. Yet Rutebeuf's intention is to offer *proven* means for overcoming pride. His *Voie* thus seems closer to a sermon than to a narrative in which the author seeks to interest us in the action itself. Indeed, Rutebeuf describes *Envie's* acts in the present tense and with expressions like "soventes foiz, toz jors"; in this way he shows that these are typical acts of *Envie,* so that men may recognize *Envie* when they or others behave like her:

> Li cors ou Envie s'embat
> Ne se solace në esbat;
> Toz jors est ses viaires pales,
> Toz jors sont ses paroles males;
> Lors rist il que son voisin pleure
>   • • •
> Envie fet hommes tuer
> Et si fet bonnes * remuer   * boundary stones
> Envie fet rooingner terre,
> Envie met ou siecle guerre,
> Envie fet mari et fame
> Haïr, Envie destruit ame. (vv. 337–41, 347–52)

Rutebeuf even describes the expressions and bodily movements of the vices, so that his hearer will recognize his feelings when he makes the same physical movements:

> Ire, que est male et vilaine,
> Ne set pas tant d'escharpir * laine

Comme ele set de cheveus rompre.
Tout ront quanqu'ele puet arompre;
Tant a corouz, tant a dolor
Qui tant li fet muer color,
Que toz jors sont ses denz serrees,
Qui ja ne seront desserrees
Se n'est por felonie dire;
Car tels est la maniere d'Ire
Que toz jors vuet les denz estraindre
Et souspirer et parfont plaindre
Et coroucier a li meïsme. (vv. 231–43)

Some of Rutebeuf's visual images of the vices resemble their representation in the plastic arts, where characteristic attitudes and actions identified the various figures. Thus Ire is often represented tearing her hair in spiteful anger, Avarice crouching greedily upon her coffer (v. 210).[57]

When Rutebeuf wishes to show how one sin or virtue may lead to another, he not only uses visual images but also multiplies the elements in his basic metaphor. *Ire's* house, for example, has walls crumbling with "Vilonie," sills of "Desesperance," roof beams of "Mescheance," and mortar of "Haine." All of these subvices are a result of *Ire* or create *Ire;* their relation is demonstrated through the elaborated description of the house. Groups of vices and virtues can be shown as a family: *Pitié* has a wife, *Charité;* a niece, *Larguece;* an aunt, *Humilitez*—and these virtues sustain each other. Other groups are portrayed as mistress and servants: *Luxure* has a chambermaid, *Rousee* ("Pimpleskin"), and a chamberlain, *Fouss'i-fie*. Figures can be dressed in symbolic clothing as *Humilitez* is clad in "Bon Eür."

Rutebeuf is far from exhausting the systems of relationships available in both the Latin and the French medieval allegorical tradi-

---

57. See Emile Mâle, *The Gothic Image: Religious Art in France of the Thirteenth Century*, trans. D. Nussey (New York, 1958), pp. 113, 117; and Katzenellenbogen, *Allegories*, p. 77; see also Bloomfield, *Sins*, p. 103, and his chap. 5, "The Chief Sins in Continental and 13th Century English Literature," pp. 123–55.

tion.[58] The delights of allegorical meals, for example, are only suggested when Rutebeuf says he had "povre pitance" in the city of
Penitance. The pilgrim of the *Voie* attributed to Raoul de Houdenc
ate a tearful repast in the house of *Contrictions:*

> Seglous * éûmes à foison   * sobs
> Angoisses & lermes béûmes,
> De quoi moult grant plenté éûmes
> Chaudes coranz aval la face. (vv. 195–98)

The Devil's menu in Raoul de Houdenc's *Songe d'Enfer* offers such
dishes as

> Bediaus brulez, bien cuiz en paste,
> Papelars à l'ypocrisie,
> Noirs moines à la tanoisie;
> Vielles prestresses au civé
> Noires nonnains au cretonné
> Sodomites bien cuiz en honte.[59] (vv. 590–95)

Groups of allegories serve moralization rather than unity or logic
in Rutebeuf's *Voie.* Some minor figures appear in several roles:
Felonie, for example, appears as a wall in *Envie's* house (v. 262)
and as *Orguex's* father-in-law (v. 127). Some houses are described
with full allegorical components, others with ordinary adjectives,
others in terms of the life one may lead in them. Rutebeuf does not
attempt consistent parallelism in the various descriptions, but uses

58. Other possible groupings include allegorical heraldic devices as in Huon de
Meri's *Tournoiement de l'Antechrist,* symbolic feathered wings as in the *Roman
des eles* of Raoul de Houdenc (*Trouvères belges,* ed. Aug. Scheler [Nouvelle série,
Louvain, 1879], pp. 248–71); see also the *Opusculum de sex alis cherubim* of
Alanus de Insulis (*Patrologia latina,* CCX, cols. 265 ff.). The monk Raoul de-
scribes the rungs of a symbolic ladder to heaven (vv. 649–769) in imitation of
Honorius of Autun's *Scala coeli minor* (*Patrologia latina,* CLXXII, cols. 869 ff.; see
also Katzenellenbogen, *Allegories,* figs. 23–26, 48).

59. Ed. and trans. Philéas Lebesque, pp. 112, 89–90. The rowdy guest-list of
Gluttony in another *Voie de Paradis* is particularly entertaining: "Gorge-Alumée,
Trop-Boire-A-La-Vesprée, Matin-Menger, Suer-Par-Force-De-Mangier, Poctrine-De-
Saulce-Soillée, Pisser-Dessoubs-La-Table, Mal-Au-Coeur, Grant-Rot-Notable, and Vo-
mir" (cited by Daniel A. Augsburger, "Rutebeuf et la *Voie de Paradis* dans la
littérature française du moyen âge" [unpublished doctoral dissertation, University
of Michigan, 1949], p. 76).

whatever development best fits his didactic purpose at a given point in his exposition of the nature of sin and virtue.

Rutebeuf's description of good and evil not only is psychological and moral, but includes occasional references to historical events and figures as examples of the truths he preaches (see FB, *1*, 337–38). Preachers also used contemporary events as well as exempla drawn from religious and profane writings to illustrate their exhortations.[60] Writers of allegories had long mixed real figures together with personified abstractions, thus giving a literal and concrete interpretation to the expression that men "follow" ideas. Huon de Meri's *Tournoiement de l'Antechrist,* for example, an allegorical battle between the powers of Heaven and Hell, has political reference to the war between Louis IX and the Counts of Toulouse and Foix (1234–35).[61] As each vice steps forward, it is followed by a group of real men: the Burgundians follow *Felonie;* the Normans, *Boban;* the Romans, *Avarice.* The poet himself was in Louis' army at the time of his "vision," and paints a humorous portrait of himself as a coward who gets hit by one of Venus' arrows during the battle between *Sainte Foy* and *Ypocrisie* (*i.e.* the Albigensians). Huon is, however, as Tarbé notes, more of a moralist than a chronicler, and he includes real men for their exemplary, rather than for their historical, interest.

The use of historical example to illustrate an idea may be contrasted with Dante's use of historical figures to represent certain human ideas, attitudes, strengths, or weaknesses. Dante does not reduce men to their ideological significance; their full human and historical identity is preserved, although they serve as didactic models for all men.[62] In like manner, historical figures exemplify virtues in Rutebeuf's poetry on the Crusades; yet our attention is focused, in the Crusade poems, as much on the historical as on the moral world.

RUTEBEUF'S CRUSADE POETRY   The poet-moralist attempted to intervene actively in the movement of history when he

---

60. See Walter, *L'Exemplum,* chap. 2, "Sources des *exempla,*" pp. 83–108.
61. Tarbé, ed., Introduction, p. xvi.
62. See Auerbach's remarks on Dante, *Literary Language,* pp. 302–03.

wrote poems on the Crusades. These works not only referred frequently to contemporary historical events—to the campaigns in Italy and *outre-mer;* they also invited men to a specific historical act, to take the Cross, as well as to reflection on moral verities and self-amendment.

Rutebeuf's Crusade poetry must be seen as part of a propagandizing campaign made by the papacy to revive flagging support for the overseas venture. I shall discuss in Chapters 2 and 3 the new importance given, during the thirteenth century, to arousing and orienting public opinion. But Throop has already proved, in his *Criticism of the Crusades,* that a formidable effort was made during the thirteenth century to evaluate widespread opposition to the Crusades, and to combat public indifference.[63] In the same Lateran Council of 1215 which had recommended instruction of the people, and in the Second General Council of Lyons (1274), the Popes had asked the prelates for memoranda: the extant papers are veritable polls of public opinion, which make suggestions for reviving a wide base of support as well as outlining reforms in the administration of the Crusades.[64]

Throop has further analyzed at length a large body of thirteenth-century Provençal, French, and German Crusade poetry which reflected the movement of public opinion.[65] Opposition was especially strong in those countries whose national interest was most threat-

63. Palmer A. Throop, *Criticism of the Crusade: A Study of Public Opinion and Crusade Propaganda* (Amsterdam, 1940). This study, not cited in FB, is an essential complement to the FB *Notices* to Rutebeuf's Crusade poetry.

64. The memorandum from the Lyons Council by Gilbert of Tournay, *Collectio de scandalis ecclesiae,* Bishop Bruno of Olmütz' memoir, the *De statu saracenorum* of William of Tripoli, and Humbert of Roman's *Opus tripartitum* are discussed at length in Throop's *Criticism,* chaps. 3–7.

65. Throop, *Criticism,* chap. 2, "Independent Criticism, pp. 26–68. F. W. Wenzloff-Eggebert's *Kreuzzugsdichtung des Mittelalters. Studien zu ihrer geschichtlichen und dichterischen Wirklichkeit* (Berlin, 1960) mentions no French works later than 1220. The moralizing, satirical, and polemical works discussed by Throop are quite different from the courtly songs edited by Bédier and Aubry in their *Chansons de croisade* (Paris, 1909); the latter lament the sorrows of parting lovers and exhort men to take the Cross, but form "un petit genre littéraire à part qui a sa technique propre et ses traditions" (p. x). Bédier specifically excludes Rutebeuf's Crusade poems which represent "d'autres formes littéraires, complaintes, dits et débats" (p. xi and n. 1).

ened by the Crusades. The Provençal works generally opposed the Crusades as well as the French kingdom and the papacy, after the invasion of their homeland in the Albigensian Crusades. German works reflect the nationalistic drives awakened in Germany by the Hohenstaufen feud with the papacy. Opposition grew in Northern France as well, based on resentment of clerical abuses, papal interference in the prosecution of the wars, and discouragement over the many defeats of the Crusade armies.

Matthew Paris, writing about the disaster at Mansourah, sums up the popular reaction: "At this time [1252], too, the name of the French king began to be held in very small esteem in that kingdom, and to become hateful and disreputable amongst both the nobles and the common people . . . because he had been shamefully defeated by the infidels in Egypt." [66] Matthew Paris further says that even in 1245 Louis IX had to trick men into taking the Cross by giving them cloaks with crosses already sewn on, which they were then ashamed to remove.[67] Joinville's reluctant decision not to join his beloved king on the Tunis Crusade of 1270 is famous; but he also reports public resistance to Louis' pressure upon his nobles in 1270.[68] Only the resourcefulness of the papacy and the moral prestige of Louis IX kept the doomed Crusade effort alive; and Louis' death in Tunis marked the end of the Crusades.[69]

Rutebeuf does not belong to the generations of poets who went

66. *English History*, 2, trans. J. A. Giles (London, 1853), 479. Compare with Moniot d'Arras' poem on the fall of Damietta (1221) and the defeat of the French in Languedoc in 1219: "Bien mostre Dieux apertement/ Que n'ovron mie a son plaisir" (A. Jeanroy and Arthur Långfors, eds., *Chansons satiriques et bachiques du XIIIe siècle* [Paris, 1921], p. 10, No. VI).

67. *English History*, 2, 128.

68. "Endementres que li roys venoit aval, dui chevalier, qui estoient de son consoil, commencierent à parler li uns à l'autre, et dist li uns: 'Jamais ne me créez, se le roys ne se croise illec.' Et li autres respondi que 'se li roys se croise, ce yert une des douloureuses journées qui onques fust en France. Car se nous ne nous croisons, nous perderons le roy; et se nous nous croisons, nous perderons Dieu, que nous ne croiserons pas por li, mais pour paour dou roy'" (*Saint Louis*, ed. Natalis de Wailly, p. 398, par. 733).

69. In spite of Pope Gregory X's efforts, there was no general passage in 1277 as planned; the Tunis Crusade was the last great expedition to go *outre-mer*. (See Throop, *Criticism*, pp. 276 ff.; and Steven Runciman, *History of the Crusades, 3* [Cambridge, Eng., 1954], 387–480.)

along on the Crusades, as did Guiot de Provins at the end of the twelfth century, or as Jean Bodel had intended to do before he was stricken with leprosy in 1205. Indeed, he insists that his only contribution can be his verse:

> Diex gart Jasphes, Acre, Cesaire!
> Autre secors ne lor puis faire,
> Que je ne sui més hom de guerre.[70]
> (*Complainte de Constantinople*, vv. 28–30)

His poems refer mostly to events touching the Crusades which took place in Paris or France: he celebrates important men who have recently taken the Cross;[71] he eulogizes dead heroes when the news of their death reaches Paris.[72] When such Crusade leaders as Guillaume de Beaujeu, Grand Master of the Knights Templas, come to France, Rutebeuf exhorts others to support them.[73] His knowledge of Crusade personalities and issues derives, therefore, from news available in Paris,[74] or from papal directives on Crusade preaching sent to Paris.[75]

Rutebeuf's Crusade poetry seems directly inspired by the papal campaign which sought to answer criticism of the Crusades. Indeed,

---

70. The word *més* in verse 30 is translated "aucunement" by FB (*1*, 425 n.); both Alfred Foulet and Edward B. Ham prefer the translation "ne . . . plus" (Foulet's review of FB in *Speculum, 36*, No. 2 [April 1961], 330; Ham's in *Romance Philology, 16*, No. 3 [February 1963], 310). Foulet further proposes that Rutebeuf might have been too old to bear arms. I think Rutebeuf might be anticipating the reproach from his audience that he should practice what he preaches; we will see a similar self-defense below, p. 120, n. 9. In any case, there is no evidence to support Kressner's suggestion that Rutebeuf might have been a Crusader ("Rutebeuf als Satirendichter," *Franco-Gallia, 11*, No. 2 [February 1894], 21).

71. See FB, *1*, 453–54, 461–62, 494–95.

72. See Rutebeuf's vivid evocation of the spreading of the news of Alphonse's death in *Complainte du comte de Poitiers*, vv. 123–34.

73. See FB, *1*, 495–96.

74. See, for example, Rutebeuf's reference to a "maitre Jehan de Paris" who provided him with information about Thibaut de Champagne's conduct in Tunis (vv. 119–24, *Complainte du roi de Navarre;* see FB, *1*, 479–80).

75. See FB, *1*, 431–32, 435–36, 443–44. Information on the contents of these papal directives is given in P. Gratien, *Histoire de la fondation et de l'évolution de l'ordre des Frères Mineurs au XIIIe siècle* (Paris and Gembloux, 1928), pp. 643 ff.

his *Disputaison du Croisé* corresponds point by point with the refutations of Crusade critics by the Dominican Crusade preacher Humbert de Romans.[76] Although there has been considerable discussion of Rutebeuf's true opinion of the Crusades,[77] in point of fact, every one of his 11 Crusade poems is favorable not only to the Crusades but to the papal policies behind them. His Crusade poems cover more than a twenty-year period (1255–77), and, except for the eulogies of recently fallen Crusade heroes, each coincides with a new papal move to find backing for another Crusade venture.[78] Rutebeuf even supports Crusade policy and interests over and against what many saw as the national interest of France.[79] His *Chanson* and *Dit de Pouille* support Charles of Anjou's papal-inspired ambitions in Apulia and Sicily, which even Louis IX only reluctantly approved.[80] It is significant, too, that Rutebeuf, no ally of the papacy

76. See FB, *1*, 38–39, 469–70; and Throop, *Criticism*, pp. 151 ff., who cites Rutebeuf extensively. A résumé of Humbert's *De praedicatione crucis* is given by A. Lecoy de la Marche, "La Prédication de la croisade au XIIIe siècle," *Revue des Questions Historiques, 48* (July 1, 1890), 5–28.

77. LeGrand d'Aussy thought Rutebeuf opposed the Crusades, because the *Croisé* in the *Disputaison* offers only devout reasons for taking the Cross (*Fabliaux et contes, 2* [3d ed. Paris, 1829], 218, n. 4); yet there is only one reason for going overseas, but that one supreme: salvation. Léon Clédat said that Rutebeuf supported the Crusades (*Rutebeuf* [4th ed. Paris, 1909], pp. 119–20), while Edward B. Ham believed that Rutebeuf was never more than a half-hearted believer in the Crusades to which he paid lip service. See Ham's *Rutebeuf and Louis IX,* Univ. of North Carolina Studies in the Romance Languages and Literatures, XLII (Chapel Hill, 1962), pp. 21 and 33; Ham's edition of *Renart le Bestourné,* The University of Michigan Contributions in Modern Philology, IX (April, 1947), p. 46; and his "Rutebeuf: Pauper and Polemist," *Romance Philology, 11,* No. 3 [February 1958], 234–39. Ulrich Leo believes that Rutebeuf's attitude toward the Crusades changed and developed (*Studien zu Rutebeuf,* Beihefte zur Zeitschrift für romanische Philologie, No. 67 [Halle, 1922], p. 127). Faral suggests that Rutebeuf borrowed his ideas on the Crusades from Crusade preachers, but insists perhaps excessively on the Crusade poems as vehicles of attack against the Mendicants (FB, *1*, 39, 48, 64).

78. See FB *Notices* to Crusade poems, and n. 75 above.

79. See Throop, *Criticism,* pp. 58–59. As early as 1248, Matthew Paris reports criticism by Louis IX's nobles as to the political wisdom of the monarch's leaving France for the Crusades (*English History, 2,* 253–54); see also above, p. 41, and n. 68.

80. See Steven Runciman, *The Sicilian Vespers: The Rising Which Brought About the Overthrow of the Universal Papal Monarchy* (Middlesex and Baltimore, 1958), pp. 90–93, 103–19.

and ultramontane intervention in the University quarrel, should avoid mentioning the suspicions circulating everywhere that the papacy was using the Crusades to consolidate temporal power.[81] I believe, in conclusion, that Rutebeuf's patrons for some Crusade poems may have been papal emissaries to France who paid him to add his talents to the propagandist campaign already being carried out by the Mendicant preachers.[82]

Faral's supposition, however, that exhortations such as Rutebeuf's and those of Crusade preachers helped create an "état d'esprit" favorable to the Crusades (FB, *1*, 64) goes against evidence that both sermons and poems fell upon deaf ears. Influential as were the Mendicants, who assumed the burden of Crusade preaching,[83] they did not equal the successes of such twelfth-century figures as Saint Bernard, who said in 1146, "I opened my mouth, I spoke, and at once the crusaders were infinitely multiplied." [84] Etienne de Bourbon could still say of Jacques de Vitry, who preached in the early thirteenth century, that "he moved all France." [85] But a passage from the Franciscan chronicler Salimbene shows that there was a direct and violent popular reaction against those who preached the disastrous 1248 Crusade.

The common Folk of France . . . were terribly provoked against the Religious, more especially against the Friars Preachers and Minors, for that they had preached the Crusade and given men crosses to go beyond the seas with the King, who had now been conquered by the Saracens. So those French

81. Throop, *Criticism*, pp. 26–34, 68.

82. Faral suggests Simon of Brie, future Pope Martin IV and the papal legate in France during the 1260s, as a possible patron for the *Chanson de Pouille*, or perhaps Gui Folcodi, future Pope Clement IV, or Erart de Lézinnes, nephew of the Bishop of Auxerre, Gui de Mello, himself an ardent Crusader (FB, *1*, 432). Throop points out that the Provençal poems were often paid polemics (*Criticism*, p. 387). We may assume that the elegies of Crusade heroes were rewarded by the mourning families as well as by the Crusade propagandists (see FB, *1*, 455).

83. See Gratien, *Frères Mineurs*, for the Mendicant's sermons on Crusades as well as the participation of Mendicants in the Crusades themselves (pp. 642–49, 655–65).

84. Cited by Bédier (in French), *Chansons de croisade*, p. 4.

85. "Totam commovit Franciam," *Exempla*, ed. Crane, p. xxvii.

who were then left in France were wroth against Christ, to such a degree that they presumed to blaspheme His Name, which is blessed above all other names. For in those days when the Friars Minor and Preachers begged alms in France in Christ's name, men gnashed with their teeth on them; then, before their very faces, they would call some other poor man and give him money and say, 'Take that in Mahomet's name; for he is stronger than Christ.'[86]

Rutebeuf himself criticized Mendicant orders after 1261. He reproached them for their bungling interventions into affairs of state for which they were ill-fitted, as well as for their role in the University controversy.[87] He also protested their misappropriation of legacies left for the Crusades[88] and their lucrative practice of ab-

86. G. G. Coulton, trans., *From Saint Francis to Dante: Translations from the Chronicle of the Franciscan Salimbene (1221–1288)* (2d ed. London, 1907), pp. 187–88. Matthew Paris reports similar "words of raving [which] resounded from the tottering faith" (*English History, 2,* 335–36). Only the lowest social levels still responded emotionally to the itinerant preachers who had formerly moved nobles and kings. The urban proletariat, the rural poor, excluded from such lay Crusades as the Fourth, were swept by messianic hopes and bedazzled by the dream of Jerusalem as a heavenly city. They gathered repeatedly during the 13th century in periodic outbreaks of social unrest, but few ever actually reached the Holy Land. (See Cohn, *Millennium,* "In the Backwash of the Crusades," pp. 77–98; and Runciman, *Crusades, 3,* 279.)

87. See above, Chaps. 2 and 3; Ham, "Rutebeuf and Louis IX" (op. cit.), and "Rutebeuf and the Tunis Crusade," *Romance Philology, 9,* No. 2 (November 1955), 133–38; see also FB, *1,* 421–23, 533–35, and vv. 86–106 of *Renart le Bestourné.*

88. See vv. 109–120 of the *Complainte de Constantinople,* protesting the friars' absolution of heretics and usurers for their own profit:

> Que sont les deniers devenuz
> Qu'entre Jacobins et Menuz
> Ont receüz de testament
> De bougres por loiaus tenuz
>
> . . .
>
> Dont il ont grant aünement
> Dont li ost Dieu fust maintenuz?
> Més il le font tout autrement
> Qu'il en font lor grant fondement
> Et Diex remaint la outre nuz.

See also *Des Règles,* vv. 19–64, and compare with the poem *De Nostre Seignour* cited by Jubinal (*O.C., 1,* xxxviii, n. 1). Throop notes that Gregory X did excommunicate several Dominicans who refused to hand over Crusade funds (*Criticism,* p. 214).

solving men from their Crusade vows.[89] It would seem, then, that
Rutebeuf wrote admiringly of the friars as long as they limited
themselves to preaching,[90] but protested when they endangered the
Crusade effort.

In contrast with the reflective, impersonal tone of his moralizing
poems, Rutebeuf speaks directly in his Crusade works to his hearers,
as would a preacher exhorting his flock. Indeed, Rutebeuf even calls
his own Crusade poems sermons.[91] The basic theme of the menace
of approaching death, the necessity to win Paradise, is familiar
from moral works. But the note in the Crusade poems is more
urgent: Paradise is to be not merely earned but conquered. The
damning sins are cowardice and indifference to the Holy War, the
brightest virtues, courage and sacrifice.[92] The moralist's image of
a world where one strives for salvation takes on a martial air: "Cilz
siecles n'est pas siecles, ainz est chans de bataille." [93] The poet no

89. Verses 94–96 of the *Bataille des Vices contre des Vertus:*
> Se sainte Yglise excommenie,
> Li Frere pueent bien assaudre,
> S'escommeniez a que saudre,

are not a break in the ironic tone, as FB suggests (*1*, 308 n.); nor do they mean,
"Les Frères peuvent absoudre, à condition que les excommuniés soient à même de
leur rendre la pareille" as Ham suggests ("The Rutebeuf Corpus," *Romance Philology, 16*, No. 3 [February 1963], 306). Instead the verses clearly and sarcastically
refer to redemption of Crusade vows, which were often imposed as a penance; I
would translate: "Les Frères peuvent bien absoudre, si l'excommunié a de quoi
payer." Throop indicates that redemptions of Crusade vows were an important
source of income for the papacy, and that the cost of payment was often stipulated
in advance (*Criticism*, pp. 82–96). Matthew Paris describes this practice as one of
"the divers traps by which the Roman court endeavoured to deprive the simple
people of God of their substance" (*English History, 1*, 261 [Year 1240]). See also
the *Complainte de Jérusalem* cited by Bédier, *Chansons de Croisade* (p. 147):
> Rome, on set bien a escient
> Que tu decroisas por argent
> Ciax qui por Deu erent croisié.

On Crusade vows imposed as penance, see FB *1*, 422, and Br. I of the *Roman de
Renart*, where the fox's death sentence is commuted to a crusade vow (ed. Martin,
vv. 1388 ff., *1*, 39).

90. See the *Complainte d'outremer*, vv. 156–58.

91. *Nouvelle Complainte d'outremer*, v. 366. For Rutebeuf's imitation of exhortations and images sent by the Popes to the Mendicants, see FB, *1*, 37–39, 431,
442–44, 462, 496–97, and above, nn. 75, 76, and 83.

92. See *Voie de Tunes*, vv. 104, 93.

93. *Dit de Pouille*, v. 29.

longer merely counsels repentance to humble sinners like himself;
his words, like those of the preachers, carry the weight of papal
authority to promise absolution to those who take the Cross. In
sweeping verses like those beginning the *Dit de Pouille:*

> Cil Damediex qui fist air, feu et terre et meir,
> Et qui por notre mort senti le mors ameir,
> Il doint saint paradix, qui tant fait a ameir,
> A touz ceulz qui orront mon dit sans diffameir! (vv. 1–4)

one feels that the transcendent historical adventure of the Crusades
has excited the fervor of the moralist and the imagination of the
poet.

The call to the Holy War gives a special poignancy to commonplace moralizing themes. Rutebeuf had portrayed in his *Voie* (vv.
774–82) malingering monks who avoid matins because they fear
the night's chill. Using the same theme in the *Complainte d'outremer*
to attack sensual prelates, Rutebeuf brings the criticism into sharp
relief by contrasting their pleasures with what is truly required of
them, by contrasting a chilly breeze with the expansive image
of the open sea:

> Ahi! prelat de sainte Yglise
> Qui, por garder les cors de bise,
> Ne volez aler aus matines,
> Mesires Giefrois de Surgines
> Vous demande dela la mer.[94] (vv. 87–91)

The rather diffuse and abstract description of the punishment in
Hell awaiting the rich clerks of *Les Plaies* (vv. 35–88) may also be
compared with the briefer and more pungent images which end
the *Complainte de Constantinople*. Once again a true Crusader is
contrasted with the shirkers Rutebeuf attacks·

> Mesire Giefroi de Surgines,
> Je ne voi més deça nus signes

94. See FB, *1,* 411–13, for the exploits of this famous Crusader, and below, pp.
56–58.

Que l'en des or més vous sequeure.
Li cheval ont mal es eschines
Et li riche homme en lor poitrines.
Que fet Diex qui nes paraqueure? *   * exterminate
Encor vendra tout a tens l'eure
Que li maufé noir comme meure
Les tendront en lor desciplines;
Cels apeleront 'Chantepleure,'
Et sanz sejor lor corront seure
Qui lor liront longues matines. (vv. 169–80)

The poet answers the excuses offered by the reluctant with supple and piercing irony, summoning up a vision of restless demons impatient to receive these laggard souls into their infernal novitiate.

Rutebeuf's last Crusade poem, the *Nouvelle Complainte d'outremer,* uses almost all the themes and techniques of the earlier Crusade and moral works, and is not only one of the most typical but also, in my opinion, the finest of his Crusade exhortations. The poem is composed around three themes of time passing: time is running out for the defense of the Holy Land;[95] man's life span must be spent in winning salvation; God's Last Judgment will not be delayed forever.

Rutebeuf begins with lines of anguish and anger over the delays which have prevented Crusaders from leaving to fight (vv. 1–21; see FB, *1,* 496–97). After defining God's qualities as judge,[96] Rutebeuf turns from indirect statements on the brevity of "cest morteil vie" and an evocation of the Day of Judgment[97] to a series of direct questions to his hearers, such as:

95. It was true that the Holy Land as well as all the Near-Eastern and North-African fortresses were under constant pressure from the Sultan Baibars; Baibars died July 1, 1277, after reducing the Frankish domains to a few cities along the coast (Runciman, *Crusades, 3,* 315–48).

96. See FB, *1,* 496, on Rutebeuf's use of the sermon technique of *divisio per verba* to explain God as a judge "fors et poissans/ Et sages et bien connoissans" (vv. 34–50).

97. Vv. 51–82; see FB, *1,* 500, note to vv. 73–78, for sources of Rutebeuf's imagery.

> Que n'entendeiz a votre afaire
> Tant com de vie aveiz espace?   (vv. 68–69)

He thus creates a responsive attitude in his hearers, who must themselves find answers to these difficult questions of life and death.[98]

Rutebeuf appeals first to the young Kings Philippe le Hardi
and Edward I. The time of their youth, of their reign, must serve to
save the Holy Land:

> Rois de France, rois d'Aingleterre,
> Qu'en jonesce deveiz conquerre
> L'oneur dou cors, le preu de l'ame
> Ains que li cors soit soz la lame
>
>   · · ·
>
> Si secoreiz la Terre sainte
> Qui est perdue a ceste empainte,
> Qui n'a pas un an de recours
> S'en l'an meïmes n'a recours.
> Et s'ele est a voz tenz perdue,
> A cui tens ert ele rendue?   (vv. 83–86, 89–94)

Rutebeuf completely identifies human salvation with the rescue
of the lands overseas. Intertwining the two themes, he insists on the
imminent menaces to the Holy Land[99] and on the shortness of
man's life span, for which he must render an accounting before
God. Many of the expressions of time—"espace, saison, votre tens"[1]
—suggest blocks of time which man receives from God as the
sculptor receives his marble, the poet his theme. Man, by his actions,

98. See also vv. 63–67, 75–78, 79–82.
99.   Baron, qu'aveiz vos enpancei?
                     Seront ja mais par vos tensei
                     Cil d'Acre qui sunt en balance,
                     Et de secorre en esperance? (vv. 103–06)
1. See for example, vv. 95–97:
                     Rois de Sezille, par la grace
                     De Dieu qui vos dona espace
                     De conquerre Puille et Cezille,
or vv. 119–20:
                     Vous despandeiz, et sens raison,
                     Votre tens et votre saison.

can spoil his lifetime or exploit it to the fullest extent. He can extract the "noiel" instead of choosing "l'escrasche" ("hull," v. 122);
he must honor God's gift by enhancing the worth of the moments
given him.

Images of youth and old age recur throughout the poem.[2]
Rutebeuf stresses physical decrepitude when he addresses the "jone
escuier au poil volage" (v. 135):

> Il ne vos chaut que vos faciez
> Tant que viellesce vos efface,
> Que ridee vos est la face,
> Que vos iestes viel et chenu
>
> . . .
>
> Quant vostre tenz aveiz vescu
> Qu'ainz paiens ne vit votre escu,
> Que deveiz demandeir celui *   * Christ
> Qui sacrefice fist de lui? (vv. 164–67, 177–80)

He touches on the wrinkles, the white hair; these are the outward,
visible signs of the invisible passing of time. The poet's quick leap
over the years, his vision of the sudden aging of the fair young faces
before him, bring out a sense of urgency in the poet's call to
action,[3] as he points to their shields, symbols of their untried
bravery.

The poet speaks to each group of men in terms most apt to
touch them, to make them feel the brevity of life and the uncer-
tainty of worldly goods. He compares the young squires to their
hunting hawks, more brave and more obedient than they themselves
to their Master:

> Vostre esprevier sunt trop plus donte *   * trained
> Que vos n'iestes, c'est veriteiz;
> Car teil i a, quant le geteiz,
> Seur le poing aporte l'aloe.* (vv. 144–47)   * lark

2. See vv. 8–12, 84, 120, 191–92, 305 ff.

The mock-heroic epithets fall particularly heavily on those who
should be showing true warlike valor: "Prelat auz palefrois
norrois," "Chevalier de plaiz et d'axises," "Riche borjois d'autrui
sustance" (vv. 197, 245, 281). Rutebeuf evokes at length the activities of the "riche borgois d'autrui sustance," using a mercantile
vocabulary: "lagan [salvage], mestier, afaire, vendre, lettre, plege,
nans [guarantee], acheteir, uzerier." Rutebeuf does not attempt to
frighten these fat businessmen with physical decrepitude. Instead,
he shows how their children will dissipate their fortunes; all their
laborious piling up of gold will go for naught when they die:

> Ja puis n'en iert contes tenuz.
> Quant li enfant sunt lor seigneur,
> Veiz ci conquest a grant honeur:
> Au bordel ou en la taverne
> Qui plus tost puet plus s'i governe.
>   . . .
> Teiz marchiez font com vous eüstes
> Quant en votre autoritei fustes.
> Chacuns en prent, chacuns en oste;
> Enz osteiz pluet, s'en vont li oste.
>   (vv. 308–12, 315–18)

In the passage Rutebeuf shows the vanity of human ambition by
contrasting the titles of power—"seigneur, honeur, autoritei"—with
the concrete images of helpless loss: the dissolute children, the
greedy hands reaching into the coffers, and finally, the empty house
under the rain.[4]

One admires again in the *Nouvelle Complainte* the striking renewal of commonplace satirical themes such as that of the boastful

3. Compare with similar themes in *Voie de Tunes*, st. XXII, and *Chanson de
Pouille*, sts. II and VII, where the poet uses moralizing generalizations instead of
precise images.
4. Compare with *Voie de Tunes*, vv. 90–92:
> Je voi aucun riche home faire maisonnement:
> Quant il a assouvi trestout entierement,
> Si li fait hon un autre, de petit coustement.

bravery of drunkards;[5] Rutebeuf himself sketched the theme in his *Complainte du comte Eudes de Nevers* (vv. 157–61). But in the *Nouvelle Complainte* he returns in a wonderful passage to attack knights whose bravery is in their cups.

> Quant la teste est bien avinee,
> Au feu deleiz la cheminee,
> Si vos croiziez sens sermoneir;
> Donc verriez granz coulz doneir
> Seur le sozdant et seur sa gent;
> Forment les aleiz damagent.
> Quant vos vos leveiz au matin
> S'aveiz changié votre latin.
> Que gari sunt tuit li blecié
> Et li abatu redrecié.
> Li un vont au lievres chacier,
> Et li autre vont porchacier
> S'il panront un mallart ou deux
> Car de combatre n'est pas geux. (vv. 251–64)

Rutebeuf sets the stage carefully, painting the cozy scene which warms the imagination of these bedtime Crusaders to swift and effortless action. Instead of the rather clumsy phrase of generalization which ends the scene in the *Complainte d'Eudes de Nevers*— "Teil coutume a et clers et lais" (v. 162)—Rutebeuf expresses indirectly his moralization on such drunkards' dreams of glory by portraying "the morning after." The poet runs the scene backward: the opened wounds close; the fallen rise up. The gay, comradely group disperses, as do the winey fumes and the fine deeds; each goes to face an enemy worthy of his courage: hares and ducks![6]

---

5. F. Lecoy cites eight such works, "Notes de lexicographie française," *Romania*, 70, No. 3 (1948–49), 347–48. See also FB, *1*, 459, note to vv. 157–61; and the passage from Pierre de Blois cited by Kilgour, *The Decline of Chivalry* . . . (Cambridge, Mass., 1937), p. 5; as well as a criticism by Gilbert of Tournay in his memoranda for the Lyons Council of 1274 cited by Throop (*Criticism*, p. 103).

6. A knight shying away from a hare often served to represent Cowardice in medieval art; see Mâle, *Gothic Image*, pp. 122–23 and figs 65–67.

One of the stylistic constants in the *complainte* form was the apostrophe, a form of direct address or exhortation repeated at intervals throughout the poem.[7] Apostrophe enables Rutebeuf to shift easily, as he does in the *Nouvelle Complainte,* from one group or person to another without breaking the fundamental unity of his poem, simply because the *complainte* is basically a series of exclamations. In the *Nouvelle Complainte* Rutebeuf calls out only to individuals or groups of men: "Prince! Baron! tournoiëur!" In other poems he calls upon cities, countries, the earth, and death itself.[8] By commencing a new apostrophe the poet can introduce virtually any new theme, shift rapidly from one subject to another. The apostrophe further maintains an exalted emotional tone; it prevents a poem as long as the *Nouvelle Complainte* (366 verses) from declining into discursive monotony by beginning anew at intervals with fresh matter and by striking again the original note of intensity.

The *Nouvelle Complainte* draws to a close with a marvelously evocative phrase of appeal which Rutebeuf had already used in the *Complainte d'outremer* (v. 16): "Recoumanciez novele estoire!" (v. 341). The final exhortations seem to turn on the several meanings of *estoire:* race, story, epic, and history (vv. 327–56). Rutebeuf invites his hearers to repeat the exploits of the first generation of Crusade heroes, the race of "li preudome de jadiz,/ Godefroiz, Buemons et Tancreiz" (vv. 334–35). He urges them further to imitate the sacrifices of God's saints, whose story he recalls (vv. 344–46). His hearers must rewrite the epics of the past[9] and start

---

7. See Edmond Faral, *Les Arts poétiques du XIIe et du XIIIe siècle* . . . (Paris, 1923), p. 72; see also below, p. 164.

8. See *Complainte d'outremer,* v. 149; *Eudes de Nevers,* v. 49; *Complainte de Constantinople,* vv. 43, 73.

9. In the *Complainte d'outremer* Rutebeuf specifically states that no epic heroism should move men as much as the Crusades and the Crucifixion (vv. 1–20, 57–63). The theme was a common one in sermons and didactic works. Add to the examples cited FB, *1,* 446: the Prologue from the *Passion des jongleurs* (cited by Grace Frank, *Medieval French Drama* [Oxford, 1960], p. 125); a text from Pierre de Blois ending, "Qui compateris Deo, compateris et Arturo," cited, with very interesting discussion, by Auerbach (*Literary Language,* pp. 303–06). Epic heroes served,

THE POET AS MORALIST

a new age to recover the supreme heroic values lost in history. Finally, the phrase turns the central theme of time into an urgent imperative: those lords and knights upon whom he calls must make history, must give shape, meaning, and value to the measure of hours given them.

THE ART OF CHARACTERIZATION IN RUTEBEUF'S CRUSADE AND DIDACTIC WORKS   Rutebeuf's Crusade poetry is entirely centered around men and the humanized figure of God as judge and leader. Those who died on the Crusades are exalted heroes who have, by their personal sacrifice, imitated the supreme sacrifice of Christ. The poems show that the same chance for glory and salvation awaits each man to whom Rutebeuf speaks. The wars overseas, therefore, are not portrayed in terms of strategy or politics nor even of sweeping scenes of military splendor. Rutebeuf is unfamiliar with the majesty of a fleet setting sail, with the cry "Faites voile, de par Dieu," and a thousand voices as one singing "Veni creator Spiritus." [10] He composes his battle scenes to illuminate one central figure. Geoffroi de Sergines, for example, appears with his men:

> Més sanz lui ne s'osent combatre:
> Par lui joustent, par lui guerroient,
> Jamés sanz lui ne se verroient

nonetheless, as standards for the bravery required of Crusaders; see the *Dit de Pouille,* favoring Charles of Anjou:
> Trop at contre le roi d'Yaumons et d'Agoulans;
> Il at non li rois Charles, or li faut des Rollans. (vv. 23–24)
Compare with Adam de la Halle's *C'est du roi de Sezile;* where a Virgilian note creeps in:
> La matère est de Dieu et d'armes et d'amours,
> Et du plus noble prinche en prouesche et en mours
>   . . .
> Mais s'encore fust Charles en Franche le roial
> Encore trouvast-on Rolant et Parcheval.
> (vv. 10–11, 49–50; E. de Coussemaker, ed., *Œuvres complètes*
>   [Paris, 1872], pp. 283–84).

10. Joinville, *Saint Louis,* p. 70, par. 126.

En bataille ne en estor,
Qu'il font de lui chastel et tor.
A lui s'asenent et ralient,
Quar c'est lor estandart, ce dient.
C'est cil qui du champ ne se muet:
El champ le puet trover qui veut,
Ne ja, por fais que il soustiengne,
Ne partira de la besoingne.
            (*Complainte de Geoffroi de Sergines,* vv. 134–44)

The attacking pagans, the rallying soldiers, all swirl around one
central figure who towers, immobile. Geoffroi is the incarnation of
courage, the sign of victory.

Throop has shown how effective was the example of noble
Crusaders admired by all in persuading the reluctant to take the
Cross.[11] Rutebeuf's glorification of past and present heroes, then,
was partially determined by his didactic intention. The thirteenth-
century portraitist, whether painter, sculptor, or poet, was, moreover, generally less interested in rendering individual peculiarities
of one man than in drawing out the eternal significance of an individual life.

The significance of a man's life, however, depended on the moral
aim of the artist. Alphonse de Poitiers, for example, brother of
Louis IX, was stricken with palsy in 1252. Matthew of Paris, un-
sympathetic to Alfonse, says of his illness that "perchance [Al-
phonse] was struck by the Divine vengeance, for when his
brother the king was placed in a very critical position, he did not
assist him as he had promised to do." [12] Rutebeuf reports the same
illness but turns it to the advantage of Alphonse in his eulogizing
Complainte du comte de Poitiers, interpreting it as a trial sent by
God for the health of Alphonse's soul:

> Dieux le tanta par maintes fois
> Por connoistre queiz ert sa fois,

11. *Criticism,* pp. 201–02.
12. *English History,* 2, 506; on the promised help Alphonse was to send to Louis
in Egypt in 1250, see Matthew Paris, ibid., p. 506, and Runciman, *Crusades, 3,* 279.

Si connoist il et cuer et cors
Et par dedens et par defors:
Job le trouva en paciance
Et saint Abraham en fiance.
Ainz n'ot fors maladie ou painne,
S'en dut estre s'arme plus sainne. (vv. 101–08)

Such details of portraiture are, then, realistic in the sense that the poet uses historical details from a man's life. Yet the artist paints with moralistic colors; although the individual is present, our attention is turned to the lesson his life can teach us.

Rutebeuf's descriptions of Crusade heroes are further determined by the conventions of rhetoric (see below, pp. 197 ff.). The poetic arts of medieval theoreticians prescribed that authors consider the name, nature, life, social condition, acts, and words of their models,[13] although in practice such rhetorical rules were applied with great flexibility in vernacular texts. Moreover, certain virtues were conventionally attributed to certain types: the poet praised the prelate for his faith, the hero for his strength and wisdom, a woman for her beauty and seriousness, a prince for his administration of justice.[14] I do not, however, believe with Faral that "la formule empêche la vie de se manifester,"[15] but rather that historical reality is cast in a particular mold, suitable to the model. In the hands of a master like Chrétien de Troyes, for example, the type of the perfect knight is subjected to subtle modulations. All of the names of the great roster of the Round Table—Gauvain, Erec, Yvain, Lancelot, Perceval—evoke the image of the perfect knight. Yet we distinguish clearly each one as a special facet of the lovely jewel of knighthood, just as Iseut, Guinevere, and Enide exemplify feminine beauty, yet live as unforgettable and unique heroines.

In his panegyric of Geoffroi de Sergines, defender of Jaffa and Acre, Rutebeuf uses the topic of *sapientia* and *fortitudo,* appro-

13. Faral, *Arts poétiques,* pp. 77–78; see also Charles Baldwin, *Medieval Rhetoric and Poetic* . . . (Gloucester, Mass., 1959), p. 267. On the practical application of rhetorical rules, see Alice Colby, *The Portrait in Twelfth-Century French Literature* (Geneva, 1965), esp. pp. 3–22.
14. Faral, *Arts poétiques,* pp. 78–79.
15. Ibid., p. 79.

priate to the ideal hero.[16] Instead of reducing the *topos* to a mere formula, however, as in the *Complainte du roi de Navarre*,[17] Rutebeuf expands it as his central theme, using the concrete images of body and soul.[18] After a moralizing introduction on the sin of sacrificing "le preu des ames por le cors," Rutebeuf casts the theme into the first person, as he did in his didactic *Voie de Paradis;* the poet himself serves as a foil to reveal Geoffroi's greatness to those who should imitate him:

> De ses teches * vous vueil touchier   * qualities
> Un pou, selonc ce que j'en sai;
> Quar, qui me metroit a l'essai
> De changier ame por la moie
> Et je a l'eslire venoie,
> De toz cels qui orendroit vivent
> Qui por lor ame au siecle estrivent,
> Tant quierent pain trestoz deschaus
> Par les granz froiz et par les chaus
> Ou vestent haire ou çaingnent corde
> Ou plus facent que ne recorde,
> Si penroie ainz l'ame de lui
> Plus tost, je cuit, que la nului. (vv. 36–48)

16. See Curtius, *European Literature,* chap. 9, "Heroes and Rulers," esp. pp. 174–76. Rutebeuf interprets *sapientia* as both wisdom in counsel and as goodness of soul in a specifically Christian sense. "Bonté d'ame" (v. 57) for Rutebeuf included chivalric courtesy, justice, and charity, together with religious piety. The spiritual and physical qualities of the hero became in fact meritorious only as they were offered in God's service; see, for example, vv. 57, 68–71, 90–91, 104–05, where the *topos* of wisdom and courage is repeated; see also FB, *1,* 412, for reappearance of the *topos* in both Joinville's and Guillaume de Nangis' descriptions of Geoffroi: "le bon chevalier et le prudhome"; "virum sapientem et fidelem et in armis strenuum."

17.   Boens en consoil et bien meürs,
              Auz armes vistes et seürs. (vv. 67–68)

18. The keys words *cors* and *ame* appear 15 times in the first 61 verses and reappear in the final prayer:

              Or prions donques a celui
              Qui refuser ne set nului

                . . .

              Le cors a cel preudomme gart
              Et l'ame reçoive a sa part. (vv. 157–58, 165–66)

Rutebeuf's statement that he would trade his soul for that of
Geoffroi [19] is drawn out over a long sentence of ten verses evoking
the sufferings of the holy Mendicants and accumulating visual
images of mortification: "deschaus, granz froiz, chaus, haire,
corde." Geoffroi's greatness is thus first stated indirectly, through
comparison with the humble poet, then with the toiling Mendicants.
After such praise of Geoffroi's soul, Rutebeuf celebrates his physical
prowess:

> D'endroit du cors vous puis je dire
> Que, qui me metroit a l'eslire
> L'un des bons chevaliers de France
> Ou du roiaume a ma creance,
> Ja autre de lui n'esliroie.
> Je ne sai que plus vous diroie,
> Tant est preudom, si com moi samble,
> Qui a ces deus choses ensamble:
> Valor de cors et bonté d'ame. (vv. 49–57)

The poet no longer attempts to compare himself to his model.
Rutebeuf appears only as witness, elector of the elect, to attest to
the growing fame of Geoffroi, who surpasses all the other knights
in France. Only after building a long series of comparison does
Rutebeuf directly state the supreme merits of Geoffroi himself; thus
the topic "valor de cors et bonté d'ame" (v. 57) comes as a necessary result of the preceding description. Clearly, the conventional
topos of physical and spiritual heroism is in no way forced upon
the poem, but, rather, the poem grows naturally around it and
out of it.

Rutebeuf's *Complainte du comte de Poitiers* is a splendid eulogy
of his former protector (FB, *1,* 486), whom the poet extols in
accordance with the *topos* of the just prince, as an equitable lord

---

19. The theme of changing souls seems to be a topic also: compare vv. 4–5 of the
Complainte du comte Eudes de Nevers:
> . . . l'un de ceulz que plus amoie
> Et que mieux recembleir vodroie.
or vv. 32 and 92–94 of the *Complainte du comte de Poitiers.*

of his lands. Alphonse, palsied and partially blind, had followed his brother on the disastrous Tunis Crusade, only to die in Savona on the sorrowful return journey. Rutebeuf ornaments his poem, therefore, with military imagery to celebrate the count who had truly given "por Dieu le cors en guerre" (v. 20).

The *Complainte* opens with an image of Christ as man's armor against sin. He protects the weak sinner with the helmet, shield, and hauberk of His own body. Paradise may be earned by imitating Christ's supreme sacrifice, moralizes Rutebeuf, citing him who "de legier laisse peire et meire/ Et fame et enfans et sa terre" (vv. 18–19). Only after this description of the supreme knight, Christ, and the ideal knight, who leaves all for God's war, does Rutebeuf name the Count of Poitiers. Alphonse thus appears endowed with all the qualities of the preceding verses. He is painted in a moment of knightly splendor:

> Ainsi fut li cuens de Poitiers
> Qui toz jors fu boens et entiers,
> Chevaucha cest siecle terrestre
> Et mena paradix en destre. (vv. 25–28)

The good Count is a mounted knight, already beyond earthly limits. He sits astride the world, leading his hopes of Paradise like a magnificent warhorse reserved for battle, ready for his triumphant and merited entry through the gates of Paradise.

The imagery of the armed Crusader is carried through the whole poem. Just as Christ's flank shields sinners, Alphonse was "boen escu" for poor men (v. 70); his generosity and piety rendered him "miraours de chevalerie" (v. 69). This continuity of image exalts Alphonse to the point that the Count's voyage to Tunis is finally depicted as a more than human venture. Rutebeuf never says, in fact, that Alphonse is dead, but rather that his voyage became a sublime road to Paradise:

> . . . en la voie
> De Tunes, en son revenir,
> Vout Dieux le conte detenir. (vv. 128–30)

Rutebeuf figures in his poem, as he did in the *Complainte de Geoffroi,* to testify to the truth of what he says about Alphonse.[20] He chooses to eulogize Alphonse's courteous charity, another common *topos* of praise, pointing out the surpassing merit of Alphonse by means of comparison with a famous historical example:[21]

> Hom nos at parlei d'Alixandre,
> De sa largesce, de son sans
> Et de ce qu'il fist a son tans;
> S'en pot chacuns, s'il vot, mentir,
> Ne nos ne l'osons desmentir
> Car nous n'estions pas adonc;
> Mais se por bontei ne por don
> A preudons le regne celestre,
> Li cuens Aufons i doit bien estre. (vv. 80–88)

By painting himself with his patron, Rutebeuf is able to praise him, yet adeptly avoid the appearance of hyperbole.

As in the *Complainte de Geoffroi,* conventional topics are used, but with such art that they orient the flow of the poem without blocking it. One does not have the impression that Rutebeuf is forcing his model to fit a pattern, but that the pattern serves as a means for understanding the worth of Count Alphonse. Funeral laments, for example, usually end with a prayer for the soul of the dead hero.[22] Yet the last verses of the *Complainte du comte de Poitiers* are:

> Ne croi que priier en conveigne:
> Prions li de nos soveigne! (vv. 143–44)

20. See vv. 37–38 and 61:
        Por ce qu'il me fist tant de biens
        Vo vuel retraire un pou des siens.

          . . .

       Ce que je vi puis je bien dire.
21. See Curtius, *European Literature,* chap. 8, "Poetry and Rhetoric," p. 6, and "Outdoing," pp. 162–66. See also Rutebeuf's *Dit d'Aristote,* where he celebrates the legendary generosity of Alexander.
22. See the final verses of the *Complaintes du roi de Navarre, Eudes de Nevers,* and *Anceau de l'Isle.*

Rutebeuf here suggests that Alphonse is already among God's elect, with the saints and martyrs, and thus even the closing prayer is skillfully turned to honor the Count.

Some important generalizations about Rutebeuf's art of characterization emerge from our reading of his panegyrics of Crusade heroes. We have seen that his portrayal of character is guided to a great extent by moral concerns and that these are, in turn, codified by rhetorical usage. In the words of Faral: "Dans toute la littérature du moyen âge, la description ne vise que très rarement à peindre objectivement les personnes et les choses. . . . [Elle est] toujours dominée par une intention affective qui oscille entre la louange et la critique."[23] By "affective," however, I believe we must understand a moral point of view, which is only given as the author's own (see below, Chap. 5).

The medieval poet-portraitists felt further that individual peculiarities were a hindrance to their desire to portray exemplary types.[24] Each individual was to be seen as a representative of a certain group; it was when the individual could be shown to be typical that he was interesting, because his particular self revealed a greater truth, taught a general lesson. This is as true of the negative portrait Rutebeuf paints of himself in his poems of misfortune (see below, Ch. V) as it is of the splendid heroes of the Crusade poems. The former portray the type of the miserable and impoverished sinner, the latter, models of perfection and merit.

The artist may describe intimate sides of a great man, as Joinville shows us Saint Louis in moments of relaxation and gaiety.[25] Yet intimate details are never included for their own sake, but only as illustrations of a moral point. Thus Rutebeuf describes in his *Complainte du roi de Navarre* the return of Count Thibaut V to his camp from the battlefields of Tunis:

23. *Arts poétiques,* p. 76.
24. An interesting example of a medieval biographer eliminating nonexemplary details from his story of his subject's life is to be found in the changes Bonaventura made in his life of St. Francis. Homely details, such as the story of Francis dancing before the Pope, are excluded as unworthy of the Saint. (See John R. H. Moorman, *Sources for the Life of S. Francis of Assisi* [Manchester, 1940], p. 147.)
25. See, for example, Louis' *tenson* with Joinville (*Saint Louis,* par. 23).

> Quant il estoit retornei,
> Si trovoit hon tot atornei:
> Tables et blanches napes mises.
> Tant avoit laians de reprises *   * lessons
> Donees si cortoisement,
> Et roi de tiel contenement,
> Qu'a aise sui quant le recorde. (vv. 97–103)

The passage illustrates the virtues of courtesy and generosity by depicting Thibaut himself gently instructing his followers in the art of courtly behavior.

Didactic and moral concerns explain why Rutebeuf deliberately turned away from the picturesque aspects of the life of Saint Mary the Egyptian. He does not insist, as did his sources, on the beauty of the repentant prostitute or on her pleasure in wickedness.[26] The only lengthy physical portrait he preserves is the edifying description of her hideous physical decadence after her years of mortification in the desert:

> Char ot noire com pié de cigne;
> Sa poitrine devint mossue,
> Tant fu de pluie debatue.
> Les braz, les lons dois et les mains
> Avoit plus noirs, et c'ert du mains,
> Que n'estoit pois ne arremenz.
> Ses ongles rooingnoit aus denz.
> Ne samble qu'ele ait point de ventre,
> Por ce que viande n'i entre.

26. See Rutebeuf's source MS T, in A. T. Baker, ed., "Vie de Sainte Marie l'Égyptienne," *Revue des Langues Romanes*, 59, Nos. 3–6 (1916–17), 292–94, vv. 159–206. On Rutebeuf's use of sources for *Marie l'Egyptienne*, see FB, 2, 10–13, and the edition by Bernadine A. Bujila (*The University of Michigan Contributions in Modern Philology*, No. 12 [June 1949], pp. 21–26). See also Robson's excellent review of Bujila's edition in *Medium Aevum*, 20 (1951), 88–91, in which he suggests Rutebeuf worked from a text he knew by heart rather than from written sources, and Ulrich Leo's interesting remarks in "Rutebeuf: persönlicher Ausdruck und Wirklichkeit," *Saggi e ricerche in memoria di Ettore Li Gotti*, 2 (Palermo 1962), 157–61.

> Les piez avoit crevez desus,
> Desouz navrez que ne pot plus
> Ne se gardait pas des espines.[27] (vv. 452–63)

In spite of the accumulation of repulsive details, this is not a realist's portrayal of a woman's suffering but a moralist's representation of the spiritual worthlessness of the human body. Mary had to endure—indeed, had to impose such wounds upon her body —so that her soul might be freed of its earthly prison, might finally slip through her worn flesh to rejoin her Creator. Laved by the rain, pierced by thorns, hollowed by starvation, she truly underwent purification and could finally pray God for death:

> . . . Biaus douz Pere
> Toi pri que ta bontez me pere.
> Quarante et neuf anz t'ai servi,
> A toi ai mon cors asservi.
> Fai de ta fille ton voloir. (vv. 1087–91)

Rutebeuf brings out this didactic value of his story by repeating the key terms "cors" and "ame" throughout his story.[28] Thus he constantly keeps his moral goal in the foreground and imposes a significant order on the narrative.

Several critics have thought that the characters in Rutebeuf's *Miracle de Théophile* were thinly portrayed and that the psychological motivation was poorly prepared.[29] I find Lemaître's description of the characterization almost entirely accurate:

> Théophile et les autres sont, en effet, des âmes très simples. Ils n'éprouvent qu'une impression à la fois. Leurs sentiments ne

---

27. Compare with Sources MS T, vv. 633–80 (ed. Baker, pp. 318–21), which brings out specifically the value of this mortification in these lines:
> . . . uns de ses pecies li caoit
> Quant une espine le poignoit,
> Por ce estoit ele molt lie
> Quant ele soffroit tel hascie. (vv. 671–74)

28. See, for example, vv. 216–29, 287–88, 1126–32.

29. See, for example, Léon Clédat, *Rutebeuf*, p. 47; and Frank, *Medieval French Drama*, p. 110.

sont que successifs, jamais simultanés. . . . [Théophile] passe
de la joie du crime au remords, directement, sans aucune espèce
de préparation. . . . Chacun de ses sentiments est détaché de
celui qui précède et paraîtra ignoré de celui qui suivra.[30]

Lemaître's explanation, however, of this succession of simple states
of being shows a fundamental misunderstanding of the nature and
intent of the *Miracle*. He says that the simplicity of character portrayal is due to Rutebeuf's own simplicity and incapacity for feeling more than one emotion at a time. In reality, the *Miracle de
Théophile* is a series of didactic tableaux, illustrating, through a
succession of images and attitudes, a story well known to the
medieval audience.[31] Only the exemplary moments are staged;
they are juxtaposed in much the same manner as a miracle would
be "narrated" in a stained-glass window or a sculpture. There is
no realistic psychological continuity between the scenes; there are
only typical gestures which illustrate clearly the value of Théophile's
acts at significant moments:[32] Théophile the sinner kneels to pay
homage to the Devil; a defiant Théophile in the Devil's power
quarrels with his friends; a penitent Théophile weeps before the
Virgin.[33]

The psychological continuity between these instructive scenes
was provided not by the text but by the spectators themselves.

30. Review of Clédat's *Rutebeuf* in *Journal des Débats Politiques et Littéraires*
(July 6, 1891), pp. 1–2. Only the verses in which Théophile "pense que trop a
grant chose en Dieu renoier" (vv. 101–43) show indecision and debate within one
scene; by presenting here alternatives, Rutebeuf underlines, I believe, the enormity
of Théophile's sin.

31. See FB, 2, 169, 173–74.

32. Rutebeuf's dramatic technique seems to derive from the archaic paratactic
technique described by Auerbach in his analysis of *Saint Alexis;* the early saint's
life removed events from their temporal context so that they became "impressive
gesturally, so that they appear as exemplary, as models" (*Mimesis*, pp. 97–107).
Compare with the more realistic setting of Rutebeuf's *Sacristain* miracle, where he
provided fuller psychological motivation and continuity (see below, p. 242).

33. Compare with the description of the sculptural representation of the legend
of Théophile at Notre-Dame de Paris (FB, 2, 169). Five significant scenes show
Théophile's fall, penitence, and pardon. See also Ernest Faligan, "Des Formes
iconographiques de la légende de Théophile," *Revue des Traditions Populaires, 5,*
No. 1 (January 15, 1890), 1–14; and the bibiliography cited by FB, 2, 169, nn. 1–2.

Rutebeuf inspires a succession of reactions in his audience through the vivid dramatization of exemplary and timeless moments. Indeed, in a truly didactic work it is the audience as well as the characters who must experience a convincing realization of sin and repentance; the didactic and intentional work of art is only complete as it affects the audience.

Some moral commentary and orientation for the spectators is provided within the text itself. Thomas, for example, reproaches Théophile with his extravagant Devil-inspired behavior, saying "vous n'estes pas bien sages" (v. 375). Théophile himself insists on the magnitude of his sin in his repentance scene of self-condemnation (vv. 384–539). Both Théophile and the Bishop appear at the end to recapitulate the story and draw the moral (vv. 602–63).

Yet the simple symbolism of the staging itself was largely sufficient to guide the spectator's reaction to each scene. The stage was arranged with the Virgin at stage (and moral) right and the Devil to the sinister stage left; the Bishop, Pinceguerre, Thomas, and Pierre remain in the terrestrial middle, between Heaven and Hell.[34] The spectators could judge the value of Théophile's actions by his position on the stage and by his movements to the right or left between the scenes. Familiar as they were with spiritual topography,[35] the spectators would tremble fearfully with Théophile as he moved toward the Devil; they would not need to be told Théophile desired to repent when they saw him move from left to right.

It becomes clear, in conclusion, that we must approach Rutebeuf's moralizing poetry through a definition of his didactic intent. If we impose our own desire for a continuous narrative in the *Voie de Paradis,* for psychological flexibility in *Théophile,* and for realism

34. See Gustave Cohen, "Les Chefs-d'œuvre animés au souffle de la jeunesse; la plus ancienne pièce de notre théâtre en France, *Le Miracle de Théophile,*" *Conferencia, 31,* No. 2 (January 1, 1937), 87–89. The positions indicated in FB, *2,* 172 are not only wrong in that they place the Virgin in the center instead of in her *right*ful place; the editors' suggestion that the left to right order could be reversed is theatrically inexact and even spiritually dangerous! (See Grace Frank, *Medieval French Drama* [Oxford, 1954], p. 111 and note 1.)

35. See, for example, the "geography" of Rutebeuf's *Voie de Paradis* above, p. 30.

in his portraits, we miss the essential elements of the medieval moralist's art. It is an art that must always be seen in relation to the poet's aim of affecting his public and in relation to a literary and moralizing tradition which the poet preserves while renewing its forms and themes. The high points of these poems may be for us the occasional vivid flash of human life, seen through a mesh of moralizing generalizations. Yet even when, as we shall see in the next two chapters, the poet used moral concerns as a means to a political end, the moral meaning of every subject was the first concern of the poet and his hearers. The art of the medieval didactic poet lay in his ability to reveal effectively to his hearers the significant lesson to be drawn from historical events and human lives.

CHAPTER TWO: THE MORALIST
TURNS PROPAGANDIST

ISTORY AND MORALITY Some useful distinctions and definitions may now be made to elucidate the processes at work in Rutebeuf's didactic and satirical poems as well as in his polemical verse. History forms an integral part of all these types of poetry. In them living persons are portrayed and contemporary events are mirrored in terms of moral attitudes and ethical evaluations. Yet the intentions and objects of each kind are different and affect the poetic structure of each poem, although the apparent concern with human salvation never varies.

The medieval historian is, in fact, never far from the moralist. He is intensely preoccupied with *truth,* not to determine as exactly as possible what happened, but to discover behind the events the moral lesson to be drawn from history and to reach an understanding of God's purpose within human time. As Collingwood says:

> In their anxiety to detect the general plan of history, and their belief that this plan was God's and not man's, [the medieval historians] tended to look for the essence of history outside history itself, by looking away from man's actions in order to detect the plan of God; and consequently the actual detail of human actions became for them relatively unimportant.[1]

They show little concern with "objectivity," for objectivity would be a spiritually dangerous neglect of God's immanent presence within history or of the transcendental meaning of men's actions.[2]

Since a superior causality was behind all historical events, God's will was evident in the outcome of battles, in the death of great men. It is natural, then, that historiography in France should appear with the Crusades, since they were an extraordinary manifesta-

1. R. G. Collingwood, *The Idea of History* (New York, 1956), p. 55.
2. Baldwin's description of medieval preaching as "a sustained and consistent call to see through the facts" could characterize the medieval approach to history and contemporary reality (*Medieval Rhetoric and Poetic*, p. 241).

tion of God's will being accomplished in the world. This exemplary venture prompted Villehardouin, Robert de Clari, and Joinville to record an event worthy of consideration, the great effort to recapture and hold God's city, Jerusalem.

When historical elements first appear in literature, they are almost entirely subordinated to the author's moral or didactic intentions. History is the ostensible subject of epics, yet the *Chanson de Roland* recounts not the inglorious defeat of Charlemagne's rear guard by a group of Christian Basque bandits but the stunning triumph of Christians over pagans, of right over wrong. Even some novels such as Chrétien de Troyes' *Cligès* use historical figures, but as a point of departure for rather didactic studies in human relations between courtly types.[3] In epics and novels, as in history, the work tends toward goals outside of history, toward "correct" social behavior, toward salvation, toward an understanding of God's purpose in history. All recount in order to organize the events of the past in a comprehensible pattern which then stands as a static model, raised to the level of an ideal example of absolute standards of behavior to guide men within history.

The satirists and moralists, on the other hand, start off from an elevated moral plane, saying "this is the way things should be." They then dip down into history for examples of virtue rewarded and wrong-doing punished. The moral questions involved are still familiar to us, and we can read such works without reference to the historical background, since it is the interpretation, not the facts of history, which is important. History serves essentially to illustrate the moral ideal and to orient men's behavior toward that ideal. The object of the satirist or moralist is again an absolute standard of ethical perfection.

Both the moralist and the historian of medieval Western Europe could count on some common basis of agreement between author and public as to the nature of the moral values or ideal proposed.

3. See Henry and Renée Kohane, ("L'Enigme du nom de Cligès," *Romania, 82,* No. 1 [1961], 113–21), who identify Cligès with Kilidj Arslan II, Sultan of Iconium (1156–92).

All agree that Charlemagne's victory was a fine success for Christendom; all agree that Hell is to be feared and salvation cherished. No matter how great the separation between ideal and practice, sins such as pride, greed, and envy were universally condemned. Even heresies are often only an exaggeration of Christian beliefs, and heretics sometimes catechize the orthodox. The Dominicans' original adoption of apostolic poverty was, according to legend, inspired by the Albigensians. The Dominican Etienne de Bourbon tells us in an exemplum that Diego, Bishop of Osma, came to Southern France with much pomp. Reproached by a heretic for preaching humility and poverty, yet having such a great train, Diego was confounded; immediately dismissing all his followers and sending away all his horses, he set out on foot to preach with Saint Dominic. "Et hoc fuit causa ordinis nostri instituendi," concludes Etienne.[4] The tremendous Franciscan revival was strong because the importance of their ideal of voluntary poverty instantly struck all who heard about it; the moral ethic the Franciscans preached proved an irresistible call to the best minds of the century —"Oh ignota ricchezza, o ben ferace!" said Dante[5]—and when the Franciscans faltered in their zeal, they were judged by the very standards they had set.

When, at the end of the twelfth and all during the thirteenth centuries, we find poems which we may call political—that is, which have to do with the administration of the temporal affairs of Church or state—and which are used for propaganda purposes, we note a significant change. The poet seemingly interprets historical events according to moral standards, but there is no longer a consensus as to the ideal. The poet must *convince* his hearers that what he calls right is indeed right. When twelfth-century poets wrote about the Crusades, their task was to remind their audience

4. *Anecdotes historiques*, p. 79, No. 83. Bennett concludes that the Dominicans conceived of poverty as a tactic rather than as an end in itself, but that the moral appeal and the example of St. Francis touched Dominic, who eventually felt an inner conviction of the blessings of austerity (R. F. Bennett, *The Early Dominicans* [Cambridge, Eng., 1937], pp. 36–37, 43–44).

5. *Paradiso*, XI, 82.

of the essential rightness of the Crusades, to bring this conviction to the fore, then to persuade hearers to act upon their own convictions. But when the absolute moral values of the Crusades had ceased to be taken for granted, as in Rutebeuf's time, the poet (or preacher) had to reconvince, to prove as well as exhort.

When, however, the question at hand was not the long-desired deliverance of Jerusalem but a novel one, such as the right of the Mendicant orders to live without working, the polemicists had to make a great effort to find biblical or historical precedents to justify the "rightness" of their position. The authors first had to connect their ideas with preestablished modes of thinking about right and wrong; they had to lead their hearers to think about the new question with the same force of moral conviction as about sin, the Crusades, or salvation. They still interpreted events from a moral viewpoint, but their intent was secular and polemical; they spoke for a faction of men, not for God.

For political works do not lead the hearer to contemplation of a moral ideal, but return him to historical reality and to an action which the poem has shown to be necessary and right. Once the moral conviction was established, the poet or polemicist was justified in asking the audience to act upon such convictions for an earthly, not heavenly, future. Factional disputes are cloaked in morality, idealized, not to lead the hearer to a timeless ideal but to persuade him to modify the course of history. The moralizing interpretation is not, then, the main object but rather the means of convincing an audience of the real, historical aim of the poem and the modern reader must first be acquainted with the polemical ends in order to understand the poem.[6]

The reader must understand, however, that power, in the Middle Ages, is first and foremost moral power. It is apparent in almost

---

6. We cannot "read," for example, Rutebeuf's poems about Guillaume de Saint-Amour without referring to the social and political environment in which they were written, and which have been so magnificently and exhaustively annotated by Edmond Faral.

every form of human dealings that this was a fundamental and
vital concept. Jurisprudence, for example, was founded on the idea
of absolute right and wrong; no form of compromise was legally
possible.[7] The strength and justification of political maneuvers derive directly from the effectiveness of the moral cast imposed upon
events. We have seen the effect Louis IX had upon the Crusade
expeditions through the force of his moral example. Those who
sought to influence the course of events were able to do so because
they insured support for themselves by interpreting their acts as
the "right" acts. Even Frederick II, the most secularized of
thirteenth-century leaders, exploited the messianic hopes centered
on him for political ends, and perhaps believed himself in his
divine mission;[8] those who opposed him did so on religious
grounds, although acknowledging the dazzling power of the man,
as did Salimbene, who said: "Had he but loved God and his
church and his own soul, he would have had few equals."[9]

THE POLITICAL POEM   The poetic tradition of intervention
in secular affairs appears virtually at the same time as the didactic
vernacular works so heavily influenced by the *sermones vulgares.*
Used by various political factions or powerful individuals, these
political poems were written to arouse public opinion as a base of
support. But where moral poetry, such as Rutebeuf's *Voie de
Paradis,* asks the individual to consider self-amendment, the polemical poem uses moral considerations as a means to move both in-

---

7. See Howland, *Ordeals,* p. 2. Law, with the introduction in the 12th century of
a purely secular civil code, Roman law, into a discipline hitherto limited to canon
law, was the first humane science to become secularized (Haskins, chap. 7, "The
Revival of Jurisprudence," in *The Renaissance of the Twelfth Century,* pp. 193–
223). Ordeals, which submitted all litigation to an immediate execution of justice
by God Himself, were prohibited by Innocent III in 1215; St. Louis' substitution of
witnesses for judicial combats represents a further submission of moral questions
to human rather than divine justice. Yet even today the witness swears on the
Bible.

8. Cohn, *The Pursuit of the Millennium,* pp. 103–04.

9. *Chronica,* p. 349, trans. Haskins, in *Medieval Culture,* p. 124.

dividuals and groups toward a political goal. The poet was hired for such a purpose.

Although many have described Rutebeuf's political poems, such as those about the struggle between the masters of the University of Paris and the Mendicant orders, as reflecting his own beliefs and feelings, the poet's intentions and opinions are not his own but those of a group who paid him—in Rutebeuf's case, those of the University secular masters. Critics have repeatedly confused modern notions of sincerity and personal conviction with an appraisal of Rutebeuf's art.[10] The poems about the University quarrel are certainly one-sided in that they defend a side which is presented as "right," but political bias attributed to a group or faction must not be confused with subjectivity, as Leo has implied. The whole question of Rutebeuf's own beliefs is not really a very useful critical means for studying his polemical poems. As we shall see, Rutebeuf's poetical *matière* in these works, as in his Crusade poems, derives largely from a literary, moral, or polemical tradition and a pre-existing body of ideas, arguments, and poetry. What interests us is how he incorporated such elements into effective works of art.

The poet may serve as an intermediary between a faction and the

10. Dehm speaks of Rutebeuf's hotly passionate involvement in political matters (*Studien zu Rutebeuf*, p. 62), as does Ulrich Leo (*Studien zu Rutebeuf*, pp. 130 ff.), who describes his poetry as anger-inspired. Ham believes that Rutebeuf's personal grievances inspired some of his works ("Rutebeuf and the Tunis Crusade," pp. 134–35), and both Jubinal and Faral suggest that Rutebeuf felt an inner hostility to the Mendicants (see, for example, FB, *2*, 282; Faral, *Les Jongleurs en France au moyen âge*, p. 162; Jubinal, "Notice sur Rutebeuf," *O.C.*, *1*, xlii). Yet Faral has also noted: "il est difficile de trouver chez Rutebeuf un fond d'idées ou de sentiments qui lui soit vraiment personnel" (FB, *1*, 57), and he hesitates to decide whether Rutebeuf wrote from "libre conviction" or "intérêt" (FB *1*, 46). Monsignor L. G. Pesce states categorically that Rutebeuf's attacks on Mendicants "ne trouvent d'autre explication que dans sa rancune" ("Le Portrait de Rutebeuf," *Revue de l'Université d'Ottowa*, *28*, No. 1 [January–March 1958], 63); Kressner rightly doubts that we can determine Rutebeuf's own convictions ("Rutebeuf, ein Dichterleben im Mittelalter," *Franco-Gallia*, *10*, No. 11 [November 1893], 168). Certainly Rutebeuf is not of the intellectual caliber of Roger Bacon (who was, after all, a Franciscan), nor can he be seen as a 13th-century Bossuet, as Keins suggested ("Rutebeufs Weltanschauung im Spiegel seiner Zeit," *Zeitschrift für romanische Philologie, 53*, Nos. 5–6 [1933], 572–75).

general public, yet his critical attitude and his ideas are not personal but part of a collectivity. Faral has conclusively demonstrated, for at least one of Rutebeuf's poems, that every idea, and even much of the language used to formulate those ideas, derives from the writings of the University of Paris masters who rose to defend their exiled rector, Guillaume de Saint-Amour.[11] Rutebeuf's originality lies not in his thinking but in the powerful impulse he was able to give to the ideas of the masters through his poems. Like the knights who fought in trials by combat to defend causes not their own, the poet wields his pen in the service of others. In every case a political poem by a professional poet like Rutebeuf can be shown to presuppose an interested public and a group or a man advocating the ideas expressed and willing to pay for such works.

Rutebeuf's earliest known work, the *Dit des Cordeliers* (1249; FB, *1,* 231–37), is just such a political work. Written not in Paris, as his other poems apparently were, but in Troyes, Champagne, the poem defends a convent of Franciscans against the local parish priest, who, together with some Benedictine nuns, tried to prevent the monks from moving their convent within the city walls to confess the faithful. The poem is divided into two parts and skips from subject to subject. Yet, for all its apparent incoherence of structure, it holds together not because of an interior unity of theme or image but because it is entirely aimed at winning the public to the Franciscan side.[12] Rutebeuf praises the friars and their good

11. Édmond Faral, "Pour le Commentaire de Rutebeuf: *Le Dit des Règles*," *Studi Medievali*, Nuova serie, *16* (1943–50), 176–211. See also the Introduction to his edition of Rutebeuf and the *Notice* and notes to relevant poems, where he gives exhaustive references to Rutebeuf's sources for ideas and terms. Arié Serper's article, "L'Influence de Guillaume de Saint-Amour sur Rutebeuf," *Romance Philology, 17,* No. 2 (November 1963), 391–403, adds little to Faral.

12. In this subordination of logical perfection to his urgent desire to convince, Rutebeuf again is close to the technique of medieval sermons. See the interesting article of Etienne Gilson, "Michel Menot et la technique du sermon médiéval," in his *Les Idées et les lettres* (Paris, 1932), pp. 193–94. The initial intention and essential function of the sermon was to speak to win souls for God (ibid., p. 149), and rhetorical effects were admitted for didactic purposes, in order that the speaker might "auditorium emolliat, excitet mentem" (ibid., p. 99, n. 2).

works to identify them with a moral ideal; their enemies are slandered to make it abundantly clear that there is only one "right" side to the quarrel.

The first part of the *Dit des Cordeliers* (sts. I–XI) is thus a general praise of the Franciscan order, having no reference to the local squabble. Rutebeuf describes the order's desire to sacrifice all to save man from the Devil; he notes the favor God showed to Francis by giving him the stigmata; he explains the meaning of the triple cord with its triple knots which scourge "le Mauffé . . . et tot son fet" (v. 26). He then interprets the name *Menor* by giving the symbolic interpretation of each letter.[13] The word starts, for example, with M (*âme*) because thought for the soul must come before any other concern. The stanza on E is a fair sample of the theological and linguistic intricacies involved in this interpretation:

> E senefie plaint: par 'E!' se doit on plaindre;
> Par E fu ame en plaint, Eve fit ame fraindre.
> Quand vint Filz d'M a point, ne sofri point le poindre:
> M a ame desjoint dont Eve la fit joindre. (vv. pp. 33–36)

A stanza interpreting R lacks, and stanzas XII–XIII plunge us in medias res, or rather, set us down in the "Espicerie," the marketplace of Troyes, next to the church Saint-Jean-au-Marché, where the good Franciscans are attempting to preach while a noisy, quarrelsome abbess drowns them out with her convent bells. Rutebeuf cites this raucous scene to condemn the unjustifiable hostility of the abbess (and her right-hand man, the *curé* Ytiers of Saint-Jean-au-Marché), since after establishing how good the Franciscans are, how they struggle against evil everywhere, he suddenly shows them at grips with an abusive female! How can they peddle their valuable wares through a crowd of fur-cloaked nuns who are trying to "skin" the good friars?

---

13. Interpretation *per litteras* is a favorite device of medieval moralists and satirists in both Latin and French. Långfors gives a listing of such alphabet poems in his Introduction to Huon le Roi de Cambrai's *Li Abecés par ekivoche* (*Œuvres, 1* [Paris, 1913], iii–x), as does Jubinal in *Nouveau Recueil, 2, 428–29*.

[D]evant l'Espicerie vendent de lor espices:
Ce sont saintes paroles en coi il n'a nul vices.   words
Tote [14] lor a fet tort, et teles an pelices
Les ont ci peliciez qu'entrer n'osent es lices. (st. XII)

Rutebeuf expends four stanzas to list the grievances of the friars against the abbess: her theft of a door, in order to stop the friar's new constructions, and of some cheese offered to them; her vociferous plaints which so delayed the bishop's hearings on the matter that no settlement could be reached even after three or four days of hearings (sts. XIII–XVI). After showing us how petty and troublesome these nuns are, Rutebeuf returns to his original theme of the good works of the Franciscan order, speaking of man's (or woman's) willful blindness to his own good. These apparently lowly friars are like the horse's tail, which, although "li plus vilz membres," protects the whole body from the "flies" of sin. A sick man should want the doctor at his side; we are sick with sin, yet "n'avons cure dou mire" (sts. XIX–XXI). The polemicist has thus proved his point: the fight against sin waged by the friars must be carried within the walls, since the sinners are (obviously) in the city, even if the Franciscans must endure "mainte parole dure":

[L]a deüst estre mires la ou sont li plaié;
Car par les mires sont li navré apaié.
Menor sont mire, et nos sons par eus apaié:
Por ce sont li Menor en la vile avoié.

[O]u miex de la cité doivent tel gent venir;
Car ce qui est oscur font il cler devenir,
Et si font les navrez en senté revenir.
Or les veut l'abeesse de la vile banir. (sts. XXII–III)

---

14. Faral reads "tote" as "torte" ("the lame woman"), with a play on "tort" ("wrong") (FB *1*, 234, note to v. 47); the abbess was Alix de Villy, daughter of the chronicler Geoffroi de Villehardouin (ibid.); thus Rutebeuf is attacking a lady of consequence!

With such irrefutable moral proofs, Rutebeuf leaves the bell-ring-ing, limping, wrong-doing abbess confounded. He need say no more, for the moral point is indeed "cler."

While he has a captive audience, however, Rutebeuf adds a parting shot to destroy the reputation of the *curé* Ytiers, the abbess' henchman, who had been saying he'd rather eat leaves and branches then let the Franciscans hear confessions in his church, and that he was sick and tired of conciliatory meetings. (st. XXIV). Rutebeuf warns that he had better suffer in silence or he will say something about all those feasts and livestock Ytiers has been lavishing on his relatives, ending his poem with a triumphantly stinging witticism:

> [B]ien le deüt sosfrir mes [*sire*] Ytiers li prestres:
> Paranz a et parentes mariez a grant festes;
> Des biens de Sainte Yglise lor a achetez bestes:
> Li biens esperitiex* est devenuz terrestres. (st. XXV)
>
>   * spiritual; ecclesiastical

Le Dit des Cordeliers is a good illustration of the political poem, since, in spite of its "moral" intention, it cannot be understood without reference to local topography and personalities and to its polemical aim. The poet uses a variety of materials as ammunition: bits of dialogue, extracts from official documents, personal slanders, proverbs, and puns, to make a lively mixture of enough local scandal and verbal wit to entertain an audience, together with enough lofty moralizing to whitewash its clear polemical intent and to convince its hearers.

As Faral has said, this poem presupposes a milieu where poetry is conceived of as something more than an intellectual game—rather, as a vehicle for opinion and debate—and presupposes also not only factional groups but the existence of a force of public opinion which, when aroused, could play a role in determining the outcome of this local quarrel.[15] In the *Dit des Cordeliers* we find evidence of such popular reaction. The friars' new convent within the walls

15. Edmond Faral, *"Le Dit des Cordeliers* de Rutebeuf," *Romania, 70* (1948–49), 331.

had evidently aroused much public discussion, for in stanza XVII Rutebeuf says:

> Or dit la laie gent que c'est par couvoitise
> Qu'il ont *ce* leu lessié et autre place prise. (vv. 67–68)

Nonsense, says Rutebeuf. The friars' convent outside the walls was "trop biau leu a devise" (v. 66), and the "laie gent" or the uninformed have been misled by the hue and cry of the talkative abbess. Stanza XVIII shows that at least some of the common folk, "fole gent," have been able to see the friars' real intention,

> [S]e cil leuz fust plus biaus de celi qu'il avoient,
> Si le poïst on dire; mais la fole gent voient
> Que lor leus laissent cil qui desvoiez avoient *   * put back on
> Por oster le pechié que en tel leu savoient.   the right
>   track

Rutebeuf uses, cites, public approval of the friars as a support for his attack directed against the abbess, adding it as one more weapon in his attack. The protagonists—the Franciscans and their enemies —are in the poem in two ways: as characters and as a public who sees itself mirrored in the poem; the "text" is completed by its "context."

Until propaganda efforts such as Rutebeuf's bore fruit, the populace was probably indifferent to such questions as the transfer of a Franciscan convent, the awarding of a chair in the Faculty of Theology of the University of Paris, or the succession of the Sicilian throne. Rutebeuf attempts to explain such events through biased simplifications and strong moral and emotional appeals so as to bring pressure to bear upon the "enemy." I disagree, therefore, with Faral's view of Rutebeuf as a representative of popular opinion, carrying the people's case before influential men. Faral concludes:

A bien y réfléchir, tous ces poèmes qui appellent à la croisade ou qui incitent à la résistance contre les Ordres mendiants n'auraient eu nulle raison d'être si l'auteur n'avait pas considéré que ces princes, ces barons, ces prélats, auxquels il s'adressait, reconnaîtraient en sa voix chétive l'écho du cri populaire.[16]

In my opinion, the poet is not so much a delegate of the people to represent them before great lords, as a "lobbyist" for one faction of the great who are attempting to manipulate public opinion for their own ends.

The primary intent of political poems is, in effect, to encourage the partisans of a political idea and to attack and destroy the opposition. Rutebeuf and his patrons did indeed intend to influence kings, princes, and prelates and men of high position by means of a popular outcry which was not spontaneous but adroitly contrived and encouraged. Rutebeuf's poems, therefore, do not reflect popular opinion, but are an effort to encourage partisans to act, and then to influence a general mass of uninformed and indifferent people to take sides and exert their force of public opinion and moral pressure.

Such use of public pressure as a political weapon was a favorite technique of those who could command widespread attention. Pope Paschal II laid all of France under interdict, ostensibly because of Philippe I's adulterous marriage, but really as a move in the struggle for power in the Investiture Contest which opposed popes, kings, and emperors throughout the twelfth century. By excommunicating the whole kingdom and denying the sacraments to

16. FB *1*, 56. Faral says, however, discussing Rutebeuf's *Complainte de Constantinople*, that Rutebeuf did not speak for the barons and against the King "selon les sentiments du peuple" in that poem, although he was an "homme du peuple." Faral suggests in this article that Rutebeuf wrote to order as the "client de plusieurs hauts personnages, clercs ou laïques" ("Le Procès d'Enguerran IV de Couci," *Revue Historique de Droit Français et Étranger*, 4e série, 26, Nos. 3–4 [1948], 258). My intention is not to point out inconsistencies in the admirable work of Faral, but to discuss the poet's technique, conception, and intention of his work. By determining now that the poet wrote for money rather than out of conviction, we shall be in a position to understand that apparently gratuitous or misplaced rhetorical effects are actually signs of a polished poetic technique which gave the client his money's worth of effective verse. (See below, Chaps. 3 and 4.)

everyone, the Pope hoped to create an irresistible tide of public
pressure to force the King to acquiesce to his wishes.[17] Here again,
the people are conceived of as a tool to gain political ends. However, whenever popular movements ran counter to the wishes of
all the great, of every powerful faction, as was eventually the case
with the Pastoureaux or Shepherd Crusaders, they were quickly
suppressed.[18]

Although we are mainly interested here in politically oriented
poetry, it is important to note that the theater also served as a
vehicle for political commentary.[19] Faral cites the mimes *La Paix
aux anglais, La Charte,* and *La Nouvelle Charte de la Paix aux
anglais,* which reflect the political rivalry between England and
France during the thirteenth century (FB, *1,* 56), as do short poems

17. See Howland, *Ordeals,* p. 29, where he discusses interdict and excommunication as political weapons. Gregory IX tried to wrest away the temporal power of
Frederick II by excommunicating him in 1227, as did Innocent IV in 1245, and
there was public confusion when the excommunicate Emperor negotiated Jerusalem
back into Christian hands (Howland, p. 24; see also chap. 3, "The Emperor
Frederick," in Runciman, *History of the Crusades, 3,* 171–204). Excommunication
degenerated occasionally into a sort of magic anathema; Howland cites an example
of an infestation of locusts and caterpillars being laid under interdict in the diocese
of Troyes; "the aforesaid animals should be warned by us and compelled, by threats
of ecclesiastical punishment to depart," on six days' notice (pp. 25–26)!

18. "Soudainement ilz evanouÿrent comme fumée," says the author of *Renart le
contrefait, 1,* Gaston Raynaud and Henri Lemaître, eds. (Paris, 1914), 294. Matthew
Paris notes for the year 1251 the "modest" reply of Queen Blanche to protests
against the Pastoureaux. "As the Lord knows, I believed that they in their simplicity
and sanctity would gain possession of the entire Holy Land; but since they are
deceivers, let them be excommunicated, seized and destroyed" (*English History, 2,*
455). For an example of how an apparently popular revolt conceals political maneu-
vering, see the story of a minstrel who pretended to be Baldwin IX, on the
instigation of a group of Flemish burghers supported by Henry III of England; he
was crowned Count of Flanders and Hainaut and Emperor of Constantinople and
Thessalonica in 1225, became a popular hero, and had to be put down by Louis
VIII (Cohn, *Pursuit of the Millennium,* pp. 77–81).

19. A solemn liturgical drama is weighted with nationalistic praise of Frederick
Barbarossa (*Ludus de Antichristo* (ca. 1160), ed. Karl Young, in *The Drama of
the Medieval Church, 2* (Oxford, 1933), 369–95. Howard G. Harvey shows how
medieval theatre duplicates the themes and language of satirical and moralizing
poetry (*Theatre of the Basoche* [Cambridge, Mass., 1941], pp. 28, 68); Adolphe
Fabre cites an allegorical morality commissioned from Gringoire by Louis XII as a
contribution to his campaign against Pope Jules II (*Les Clercs du palais* [2d ed.
Lyon, 1875], p. 206).

like the *Roman des français,* a comic account in Anglo-Norman of King Arthur's conquest of France, intended to humiliate and provoke the French, and the chauvinistic *Chronique des rois de France,* which starts out bravely, "Honis soit li rois d'Ingleterre."[20] Thirteenth-century Arras was a hotbed of poetic and theatrical political commentary, enlivened by a juicy scandal over the local *échevins* and their system of tax collection.[21]

Vernacular polemical poets were, of course, imitating their clerical predecessors who wrote in Latin similar political tracts also disguised as eternal moral verities. A tremendous struggle for control of the order between the Grandimontine monks and their lay administrators (1185–88), for example, produced a spate of angry verses such as these attacking the laymen:

> Sic dominari laicos
> Est sanctum dare canibus.[22]

When Innocent III decreed against clerical marriages in the Third Lateran Council (1179),[23] Latin poems show spirited resistance from the priests:

---

20. Jubinal, ed., *Nouveau Recueil, 2,* 1–17, 18–22. Faral has edited the mimes mentioned, giving the necessary background of their historical context in his *Mimes français* (Paris, 1910), pp. 29–51.

21. Texts edited by A. Jeanroy and A. Långfors, *Chansons et dits artésiens du XIIIe siècle* (Bordeaux, Marseille, Montpellier, Paris, and Toulouse, 1898). The best discussion of these rather controversial poems is found, I believe, in A. Guesnon's review of Jeanroy and Långfors' edition, *La Satire à Arras au XIIIe siècle* (Paris, 1900; excerpt from *Moyen Age* [1899–1900]), and Henri Roussel's review of Marie Ungureau's *La Bourgeoisie naissante: Société et littérature bourgeoises d'Arras aux XIIe et XIIIe siècles* (Arras, 1955), "Notes sur la littérature arrageoise du XIIIe siècle," *Revue des Sciences Humaines,* Nouvelle série, Fasc. 87 (July–September 1957), pp. 249–86, esp. 256 and 280. Roussel also criticizes the articles of P. Paris, Henri Guy, Guesnon, and E. Langlade on Arras satirical poetry (pp. 251–56). Sutherland's excellent article "Fact and Fiction in the *Jeu de la Feuillée*" (*Romance Philology, 13,* No. 4 [May 1960], 419–28) studies Adam's use of the Wheel of Fortune (vv. 766–823, *Jeu de la feuillée,* ed. E. Langlois [Paris, 1951]) as "a way of indicating who is up and who down in the political world of Arras at the time when the play is written" (p. 424).

22. Dobiache-Rojdestvensky, *Poésies des goliards,* p. 151; see pp. 150–54, "De scismate grandimontanorum."

23. Ibid., p. 119.

Non est Innocentius, immo nocens vere,
Qui, quod facto docuit, verbo vult delere,
Et quod olim iuvenis voluit habere,
Modo vetus Pontifex student prohibere.[24]

The Church hierarchy will be observed, but let it be with additions
to the clerical harem according to rank!

Habebimus, clerici, duas concubinas;
Monachi, canonici totidem, vel trinas;
Decani, prelati quatuor, vel quinas:
Sic tandem leges implebimus divinas! [25]

The *carmina rebelli* of the Goliards achieved heights of moral reproach about ecclesiastical abuses, and depths of scandal in pamphleteering against leaders such as the Regent Queen Blanche.
Matthew Paris quotes a ditty composed against Blanche and her
supposed paramour, the Cardinal Legate Saint-Ange, held re-
sponsible for the University strike of 1229:

Thus, the clerics, therefore, retreating from the city of Paris,
spring of philosophy and well of learning, and cursing the
Legate, reviled the feminine frivolity of the Queen, and their
infamous alliance too. Moreover, some lackeys and toadies of
those who fled, those whom we are wont to call Goliards, composed ribald verses, saying:
Heu morimur strati, vincti, mersi, spoliati;
Mentula legati nos facit ista pati.

24. "Prisciani regula penitus cassatur" (ibid., p. 127). The grammatical euphemism
which runs "Sacerdos per *hic* et *haec* olim declinabatur;/ Sed per *hic* solummodo
nunc articulatur,/ Cum per nostrum praesulem *haec* amoveatur" (p. 127) appears
also in "Clerus et presbyteri nuper consedere," st. 43 (p. 134), and again in Gautier
de Coinci's attack on sodomy in his *Sainte Léocade* (vv. 1232–46, p. 172). This is a
good example of what we will see to be a tendency for satirical or polemical
formulas to be repeated and reused in new circumstances.
25. "Clerus et presbyteri nuper consedere" (st. XLV, Dobiache-Rojdestvensky, p.
134). This poem, "Prisciani regula," and a third similar poem, "Rumor novus
angliae," are edited also by Wright, *The Latin Poems Commonly Attributed to
Walter Mapes,* pp. 171–82.

However, another more decorous verse-writer says, as if the city of Paris were speaking to a weeping clergy:

Clere, tremisco metu, quia vis contempnere me tu
Perfundor fletu, mea dampna fleo, tua fle tu.[26]

By 1229, however, most pamphleteering was done in the vernacular. We can perhaps account for the Latin verses cited by Matthew Paris by noting that clerics must have been especially interested in the scandal, since it involved a papal legate. Most polemical verses of the period, nevertheless, even when they involve ecclesiastics, are no longer in Latin.

The Provençal poets wrote the first vernacular political polemics and polished the *sirventés* as a useful political weapon during the twelfth century.[27] Marcabru's *vida* says that he was killed by the

26. *Chronica majora, 3,* ed. Henry R. Luard (London, 1872–83), 168–69: "Sic ergo a nutrice philosophiae et alumpna sapientiae civitate Parisiaca recedentes clerici, legatum Romanum execrantes, reginae muliebrem maledixerunt superbiam immo eorum infamie concordiam. Recedentium autem quidam famuli, vel mancipia, vel illi quas solemus goliardenses appelare, versus ridiculos componebant, dicentes . . . Quidam autem honestior versificator per apostrofam, id est, informationem personae, ut si loqueretur urbs Parisius clero sub planctu, ait." See Helen Waddell, *The Wandering Scholars* (New York, 1961), p. 202 and n. 82. For representative Latin texts of the 12th and 13th centuries, see Dobiache-Rojdestvensky, *Poésies des goliards;* Thomas Wright, *Anglo-Latin Satirical Poets;* and Raby, *Secular Latin Poetry,* pp. 45–54 on French satirical poets, pp. 89–102 on English satirists and epigrammatists, and all of chap. 13, "The Latin Lyric (I)," pp. 171–235. Lecoy de la Marche seems somewhat blinded by 19th-century chauvinism to the value of the goliardic political and satirical poetry. He dismisses them as "grossier," and adds "mais empressons-nous de le dire, les principales de ces compositions sont dues à des plumes anglaises ou allemandes: aussi se distinguent-elles plutôt par la brutalité que par la finesse. Et puis il y a autre chose; elles sont presque toujours jointes au dénigrement ou à la caricature de la papauté" (*Le Treizième Siècle littéraire et scientifique* [Bruges, 1894], p. 177). He misinterprets the serious reforming purpose behind the Latin satires and overlooks the giants of Latin satirical verse in 12th-century France: Hugh Primas d'Orléans, Gautier de Châtillon, and Philippe Chancellor, who certainly rank with the best English and German satirists. Latin satirical verse persists longer in England than in France, however, where it is replaced by vernacular poems; see Thomas Wright, *Anecdota literaria* (London and Paris, 1844), p. 38, on the large number of 13th-century English manuscripts containing Latin satires.

27. On the Provençal *sirventés* see Alfred Jeanroy, *La Poésie lyrique des troubadours, 2,* 174–237. Gallego-Portuguese poets, including the Castillian king Alfonso X el Sabio, cultivated a poem of personal reflection, invective, and political commentary during the 13th century, the *cantar d'escarnio (cantigas d'escarnho),* dis-

chatelains of Guyenne because he was so "mal dizens"—that is, because of his polemical works of praise and attack.[28] The *vida* of Bertran de Born shows how he intrigued through his *sirventés* to foment war between Henry of England and Henri au Court Mantel, and between Richard the Lion-Hearted and Alphonse II.[29] These Provençal poets are Court polemicists, as was Walther von der Vogelweide (ca. 1170–ca. 1228) who wrote partisan pieces for the Imperial Court of Germany.[30]

French propaganda poets apparently enjoyed an international reputation as early as 1191. William Longchamp, Bishop of Ely and Chancellor of England under Richard the Lion-Hearted, was an extraordinarily powerful political figure who imported French poets to sing his praises and maintain his reputation against the attacks of his numerous enemies. Roger de Hoveden includes in his *Chronica* a very hostile letter written in 1191 by Hugh de Nunant, Bishop of Coventry, describing William Longchamp and his "ad-men," and gloating over his downfall:

> He moved pompously along, bearing a sneer in his nostrils, a grin on his features, derision in his eyes, and superciliousness on his brow, by way of fit ornament for a priest. For his own aggrandizement, and for the glorification of his name, he was in the habit of getting up verses that he had picked up by begging, and adulatory jingles, and enticed jesters and singers from the kingdom of France by his presents, that they might

cussed in Menendez Pidal in his *Poesía juglaresca* (Madrid, 1957), pp. 160–61, and edited by Manuel Rodrigues Lapa, *Cantigas d'escarnho e de mal dizer* (Coimbra, 1965).

28. Marcabru's *vida* reads: "Et fo mout cridatz et ausitz pel mon, e doptatz per sa lenga; car el fo tant maldizens que, a la fin, lo desfeiron li castellan de Guian[a], de cui avia dich mout gran mal" (*Biographies des troubadours*, ed. Jean Boutière and A.-H. Schutz [Toulouse and Paris, 1964], p. 12).

29. The *Vida* of Bertran de Born reads in part: "Mas totz temps volia que ill aguessen guerra ensems, lo paire e·l fils e·l fraire, l'uns ab l'autre. E toz temps volc que lo reis de Fransa e·l reis d'Engleterra auguessen guerra ensems. E s'il aguen patz ni treva, ades se penet ab sos sirventes de desfar la patz e de mostrar com cascuns era desonratz en aquella patz" (Boutière and Schutz, *Biographies*, p. 65).

30. *Gedichte*, ed. Carl V. Kraus (Berlin and Leipzig. 1936).

sing about him in the streets; and but lately it was everywhere said that there was not such a man in the world.[31]

Rutebeuf's work is largely nonlyric (FB *1,* 209-11), but many French polemicists use the song form.[32] One of the earliest series of French political songs are a group of scurrilous verses written against Blanche of Castille during her regency (1226–35) at the instigation of the faction of rebellious barons. Here again one sees that the poems reflect not popular outcry but a struggle for power where public opinion is mobilized to favor one faction over another. Blanche was variously accused of being the mistress of Thibaut de Champagne (in turn accused of poisoning Louis VIII), as well as of the Papal Legate, and of representing dangerous foreign interests. In three songs by Hues de la Ferté,[33] whose tunes must have been heard everywhere—easy to sing and to remember—one would have had only to hum:

31. Roger de Hoveden, *The Annals, Comprising the History of England and of Other Countries of Europe from A.D. 732 to A.D. 1201,* 2, trans. Henry T. Riley (London, 1853), 232. William Longchamp was the reforming bishop to whom Nigel Longchamp dedicated his *Speculum stultorum* and his *Contra curiales et officiales clericos* (see below, p. 97, n. 61).

32. Leo Schrade ("Political Compositions in French Music of the 12th and 13th centuries: The Coronation of French Kings," *Annales Musicologiques, moyen âge et renaissance, 1* [Paris, 1953], 20) has studied a group chosen from among the Latin *conductus*-type hymns of a political character—panegyrics, admonitions, laments, celebrations—and found that the hymns use the same music as French poets did for their courtly lyrics, just as the pious songs to the Virgin imitated the profane lyric (see below, pp. 219–21).

33. *Altfranzösische Lieder, 1,* ed. Friedrich Gennrich, Sammlung Romanischer Übungstexte, gen ed. Gerhard Rohlfs (Halle, 1953), 15–21; and Leroux de Lincy, ed., *Recueil de chants historiques français, 1* (Paris, 1841), 165–75. Although the bibliographical and historical information needs to be brought up to date, the fullest account of the French tradition of political song which I have been able to find is in C. Lenient's *La Satire en France au moyen âge* (3d ed. Paris, 1883), chaps. 9–18, which gives a lively evocation of the developing tradition, its effect, and historical context. Some of the texts may be found in Leroux de Lincy's *Chants historiques,* others through references in Lenient or in Victor le Clerc's "Poésies historiques," *Histoire littéraire de la France, 23* (Paris, 1856), 336–511.

for all to snicker at the culpable Count Thibaut and that foreigner,
Blanche. Hues' tone, as Rutebeuf's, alternates between heavy sarcastic attack in verses such as:

> De ma dame, vous di-je vraiement
> Qu'ele aime tant son petit enfançon,*   *Louis IX
> Qu'el ne veut pas qu'il se travaut souvent
> En departir l'avoir de sa maison.
> Maiz ele en doune et depart a fuison:
> Mout en envoie en Espagne,
> Et mout en met en esforcier Champaigne,

and inflammatory exhortations directed at the barons themselves:

> Bien est France abastardie,
> Seignors barons, entendez,
> Quant feme l'a en baillie,
> Et tele com bien savez.

The wide diffusion of the songs against Blanche is attested by remarks made about them in various chronicles. Leroux de Lincy
cites three chronicles which report the rumors about Blanche and
Thibaut.[34] The fourteenth-century author of the *Chronique des
évêques de Liège,* Jean de Hocsem, wrote almost a full century after
the events (and, indeed, confuses Blanche's two regencies of 1226–
35 and 1248–52), yet the scurrilous pamphlets which had circulated
in the streets and public places still drew his attention: "The nobles
having aroused ill-will against her, most evilly stirred up scandal,
stealthily strewing diffamatory pamphlets along the highways and
byways, so that they made a chaste queen seem a loose woman." [35]

The political struggles between Louis IX and his barons gave rise

---

34. *Chants historiques, 1,* 154–59: Matthew Paris (year 1256), the *Chronique
en vers dite de Sainte-Magloire* (year 1230), and Philippe Mouskes' *Chronique
rimée.*

35. Ed. Godefroid Kurth (Brussels, 1927), p. 10: "Cujus rei proceres invidia
excitati contra eam furtive libellos diffamatorios spargentes in viis et plateis
detractionis improbissime excitaverunt scandalum, ut castissime regine imponerunt
velut commune carnis ludibrium."

to an outburst of political poems which Faral has studied in his article on the rebellious Enguerran IV de Couci. Verses 136–41 of Rutebeuf's *Complainte de Constantinople,*

> Li rois ne fait droit ne justize
> A chevaliers, ainz les desprize
> (Et ce sunt cil par qu'ele est chiere),
> Fors tant qu'en prison fort et fiere
> Met l'un avant et l'autre ariere,
> Ja tant n'iert hauz hom a devise,

protest the King's excessive dependence on the clergy, and his reforms of judicial procedure which broke the feudal relationship between the King and his lords. The anonymous song, "Gent de France, mult estes esbahie!" was a clarion call to the barons with its trumpeted first notes:

36

As Faral comments, the melody and even some of the expressions used came from a song by the courtly poet Blondel de Nesle, and had been imitated by Thibaut de Champagne in a *jeu-parti* as well as by Gautier de Coinci in a song to the Virgin. Certainly imitation was part of the entertaining effectiveness of the poem as propaganda, as Faral says: "C'était là le piquant de sa chanson et qui pouvait la faire courir. Aux premières attaques de l'archet sur la viole et aux premières paroles du chanteur, chacun reconnaissait l'intention parodique." [37]

I believe we can identify another propaganda campaign in the poems called *Complainte* and the *Jeu de Pierre de la Broce.*[38] Pierre de la Broce was an extraordinary *arriviste* who attained an extremely influential position—and heavily feathered his nest—as the

---

36. Gennrich, *Altfranzösische Lieder, 1,* 21–23, and Leroux de Lincy, ed., *Chants historiques, 1,* 215–20.

37. "Le Procès d'Enguerran IV de Couci," *Revue Historique de Droit Français et Étranger, 26,* 255; see pp. 248–58.

38. F. Ed. Schneegans, ed., in *Romania, 58* (1932), 520–50.

companion and chamberlain of Philippe le Hardi at the beginning of his reign. Pierre overreached himself when he accused Queen Marie de Brabant of poisoning her stepson Louis, heir to the throne, and he was discredited and eventually executed through the efforts of the Queen's faction. The *Chronique de Saint Denis* describes the popular reaction to his hanging in 1278: "Le peuple de Paris s'esmut de toutes pars, et coururent hommes et femmes aprèz, car il ne povoient croire en nulle manière que homme de si haut estat fut devalé si au bas." [39] The two poems, written shortly after the execution, must have been intended to eradicate any lingering partisanship for Pierre, since in penitently moral terms "Pierre" accuses himself in the *Complainte* of the very crimes for which he was executed: false accusation of the Queen, secret correspondence with enemy Aragon, as well as greed. In the *Jeu* "Pierre" disputes with *Fortune,* and *Reson* renders judgment against him; Pierre has fallen not because of *Fortune's* caprice, but because of his own misdeeds and betrayal of his lord. The specifically informative character of the poems, their careful explanation of the reasons behind Pierre's condemnation, prove that these poems are not using Pierre to moralize about Fortune, but that they are part of a factional effort to orient public opinion and consolidate it in favor of the Queen.

The political song continued to flourish throughout the fourteenth and fifteenth centuries, yet both the themes and the poets' conception of history became progressively more secularized. The thirteenth-century desire to accomplish God's kingdom on earth, which masked so many worldly longings, yielded to an open European rivalry for political supremacy, and the later songs used strongly na-

39. Cited by Jubinal in his edition of the three poems (Paris, 1835), p. 13. See the *Chronicon* of Guillaume de Nangis (ed. H. Géraud [Paris, 1843], *1,* 249–50). In the prose chronicle inserted in *Renart le contrefait* (*1,* 290, par. 147) we read: "Ce Pierre haioit la roÿne . . . Et enquist le roy dillagamment se la roÿne estoit coupable de ce que le dit Pierre lui avoit mis sus, mais elle fut trouvée innocent. L'an .M..IIᶜ..LXXVIII, l'endemain de la feste saint Pierre et saint Pol, le dit Pierre de la Broce fu pendu en la presence des gens, qui ne s'en pouoient assés esmerveillier comment si grant homme et de si grant auctorité vint a tel fin. Entre les aultres choses que on lui mettoit sus, unez lettrez furent trouvées scellées de son scel, esquelles estoit contenu traÿson, laquelle il ne pouoit nÿer."

tionalistic, not eschatological, terms.[40] The police, not the moralists or the Church, saw to it that the population was not too stirred up by the polemicists; during the troubled last decade of the fourteenth-century, when a madman sat on the throne of France and an anti-pope at Avignon, a police ordinance forbade poets to write, say, or sing any works mentioning the Pope, King, or schism.[41] In 1396, when the melancholy Plantagenet, Richard II, was to marry the seven-year-old Isabella of France, the "chifrineurs et chanteurs" of Paris asked permission to sing songs on the event and on any other noble deeds which might be done, "comme, de si long temps qu'il n'est memoire du contraire, ilz aient acoustumé à l'onneur de vous [Charles VI] et de vostre royaume." Permission was granted, but only for songs "touchans la feste de la reyne," added the wary officials.[42]

A NEW ROLE FOR THE POET Medieval moralizing texts reflect the changing concept of the poet's role in society. Faral's Appendix III to his *Jongleurs en France au moyen âge* [43] gives a series of texts from the late twelfth and thirteenth centuries which show recognition of the poet's new role as pamphleteer. Twelfth-century texts may decry the jongleur as a corrupter of morals and a ribald, but essentially he was then seen as, and thought of himself as, either an entertainer or a moralist with a reforming mission. The minstrels invited to the wedding of Erec and Enide are typical entertainers:

40. See Lénient, *La Satire*, pp. 164–278, and Leroux de Lincy, ed., *Chants historiques*, *1*, 231–409, covering songs on the Hundred Years War, the Babylonian Exile and Schism, the defeats of French knighthood at Crécy, Calais, and Poitiers, and the *frondeur* rebellion of the war of the *Bien Public* (1465). A secular poetry of economics begins to appear in the early 14th century with works like "Dou Pape, dou roy et des monnoies," which joins traditional anti-Roman satire to criticism of the inflationary fiscal policy of Philippe le Bel (ed. Chabaille, *Bulletin de la Société de l'Histoire de France, 2*, 2e partie [1835], 221–24).

41. Text given by B. Bernhard, "Recherches sur l'histoire de la corporation des ménétriers . . . ," *Bibliothèque de l'Ecole des Chartes, 3* (1841–42), 404.

42. Texts given by Gustave Fagniez, "Les Ménétriers parisiens," *Bulletin de la Société de l'histoire de Paris et de l'Ile de France, 2* (1875), 103–04 (FB, *1*, 55, n. 1, erroneously give *Bulletin . . . . Histoire de France*), and in Gautier, *Les Epopées, 2*, 120–22.

43. Pp. 272–327.

An la sale molt grant joie ot,
chascuns servi de ce qu'il sot:
cil saut, cil tunbe, cil anchante,
li uns sifle, li autres chante,
cil flaüte, cil chalemele,
cil gigue, li autres vïele;
puceles querolent et dancent;
trestuit de joie fere tancent.
Riens n'est qui joie puisse fere
ne cuer d'ome a leesce trere,
qui as noces ne fust le jor.[44]

Texts written in a more negative spirit disparage the jongleur as a corrupter of morals and a purveyor of human vanity. Thus John of Salisbury says disapprovingly in his chapter "De histrionibus et mimis et praestigiatoribus" that "the whole stage of jokers . . . pollutes the keen and shames the sheltered," adding that they should be excommunicated "as long as they persevere in their wickedness." [45]

But in thirteenth-century texts the poet was also said to be a slanderer, which is really just a negative way of describing his polemical role. The description of jongleurs given by the English Bishop Thomas of Cabham in his *De poenitentia* (after 1250) distinguishes three types: first, the mountebanks or buffoons; second, the singers, whom he subdivides into those who sing good songs, such as saints' lives and epics, and those who sing evil, lascivious songs; and the third type is described as follows:

There are, moreover, others who work at nothing, but behave in an accusatory way; these do not have a fixed domicile but follow the courts of great men and dishonor and reproach absent men to please others. Such are also damnable . . . and

---

44. Ibid., p. 286, No. 68. I cite the recent edition of Mario Roques (Paris, 1955), vv. 1987–97. Compare the boastful self-advertising of the buffoons in the two poems called *Deus Bordeors* [or *Troveors*] *Ribaus* (*O.C., 3,* 2–14, or Montaiglon and Raynaud, eds., *Fabliaux, 1,* 1–12).

45. Faral, *Jongleurs,* pp. 285–86, No. 66 (*Policraticus,* I, p. 8 [*Patrologia latina,* CXCIX, col. 405]).

such are called wandering songsters because they work only at eating and slandering.[46]

A *Summa de arte prosandi* (ca. 1275) gives an equally hostile description of jongleurs, comparing the poets and panhandlers who flock to courts to vultures preying on a cadaver or flies around sweet things; the list of insulting epithets also includes references to poets who try to affect reputations. To the courts come

forsooth, the paupers, the weak, the blind, the lame, cripples . . . Jongleurs, dancers, harpers, pipers, lute-players, trumpeters, hornplayers, actors, mimes, tricksters, spongers, freeloaders, liars, buffoons, ribalds, *buflardi* [?], flatterers, jailbirds, betrayers, traitors, slanderers, gossips, apostate sons of perdition . . . and other vile sorts of men, too numerous to list.[47]

Considerable attention, then, is given by moralists not only (as in the past) to the loose morals of jongleurs, but also to their scandalmongering and backbiting. About 1219 a bishop of Lodève in Languedoc wrote an invective against the Goliards, deploring their vices, their wanderings, and, above all, their songs, "which prick like thistles"; he ends with the warning, "Nulli noceat tua Musa."[48] Around 1277 a Dominican preacher condemns "histrions who deride and condemn the virtues of others, and do nothing praise-

46. Cited by Léon Gautier, *Les Epopées françaises,* 2 (2d ed. Paris, 1878–92), 22, and nn. 1 and 2. See Faral, *Jongleurs,* p. 290, No. 102; and Waddell, *Wandering Scholars,* p. 291: "Sunt etiam alii qui nihil operantur, sed criminose agunt, non habentes certum domicilium, sed sequuntur curias magnatum et dicunt opprobria et ignominias de absentibus ut placeant aliis. Tales etiam damnabiles sunt . . . et dicuntur tales scurrae vagi, quia ad nihil aliud utiles sunt, nisi ad devorandum et maledicendum."

47. Faral, *Jongleurs,* p. 323, No. 267: "silicet pauperes, debiles, ceci, claudi, manci . . . joculatores, saltatores, fidicines, tibicines, lyricines, tubicines, cornicines, hystriones, gesticulatores, nebulones, parasiti, umbre, mensiuagi, scurre, ribaldi, buflardi, adulatores, carciones, proditores, traditores, detractores, susurrones, filii perditionis apostate . . . et alia uilium hominum genera, que longum est explicare."

48. Dobiache-Rojdestvensky, *Poésies des goliards,* p. 22.

worthy."[49] Harsh words, indeed, but we can understand them as a moralist's way of describing a polemical writer whose work was intended to affect public opinion.

On the simplest level of propaganda, poets could be paid to include a patron's name in a song, thus increasing his fame. Gautier quotes in *Les Epopées* the story of a jongleur who asked Arnoud II, Count of Ardres, for a pair of scarlet pantaloons for including his name in the *Chanson d'Antioche;* the chronicler violently condemns "eidem scurrae, qui nullo nomine dignus habetur," with fiery Latin expostulation: "O gartionum et ministralium, immo adulatorum injuriosa laudatio! O inertium principum indigna et inanis exultatio"![50] Baudouin de Condé, a contemporary of Rutebeuf, writes a long diatribe against poets who thus prey on the vanity of silly men in his *Contes des hiraus;* after describing three types of mimes, he speaks of

> Li quars, ki onques riens ne sot
> D'armes, s'en parole et raconte
> De ce preu duc, de ce preu conte,
> De che preu riche homme ensement,
> Dont on set bien que il se ment
>
> . . .
>
> Si fait de noient grant renon:
> Celui fait preu, cel autre non;
> Celui loe, cel autre blasme,
> Et vent honour et done blasme.
> Sès tu coment, à voir retraire,
> Il vent honor? Il set bien traire
> Des fols riches hommes son preu,
> Si lor fait croire qu'il sont preu,

---

49. *La tabula exemplorum secundum ordinem alphabeti,* ed. Welter, p. 54, No. 202.

50. *Les Epopées, 2,* 120, n. 1. Gautier also cites a letter from the *Dictamen rectorica magistri Guidonis,* recommending a jongleur, which says, "De honore vestre persone, sicut de proprio, gratulantes, talem doctorem, quem ad nos munerandum misistis, sic licenciare curavimus magnis quod cantando ubique magnificet nomen vestrum" *2,* 108, n. 1).

Tant qu'il a dou leur por le vent.
Vesci l'onour, tele le vent.[51] (vv. 66–70, 73–82)

Baudouin compares such poets to stinging flies and contrasts their lies with the "biaus mos et biaus dis," which really amuse others (vv. 220–21). In his *Contes dou wardecors* he criticizes greedy poets who are paid to ruin reputations and are even paid by those who are afraid the poet might speak ill of them:

Ciaus doune on pour ce c'on les doute,
Les autres por çou c'on ascoute
Volentiers ce qu'il sèvent dire.
Mais cil qui siervent de mesdire,
Que vous diroie je d'iaus el?
Ce ne sont mie menestrel,
Ains sont tahon qui les gens mordent.[52] (vv. 83–89)

The courtly *losengier*, the Provençal *lauzengier*, although portrayed as an envious slanderer, refers only to a courtly type figuring in a love triangle. It is his role to envy the success of the discreet true lover. He does not so much ruin reputations as try to spoil the perfect secrecy and trust upon which love depends by his spying and gossip.[53]

Médisance becomes, by the end of the century, a standard reproach leveled against poets. Adenet pontificates in *Cléomadès* (ca. 1280): "Drois menestrex se doit garder/ De mesfaire et de mesparler." [54] Watriquet de Couvins, minstrel of Count Gui de Blois at the beginning of the fourteenth century, thinks that such poets are

51. *Dits et contes de Baudouin de Condé et de son fils Jean de Condé, 1,* 155–56.
52. Ibid., *1,* 20. The anonymous author of the *Couronnement Renart* fills the Court of his fox-king with "mesdisans [qu'il] amoit por mesdire/ Par le roiaume et par l'empire" (ca. 1263, ed. Alfred Foulet [Princeton and Paris, 1929], vv. 2921–22).
53. See Alfred Jeanroy, *La Poésie lyrique des troubadours, 2* (Toulouse and Paris, 1934), 113; and Erich Koehler, "Observations historiques et sociologiques sur la poésie des troubadours," *Cahiers de Civilisation Médiévale, 7,* No. 1 (January–March 1964), 43–44.
54. Faral, *Jongleurs,* p. 324, No. 273.

worse than "murdriers" since, although they may put their arms around a count's neck, they smile in the face of those they hate within their hearts:

> . . . entrer ne doit en haute court
> Menestrel qui soit mesdisanz,
> Car mauvais est li mesdisanz
> Chose qui autrui puet grever.
> Jà ne verrez pris alever
> De menestrel qui soit janglerres
> Seur autrui: il vaut pis que lerres,
> On ne se puet de lui garder.[55] (vv. 4-11)

Such fear of the power of the poet's tongue appears in the *Droiz au clerc de Voudai*:

> Droiz dit c'uns mesdisanz vaut pis
> Qu'avoir deus mortex anemis,
> C'on en het la gent sans réson.[56]

"Sans réson" meant without moral justification; effective polemicists always screened their comments with some sort of didactic pretext or edifying pretension, thus portraying political events and personalities in sharply moral terms.

Rutebeuf seems to be quite aware that his polemical poems could be described as *médisance*. In his *Bataille des vices et des vertus*, where he pretends to be against those who condemn the Mendicant friars and to repent of his own attacks on them, he qualifies his own criticism as scandal-mongering. The friars are really fine fellows,

> Maugré toutes les langues males
> Et la Rustebuef tout premiers,
> Qui d'aus blasmer fu coustumiers. (vv. 82-84)

---

55. "Dit du fol menestrel," *Dits*, ed. Aug. Scheler (Brussels, 1868), p. 367. Compare with Hue Archevesque, who starts his *Dit de larguece et de debonereté:* "Se vilonie di, fetes le moi desfendre/ C'on doit bien le mesdit au mesdisant reprendre" (*Dits*, ed. A. Heron [Rouen, 1885], No. I, vv. 3-4).
56. Jubinal, ed., *Nouveau Recueil, 2*, 136-37.

He doesn't agree at all that the King does too much for the friars nor with

> . . . aucun mesdisant
> Qui par le païs vont disant
> Que, se Diex avoit le roi pris,
> Par qui il ont honor et pris,
> Moult seroit la chose changie
> Et lor seignorie estrangie. (vv. 107-12)

Again, as part of the repentance theme of his *La Mort Rutebeuf* (vv. 37-40), his *mea culpa* contains the standard accusations of riotous living, but also remorse for his partisan writing, now described as the Devil's work (see below, pp. 274-76). No moralist is more severe than Rutebeuf in condemning the envious backbiters who crowd around rich men to flatter them while reviling them in their hearts. He who seeks wealth will find

> Qu'il at mesdizans d'avantage
> Qui de ligier li font damage,
> Et si est touz plains d'envieux,
> Ja n'iert tant biaux ne gracieux.
> Se dix en sunt chiez lui assis,
> Des mesdizans i avra six
> Et d'envieux i avra nuef.
> Par derrier nel prisent un oef
> Et par devant li font teil feste
> Chacuns l'encline de la teste.
> (*Testament de l'âne*, vv. 5-14)

Here it is clear that Rutebeuf is thinking of *médisance* as false flattery provoked by sinful envy and greed.

Médisance, from another point of view and in other circumstances, can be considered salutory truth, painful only to those whose faults are publicly exposed. The poet thus speaks as a fearless truth-teller. In a revealingly self-conscious passage of *Le Dit d'Hypocrisie* Rute-

beuf imagines he meets a stranger who knows him by reputation
and who greets him with the following words:

> Rutebeuf, biaux tres doulz amis,
> Puis que Dieux saians vos a mis,
> Moult sui liez de votre venue.
> Mainte parole avons tenue
> De vos, c'onques mais ne veïmes,
> Et de voz diz et de voz rimes
> Que chacuns deüst conjoïr. (vv. 47–53)

All should appreciate Rutebeuf's poems against hypocrites, but
cowards are afraid to hear them in public, "por ce que trop i at de
voir" (v. 55); the hypocrites themselves listen most unwillingly,
since "il n'est ne biau ne gent/ Qu'il les oent, ses oent il" (vv. 68–
69). Only brave persons who are really interested in truth welcome
Rutebeuf's poems:

> Si ra de teilz cui il ne chaut
> S'ypocrite ont ne froit ne chaut
> Ne s'il ont ne corroz ne ire:
> Cil vos escoutent bien a dire
> La veritei trestoute plainne. (vv. 75–79)

It is clear that, with such justification, *médisance* is not only good
but that the poet has a moral mission to write. Rutebeuf here assumes a pose of didactic dignity adopted by moralists since the beginning of time and parodied by the Goliard whose credo, "Cum
in orbem universum," ended with a joyously blasphemous call to
reform:

> Give to any folk you meet
> Reasons for your questing
> As that men's peculiar ways
> Seem in need of testing:
> 'Probity from pravity

Seeking to unravel
Reprobates to reprobate
That is why I travel.'[57]

The Goliard's ambiguous wink, which undermines his solemn expression, is, however, unlike Rutebeuf's rather straightforward expression of moral intent. Indeed, Rutebeuf, like most medieval satirists, did not really distinguish between politics and morality; when we speak of polemical intentions being cloaked by didacticism, it is we, not the medieval poet, who make the distinction. Bédier's glorious style is misleading, however, when he denies that Rutebeuf had "la conscience qu'il jouait un rôle, exerçait une influence." The *Dit d'Hypocrisie* shows that the poet is conscious of the effect of his art upon a real world of human experience, and such effect is consciously valued and sought. He sang for something more than "la joie des écoliers de l'Université de Paris et pour l'ébaudissement des bourgeois de la Cité."[58] When he wrote about a purely political quarrel on an explicitly moral level, Rutebeuf surely defined his own polemical works as being as edifying as his *Voie* or Crusade poems.

THE QUARREL BETWEEN THE UNIVERSITY OF PARIS AND THE MENDICANT ORDERS In the quarrel between the secular masters of the Theology Faculty of the University of Paris and the encroaching Mendicant friars, there is evidence of an extensive and effective propaganda campaign, reflected in Rutebeuf's work. We shall see that nine of his poems[59] are directly connected

---

57. "Ad quos preveneritis,/ his dicatis, quare/ singulorum cupitis/ mores exprobare:/ "Reprobare reprobos/ et probos probare,/ et probos ab improbis/ veni segregare" (ed. and trans. George F. Whicher, *The Goliard Poets* [New York, 1949], pp. 278–79). The Goliard is parodying Matthew 25:32-33.

58. Joseph Bédier, *Les Fabliaux: Etudes de littérature populaire et d'histoire littéraire du moyen âge* (4th ed. Paris, 1925), p. 417.

59. *La Discorde de l'Université et des Jacobins, Le Dit de Guillaume de Saint-Amour, Du Pharisien, Complainte de Guillaume, Des Règles, Le Dit de Sainte Église, Le Dit d'Hypocrisie, La Bataille des Vices contre les Vertus, Des Jacobins.* Several other poems, such as *Les Ordres de Paris*, make reference to the quarrel but seem to be satirical rather than directly polemical in intent.

with this quarrel and may well be described as political pamphlets. Rutebeuf is not the first poet to rhyme in favor of philosophers against monks. The twelfth-century author of the *Metamorphosis of Golias* hotly defends philosophers against the censures of Saint Bernard, who repeatedly pursued Abélard (in 1121 and 1140).[60] He ends his poem with eloquent praise of humanistic studies and an attack on Bernard's monastic superstitiousness:

> Clamant a philosopho proles educati,
> Cucullatus populi primas cucullati;
> Et ut cepe tunicis tribus tunicati,
> Imponi silentium fecit tanto vati.
> Grex est hic nequitiæ, grex perditionis;
> Impius et pessimus hæres Pharaonis,
> Speciem exterius dans religionis,
> Sed subest scintillula superstitionis.
>
>   . . .
>
> Cucullatus igitur grex vilipendatur,
> Et a philosophicis scolis expellatur.[61]

The University quarrel is, then, part of a continuing history of rivalry between different ecclesiastical branches. McKeon's useful article on the quarrel sets it in this larger context: he shows how the papacy first encouraged the foundation of universities in a move "aimed at destroying the local limitations and hence controls" of royalty and local Church officials, and at sustaining ortho-

---

60. See Raby, *Secular Latin Poetry,* 2, 219–22.

61. "People educated by the philosopher call him cowled primate of the cowled people, and like an onion tunicked with three tunics, they impose silence on many poets. Here is a wicked flock, a flock of perdition, the impious and most evil heir of Pharoah, giving an outward appearance of religion, but the little spark of superstition is within. Therefore let the cowled flock be reviled and driven from the philosophical schools" (ed. Wright, *Walter Mapes,* p. 30). An interesting article by B. Landry, "Les Idées morales du XIIᵉ siècle: Les Ecrivains en latin; satiristes et fabulistes" (*Revue des Cours et Conférences, 40,* No. 13 [June 15, 1939], 432–48), discusses Nivard's *Ysengrinus,* Map's *De nugis curalium* (ed. M. R. James [Oxford, 1941], and Niegel's *Speculum stultorum,* all of which show hostility to St. Bernard.

doxy by training the clergy.[62] By 1250 the University felt itself to be an autonomous body and sought freedom from both local ecclesiastical and papal controls.[63] Papal support of the new Mendicant orders' desire to enter the closed circle of the Theology Faculty appeared, according to McKeon, as a "reaffirmation of papal supervision and control." Matthew Paris, an ardent Anglican and no admirer of the sort of royal presumption evinced by Henry III, states clearly what must have been common opinion among rather na-

62. Peter R. McKeon, "The Status of the University of Paris as *Parens Scientarium*: An Episode in the Development of Its Autonomy," *Speculum, 39*, No. 4 (October 1964), 651. The article is an excellent study of the political implications of the University quarrel and is a necessary complement to the extremely accurate but somewhat limited survey of the quarrel by Faral (FB, *1*, 65–82), who gives full references to all relevant documents. Other useful recountings of the historical events are to be found in: Maurice Perrod, "Etude sur la vie et sur les œuvres de Guillaume de Sainte-Amour, Docteur en théologie de l'Université de Paris, Chanoine de Beauvais et de Mâcon, (1202–1272)," *Mémoires de la Société d'Emulation du Jura*, 7e série, 2 (Lons-le-Saunier, 1902), 61–252; *Rutebeuf: Poèmes concernant l'Université de Paris*, ed. H. H. Lucas (Paris, 1952), pp. 9–25, gives an account somewhat inaccurate in the details (see Faral's critical review, *Romania, 74* [1953], 109–20); Le Nain de Tillemont's *Vie de Saint Louis, 6* (Paris, 1851), 135–228 is an interesting 17th-century account of the affair by the Jansenist priest. Documentary source material formerly taken from C E. DuBoulay's *Historia Universitatis Parisiensis* (Paris, 1666), Vol. 3, is now replaced by the *Chartularium Universitatis Parisiensis, 1*, ed. Henri Denifle and Emile Chatelain (Paris, 1889), 1200–86. See also: Louis Petit-Radel, "Guillaume de Saint-Amour," *Histoire littéraire, 19* (Paris, 1838), pp. 197–215; Hastings Rashdall, "The Mendicants and the University," *Universities, 1*, 345–92; McDonnell, "The Hierarchy Undiminished" and "The Protest of Rutebeuf" (*Beguines*, pp. 456–73), relating the criticism of Guillaume de Saint-Amour, Rutebeuf, and Jean de Meun to the *béguine* movement; Christine Thouzellier, "La Place du *De Periculis* de Guillaume de Saint-Amour dans les polémiques universitaires du XIIIe siècle," *Revue Historique, 156*, No. 310 (September–October 1927), 69–83; P. Anastase Van den Wyngaert, "Querelles du clergé séculier et des ordres mendiants à l'Université de Paris au XIIIe siècle," *La France Franciscane, 5* (1822), 257–81, 369–97, and 6 (1923), 47–70, gives a complete bibliography of all the Latin polemical writings on both sides (p. 397). Extracts of the relevant Latin polemical texts are given by Max Bierbaum, *Bettelorden und Weltgeistlichkeit an der Universität Paris. Texte und Untersuchungen zum literarischen Armuts- und Exemptionsstreit des 13. Jahrhunderts, 1255–1272 (Franziskanische Studien*, Beiheft 2; Munster-inWestf., 1920).

63. Mandonnet, the Dominican historian of 13th-century intellectual history, has clearly established that the University faculties were under the direct control of the Bishop of Paris and his Chancellor, who alone had the right to name professors ("De l'Incorporation des Dominicains dans l'ancienne Université de Paris, 1229–1231," *Revue Thomiste, 4*, No. 2 [May 1896], 148–52). Mandonnet also studies the Pope's role in the University organization, pp. 145–47.

tionalistic secular clergymen: "A great dispute arose between the scholars of the University of Paris and the preacher brethren, who had become so numerous and so elevated at being the confessors and advisors of kings, that they refused to submit to the old and approved customs and rights of the scholars." [64] These "old and approved customs" dated at the most from a half-century before the admission of the first Mendicant professor (1229), and thus we can see the strong tendency toward conservation of exclusive privilege, evident in the Church hierarchy, at war with tendencies toward reform and centralization.

Briefly, the quarrel between the University masters and the Mendicant friars was as follows.[65] In 1252 the Mendicant orders, who had arrived in Paris during the second decade of the century [66] and had been progressively encroaching on the privileges and revenues which the parish clergy derived from rights of sermons, burials, confession, and administration of sacraments, came into conflict with the secular masters of the Faculty of Theology. During a strike by the secular masters in 1229–31, the friars had obtained three chairs in the Theology Faculty,[67] but refused to submit to University statutes

64. *English History, 3,* 57. Christine Thouzellier misinterprets Guillaume's aims when she says he wants to "maintenir l'intégrité du pouvoir pontificale contre toute tentative d'usurpation" ("La Place du *De periculis*," p. 73). Guillaume really sought to remove the University from papal and Mendicant influence and control.

65. The following résumé of events in the university quarrel is based on the studies listed above, n. 62, and is given to facilitate reading for those who do not have FB at hand.

66. See Bennett, *The Early Dominicans, 1,* pp. 52–54, and FB, 65–66. The Dominicans first occupied a rented house, then the former "parloir aux bourgeois" of the Town Council, and after spending some time in a castle belonging to the Lord of Hautefeuille, they accepted the Saint-Jacques hospice in 1218 from Jean de Burastre, chaplain of the King and Regent of the University (whence their name, "Jacobins"). The University ceded its rights to the Saint-Jacques chapel in return for prayers offered by the Dominicans (Perrod, "Guillaume de Saint-Amour," p. 99). The University thus considered itself the patron of the Dominicans.

67. During the 1229–31 strike, the master Jean de Saint Giles taught at the Dominican convent, and Friar Roland of Cremona was accepted as a master; Jean de Saint Giles himself, while preaching at the Dominican convent in 1231, was evidently moved by his own rhetoric, stepped down from the pulpit, donned the Dominican habit, then finished his sermon; he retained his University chair, as did the Master-Regent Alexander of Hales, who took the Franciscan habit in the same year of 1231 (Bennett, *Early Dominicans,* pp. 53–54; Perrod, "Guillaume de Saint-

or to join the secular masters in an official protest concerning four students who had been illegally arrested by the civil police of Paris (1253), and protested efforts of the Theology Faculty to take away one of the Dominican chairs. Early in 1254 the secular masters of the University, led by the eloquent doctor of theology Guillaume de Saint-Amour, Master-Regent of the Faculty of Theology, joined forces with the parish clergy and sent a "manifesto" to all the Church prelates exposing the wrongs done them by the Dominicans over more than two decades.[68] In this letter they spoke of the friars' ingratitude to the secular masters who had helped them in their humble beginnings, of their ambitious intriguing for University chairs, of their refusal to join with the other masters in the protest over the students' arrest, and of their refusal to obey the University statutes.

During the summer of 1254 the University sent a delegation of masters,[69] led by Guillaume de Saint-Amour, to plead their cause before Pope Innocent IV, who judged in their favor.[70] Innocent, however, died 17 days after issuing the bull favoring the masters, and his successor, Alexander IV, quickly reversed the decision in his "Quasi lignum" of April 14, 1255,[71] ordered the University to accept the Mendicant professors, and limited the powers of the secular masters.

The masters, unwilling to acknowledge defeat and trying to strike at the roots of the Mendicants' power—that is, at their papal support—seized upon an apocalyptic work written by a Franciscan, Gerard of Borgo San Donnino, the *Liber introductorius* or *Eternal Gospel*, in which he exposed the doctrine of Joachim of Floris.[72]

Amour," pp. 11–15; P. Gratien, *Histoire de la fondation et de l'évolution de l'ordre des Frères Mineurs*, pp. 130–32). Other friars already taught on other faculties prior to 1229 (Perrod, "Guillaume de Saint-Amour," pp. 111–12).

68. *Chart. Univ., 1,* 252–58, No. 230.

69. The delegation included the Masters Odon de Douai, Chrétien de Beauvais, and Nicholas de Bar-sur-Aube, who returned with Guillaume to Italy in 1256.

70. Bull entitled "Etsi animarum," *Chart. Univ., 1,* 267–70, No. 240.

71. *Chart. Univ., 1,* 279–85, No. 247.

72. Gerard's *Liber introductorius* was lost. Emmanuel Aegerter made a partial translation of Joachim's own writings, *L'Evangile éternel*, Les Textes du christian-

Joachim, a Cistercian monk of the end of the twelfth century, had predicted the arrival of a new reign of the Holy Spirit for the year 1260 during which the monastic orders would replace the existing Church hierarchy.[73] Although the University faction tried to smear all the Mendicants with this heretical doctrine, only a few Franciscans, among them influential men like John of Parma, Master General of the order, actually subscribed to it. The secular masters, under the direction of Guillaume, wrote a pamphlet listing the errors of the *Eternal Gospel*, the *Tractatus de periculis novissimorum temporum ex Scripturis sumptis* (1255),[74] turning the apocalyptic prophecies against the friars themselves, denouncing them as the false apostles who were to appear before the Antichrist in the Last Days. Guillaume, together with the masters and students, wrote again to Alexander IV, attacking the friars and again requesting the Pope to grant them all rights of control over the University chairs and courses, as well as the exclusion of the Mendicants.

Guillaume preached sermons defending the University cause in Paris and in the provinces from the fall of 1255 to the spring of

---

isme, III and IV (Paris, 1928). A good résumé of the doctrine and its importance is to be found in Karl Löwith, *Meaning in History* (Chicago, 1949), pp. 145–59. Cohn, *Pursuit of the Millennium*, offers an interesting discussion of Joachism as a factor in the political career of Frederick II (pp. 99–107).

73. Matthew Paris, *English History, 3*, 454, shows how apocalyptic rumors as well as political opinions were spread by song: "In these times, also, on account of terrible rumors of this kind [about the imminent Tartar menace of 1242] the following verses, declaring the coming of the Antichrist, were spread about.

    Quum fuerint anni transacti mille ducenti
    Et quinquaginta, post partum Virginis Almae
    Tunc Antichristus nascetur daemone plenus."

74. Guillaume de Saint-Amour, *Opera omnia quae reperiri potuerunt*, ed. "Alithophilos" [Valérien de Flavigny, docteur en Sorbonne, professeur au Collège Royal (Constance, 1632)], pp. 17–71. Perrod suggests that this, the first and only printed edition of the complete works of Guillaume, was actually printed in Paris, under the false rubric of "Constantiae," since Guillaume's works were still under interdict ("Guillaume de Saint-Amour," p. 247)—a useless precaution, since the edition was condemned by the Royal Council in an edict of July 1633: "Veu l'exemplaire du livre susdit de 1256 [*De periculis*] la bulle de nostre sainct père le pape, Alexandre, quatriesme année de son Pontificat, qui estoit l'année mil deux cent cinquante six, portant condamnation du traicté susdit comme meschant et exécrable" (Perrod, p. 249).

1256.[75] An effort made by the King to arbitrate the question in a council held by the Archbishops of Bourges, Rheims, Sens, and Rouen, together with many bishops, the "Amiable Conciliation" of March 1, 1256, was rejected out of hand by the Pope. Summoned to Italy by the Dominicans and Alexander IV, Guillaume and three other masters arrived just after the *De periculis* had been condemned, but in time to see the tract publicly burned, whereupon all the masters except Guillaume capitulated to the Pope's authority. The *Eternal Gospel* was also condemned to destruction, but secretly and quietly, since the Pope did not intend to undermine the friars' position.[76]

Guillaume, detained in Italy by illness, was unable to leave for France until August 1257. While Guillaume was safely under his eye, the wily Pope carefully consolidated his position. He wrote more than twenty letters between April 1256 and July 1257 to the archbishops of France, to the Bishop and Chancellor of Paris, to Louis IX, and to the masters and students at the University, cajoling, threatening, and ordering obedience to the "Quasi lignum" bull and insisting on the friars' admission to the University. He had already suggested, in honeyed words, that Louis exile or imprison Guillaume,[77] but he sought to quash public outcry before moving against Guillaume himself.

In the second and third week of August 1257 Alexander struck quickly and brutally. Guillaume was stopped by messengers as he was on the road home to France, and was told that he was not only exiled from France but forbidden on pain of excommunication to teach or preach by virtue of a papal order sent to Louis IX and

75. See Perrod, "Guillaume de Saint-Amour," pp. 139–43. Texts of two extant sermons, *De pharisaeo et publicano*, and *Sermo magistri Guillielmi de S. Amore, in die Sanctorum Apostolorum Jacobi et Philippi* in his *Opera omnia*, pp. 7–15 and 491–504.

76. The Franciscans themselves tried to expel the Joachites from their midst: Gerard of Borgo San Donnino refused to retract his erroneous beliefs and was condemned to perpetual imprisonment in 1258; John of Parma resigned as Master General in 1257 and was succeeded by Saint Bonaventura. John withdrew to a solitary hermitage in Greccio after being exonerated by a tribunal (Gratien, *Frères Mineurs au XIIIe siècle*, pp. 276–77).

77. *Chart. Univ.*, *1*, No. 282.

Reginald, the Bishop of Paris.[78] Rutebeuf's *Dit de Guillaume* (1257) is one of the very few texts illustrating the abortive movement of reaction over Guillaume's abrupt exile; Alexander had recognized the dangers of public protest and laid his ground well. It was not until early in 1259, when the Pope had relaxed his vigilance, that open opposition reappeared. Immediately the Pope reacted, sending strong letters to the Bishop, King, and students, deploring scandal, turbulence, and dissension, and forbidding agitation in favor of Guillaume, "qui nulla penitentia signa monstratur."[79]

It is clear that although the *Eternal Gospel* presented a threat to orthodoxy, Guillaume, his *De periculis,* and the University rebellion represented an immediate menace to the orderly exercising of papal power. The Pope made little effort to curtail the rumor that *De periculis* had been condemned for its heresy, thus masking the struggle for secular power, which was the real issue. Guillaume de Nangis in his *Chronicon* states the matter clearly: "It was condemned to the flames by the Pope . . . not because of heresy, as some say, which he was guilty of, but because it was thought to incite treachery and scandal against the aforesaid monks."[80]

Guillaume had also faced extraordinarily powerful adversaries in Italy. Perrod recounts vividly how the friars had brought their most powerful voices to Anagni: Saint Bonaventura represented the Franciscans together with Friar Bertrand d'Aquitaine, also known as Bigle de Bayonne, a former colleague of Guillaume's noted for

78. Ibid., Nos. 314–16.
79. Ibid., p. 382, No. 332.
80. *Chronique latine . . . de 1113 à 1300 avec les continuations de cette chronique de 1300 à 1368,* ed. H. Géraud, 2d ed. Paris, 1843), 216–17; "Damnatus est et combustibus coram Papa . . . non propter haeresim, ut quidam dicunt, quam contineret, sed quia contra praefatos religiosos videbatur seditionem et scandalum excitare." It was popularly believed, however, that the book had been condemned for heresy; see, for example, the prose chronicle in *Renart le contrefait* (first half of 14th century), which says: "L'an .M..IIe..LII. ot a Paris monlt grant discencion entre les escolliers et les relig̈ieux, de laquelle discension fut acteur Maistre Guillamme de Saint-Amour, lequel maistre composa ung livre contre les relig̈ieux especialment Mendians; il apela le livre *Du desrenier Perl du Monde.* Mais le dit livre comme contenant erreur et heresie fust condempné par le pappe Alixandre et conmanda a ardoir" (*1,* 289, par. 144).

his eloquent disputations; for the Dominicans, came Humbert de Romans, Albertus Magnus, *and* Saint Thomas Aquinas, who drew upon their tremendous resources of learnings and intellect to refute *De periculis* and its author.[81] Guillaume's *Responsiones*,[82] or answers to the charges against him, were heard, and the *De periculis* was condemned, although Guillaume was cleared by a council hearing.

The thirteenth-century Dominican Thomas de Cantimpré recreates the atmosphere of intense partisanship and factionalism which reigned during these hearings, and shows again how public opinion was called to play a role. Recounting the first efforts of the masters, he speaks as a violent adversary of the University cause:

> Quatre maîtres principalement furent à Paris les instigateurs acharnés. Ils excitèrent férocement contre les Frères les âmes naïves des écoliers, au point que, si le très pieux et très dévot Louis, roi de France, et son pieux frère Alphonse, comte de Poitiers . . . ne s'étaient dressés comme des murailles pour la défense des Frères, ces religieux eussent été anéantis en leurs biens et leurs personnes. Alors, faute de pouvoir davantage, les maîtres en question envoyèrent à travers les pays et les royaumes des lettres diffamatoires et pleines de mensonges dirigés contre les Frères.[83]

He describes further the hearings in Rome as a sort of public combat in which the prize was popular acclamation and vindication:

> Et l'on doit noter qu'avant que maître Albert, frère de l'Ordre des Prêcheurs, se fut présenté à la cour de Rome, un certain

---

81. Perrod, "Guillaume de Saint-Amour," pp. 177–79. See the study of Aquinas' refutation of Guillaume by P. Glorieux, "Le *Contra Impugnantes* de S. Thomas; Ses sources—son plan," *Mélanges Mandonnet; Etudes d'histoire littéraire et doctrinale du moyen âge, 1* (Paris, 1930), 51–81.

82. The full title is "Casus et articuli super quibus accusatus fuit magister Guillielmus de Sancto Amore a Fratribus Praedicatoribus cum responsionibus ad singula," *Opera omnia*, pp. 88–110; recently and expertly edited by Faral in *Archives d'Histoire Doctrinale et Littéraire du Moyen Age*, 25–26 (1950–51), 336–94.

83. *Bonum de apibus*, 1. II, c. 10, pars. 23–24; cited by Faral, "Les *Responsiones*," p. 366.

maître Guillaume, avec ses complices, avait étrangement gagné à la cause de sa perversité le clergé romain et aussi le peuple, les séduisant par de nombreux discours. Mais, après les discussions dont j'ai parlé, comme, à la demande du pape et de tous les cardinaux, maître Albert avait expliqué de façon admirable, mieux que personne ne l'avait jamais fait, l'Evangile de Jean en entier et les épitres canoniques, l'affaire des Frères Prêcheurs et Mineurs fut réglée de façon si favorable, que tous leurs ennemis en furent frappés de stupeur et d'horreur, et que les partisans de la vérité purent se reposer et se réjouir dans la paix la plus complète.[84]

Faral is certainly right in saying that Thomas de Cantimpré is less than clear in his exposition of the facts;[85] but objectivity would have menaced the *truth*. Thomas de Cantimpré's recounting of events, like that of the masters, is distorted by his urgent desire to convince, to win men over to the right side—hence his jubilation at the triumph of the "partisans of the truth."

PROPAGANDA CAMPAIGN OF THE UNIVERSITY The University masters, no less than the friars, threw the combat into the public arena during the years 1254–59. They evidently tried to bring pressure on the friars from several directions at once: they sought to arouse popular hostility against them, since the Mendicants depended on public generosity for their subsistence; they attacked on theological grounds the Mendicants' right to beg; and finally, they sought to attribute to all the Mendicants the heretical tendencies of a few. The masters' task was considerable, since they had not only to win over the great power of the national Church hierarchy but also to defeat a strong pope, Alexander IV, who was supported by Louis IX within France. They did not only depend on the carefully constructed defense of *De periculis* or *Responsiones,* but turned to satire as a weapon.

84. Ibid.
85. Ibid., pp. 365–67.

Although a vernacular poet and no theologian, Rutebeuf was called upon to use his talents to popularize the cause of the secular masters. The substance of Rutebeuf's nine poems is, in every case, closely related to the Latin polemical writings of the University masters. Faral has made a special study of *Des Règles* proving that "toute la doctrine de la pièce procède de celle qu'on trouve exprimée dans la littérature de combat du même temps, qui en fournit sur beaucoup de points, comme on le verra dans nos notes, le commentaire indispensable."[86] Faral does not suggest that Rutebeuf composed his poem with the Latin documents in hand, but rather that Rutebeuf is, "quand il écrit sur des questions débattues, un homme informé de beaucoup de choses, plongé en un certain milieu intellectuel et social, épousant les idées d'une partie de l'opinion et les reflétant en leur complexe diversité."[87] Rutebeuf himself contributed no new ideas, no new arguments; his role in the University quarrel was strictly that of propagandist or publicist. He adapted the essential elements of the polemical effort into French verse, into vivid and forceful poems designed to arouse fervent support for the masters of theology.

The poems could have been circulated either in writing or orally. Rutebeuf himself consistently uses the verbs "listen" and "hear" when he speaks to his audience, but these are time-honored formulas in medieval poetry. Speaking of Rutebeuf's Crusade poems, Nykrog asserts that they must have circulated "sous la forme de feuilles volantes" in order to affect a sufficiently large public, and that oral recitations would not have reached enough people.[88] Nykrog exaggerates, I believe, the size of Rutebeuf's public; his activities and influence as poet seem generally restricted to Paris (see below, Chap. 3), and the poems on the University quarrel are even further limited to a few interested groups such as the masters themselves, the prelates, the students, and the friars, and only secondarily

86. FB, *1, 268.* See above n. 11, and the Tübingen dissertation of Tiberius Denkinger, "Die Bettelorden in der französichen didaktischen Literatur des 13. Jahrhunderts, besonders bei Rutebeuf und im *Roman de la Rose,*" *Franziskanische Studien,* 2 (1915), esp. 73–109, on Rutebeuf.

87. Faral, *"Le Dit des Règles,"* p. 206.

88. Per Nykrog, Les Fabliaux: Etude d'histoire littéraire et de stylistique médiévale, p. 50 n.

to the general public. But a text from Alfonso X El Sabio's *Siete Partidas,* the great vernacular codification of the legal heritage of Rome, dated 1256, confirms Nykrog's theory in a most interesting passage, showing not only the common existence of partisan verse but also giving information on how the poems were spread about:

"De la deshonra que face un home á otro por cántigas ó por rimas."

Enfaman et deshonran unos á otros non tan solamente por palabra, mas aun por escriptura faciendo cántigas, ó rimas ó dictados malos de los que han sabor de enfamar. Et esto facen á las vegadas paladinamente et á las vegadas encubiertamente, echando aquellas escripturas malas en las casas de los grandes señores, ó en las eglesias, ó en las plazas comunales de las cibdades ó de las villas, porque cada uno lo pueda leer: et en esto tenemos que reciben muy grant deshonra aquellos contra quien es fecho. . . . Et tales escripturas como estas dicen en latin *famosos libellos,* que quiere tanto decir como libro pequeño que es escripto á enfamamiento dotro. Et por ende defendieron los emperadores et los sabios que ficieron las leyes antiguas, que ninguno non debiese enfamar á otro desta manera.[89]

Alphonso's text uses the same words, "famosos libellos," to describe the polemical texts as Alexander did in his letter denouncing the campaign of propaganda in favor of Guillaume, and confirms Nykrog's belief that the partisan poems circulated as handbills. Moreover, Jean de Meun tells us that the *Eternal Gospel* could be rented for copying in front of Notre Dame:

A Paris n'ot ome ne fame,
Ou parvis devant Nostre Dame,
Qui lors aveir ne le peüst,
A transcrivre s'il l'i pleüst.[90]

89. Alfonso El Sabio, *Las Siete Partidas, 4,* ed. Gregorio López (Paris, 1851), Setena Partida, Titulo IX, Ley III, p. 504.

90. *Roman de la Rose, 3,* ed. Ernest Langlois, 216, vv. 11,807–10. We know that books were commonly rented for copying in university towns; see Charles Homer Haskins, *Studies in Medieval Culture* (Oxford, 1929), p. 99, and all the chapter

The letter from Pope Alexander to the Bishop of Paris in 1259 was part of his campaign to scotch new efforts on Guillaume's behalf, and consigns also certain libelous pamphlets and songs to the flames along with *De periculis*. After praising his "dilectorum filiorum Predicatorum et Minorum Ordinum fratrum," and condemning turbulence and scandal among the students of Paris, Alexander says:

> Moreover, in accordance with his public confession before The Apostolic Seat, we have had condemned to be burned by fire, upon the advice of our brothers, a certain famous and detestable little volume edited by the same Guillaume [de Saint-Amour], the title of which is *Tractatus brevis de periculis novissimorum temporum,* and whose beginning was 'Ecce videntes clamabunt foris,' and also certain other wretched little pamphlets [*libellos*], famous for their infamy, and slandering these same friars, published anew, as it is reported, by their rivals, in both literary and vernacular language, in indecent rhymes and songs, which you are to have brought before you, compelling those who withhold evidence to appear before an ecclesiastic censure, without appeal, and, summoning all the masters and students of Paris, you are to have these works openly and publicly burned.[91]

It is clear from this letter that factional propaganda efforts such as Rutebeuf's had received a dangerous amount of public attention.[92]

"The Spread of Ideas in the Middle Ages," pp. 92–104; as well as Auerbach, *Literary Language*, p. 289.

91. "Insuper quendam libellum famosum et detestabilem ab eodem G. editum, prout publice apud sedem apostolicam confessus extitit, quem per nos de fratrum nostrorum consilio condemnatum igne cremari fecimus, cupus titulus: *Tractatus brevis de periculis novissimorum temporum,* nuncupatur, principium autem ejus erat: *Ecce videntes clamabunt foris,* necnon et quosdam alios libellos famosos in infamiam et detractionem eorundem fratrum ab eorum emulis in litterali et vulgari sermone necnon rismis et cantilenis indecentibus de novo ut dicitur editos, quos tibi exhiberi facias, detentores ad exhibitionem ipsorum per censuram ecclesiaticam appellatione postposita compellendo, convocatis magistris et scolaribus parisius existentibus facias publice coram omnibus igne cremari" *Chart. Univ., 1,* 391, No. 342).

92. The Pope's letter possibly refers also to certain fictitious letters written in

The Pope's letter goes on to condemn a beadle named Guillot of the Picard Nation, who, "unmindful of his own salvation," says Alexander, had actually got up in the middle of a Palm Sunday sermon by Saint Thomas Aquinas and started to peddle pamphlets against the Mendicants within the church.[93]

Certainly within Paris there was always an audience in the streets and the taverns, eager for news and gossip, ready consumers for polemical works "hot from the oven" and spoken aloud. Poems such as Rutebeuf's have a dramatic, urgent immediacy; they are news. Spoken in French they could be understood by anyone, from learned clerks to guffawing ribalds. People went to taverns, especially in the student quarter,[94] to get warm in winter, to drink, but above all, to get news and discuss the latest happenings in the city. Taverns, then, were trouble spots in times of controversy, and it is with interest that we read in Guillaume de Nangis that "l'année où les troubles de l'Université eurent lieu (1255), le Roi défendait de boire dans les tavernes, autrement que debout et en passant." [95] Such precautions must have been necessary to prevent outbreaks of agitation and dissemination of rumor, and to control the oral circulation of propaganda.

One can perhaps distinguish most easily between works intended

---

Latin which were circulating in 1259, as well as to vernacular works like Rutebeuf's poems. Three are given in the University *Chartularium* (Vol. 1) which are imaginary letters from the University to the King (No. 355), from Louis IX to the masters (No. 356), and one from Louis to the Pope (No. 357). No. 356 attacks Guillaume in such violent terms, saying: "Canis, lupus et vulpecula ab humanis moribus discrepantes non sunt inter homines receptandi . . . Monstrum est in natura doctor vester, pro quo nobis noviter supplicastis" (p. 404), that the exaggerations and unpleasantness of the supposed attack, so unlike pious Louis, must have been intended to call forth first protest, then defense of Guillaume, and eventually create support for the University cause.

93. *Chart, Univ., 1, 391,* No. 342. Although deprived of his office for a time, Guillot had regained his position by 1263 (Perrod, "Guillaume de Saint-Amour," pp. 226–27)

94. See E. Chatelain, "Notes sur quelques tavernes fréquentées par l'Université de Paris aux XIVe et XVe siècles," *Bulletin de la Société de l'Histoire de Paris et de l'Ile-de-France, 25* (1898), 87–109, and, of course, that perennial barfly, Villon.

95. *Vie et vertus de Saint Louis,* ed. René de Lespinasse, Petits Mémoires sur l'histoire de France, I, gen. ed. Marius Sepet (Paris, 1877), p. 164.

primarily for oral or for written circulation by their style. The Latin polemical texts often achieve impressive rhetorical effects and proceed logically with elaborate proofs of each point by biblical texts, but they are hardly filled with catch-phrases or striking images as is Rutebeuf's poetry, which uses, as we shall see, the vivid scene, the appeal to ready-made emotional reactions, and the quick verbal wit which attracts and convinces an audience. His propaganda technique is indeed quite different from that of the University masters who try to win influential churchmen to their cause through mellifluous and leisurely prose of a sort only to be appreciated by the learned. The contrast between the masters' Manifesto of 1254 and Rutebeuf's first University poem, La Discorde de l'Université et des Jacobins, is revealing. The masters describe the arrival of the Dominicans within the University, and the kindly welcome given them, with a great flow of sentiment and adverbs:

> Novissime autem diebus nostris quidam viri regulares, qui fratres Predicatores dicuntur, Parisius in parvo numero viventes sub quadam pietatis ac publice utilitatis specie subingressi una nobiscum theologie studium ferventer et humiliter sunt aggressi, propter quod a majoribus nostris et nobis benigne recepti, sincere caritatis brachiis amplexati, in domo nostra propria, in qua usque hodie commorantur, quam eis ad inhabitandum concessimus, hospitati, alimento tam doctrine quam corporali diligentius educati . . .[96]

and the sentence is but half done! Rutebeuf takes a short-cut through the masters' elaborate proofs of the friars' treachery with his succinctly humble phrases:

96. "Moreover, most recently in our days, certain regular clerics called Preaching Brethren, living in Paris under the guise of piety and public usefulness, have joined us and have undertaken fervently and humbly the study of theology with us, because of which they have been kindly received by our elders and by us, embraced with sincere charity in our arms, in our own house, in which, as of today, they still dwell, [and] which we granted to them for their living quarters, treated as guests, and reared diligently in bodily as well as doctrinal nourishment . . ." (Chart. Univ., 1, 253, No. 230).

Chascuns d'els deüst estre amis
L'Université voirement,
Quar l'Université a mis
En els tout le bon fondement:
Livres, deniers, pains et demis;
Més or lor rendent malement,
Quar cels destruit li anemis
Qui plus l'ont servi longuement. (vv. 25-32)

Where the masters spoke of giving the friars "bodily as well as doctrinal nourishment," Rutebeuf speaks specifically and bluntly of books, money, and bread. He quickly states the facts, then punctuates them with proverbs which make the moral point.

Rutebeuf counts more on the vivid image, the detail guaranteed to wring the hearts of his hearers, than on subtle orientation of language. To show how the friars have enriched themselves at the expense of the parish priests, he compares their libraries:

Sanz avoir cure * or ont l'avoir,	* official authorization; worry
Et li curez n'en puet avoir,	or work
S'a paine non, du pain por vivre	
Ne achater un petit livre	
Ou il puisse dire complies;	
Et cil * en ont pances emplies	* friars
Et bibles et sautiers glosez,	
Que l'en voit cras et reposez. (*Des Règles,* vv. 125-32)	

The one little book the devout *curé* needs to say his evening prayers is denied him, while the friars, who do not labor long at pious tasks, have many and well-edited texts. The *curé* must struggle just to get enough bread to eat, while the friars have fat bellies below their plump and rested faces. Without work they have wealth!

This distressing contrast is followed by a marvelous description of the visit of one of these fat friars to the home of a poor priest. The passage is an excellent example of Rutebeuf's talent for turning the rhetorical Latin polemical writings into lively art. In *De periculis* and in the *Collectiones* the masters had criticized the friars who "offenduntur quando non ministrantur eis cibaria lautiora," and who "non sunt contenti oblatis cibo et potu, sed potius stomachantur vel indignantur . . . si non ministrantur eis magni pisces et optima vina."[97] Rutebeuf puts the haughtily condescending brother before our eyes and shows us the flustered parish priest doing his best to serve up the meal in style:

> Quant chiés povre provoire vienent
> (Ou pou sovent la voie tienent
> S'il n'i a riviere ou vingnoble),
> Lors sont si cointe et sont si noble
> Qu'il samble que ce soient roi.
> Or covient por els grant aroi,
> Dont li povres hom est en trape.
> S'il devoit engagier sa chape,
> Si covient il autre viande
> Que l'Escripture ne commande.
> S'il ne sont peü * sanz defaut,   * fed
> Se li prestres de ce defaut,
> Il ert tenuz a mauvés homme,
> S'il valoit saint Piere de Romme.
>
> (*Des Règles, vv.* 139–52)

What pomp in the substitution of river and vineyard for fish and wine! How unfair that the poor priest should have to pawn his cloak to set the best viands before "his nibs"! And to risk the stake if the meat is burnt! The cleverly placed comparison of the friar's regal arrogance to the truly apostolic if involuntary poverty of the priest dramatizes the scene for us and directs our sympathies while apparently entertaining us. Rutebeuf's vernacular polemic thus combines a simple explanation of the "facts," with concrete images that bring out the moral issues involved.

---

97. *Collectiones*, p. 469; cited by FB I, 274, note to vv. 139–48.

THEMES OF RUTEBEUF'S UNIVERSITY POEMS   Just as
the masters compiled a series of all-purpose texts to use against the
friars,[98] so Rutebeuf's poems about the University quarrel are built
around a limited number of themes, formulated at the very beginning of the controversy in 1254 or adapted from the general satirical
tradition.[99] These themes reappear when events such as Guillaume's
exile (1257) or renewed efforts on his behalf (1259) call for more
propaganda. The poems correspond to the stimulus of a historical
event (what Faral calls "un fait d'actualité"), yet the poet repeats,
adapts, hammers away at the same themes. Although it may seem
that repetition serves a polemical goal of convincing through emphasis, there is abundant evidence to show that repetition of theme
and formulas is characteristic of medieval poetry.[1] The poet tends to
seek the preestablished mold as naturally as water flows along a
stream bed, gradually eroding and carving new forms. All studies
of satirical and moral themes in medieval literature show this same
tendency to repetition.[2] The marvel of medieval verse is in its constant renewal, not its innovation; it is not the inner landscape but
the vision which is born anew.

In Rutebeuf's polemical verse, thematic repetition was adapted to
changing circumstances. A theme such as the ambition of the friars

98. The *Collectio catholice et canonice scripture ad deffensionem ecclesiastice
ierarchie et ad instructionem et preparationem simplicium fidelium christi contra
pericula eminencia ecclesia generali per ypocritas, pseudo predicatores et penetrantes
domos et ociosos* [var: *et criminosos*] *et curiosos et gerovagos,* printed in the *Opera
omnia* of Guillaume de Saint-Amour (pp. 111–486). Faral, (FB, *1,* 71, n. 1) asserts
that the *Collectiones* are not by Guillaume; very likely not entirely, but the *Collectiones* derive directly from his *De periculis* and *Responsiones* and are part of
the same propaganda campaign.

99. See below, pp. 183–89, for the survival of these themes after the University
quarrel was over.

1. In Chap. 4 we shall see how this formulization of themes occurs in vocabulary and sentence construction and discover rhetorical as well as thematic patterns.

2. See, for example, above, in Chap. 1, the sections on the estates and *voie*
poems, the Crusade pieces, and such studies as: Howard R. Patch, *The Goddess
Fortuna in Medieval Literature* (Cambridge, Mass., 1927); Bloomfield, *The Seven
Deadly Sins;* Yunck, *The Lineage of Lady Meed;* and for both thematic and rhetorical *topoi,* the key study of Curtius, *European Literature.*

was more amply developed as the Mendicants grew more powerful, while a theme originally treated very fully, such as the injustice of Guillaume's being exiled without a hearing, was reduced to a notation as the details of the quarrel became better known and hopes for Guillaume's return were dashed. Thus the whole of Rutebeuf's *Dit de Guillaume* (1257) is an elaborate discussion of the legality of the master's exile "sanz jugement." When the theme reappears in *Du Pharisien* (1259), these key words suffice to recall the grievance; speaking of the triumph of the friars, represented by the allegorical figure of *Ypocrisie,* Rutebeuf says:

> N'est més nus tels qui la responde *   * resists
> Qui maintenant ne le confonde
> Sanz jugement. (vv. 98–100)

Again in the *Complainte de Guillaume* (1259), *sainte Yglise* laments

> Com sont li mien mort et trahi
> Et por la verité haï
> Sanz jugement! (vv. 23–25)

Once again in *Des Règles* (1259) the poet recalls the degradation of the Church, whose best servant was exiled:

> Sainte Yglize, qui tel clerc as,
> Quant tu le lessas escillier
> Te peüs tu miex avillier?
> Et fu baniz sanz jugement. (vv. 98–101)

In like manner, the role that Louis IX and Pope Alexander IV played in this miscarriage of justice under the evil influence of the friars is thoroughly analyzed in the *Dit de Guillaume* (vv. 14–38; see below, Chap. 3) and reappears not only in 1259 in the *Complainte de Guillaume:*

> Pris ont Cesar, pris ont saint Pere,
> Et s'ont emprisoné mon pere
> Dedenz sa terre, (vv. 32–34)

but as late as 1263 in the *Bataille des Vices contre les Vertus*. In the *Bataille* Rutebeuf retells Guillaume's story for the last time, noting the death of his erstwhile supporter Chrétien de Beauvais.[3] The poet recalls in verses 198–204 his principal arguments from the *Discorde,* but ends now with a sad commentary, once again condensed in a proverb. Alluding to Guillaume's courageous defense before the Pope, he concludes:

> Més ce sachent et droit et tort
> C'on puet bien dire trop de voir. (vv. 208–09)

Rutebeuf alters his presentation of topical events such as the Amiable Conciliation of March 1256 to accommodate different objectives. We might say that the facts are made to suit the crime. In the *Dit de Guillaume* Rutebeuf wants to force the King to hold a fair hearing for Guillaume, so he accuses Louis of breaking his promise to uphold the Amiable Conciliation in order to put him under a moral obligation to act justly:

> Mestre Guillaumes au roi vint,
> La ou des genz ot plus de vint,
> Si dist: 'Sire, nous sons en mise
> Par le dit et par la devise
> Que li prelat deviseront:
> Ne sai se cil * la briseront.'   * the friars
> Li rois jura: 'En non de mi,
> Il m'avront tout a anemi
> S'il la brisent, sachiez sanz faille:
> Je n'ai cure de lor bataille.'
> Li mestres parti du palais
> Ou assez ot et clers et lais.
> Sanz ce que puis ne mesfeïst [4]

3. See FB, *1,* 305–06 and 79.
4. Rutebeuf is perhaps here suppressing some facts in the interests of absolute truth, since Guillaume actually preached inflammatory sermons against the Mendicants immediately and all during the period after the Amiable Conciliation, two of which are printed in his *Opera omnia* (see above, n. 75).

Ne la pais pas ne desfeïst,
Si l'escilla sanz plus veoir. (vv. 75–89)

Rutebeuf uses the setting of the royal palace to dramatize the scene
and even adds Saint Louis' scrupulously unblasphemous oath[5] to
accentuate the King's role in the agreement. In *Des Règles* Rutebeuf
blamed the friars for the breaking of the truce and sought to move
the prelates to protest, so here he underlines the Mendicants' treacherous disregard of the agreement and their disdain for the prelates,
and the royal scenery is completely missing; the King does not even
appear in this account:

> Je vi jadis, si com moi samble,
> Vint et quatre prelas ensamble
> Qui, par acort bon et leal
> Et par conseil fin et feal,
> Firent de l'Université,
> Qui est en grant aversité,
> Et des Jacobins bone acorde.
> Jacobins rompirent la corde.
> Ne fu lors bien nostre creance
> Et nostre loi en grant balance,
> Quant les prelaz de sainte Yglise
> Desmentirent toz en tel guise? (vv. 77–88)

Faral, noting this sort of repetition (FB, *1*, 314), calls them ideas
in germination and leftovers.[6] It is true that the poet seems reluctant
to leave out any pretested formula or any possible means of attack,
however irrelevant to his apparent central theme. But once again,
unity is found in intention, not in thematic logic,[7] and the poet who

5. Attested by the Dominican historian Geoffroi de Beaulieu, Louis' confessor
(FB, *1*, 247, note to v. 81).
6. Although Faral elsewhere speaks more accurately, in my opinion, of "pièces
préfabriquées" (FB, *1*, 59). See below, pp. 228–34.
7. Guillaume le Clerc clearly justifies the diverse subjects of his *Bestiaire* by
unity of intent:
> Nostre matire est mult estrange:
> Car sovent se diverse e change
> E neporquant si est tote une:

used the same formulas over and over again could eventually assume that his audience agreed with him on the fundamental moral notions he wanted them to take for granted.

The battle with the friars themselves, the archfoes of the masters, is the theme sounded early in the *Discorde* (1254) and is, naturally, the one most fully developed in later poems. Rutebeuf's criticisms follow consistently behind shifts in the polemic of the masters themselves. He attacks the friars first, as did the masters, for their ingratitude to their benefactors, for their reversal of the roles of master and servant. The Mendicants' change of heart is described in the third stanza of the *Discorde:*

> Quant Jacobin vindrent el monde,
> S'entrerent chiés Humilité;
> Lors estoient et net et monde
> Et s'amoient divinité.*   * theology
> Més Orguex, qui toz biens esmonde,
> I a tant mis iniquité
> Que par lor grant chape roonde
> Ont versé l'Université. (vv. 17–24)

Here Rutebeuf is using a common theme of moralizing verse, the "Bons fu, or est d'autre maniere" of his own *Etat du monde* (v. 5), a theme peculiarly appropriate for the Mendicants, who had preached such high ideals and had now sunk so low. The humble beginnings of the Dominicans are explained through brief references to allegorical figures, and their academic pretensions are illustrated through the image of the "grant chape roonde," their voluminous academic gown which has engulfed the University.

Almost a decade later, when the friars had not only won their chairs but had built themselves splendid new buildings (FB, *1*, 304), the same story is recalled in *La Bataille des Vices contre les Vertus.*

Car les essamples, qu'ele äune,
Sont totes por l'amendement
D'ome qui eire folement.
(vv. 345–50, ed. R. Reinsch [Leipzig, 1892], p. 235)

The Mendicants' ambitions are no longer limited to the University but have extended to the whole country and have swallowed up the King himself:

> Quant il vindrent premierement,
> Si vindrent assez humblement:
> Du pain quistrent, tel fu la riegle,
> Por oster les pechiez du siècle.
>   . . .
> Humilitez estoit petite,
> Qu'il avoient por aus eslite:
> Or est Humilitez greignor,
> Que il Frere sont or seignor
> Des rois, des prelas et des contes.
>   (vv. 57–60, 65–69)

Not content with their University studies, the friars now read theology in palatial luxury! The same themes recur in *Des Jacobins* (ca. 1263–65), where Rutebeuf mocks the deceptive original poverty of the friars, who now despise the poor, whose new buildings loom larger than ever, and whose academic pretensions have reached pinnacles of arrogant supremacy:

> Quant Frere Jacobin vindrent premier el monde,
> S'estoient par semblant et pur et net et monde.
>   (st. V, vv. 17–18)
> Premier ne demanderent c'un poi de repostaille
> Atout un pou d'estrain ou de chaume ou de paille;
> Le non Dieu sermonoient a la povre pietaille,
> Més or n'ont més que fere d'omme qui a pié aille.
>   (st. VI, vv. 21–24)
> . . . des basses mesons ont fet si granz palais
> C'uns hom, lance sor fautre, i feroit un eslais.
>   (st. VII, vv. 27–28)
> Divinité, qui est science esperitable,
> Ont il torné le dos, et s'en font connestable.

Chascuns cuide estre apostre quant il sont a la table,
Més Diex pot * ses apostres de vie plus metable.   * fed
(st. XV, vv. 57–60)

Through alliterations the poet underlines the false meekness of the friars, for the humble sequence "*premier, poi, repostaille, pou, paille, povre, pietaille*" explodes into haughty insolence with the last *p,* "n'ont més que fere d'omme qui a *pié* aille." The extreme contrast between the images of the poor man on foot and the armed warrior serves indeed to measure the pride of the friars, which can no longer be contained in "basses mesons" but requires "granz palais." The friars' ambition appears to reach higher with each poem: while in the *Discorde* they want to possess the University and in the *Bataille* to control the King, in *Des Jacobins* they aspire to be apostles seated with Christ himself, and think their greedy feasts to be the Holy Supper.

Faral's notes and *Notices* to his edition of Rutebeuf enable us to relate the appearance of new themes in Rutebeuf's poetry to the developing Latin polemic. The poet, however, expresses the themes in his own unique way, writes out of his experience as jongleur and polemicist. The masters, during their struggle, eventually contended, for example, that the friars should do manual work, as was customary for monks. Although their intentions seem most elevated—the masters cite Saint Paul, "If any one will not work, let him not eat"—they actually wanted to prevent the Mendicants from teaching by obliging them to live in convents and do manual work. The masters even tried to discredit the Mendicants, who traveled much and begged to live, by associating them with the *gyrovagi* or wandering clerks who had long been denounced as ruffians and a disgrace to the Church.[8]

8. See Waddell, Councils Relating to the *Clericus Vagus* or *Joculator,*" *Wandering Scholars*, pp. 269–99; and Faral, *Jongleurs*, App. III, passim. Bennett shows that discipline problems did exist within the Dominican order, and that some friars were imprisoned for being "inordinate ambulantes" (*Early Dominicans*, p. 152). Matthew Paris echoes the views of the Paris masters when he contrasts the life of the Cistercians, who lived in convents, with that of the wandering Mendicants:

Rutebeuf includes the theme of work in one of his late University poems, the *Bataille des Vices et des Vertus,* but develops it in a way particular to jongleurs. Poets were themselves frequently accused of being good-for-nothing freeloaders, and many took great pains to justify their rhyming as work.[9] The idea of work is the unifying theme running through Rutebeuf's *Vie de sainte Elysabel* (date uncertain), where the Saint is admired for her good works. The *Vie* opens with a commentary on the very quotation from Saint Paul used by the masters, here combined with Rutebeuf's hope for the moral value of his own work

> Cil Sires dist, que l'en aeure:
> 'Ne doit mengier qui ne labeure;'
> Més qui bien porroit laborer
> Et en laborant aourer
> Jhesu, le Pere esperitable
> . . .
> Que je puisse en tel lieu semer

Their honorable and orderly behavior gave pleasure to God, the prelates, and the people. They did not wander, like vagabonds, through cities and towns; nor was the ocean their barrier and limit, but they remained quietly shut up within the walls of their domicile, obeying their superior according to the rule of St. Benedict. . . . For at the commencement of it, in distinguishing the different kinds of monks, he rebukes the Sarabaitas and Gyrivagos. However these same brethren [the Dominicans], zealously pursuing their office of preaching, and weakening the authority of ordinary preachers, gained the commendation of many, whilst to many others they rendered themselves objects of reproach. (*English History, 3,* 149 [year 1255])
Rutebeuf sarcastically notes that sainthood does not come from wandering and begging good meals instead of scraps (*Complainte de Guillaume,* vv. 153–55).

9. *Joculatores* were frequently condemned together with *clerici vagi* in the texts cited by Waddell (App. E.). Defense of the entertainer's task is behind the lovely story of the *Tumbeor Nostre Dame* (ed. Erhard Lommatzsch and Max Leopold Wagner, Romanische Texte, I [Berlin, 1920]). And Watriquet de Couvins presents himself in his poem, *Li Tournois des dames,* saying: "D'autre mestier ne sai user/ Que de conter biaus dis et faire" (*Dits,* p. 245, vv. 437–38). The same phrase occurs in Rutebeuf's *Complainte de Constantinople:* Souspirant por l'umain lingnage . . ./ Vous vueil descouvrir mon corage,/ Que ne sai autre laborage" (vv. 1, 4–5). Curtius, in his *European Literature,* cites examples from classical Latin authors of what he calls the exordial topos: "Idleness is to be shunned" (pp. 88–89). Rutebeuf, then, contrives to use a preexisting poetic mold for new polemical ends.

Ma parole et mon dit retrere
(Quar autre labor ne sai fere). (vv. 1–5, 12–14)

Although there is absolutely no reference to the Mendicants here, the text might have been particularly familiar to Rutebeuf from the University controversy, for Rutebeuf contrives to use such authoritative texts for new, polemical ends. The opening verses of the *Bataille* seem intended to justify the value of the poet's work, yet because of the polemical context the words become a means of attacking the Mendicants:

> Puis qu'auteurs et auctoritez
> S'acordent que c'est veritez
> Qui est oiseus de legier peche,
> Et cil s'ame trahist et treche
> Qui sanz ouvrer sa vie fine,
> Quar tel vie n'est mie fine,
> Por ce me vueil a oevre metre
> Si com je m'en sai entremetre:
> C'est a rimer une matire;
> En leu d'ouvrer a ce m'atire,
> Quar autre ouvraingne ne sai fere.
> Or entendez a mon afere,
> Si orrez de deus Ordres saintes * (vv. 1–13)
>   * The Dominicans and Franciscans

The poet here firmly establishes his good intentions, while clearly alluding to criticism of the Mendicants.

Jean de Meun's long discussion of mendicancy [10] derives far more directly from Guillaume's writings than does Rutebeuf's poetry. Jean de Meun, the only other contemporary French author to write about the controversy in the vernacular, virtually translates passages from *De periculis* and the *Responsiones* [11] about begging. [12] Yet

10. *Roman de la Rose, 3,* vv. 11,287–491.
11. Esp. Articles 7 and 8.
12. See Langlois' notes to vv. 11,287–491, *Rose, 3,* 316–19, where he cites specific passages from *De periculis, Responsiones,* and *Collectiones.* See also Denk-

Gunn has ingeniously demonstrated how Jean de Meun included the passage on work, apparently a polemical attack on the Mendicants, as part of his larger exposition of his doctrine of generation.[13] These verses cannot be separated from their larger context. Jean de Meun treats the controversy as an academic, not a propagandistic, question. An intellectual trained in scholasticism, he divides and subdivides the question of mendicancy into logical units:

> Vez ci les cas especiaus:
> Se li on est si bestiaus
> Qu'il n'ait de nul mestier science
>   · · ·
> Ou s'il labourer ne peüst
> Pour maladie qu'il eüst . . .
>   (vv. 11,437–39, 11,445–46)

and so on through eight different categories of those who may rightfully beg. Jean de Meun's scholastic vocabulary[14] is inconceivable in the mouth of Rutebeuf, who, although a University advocate, obviously knew little of their jargon.

---

inger, "Die Bettelorden," pp. 286–313, on Jean de Meun. The résumé of Mary Morton Wood, "The Defense of Guillaume de Saint-Amour," in *The Spirit of Protest in Old French Literature*, Columbia University Studies in Romance Philology and Literature (New York, 1917), pp. 115–33, is somewhat superficial. Faral discusses the possibility that Rutebeuf might be one source for Jean de Meun (FB, *1*, 42).

13. Alan M. F. Gunn, *The Mirror of Love: A Reinterpretation of "The Romance of the Rose"* (Lubbock, Texas, 1952), p. 271; see also p. 258.

14. Examples of Jean de Meun's scholastic vocabulary:

> Mauvaisement l'ordre tendraient,
> Se tel menestrel estaient
>   · · ·
> N'i a nul qui preudon n'apere.
> Mais ja ne verreiz d'aparence
> *Conclure* bone *consequence*
> De nul *argument* que l'en face,
> *Se defauz existence efface;*
> Toujourz i trouvereiz *sofime,*
> Qui la *consequence* envenime,
> Se vous avez *soutilité*
> D'entendre la duplicité.
>   (*Rose, 3,* ed. Langlois, vv. 12,138–46)

Note the moralist's identification of "menesterel" with liars.

Rutebeuf, as propagandist, cannot afford to risk confusing his audience with such shadings or terminology. His colors are black and white: working is good; begging leads to sin; illustration—two supposedly holy orders. It is not enough, then, to say that Rutebeuf repeats a polemical theme, for he does so in his own peculiar terms. He leans on proverbs and popular stories (see below, pp. 129–36) rather than on the Church Fathers to prove his point, and speaks as a jongleur, not as a theologian or a dialectician.

The friars were not the only target of Rutebeuf's pamphlets. He also had to urge on the weak-willed masters and prelates to engage the enemy. The secular clergy did not form a close-knit group to sustain each other in moments of attack as did the Dominicans and Franciscans, and their enthusiasm for battle cooled rapidly. Guillaume himself complained about the indifference of the secular clergy to the intrusion of the Mendicant orders: "So great shall be the sloth of the prelates that the Church has no wall of defense; so great is the weakness of the doctors that there is no one who, openly preaching the truth, may dare to oppose himself to the aforesaid enemies.[15] In 1257 Rutebeuf tries to arouse them by saying that Guillaume's exile represents a humiliating assault on their ecclesiastical powers:

> Prelat, je vous faz a savoir
> Que tuit en estes avillié.
> (*Dit de Guillaume*, vv. 12–13)

By 1259 the tone has changed to one of lament over the general indifference to Guillaume's fate. *Sainte Yglise* tries to recall the Faculties of Arts, Law, and Medicine to defend their honor, and reminds them that Guillaume awaits their help:

---

15. "Tanta erit ignavia praelatorum, ut ecclesia murum non habeat defensionis; tanta doctorum infirmitas, ut portis et vectis careat, nec sit qui aperte veritatem praedicando, contra praedictos hostes se opponere audeat (*Liber de Antichristo et ejus ministris*," in *Veterum scriptorum et monumentorum, 9*, eds. Martène and U. Durand [Paris, 1733], col. 1299), now attributed to Guillaume de Saint-Amour (see FB *1*, 71, n. 1; and Mandonnet, *Siger de Brabant*, pp. cv and cix). Dated by Wyngaert as 1266 ("Querelles du clergé," p. 47, and p. 397 and n. 1).

> Hé! arcien,
> Decretistre, fisicien,
> Et vous la gent Justinien
> Et autre preudomme ancien,
> Comment souffrez en tel lien
> Mestre Guilliáume,
> Qui por moi fist de teste hiaume?
> Or est fors mis de cest roiaume
> Li bons preudon,
> Qui mist cors et vie a bandon.
> Fet l'avez de Chastel Landon
> La moquerie.
>   (*Complainte de Guillaume*, vv. 40–51)

Sainte Yglise calls upon the clergy whom the masters had helped in *their* quarrel with the Mendicants over the lucrative privileges of confession and testaments:

> Clergié, comme estes mi fillastre!
> Oublié m'ont prelat et pastre, *   * pastors
> Chascuns m'esloingne;
> A poi lor est de ma besoingne.
> Sejorner l'estuet en Borgoingne * * Saint-Amour in
> Mat et confus. (vv. 111–16) Franche-Comté

One feels that these are hopeless remonstrations; the last *preudon* is disarmed and far away. The poet soon moves to condemnation and menace, evidently his last resort to extract support for Guillaume. Thus in *Des Règles* Rutebeuf says flatly that the prelates and masters have been cowed by the Mendicants and that hell-fire awaits them for their fear of the truth:

> Nostre prelat sont enragié,
> Si sont decretistre et devin.* * theologians
> Je di por voir, non pas devin:
> Qui por paor a mal se ploie

Et a malfetor se souploie
Et por amor verité lesse,
Qui a ces deux choses se plesse
Si maint bone vie en cest monde,
Qu'il a failli a la seconde! (vv. 68–76)

The *Dit de Sainte Eglise* draws on images from previous poems.
In the *Complainte de Guillaume* Rutebeuf had said:

Li enfant que vous verrez nestre
Vous feront encor herbe pestre,
    Se il devienent
De cels * qui ensamble se tienent   * The Friars
Et cil * vivent qui les soustienent   * Alexander IV and Louis IX
    Que j'ai descrit. (vv. 183–88)

In the *Dit de Sainte Eglise* the masters are once again seen as silly
sheep, submissive to their former pupils, and content to feed wherever the friars would lead them, and they are condemned in God's
name:

Vous devin, et vous discretistre,
Je vous jete fors de mon titre,
De mon titre devez fors estre,
Quant le cinqueime esvengelitre [16]
Vost on fere mestre et menistre
De parler dou roi celestre.
Encor vous feront en chanp [p]estre,
[Si] com autre berbiz chanpestre,
Cil qui font la novelle espitre.
Vous estes mitres, non pas mestre:

16. Faral contends that "le cinqueime esvengelitre" means not the *Eternal
Gospel* but the privileges of confession, etc., seized "illegally" by the friars (FB, *1,*
280, note to v. 40), although "la novelle espitre" (v. 45) is defined in the
glossary as "l'*Evangile éternelle*" (FB, *2,* 324). Jean de Meun speaks, in the following decade, of the book as an ever-present menace: "Or ne sai qu'il en avendra,/
Ne quel chief cil livres tendra. . . . Ainsinc Antecrit atendron,/ Tuit ensemble a
lui nous tendron" (*Rose,* vv. 11,841–42, 11,845–46)

Vous copez Dieu l'oroille destre;
Diex vous giete de son regitre. (st. IV, vv. 37-48)

The rhyme in -itre and -etre is exploited to point up the difference between the friars and the masters. The former have become "mestre et menistre," teachers of a false doctrine and omnipotent in the clerical world. As for the secular masters, they are "mitres, non pas mestre," torturers and executioners whose victim is God himself. The paratactic construction of the last two verses suggests that God's retribution will be an absolutely necessary consequence of the masters' blasphemous cowardice in God's cause.

Although the prelates gave only the flabbiest of support to Guillaume, one finds especially in the 1259-63 poems, signs that the University made common cause with the local clergy against encroachments by the friars within parishes as well as in the Theology Faculty. In *Des Règles* the griefs of both parties are intertwined. The commonest criticism is that the friars seek out only the rich, and when they get their foot into the door of a wealthy man, they become dogs-in-the-manger:[17]

Encor est ceste gent si chiene,
Quant un riche homme vont entor,
Seignor de chastel ou de tor,
Ou userier ou clerc trop riche
(Qu'il aiment miex grant pain que miche),
Si sont tuit seignor de leenz:
Ja n'enterront clerc ne lai enz
Qu'il nes truient en la meson.
A ci granz seignors sanz reson! (vv. 106-14)

Rutebeuf here chooses the point of view of the outsider, insisting on what every man on the street could see for himself[18] and cor-

17. For similar theme in *De periculis* and *Collectiones*, see FB, *1*, 269-70, note to vv. 19-64, and p. 273, note to vv. 106-34; frequent elsewhere in Rutebeuf, as in *Complainte de Constantinople*, st. X; *Dit de Sainte Église*, vv. 91-96. *Faus Semblant* speciously reasons that rich men are more exposed to sin; "li riches est entechiez/ plus que li povres de pechiez,/ S'a greigneur mestier de conseil,/ Pour c'i vois, pour ce le conseil" (*Rose*, vv. 11,265-68).
18. See Leo, "Rutebeuf: persönlicher Ausdruck und Wirklichkeit," *Saggi e ricerche in memoria di Ettore Li Gotti* (Palermo, 1962), 2, 147.

roborate by his own experience. His explanation of the friars' conduct derives from this apparently "objective" description; they are powerful "sanz reson," without the right to be so, since their acts prove that they are only interested in money.

These, then, are the major themes in Rutebeuf's polemical poetry about the University quarrel: the injustice done Guillaume and the parish priests; the duplicity of the ambitious friars; their ecclesiastical, academic, and secular triumphs; the feeble resistance of the secular clergy; and the attack on the founding principles of the orders. The poet's polemical technique is a combination of a simple explanation of the issues at stake and a dramatization of their moral importance. A closer look at Rutebeuf's choice of vocabulary, images, and verse forms will show that his poetical language is the source of the effectiveness of his propaganda.

CHAPTER THREE: THE LANGUAGE
OF POLEMICS

I n all of Rutebeuf's polemical poetry he sets a concrete, immediate situation in a literary and propagandistic context through the use of readily understood moral *topoi.* The poems are studded with proverbs, familiar allegorical figures, and references to well-known stories. By using such preestablished modes of thinking about right and wrong, the poet can both explain to his audience the "true" meaning of the friars' desire to teach at the University, and use their ready-made moral response to the proverbs and stories to win their allegiance to the "right" side. The poet exploits *topoi* known to his public to inform them about new social and moral questions. Essentially this is why polemical writings tend to run to type; familiarity was a guarantee of comprehension and communication between poet and hearer, and this communicative function was valued far more than novelty.

The audience was accustomed to this technique from its experience with religious and didactic literature, which stirred emotions by appeals to a common fund of ideas, images, figures, sayings, and stories. As Baldwin has said of the figures repeated in hymns, "medieval symbolism sought to induce mood, to stir emotion, not by individualizing concrete details, but by familiar typical associations: lamb, vine, star of the sea."[1] Another critic of medieval hymns describes the technique of "calling up familiar blocks of feeling and transferring them to a higher plane."[2] Rutebeuf's purpose in appealing to a common moral viewpoint is, however, different from the preacher's. Rather than explaining a sacred mystery, he attempts to connect the friars with negative associations and to

1. Baldwin, *Medieval Rhetoric and Poetic,* p. 203. Speaking of sermons, Baldwin continues: "A medieval auditory had a great fund of conscious and unconscious associations" (ibid., p. 231).
2. Walter J. Ong, "Wit and Mystery: A Revaluation in Medieval Latin Hymnody," *Speculum,* 22, No. 3 (July 1947), 322.

explain their behavior in ways which would create hostile feelings about them. The transference of feelings is horizontal, wholly of this world.

PROVERBS AND POPULAR STORIES Proverbs, for example, provide a means to quick recognition of the moral point the author is trying to make. Since they are a common frame of reference, their truth is unquestioningly accepted.[3] In Rutebeuf's earliest University poem, the *Discorde,* the theme is stated as an illustration of the proverb, "Entre faire et dire a moult."[4] The friars have honeyed words of peace, faith, and concord on their tongues:

> Més lor maniere me recorde
> Que dire et fere n'i soit mie. (vv. 7–8)

Quickly naming the enemy, "Sor Jacobins est la parole" (v. 9), Rutebeuf labels them men who do not practice what they preach, since they say that God forbids angry quarreling as the soul's destruction, yet

---

3. Proverbs point the moral in each stanza of Huon le Roi's *Descrissons des relegions;* Guesnon, in his review of Långfor's edition of Huon le Roi, notes that proverbs are frequently used in collections of medieval sermons as well (*Moyen Age,* 2e série, *19* (January–June 1915). Proverbs are also the subject of moral (or immoral) poems like *Li Proverbe au vilain* (ed. A. Tobler [Leipzig, 1895]), Nicole Bozon's *Les Proverbes de bon enseignement* (ed. A. Chr. Thom [Lund, 1921]), and the grotesque *De Marco et de Salemons* (ed., Méon, *Nouveau Recueil, 1,* 416–36).

4. Morawski, *Proverbes,* No. 695, whose original source is Matthew 23:2–3. FB identifies most of the proverbs cited here and below in notes to the poems. Everyone would have known and could appreciate the aptness of the Bible verse applied to the Preachers: "The scribes and the Pharisees sit on Moses' seat; so practice and observe whatever they tell you, but not what they do; for they preach, but do not practice." This proverb and the appropriate "N'est pas or quanque luit" (Morawski, No. 1371) recur often; the latter is used in the Crusade poetry to distinguish true Crusaders from cowards (*Complainte d'outremer,* v. 38), in *Sainte Elysabel* (v. 732) as a comment on the Saint's wearing a hair shirt under her lovely dresses, and finally, as rueful consolation for the knight whose wife ran away with the sacristan (*Le Sacristain,* v. 428). Tjaden lists most proverbs used by Rutebeuf (*Untersuchungen über die Poetik Rutebuefs* [Marburg, 1885], pp. 65–70).

> Or guerroient por une escole
> Ou il vuelent a force lire. (vv. 15–16)

Much as a preacher might take a text and illustrate it with an exemplum drawn from daily life, Rutebeuf illustrates the truth of the proverb with the example of the Jacobins—and defines the Jacobins' nature with the proverb, thus setting the stage with the necessary moral props to enable his hearers to interpret, as he wants them to, the history of the University quarrel. He adds more proverbs in stanzas IV and V to support his central point; the Dominicans have notably proved false by turning on their benefactors:

> Quar cels destruit li anemis
> Qui plus l'ont servi longuement. (vv. 31–32)

> Quar tel herberge on en la chambre
> Qui le seignor gete du cas. (vv. 39–40)

The secular masters use the same technique, summing up their case against the friars with a vernacular proverb translated into Latin: "In quibus omnibus supradictus non sine gravi jactura sumus experti *veritatem illius vulgaris proverbii:* 'Mus in pera, serpens in sinu, ignis in gremio, male suos remunerat hospites.' " [5] While the masters add to the weight of their argument by quoting also such authorities as Solomon and Moses, only once does Rutebeuf turn to learned texts in his polemical verse. At the end of *Des Règles* he quotes first Saint Bernard on women and then Boethius on ingratitude:

> Et por ce nous dit ci la lettre:
> 'Nule dolor n'est plus fervant
> Qu'ele est de l'anemi servant.' (vv. 178–80)

Since these texts were much used by the masters in their polemical writings,[6] they show Rutebeuf's acquaintance with the Latin docu-

---

5. *Chart. Univ., 1,* 257, No. 230. The same proverbs appear in exemplum No. CIX of Jacques de Vitry (*Exempla,* p. 70).
6. Boethius, himself an exile and victim of injustice, was often cited by the

ments rather than any taste for ornamental erudition (see FB, *1, 37*). In many poems the proverb appears at the end of a passage to explain the meaning and to cast back a moral illumination on all that has been said. Thus in the *Complainte de Guillaume* Sainte Yglise says that those who pretend to be her friends are actually confounding her true defenders, and the behavior of these "supporters" is first described, then explained by proverbs:

> Tel gent se font de ma querele
> Qui me metent en la berele:
>   Les miens ocient
> Sanz ce que pas ne me desfient,
> Ainz sont a moi, si comme il dient
>   Por miex confondre
> Por ce font il ma gent repondre
> Que nus a els n'ose respondre
>   Ne més que sire.
> Assez pueent chanter et lire,
> *Més moult a entre fere et dire;*
>   C'est la nature:
> Li diz est douz et l'uevre dure;
> *N'est pas tout or quanc'on voit luire.* (vv. 8–21)

Proverbs also serve to describe attitudes in a vivid way. For example, Rutebeuf condenses the indifference of the secular masters in a brief proverb, a verbal shoulder shrug:

> Cil* ne le vont gueres requerre   * the masters
> Por qui il commença la guerre,
>   C'on nes perçoive.
> N'est més nus qui le ramentoive:
> *S'il fist folie, si la boive!*
> *(Complainte de Guillaume,* vv. 35–39)

---

secular masters. One of the fictitious letters in favor of Guillaume (see above, p. 109, n. 92), *Chart. Univ., 1,* No. 355, cites a poem from Boethius' *De consolatione.*

Proverbs also serve to replace elaborate explanations. Thus Rutebeuf exploits the inherent two-part construction of many proverbs which shows the immediate and neat relation between right and wrong, cause and effect. Is Guillaume unjustly banished? "Qui droit refuse guerre quiert."[7] Can we count on God's punishing the money-hungry friars? "Ainsi requeut qui ainsi same."[8] The proverb carries both a traditional meaning and an emotional potential; that is, it condenses beliefs and moral feelings in a pungent, rich, and concrete form, uniting the public through common feelings. Moreover, since a proverb carries the authority of tradition, if properly placed, it cannot be disputed: it is simply true.[9]

To make his point, Rutebeuf also refers to well-known stories. When in his *Discorde* he describes the friars' efforts to penetrate the University, he says:

> Chascuns a son pooir desmembre
> La mesnie saint Nicholas. (vv. 35-36)

All of his hearers knew the story of Saint Nicholas. They knew that the bishop of Myra, patron saint of students, revived the pickled pieces of three little boys, and so all could appreciate Rutebeuf's witty comment that the friars were apparently trying to "dismember" the University, "la mesnie saint Nicholas."

In the same poem Rutebeuf asks if the friars really love God as much as their habit indicates, and reminds his audience of the many "Renart" stories in which the wily fox disguises his greed under penitential clothes:[10]

---

7. *Dit de Guillaume*, v. 9.
8. *Des Règles*, v. 124.
9. Latini advises such calling on proverbs: "Quant la matire desplest as oïans . . . tu dois ramentevoir .i. essample samblable, ou proverbe ou sentence ou auctorité des sages homes, et mostrer ke ta besoigne soit dou tout *resemblable* a celui" (*Trésor*, ed. F. J. Carmody [Berkeley, 1948], pp. 340–41). Matthieu de Vendôme described proverbs as "uncorrupt truth": "communis sententia; cui consuetudo fidem attribuit; opino communis assensum accommodat incorruptae veritatis integritas adquiescit" (Faral, *Arts poétiques*, p. 113).
10. See, for example, Br. I, pp. 39–49, and Br. VIII, pp. 269–70, of the *Roman de Renart, 1* (ed. Ernest Martin [Strasbourg and Paris, 1882]).

> Quar se Renars çaint une corde
> Et vest une cotele grise,
> N'en est pas sa vie mains orde. (vv. 53–55)

In *Des Règles* the deceitful friars are again compared to the fox:

> Aussi nous prenent et deçoivent
> Com li gorpis fet les oisiaus.
> Savez que fet li damoisiaus?
> En terre rouge se toueille,
> Le mort fet et la sorde oreille;
> Si vienent li oisel des nues
> Et il aime moult lor venues,
> Quar il les ocist et afole:
> Ausi, vous di a brief parole,
> Cil* nos ont mort et afolé   * the friars
> Qui paradis ont acolé.[11] (vv. 8–18)

As for Rutebeuf's *Renart le Bestourné,* although the exact identification of the public figures who were the object of satire here have thus far escaped critics, and although the historical circumstances have been disputed, the Mendicants are clearly among those attacked.[12] Indeed, not only does the image of Renart serve to reveal

11. Although Faral refers the reader to *Physiologus* (FB, *1,* 269, note to v. 11), this story was used as a sermon exemplum and is given in Jacques de Vitry, *The Exempla* (p. 127, No. CCCIV): "Similiter ypocrite et heretici vulpecule sunt diaboli, qui se mortuos mundo fingunt et lingua venenosa et verborum blandiciis in tantos dicipiunt, similes vulpi que se simulat mortuam et dum jacet, aperto ore et lingua extracta, volucres animal mortuum reputantes, quasi ad cadaver accedunt, et videntes linguam rubeam, dum comedere volunt vulpecula dentes stringit et aves deceptas retinet et comedit." The same exemplum occurs in a collection compiled by a Franciscan (ca. 1277), which proves that didactic materials were the common property of moralists and satirists of every persuasion (No. 137 of *La tabula exemplorum*).

12. Ham, in his "Rutebeuf—Pauper and Polemist," suggests that *Renart le Bestourné* is a "cautiously veiled" attack (p. 38); yet in his "Rutebeuf and the Tunis Crusade" he says that "Rutebeuf must be credited wth having conveyed to his public a sense of complete clarity in purpose and of complete clarity in exposition," and that the language is "superficially veiled for easily understandable reasons of personal strategy" (p. 134). Ulrich Leo denies that political criticism was dangerous and suggests that the allegorical form is "ein freies künstlerisches Spiel," used because of popularity of Renart stories ("Rutebeuf: persönlicher

the real nature of those Rutebeuf attacks by identifying them with the unscrupulous, thieving fox, it also provides an entertaining means of presenting criticism of Court politics (see FB, *1*, 533–36). Moreover, it would seem that medieval authors felt they could speak not only more clearly but more safely through the mouth of an animal. The author of *Renart le Contrefait* found the allegory a fertile source of invention and a convenient shield, saying:

> Car sur Regnart poeult on gloser
> Penser, estudïer, muser
> Plus que sur toute rien qui soit.
> Qui proprement Regnart perchoit
> Le texte layt, prende la glose;
> S'il se congnoist, et dire l'ose
> . . .
> Pour ce commence cest rommant
> Pour dire par escript couvert
> Ce qu'il n'osoit dire en appert.
> (vv. 105–10, 121–22)

Renart is not the only familiar animal symbol. The masters had often used Matthew 7:15 in their denunciations of the friars: "Beware of false prophets who come to you in sheep's clothing, but inwardly are ravenous wolves; you will know them by their fruits." The masters were following a satirical convention established by twelfth-century Latin antimonastic satires such as the *Invectivo in Monachos* of Serlo of Bayeux:

> Turbæ raptorum vicinus quam monachorum,
> Rodens viventes, acuunt gens mortua dentes;
> Mortua gens mundo fremit ore vorax furibundo,

Ausdruck und Wirklichkeit," p. 152). FB, *1*, 532–36, discusses the essential questions of historical circumstances, although John Flinn adds some helpful suggestions in his *Le "Roman de Renart" dans la littérature française et dans les littératures étrangères au moyen âge* (Toronto, 1963), chap. 5. "Renart le Bestourné," pp. 174–200. Serper's recent article, *"Renart le Bestourné,* poème allégorique," (*Romance Philology, 20,* No. 4 [May 1967], 439–55) reviews all the theories of Leo, Ham, Faral, and Flinn, without arriving at any valid new conclusions.

Mitem se fingens, sic virus contigit ingens.
Hic dolus est magnus, lupus est qui creditur agnus.[13]

Rutebeuf, therefore, needed only to show a wolf's face grinning
from under the academic cope for the well-known biblical verses
and perhaps also the satirical allusion to reverberate in the mind of
his hearers:

> Se par l'abit sont net et monde,
> *Vous savez bien,* ce est la voire,
> S'uns leus avoit chape roonde
> Si resambleroit il provoire. (*Discorde,* vv. 45–48)

A veritable zoo of animals appear in moral dress in *Du Pharisien:*
demoniacal might, sin-spotted men, and deadly treachery are represented by the lion, leopard, and scorpion of verses 58–59;[14] and
in verses 80–81 the figures of the fox and the scorpion are combined
to exemplify the deceitful hypocrisy of the friars:

> Ypocrisie la renarde,
> Qui defors oint et dedenz larde.[15]

Again in the *Complainte de Guillaume,* Rutebeuf says that the
master has been assailed by "escorpion, serpent et guivre" (v. 121).[16]

13. In *Anglo-Latin Satirical Poets,* 2, 203–04. See also FB, *1,* 240, note to
vv. 41–56.

14. See Richard Thayer Holbrook, *Dante and the Animal Kingdom* (New
York, 1902), for an accurate evaluation of medieval animal symbolic values: lion,
pp. 103–04; leopard, pp. 91–93; scorpion, pp. 338–39. See also George Ferguson,
Signs and Symbols in Christian Art (New York, 1959), pp. 8, 10; although his
work is about Renaissance figures, he indicates medieval symbolic values.

15. The same image is used in the *Complainte de Guillaume,* v. 109, to
describe Fortune's treachery.

16. See also the *Dit d'Hypocrisie:* "Ours ne lyons, serpent ne wyvre,/ N'ont tant
de cruautei encemble" (vv. 260–61). In *De periculis* Guillaume speaks of "pseudo-
praedicatores . . . quasi viperae, & vulpes, & scorpiones" (*Opera,* p. 31). An interesting Latin poem against the friars by an English Goliard of the second half
of the 13th century combines most of the animal images and proverbs we have
seen in Rutebeuf. His first verse, "O spina noxia latet in lilio," recalls Rutebeuf's
"Rose est bien sor espine assise" (*Descorde,* v. 56) and "Li rosiers est poingnanz,
et s'est souef la rose" (*Jacobins,* v. 48). The Goliard develops the animal metaphor:
"In visu regulus, in cauda scorpio; in dente coluber, princeps in gladio; fuca
simplicitas in falso labio;/ dentem vipereum ubique timeo", and the theme of

Note that the process of moral judgment occurs through identification of real men with moral figures whose value is predetermined. The poet does not say that the friars are bad and *therefore* resemble foxes or vipers, but that these friars are like foxes, whom everyone *already* knows to be bad. The stories, allegories, and images are thus not merely ornamental or entertaining but, establishing guilt by association, they serve polemical ends.

ALLEGORIES   Rutebeuf also conveys moral judgment of the subject of his poems through allegorical figures. Recognizable to an unlettered audience who had met them in sermons, they were also a familiar mode of thinking for a cultivated audience.[17] Allegories are more than trimming.[18] When fully developed in a "story," they are certainly more interesting than dry dissertation, but they are also a means to moral categorizing. They translate current events into significant events.

Some of Rutebeuf's allegorical figures are barely embodied abstractions. In the *Complainte de Guillaume* the first direct statement of sadness about Guillaume's unfair exile is followed by allegorical concepts which tell us the wider meaning of Guillaume's exile:

> Quar Verité a fet son lais;
> Ne l'ose dire clers ne lais.
> Morte est Pitiez
> Et Charitez et Amistiez;
> Fors du regne les ont getiez
> Ypocrisie
> Et Vaine Gloire et Tricherie

---

ingratitude is recalled: "Nullus nocivior hoste domestico." The Goliard was obviously acquainted with the many texts used against the friars in the University controversy (*De falsis fratribus*, ed. Wright, in *Walter Mapes*, pp. 236–37).

17. Careful reading, for the medieval intellectual, meant discovering the various levels of meaning of a text: literal, allegorical, moral, and anagogical. See Harry Caplan's article, "The Four Senses of Scriptural Interpretation and Medieval Theory of Preaching," *Speculum*, 4, No. 3 (July 1929), 283–90.

18. Faral speaks of Rutebeuf's occasional desire to "enjoliver la présentation" of his poems (FB, *1*, 301).

Et Faus Samblant et dame Envie
Qui tout enflame.[19] (vv. 71–79)

This passage is a very condensed recapitulation of the preceding seventy verses. The "fors du regne" refers, of course, to the exile of Guillaume, who appears as the embodiment of truth, pity, charity, and friendship. "Verité a fet son lais" expresses the discouragement felt about the chance of the University's winning a fair hearing; "enflamme" refers to the quarrelsome friars. The five figures applied to the friars provide moral commentary on their actions just as did the proverbs at the beginning of the poem. Little effort is made to bring the allegories to life; four verbs express their "action" and there is no attempt at personification.

Now figures like *Envie* and *Vaine Gloire* were sufficiently well characterized in the *voie*-type poems for them to be familiar to any audience. Their names suffice to evoke a full range of attributes. *Ypocrisie* and *Faus Semblant,* however, were less well-established allegorical figures at the time of the University quarrel than were Pride, Avarice, or Envy. Since the masters found the former useful for denouncing the friars, they were first obliged to describe the figures as fully as possible so that their moral weight could be felt. Hypocrisy was not, of course, new in 1250. The fundamental metaphors for hypocrisy, as a wolf in sheep's clothing and an ostentatiously praying Pharisee, came from the Bible and repeatedly appear in early texts.[20]

Hypocrisy appears early in vernacular didactic writings, as in the *Castoiement d'un père à son fils,* a French imitation of the twelfth-century *Disciplina clericalis* of Petrus Alphonsus. The father counsels his son by means of examples of vice punished and virtue re-

19. In the *Dit de Sainte Eglise* we find two verses repeated: "Car veritez a fet son lais,/ Ne l'ose dire clers ne lais" (vv. 52–53). The editors did not even capitalize "veritez" here, showing how tenuously this figure maintains allegorical status.
20. Several are cited in *Roman de la Rose, 3,* 307–08. *Hypocrisy* plays a leading rôle in the 12th-century *Ludus de Antichristo* as a handmaiden of the Antichrist (see above, p. 79, n. 19).

warded—pretext for a collection of rattling good tales. He first
teaches his boy to honor God and warns him against hypocrisy,
described only as false piety:

> Beax filz, ge te pri et coment
> Que n'aimes pas Dieu faintement,
> Ne li fais semblant à nul fuer,
> Si tu ne l'aimes de bon cuer;
> Ne seroies pas por tant quites,
> Quar tu seroies ypocrites.
> Ypocrites est de-fors bel,
> De l'aignel a vestu la pel,
> Mais dedens est lou ravisant.
> De Dieu amer fait un semblant:
> Il vait volentiers au mostier
> [Pour aourer et pour prier].
> Ilueques fait ses oroisons,
> Sovent se courbe à genoillons,
> Et son pis vait molt debatant,
> Et sa bouche muet en ourant,
> Mais ses cuers est de Dieu molt loing.[21]

The wolf and the Pharisee reappear, but this portrait is a simple
warning against ostentatious, insincere religious practices, applicable
to clergy and laymen alike.[22]

The Mendicants themselves preached against hypocrisy. The
Dominican who wrote a life of Saint Dominic, probably before
1259, contrasts the saint with hypocrites:

> Il ne voloit einsi faire,
> Com li malvais faus bougre font,
> Et li hypocrite, qui sont

---

21. Barbarzan and Méon, eds., *Fabliaux*, 2, 41–42, vv. 29–45. In Rutebeuf's *Dit
de Sainte Eglise*, vv. 58–59, is the same image of a mouth praying without the
heart feeling. See above, p. 250, n. 75.

22. *Papelardie*, on the wall of Guillaume de Lorris' garden (*Rose*, 2, vv. 407–40)
represents not only hypocrisy but prudery as well, according to C. S. Lewis,
Allegory of Love, p. 127.

Et si bieles meurs par defors;
Si ont le vif dyable ou cors,
Qu'il voelent les gens decevoir,
Et gres et loenges avoir
De che ki est guile et baras.[23] (vv. 2570–77)

In the miracle *De Sainte Léocade* by Gautier de Coinci, the amiable and gifted prior of Vic-sur-Aisne (ca. 1177–1236),[24] the theme of hypocrisy is given its first extensive development. Gautier worked with a fine satirical eye and a clever pen, and is in many ways an important poet to compare with Rutebeuf (see below, Chap. 4). Gautier interrupts his miracle narrative for a long passage of satirical invective against the vices of his times, including 551 verses on *beguins* and *papelarz,* terms which he uses as synonyms for hypocrites. Only 147 of these verses are specifically devoted to ecclesiastical hypocrites, who use *papelardie* to further their ambitions; the rest apply to the holier-than-thou of any estate.[25] What interests us is that although Gautier specifically contrasts the smiling faces of the truly pious Franciscan friars with the dour expression of the sanctimonious, there are already, in *Sainte Léocade,* most of the images and rhetorical themes connected with hypocrisy which Rutebeuf used against the Mendicants. Oiling before and stinging behind (here like wasps, vv. 1324–34), hypocrites have the guile of Renart (vv. 1377, 1404, 1392, 1516). Proverbs like "All that glitters is not gold" (vv. 1483–84) appear attached to the theme, as does the hypocrite's love of luxuries like fish and wine (vv. 1580–84). In a moralizing epilogue to his *Theophilus* miracle,[26] pride and false

23. W. F. Manning, ed., *Life of Saint Dominic in Old French Verse,* Harvard Studies in Romance Languages, 20 (Cambridge, Mass., 1944), pp. 210–11. The Franciscan *Tabula exemplorum* compares hypocrites to foxes, to counterfeit money, and to crabs who retreat though seeming to advance, and denounces those who desecrate churches "sicut bubo, qui habitat in ecclesiis non propter devocionem, sed ut comedat oleum lampadarum" (No. 135, p. 40. See Nos. 136–38).
24. Ed. Eva Vilamo-Pentti (Helsinki, 1950). See Erhard Lommatzsch, *Gautier de Coincy als Satiriker* (Halle, 1913), esp. pp. 26–31.
25. *Léocade,* vv. 1147–1698.
26. *Miracles de Nostre Dame, 1,* ed. V. Frédéric Koenig (Paris and Geneva, 1955), 161–63, vv. 1855–80.

humility are called *papelardie,* and the proverb "the habit does not make the monk" appears (vv. 1855–80) with extensive glossing as in Rutebeuf. Although direct influence is, as with most medieval authors, virtually impossible to prove,[27] it is significant that the elements for an extended satire of hypocrisy existed in the didactic tradition and could be called on and expanded as need for them arose.

It is at the time of the University quarrel that the Mendicants became definitively identified as the supreme example of hypocrisy. A late thirteenth-century antifeminine poem, *L'Evangile as James,* shows that "Jacobin" has become proverbial for treacherous deceit; speaking of woman's faithlessness, the author says:

> Leur conseil est cortois et tant voir et tant fin
> Que autant font acroire comme font jacopin.
> Conseillez-vous à femme, au soir et au matin,
> Si serez tot certains de faire male fin.[28]

Rutebeuf's portrait of *Ypocrisie* in *Du Pharisien* and Jean de Meun's *Faus Semblant* are the first true full-length portraits of the allegorical figure. Rutebeuf portrays the "grant dame" and her "estre" —that is, her nature or the way of life of those who follow her— as a towering central figure in the poem. She is seen surrounded by smaller figures and scenes which illustrate her powers and activities in the world. We recognize his beginning with her "family tree" as a technique from the *voie*-type poems for indicating which vices or sins are interrelated (see above, Chap. 1):

> A vous toz faz je ma clamor
> D'Ypocrisie,
> Cousine germaine Heresie,
> Qui bien a la terre saisie. (vv. 6–9)

Rutebeuf concentrates not on a description of *Ypocrisie's* person but rather on her actions and her power. In fact, she seems deified

27. Faral affirms, nonetheless, that Rutebeuf knew *Léocade* (FB, *1,* 40).
28. *Jongleurs et trouvères,* ed. Jubinal, p. 27. The author is one "Jehans Durpain, uns moines de Vaucelles."

instead of personified, and appears of superhuman size in verses
such as:

> Partout fet més sa volenté,
> Ne la retient nonostenté
> N'autre justise;
> Le siecle gouverne et justice;
> Resons est quanqu'ele devise,
> Soit maus soit biens. (vv. 33–38)

She is even identified with the Antichrist (vv. 101–15) or perhaps
as an "Anti-Virgin" who puts souls in Hell instead of Heaven:

> Tant est grant dame
> Qu'ele en enfer metra mainte ame. (vv. 10–11)

Her rise to power is rendered in a very powerful image which contrasts, as in other poems we have seen, the ascetic ideal of the friars
with their luxurious life and ambitions:

> Gesir soloit en la vermine:
> Or n'est més hom qui ne l'encline
> Ne bien creanz,
> Ainz est bougres et mescreanz. (vv. 21–24)

She is, above all, characterized by her possessions, for she owns not
only money but men, the source of her power:

> Ses anemis ne prise gaires,
> Qu'ele a baillis, provos et maires,
> Et si a juges
> Et de deniers plaines ses huges
> Si n'est cité ou n'ait refuges
> A grant plenté. vv. 27–31)

Only after completing his portrait of this powerful lady does
Rutebeuf turn to her followers, "Qui sont si seignor et si mestre/
Parmi la vile" (vv. 46–47). He proves their hypocrisy in a passage
of violent contrasts:

> Granz robes ont de simple laine
> Et si ont de simple couvaine;
> Simplement chascuns se demaine,
> Color ont simple et pale et vaine,
> Simple viaire,
> Et sont cruel et deputaire
> Vers cels a cui il ont afaire. (vv. 51–57)

The word "simple" becomes more ironic with each repetition, and finally the truth bursts forth: the ferocious inner soul is revealed behind the "simple viaire," the deceptive appearance.

Rutebeuf's moral commentary appears in the next verses with a series of animal figures—lion, leopard, scorpion, and fox (vv. 58–59, 80–81)—and allegories to describe the virtues—that is, the prelates, who have submitted to this immensely powerful lady: [29]

> Car Verité,
> Pitié et Foi et Charité
> Et Larguece et Humilité
> Ont ja sousmise;
> Et maint postiau de sainte Yglise,
> Dont li uns plesse et l'autres brise,
> Ce voit on bien,
> Contre li * ne valent més rien. (vv. 64–71)   * Ypocrisie

A final proverb is added to drive the point home, "N'est pas tout or quanqu'il reluit" (v. 92), and the poet rests his case; the friars are harbingers of the Antichrist:

> Et par ce veez plainement
> Que c'est contre l'avenement
> A Antecrist:
> • • •
> Celui qui vient,
> Que par tel gent venir covient;

---

29. See the *Dit de Guillaume*, vv. 12–13.

Quar il vendra, bien m'en sovient,
    Par ypocrites:
Les prophecies en sont escrites.
Or vous ai je tel gent descrites.
        (vv. 101–03, 112–17)

The use of allegory is, then, no mere gratuitous ornament. The long
description of *Ypocrisie* and her followers is essential to explain
what has happened in Paris. The comparisons Rutebeuf uses to de-
pict the friars reveal their true nature and would have struck the
imagination of his hearers not as an impoverished rhetorical effort
but as a vital and vivid moral indictment.

Like Rutebeuf, Jean de Meun creates a striking allegorical figure,
Faus Semblant, as a method of exposition and moral commentary.
Treating the same subject, he does so from the *inside,* revealing the
ugly soul that *Faus Semblant* hides under his Jacobin robe. *Faus
Semblant* speaks for himself, justifying his conduct, and is con-
demned by the very words he uses:

J'ameraie meauz l'acointance
Cent mile tanz dou rei de France
Que d'un povre, par nostre dame!
Tout eüst il ausinc bone ame.
Quant je vei touz nuz ces truanz
Trembler sus ces fumiers puanz
De freit, de fain crier et braire,
Ne m'entremet de leur afaire
                    . . .
Car d'une aumosne toute seule
Ne me paistraient il la gueule,
Qu'il n'ont pas vaillant une seche:
Que donra qui son coutel leche?
        (vv. 11,241–48, 11,251–54)

Clearly, *Faus Semblant's* brazen shamelessness does not conceal Jean
de Meun's criticism. By adroit sentence construction, he makes one

feel the cold arrogance of the hypocritical friars: three lines evocative of the misery of the poor (vv. 11,245–47) are not destroyed by the brusque dismissal in the fourth (v. 11,248). Since our sympathy is held by the sufferers, we turn against the specious reasoning of *Faus Semblant*.

However, although Jean de Meun makes use of themes and vocabulary developed in the University polemic,[30] his writing about the quarrel cannot be called propagandistic. The *Faus Semblant* episode is an element in the overall didactic structure of the *Roman de la Rose*. (In contrast, Rutebeuf's poems are complete in themselves, not part of a general scheme.) Instead of using the conception of false-seeming to *explain* the conduct of the Mendicants, as does Rutebeuf, Jean de Meun refers to Guillaume de Saint-Amour and the University quarrel so that the nature of *Faus Semblant* may be understood. In like manner, *Raison* used the story of Manfred and Conradin to illustrate the capriciousness of Fortune in an earlier passage of the *Roman de la Rose:*

> E se les preuves riens ne prises
> D'ancienes estoires prises,
> Tu les as de ton tens nouveles,
> De batailles fresches e beles. (vv. 6631–34)

The story of the University quarrel is included, then, in *Faus Semblant's* "autobiography" because it would be fresh in the minds of Jean de Meun's audience; it would serve "pour prendre comun essemplaire," he says (v. 11,800). Also, the polemicist must strike quickly. The leisurely pace and lengthy discourse of the *Faus Semblant* episode makes it ill-suited for use as a quick rabble-rousing piece like Rutebeuf's.

Nonetheless, Jean de Meun reveals fervent partisanship for the secular masters, as proved by significant breaks in tone in *Faus Semblant's* discourse.[31] *Faus Semblant* starts his self-portrait, as we

---

30. As, for example, vv. 11,787–89: "Ja ne les quenoistreiz aus robes,/ Les faus traïteurs pleins de lobes;/ Leur faiz vous estuet regarder."

31. I do not agree with Gunn that *Faus Semblant's* praise of Guillaume is mere hypocrisy (*Mirror*, p. 162): the eternal hypocrite has sworn for once to

have seen, with smug contentment over his evil treachery. Then, to tell the story of Guillaume de Saint-Amour (vv. 11,488–11,508), a "je" intervenes which is not *Faus Semblant* but Jean de Meun himself, disputing with his fictional character and opposing God's commandments to his character's selfish credo. In the same contentious tone familiar to us from Rutebeuf, Jean de Meun declares his support for Guillaume in terms full of passion:

> Car je ne m'en tairaie mie
> Se j'en devaie perdre vie,
> Ou estre mis contre dreiture,
> Come Sainz Pos, en chartre ocure,
> Ou estre baniz dou reiaume
> A tort, con fu maistre Guillaume
> De Saint Amour, qu'Ypocrisie
> Fit esseillier par grant envie.[32] (vv. 11,501–08)

Perhaps the word "Ypocrisie" recalled Jean de Meun to his figure, for it is *Faus Semblant* we hear in the next verse:

> Ma mere en essil le chaça [33]
> Le vaillant ome, tant braça,
> Pour verité qu'il soutenait.
> Vers ma mere trop mesprenait,
> Pour ce qu'il fist un nouvel livre *   * De periculis*
> Ou sa vie fist toute escrivre,
> E voulait que je reneiasse
> Mendicité e labourasse,
> Se je n'avaie de quei vivre. (vv. 11,509–17)

The words "vaillant" and "verité" seem added by Jean de Meun, as do the adjectives describing the *Eternal Gospel* in verses 11,791–

---

speak only the truth, at *Amour's* command, so that *Amour's* allies may recognize him wherever he appears. (vv. 10,940–11,002).

32. Compare with Rutebeuf's statement at the end of the *Dit de Guillaume,* vv. 117–20.

33. *Faus Semblant* was engendered by *Barat* and *Ypocrisie* (vv. 10,982–83).

11,835: "Uns livres de par le deable . . . Bien est dignes d'estre brulez . . . cel orrible montre."

The character of *Faus Semblant* is more than a front for Jean de Meun's views of the Mendicants, however, for once his discourse is done, *Faus Semblant* dons the robe of a Mendicant, and, with his friend *Astenance Contrainte* dressed as a Béguine, goes on to play his part in the assault of the Castle of the Rose. He strangles the doorkeeper, *Malebouche,* and cuts out his tongue; what violence is revealed behind the humble visage of *Faus Semblant* in this act!

It would seem, however, in Jean de Meun's rendering of the University polemic, that the quarrel is over, although he does add that he does not yet know what will become of the detestable *Eternal Gospel.* (vv. 11,841-42). He describes *Faus Semblant* in the present tense, as a *being,* but the University story is told in the past. Rutebeuf, on the other hand, uses the present tense to describe *Ypocrisie,* but also uses the present and future for events connected with the University quarrel, thus creating an effect of urgent immediacy. He uses the past only when he describes events which have led to the present crisis: the breaking of the Amiable Conciliation, or Guillaume's exile. If Jean de Meun is the historian of the quarrel, Rutebeuf is the war correspondent under fire at the front lines.

Polemical use of allegory appears again in the *Dit d'Hypocrisie* which Rutebeuf wrote in the fall of 1261 to hail the election of Jacques, the Patriarch of Jersualem, as Pope Urban IV (FB, *1,* 286–87). The poet seizes the chance to denounce the greed and hypocrisy of the Curia under the late Alexander IV, protector of the Mendicants, and exploits both the vast tradition of anti-Roman satire [34] and elements from the recent polemic against the friars. The allegorical figures of the *Dit d'Hypocrisie* are less static than those of *Du Pharisien,* since they *act* in a suspenseful event—the papal conclave—and since the central allegorical figure, *Cortois,* [35] is both man and symbol. Moreover, the poet himself is not just a

---

34. See Yunck, *Lineage of Lady Meed,* pp. 198–99, who discusses the *Dit d'Hypocrisie* in terms of medieval meed satire.
35. *Cortois* is a synonym for "urbain" (FB, *1,* 287).

voice but a participant in the story, for the adventure is narrated as his own.

Rutebeuf adopts the framework of the dream journey (as in his *Voie*) for his polemic. The poet-dreamer finds his way to a "grant citei," Rome, where he finds an informant and guide, *Cortois*, who appears first simply as a "preudoume" whose name and nature are revealed by his exquisitely courteous hospitality and his well-served table. It is *Cortois*, sensible man that he is, who recognizes in turn the value of Rutebeuf's fearlessly truthful poems, in the passage I have already cited (above, p. 95).

Cortois makes a long after-dinner speech (vv. 103–220), which, although ostensibly a narrative of his unhappy experiences at Rome, is actually a moralized description of the Curia. Son of *Cortoisie*, *Cortois* came to Rome with his wife, *Bele Chiere*, who was promptly killed by the surly local folk who thought that any welcome should be well paid:

> Mais cist* l'ocistrent au venir   *the Romans
> Tantost qu'il la porent tenir.
> Qui bele chiere vuet avoir
> Il l'achate de son avoir. (vv. 115–18)

His discourse also includes some of the hoary old saws, derived from Latin and French satires, about the venality of Rome. In his verse "Mains raüngent et vuident borces" (v. 157), Rutebeuf recalls the satirical derivation of Rome from *rodit manus*[36] and he inserts proverbs which had long said that pilgrims to Rome return the poorer in pocket and spirit.[37]

> Teiz i va riches et rians
> Qui s'en vient povres mendianz. (vv. 163–64)

36. See Lehmann, *Die Parodie im Mittelalter* (Stuttgart, 1963), p. 52, and Gautier de Coinci, *Léocade*, v. 923, for examples.

37. See, for example, Morawski, *Proverbes*, No. 2198, "Renc et rime et Rome n'espargne nul home"; No. 2221, "Roe [Rota] et rogne n'espargnent nully"; and Nos. 1089 and 1869. In Leroux de Lincy, *Proverbes, 1*, 296, a 15th-century saw: "Trout arrière, trout avant/ Ceux qui viennent de Rome valent pis que devant."

Car teiz i va boens crestiens
Qui s'en vient fauz farisiens. (vv. 191–92)

Although the poem begins as a criticism of Roman politics, and
in spite of the topical references to the eight cardinals gathered to
elect a pope (vv. 294–314), one recognizes many figures borrowed
from poems criticizing the Mendicants. Rutebeuf's poem is principally aimed at the excessive greed and contaminating influence of
the hypocritical friars in Rome.[38] When he asks *Cortois* who is now
master of Rome, the answer is an indictment of the ambitious
Mendicants in familiar allegorical terms:

N'i a empereor ne roi
Ne seigneur, qu'il est trespasseiz: *   * Alexander IV (d. 1261)
Mais atendans i a asseiz
Qui beent a la seignorie.
Vainne Gloire et Ypocrisie
Et Avarice et Covoitize
Cuident bien avoir la justise,
Car la terre remaint san oir
Si la cuide chacuns avoir.
D'autre part est Humiliteiz
Et Bone Foiz et Chariteiz
Et Loiauteiz; cil sont a destre
Qui deüssent estre li mestre. (vv. 198–210)

The latter part of the *Dit* is an exploration of the nature of
Ypocrisie, who has joined *Avarice* as a "dame de la cort." The poet
does some counterintelligence work by disguising himself as a
hypocrite, in an ample robe of humble cloth, to deceive the deceivers and to penetrate to the innermost secrets, thoughts, and intentions of *Ypocrisie.* He thus inverts the proverb so often used
against the pretended austerity of the Mendicants, "L'habit ne fait
pas le moine," since *his* intentions are of the purest, although he is
dressed like a hypocrite:

38. Of the eight cardinals at the conclave, only Hugues de Saint-Cher was a
Mendicant, but four of these cardinals had sat on the council which had condemned
Guillaume's *De periculis* (FB, *1*, 297, note to vv. 294–95).

> Car bien sou faire le marmite*   * hypocrite
> Si que je resembloie hermite
> Celui qui m'esgardoit defors:
> Mais autre cuer avoit ou cors. (vv. 235–38)

In this way, Rutebeuf's *Ypocrisie* is revealed from the inside, as we have seen that Jean de Meun's *Faus Semblant* was. The poet, as *Ypocrisie's* notary, finds her to be greedy, bitter, and resentful; and her cruelty is rendered through animal figures:

> Ours ne lyons, serpent ne wyvre
> N'ont tant de cruautei encemble
> Com ele seule, ce me cemble. (vv. 260–62)

Her hardheartedness is compared to an unmeltable icicle, her treachery to the coal which burns hotter than an open flame. Fire or ice, the friars are protected from all dangers by their grey robes:

> Qui porroit teil eür avoir
> Con de lui loeir et prisier,*   * to be pleased with himself
> Il s'en feroit boen desguisier
> Et vestir robe senz coleur,
> Ou il n'a froit n'autre doleur,
> Large robe, solers forreiz;
> Et quant il est bien afeutreiz,
> Si doute autant froit comme chaut
> Ne de povre home ne li chaut,
> Qu'il cuide avoir Dieu baudement
> Ou cors tenir tot chaudement. (vv. 280–90)

The austere robe of the friars appears, as the poet dons it, to have a rich warm lining, enabling the deluded friars to hug close their cozy expectations of Heaven.

The poet's dream ends happily: *Ypocrisie* almost carries the conclave, but God intervenes in the nick of time, and *Cortois,* a compromise candidate, is elected. It is God's intervention in history which sets the moral of the story:

Mais Dieux regarda au damage
Qui venist a l'umain linage
S'Ypocrisie a ce * venist   * to the papacy
Et se si grant choze tenist. (vv. 303–06)

But it is the poet's "experience" which verifies the authenticity of what he relates; his are the feelings of joy and relief at *Cortois'* election as he returns home to Paris over the Alps:

Lors si fu Cortois esleüz
Et je fui de joie esmeüz,
Si m'esvoillai inelepas
Et si ou tost passeiz les pas
Et les mons de Mongieu sans noif. (vv. 313–17)

For all the topical allusions and the appearance of the historical figure Pope Urban, the poem is convincingly alive because of the presence of Rutebeuf himself as a character in his fiction. He is the only one who remains human, although disguised at one point in the trappings of *Ypocrisie. Cortois* is a depleted figure, robbed of human density by the way the poet maneuvers him in the poem, and is really only a mouthpiece for polemical attack, set up so that the criticism of the Curia and the Mendicants can be presented as a dialogue rather than in straight exposition. Only as host does *Cortois* seem to breathe in a human atmosphere; together, he and Rutebeuf wash up, dine side by side, and go to relax in the garden. No grief is felt, however, for the death of *Cortois'* "wife," *Bele Chiere,* who is nothing more than an abstract noun. Indeed, at one point in *Cortois'* speech the poet forgets who is speaking and inserts a verse starting "Rutebuez dit . . ." (v. 172). Of course, the poem is in no way historical in the sense that Rutebeuf might have gone to Rome and met Urban IV, as Faral clearly shows (FB, *1,* 287); yet it is one of the poems where Rutebeuf succeeds in painting a life-like fictional portrait of himself no matter how improbable the "dream" circumstances (see below, Chap. 5).

EXPLOITATION OF FAMILIAR MORAL BELIEFS The
line between moralizing and propagandizing is a thin one in many
poems, since authors use such similar techniques for both ends. In
the *Dit d'Hypocrisie, Renart le Bestourné,* and the *Bataille des Vices
et des Vertus* the poems' effect comes from the hearer's gradual
realization of its true polemical intent. The *Dit d'Hypocrisie* is
indistinguishable at the beginning from any standard "dream" poem
of didactic intent: there is a picturesque, if zoologically inaccurate,
description of crows cawing and burying nuts, as the little worms
return underground. The poet's preparation for slumber includes
a leisurely drink of a wine so good that one could believe that
"Dieux avoit plantei/ La vignë et follei le vin" (vv. 12–13). It is not
until Rutebeuf introduces himself to *Cortois* and is recognized by
his "hostes" as the redoubtable enemy of "ypocrites" that Rutebeuf's
polemical use of a didactic form becomes clear. Because the poem
seems devotional in intent at the beginning, the audience is prepared to be edified and to accept the poet's moralizing intention by
the time his polemical object comes into focus.

In the same manner, *Renart le Bestourné* starts off as a particularly lively fox tale. Rumors are flying, news is passed from mouth
to mouth:

> Renars est mors: Renars est vis!
> Renars est ors, Renars est vils:
> Et Renars regne!
> Renars a moult regné el regne;
> Bien i chevauche a lasche regne,
> Col estendu.
> L'en le devoit avoir pendu,
> Si com je l'avoie entendu,
> Més non a voir:
> Par tens le porrez bien savoir. (vv. 1–10)

By this time Rutebeuf holds his audience breathless. Enthralled,
they will only gradually realize that the entertaining story coats a

bitter pill of political truth.[39] Unlike other contemporary and later authors of longer works of propaganda using the story of Renart as framework (see below), Rutebeuf does not try to maintain attention by keeping a story going while he develops his argument; he keeps his poem short (162 verses) and, instead, attracts his audience, delivers his punch, and ends, his task accomplished. By adapting old forms to new uses, Rutebeuf has the additional advantage of allowing the audience to discover for itself his true intentions; interest must have risen as the parody or polemic appeared, just as Hue de la Ferté could count on a smile when his audience heard the new words attacking Blanche of Castille which he had set to Blondel de Nesle's tune (see above, p. 86).

This technique of involving the audience is used to great advantage in the *Bataille des Vices et des Vertus.* The poem announces a complete didactic *Psychomachia,* with the standard combats between the seven couples of vices and virtues (vv. 18–36).[40] Rutebeuf speaks with honeyed words of "deus Ordres saintes" sent by God to preserve the world from "maint grant mal" by their teachings. One is well into the poem, comfortably settled as it were, when strange things begin to happen. In the first combat between *Orguex* and *Humilitez, Humilitez* strangely resembles her archenemy. Instead of remaining humbly demure, she has become a "granz dame" (vv. 65 ff.). The poet cleverly lets the audience protest; he himself pretends, as we have seen (above, pp. 93–94), to be a reformed slanderer who has finally understood why the friars need such great palaces and why the King does well to protect them. Adroitly, he phrases the accustomed criticisms as questions, and answers them with heavy sarcasm, letting his hearers draw their own conclusions about the absurd spectacle of *Humilitez* ensconced in royal splendor. Slyly he says:

39. In similar fashion, the friars often attracted an audience to a sermon by starting off in an epic or chivalric vein, then switching to their didactic matter; see the example cited by Pfander, *The Popular Sermon,* pp. 25–26.

40. In *Des Jacobins* the *psychomachia* theme reappears, but the battlefield is a dicing table (vv. 5–8).

Et or est bien droiz et resons
Que si granz dame ait granz mesons
Et biaus palais et beles sales,
Maugré toutes les langues males
Et la Rustebuef tout premiers,
Qui d'aus blasmer fu coustumiers.
Ne vaut il pas miex c'umilité
Et la sainte divinité
Soit leüe en roial palais,
C'on fist d'aumosnes et de lais
Et de l'avoir au meillor roi
C'onques encor haïst desroi,
Que ce c'on secorust la terre
Ou li fol vont folie querre,
Constantinoble, Rommenie? (vv. 79–93)

The heavy insistence on the adjectives "granz, biaus, beles, roial" makes the friars' new schools appear ridiculously luxurious. The feigned repentance of the poet; the friars' greed for alms, legacies, and riches, hidden behind the figure of pious Saint Louis; the apparent dismissal of the Crusades as a fool's errand—all permit the audience to give free rein to their own angry protests, while the poet transparently veils his own attitude.

The justifications Rutebeuf cites for the friars' anxious rapacity are patently absurd. They do well, says he, to feather their nests while the King lives, since all men prepare for the worst. Surely, "il n'en font de riens a blasmer" (vv. 117–27). Certainly they should be permitted to ferret everywhere, discover all secrets, and control the kingdom, for don't they wear a habit in which God dwells? "Et si fet il, je n'en dout mie," Rutebeuf hastens to add (vv. 143–57). The poet never quite abandons the pretense that he is actually writing an edifying treatise. He sprinkles the poem with military touches to maintain the theme of a combat between vices and virtues, yet with a sarcastic tone. Pride sounds the retreat, "Orguex

s'en va, Diex le cravant." Yes, let God crush Pride, however disguised! *Larguece* fearlessly runs down *Avarisce,* "lance sor fautre,"
just as the friars have fearlessly run down heretics and given goose-
pimples to all the "mauvés" (vv. 159-63). The friars, triumphant,
fear no one, and indeed, after successfully pulling the wool of their
humble cloak over the eyes of King and Pope, whom should they
fear?

Rutebeuf uses the ironic tone and allegorical framework only so
long as it suits his polemical purpose. We see only three of the
promised seven combats, and in the third, between *Debonereté* and
Ire, when the poet recalls Guillaume's fruitless trip to Rome in
1256 and his shameful banishment, he abandons the pretense of
being on the friars' side to anathematize Pope, King, and friars.
He portrays them all as arbitrarily making and breaking judg-
ments and incapable of attaining true justice:

> Cil de cort ne sevent qu'il font,
> Quar il font ce qu'autres desfont
> Et si desfont ce qu'autres fet:
> Ainsi n'avront il jamés fet. (vv. 217-20)

The poem thus ends on an inconclusive note. The battle between
Debonereté and *Ire* remains unresolved, although death and exile
have decimated the ranks.[41]

Rutebeuf frequently uses the technique, dear to politicos, of
leading an audience to discover for itself a desired truth.[42] In the
Discorde he feigns an open mind and twice invites his audience to
draw their own conclusions—making sure, however, that they reach
the right ones. We are all free to think the Jacobins are fine, up-
standing men, says Rutebeuf:

41. Vv. 178-84; reference to the death of Chrétien de Beauvais (FB, *1,* 79 and
305).

42. See Brunetto Latini's advice in his chapter, "Comment on doit commencier
son prologue quant li oïeur croient a son adversaire": "Et quant celui a qui tu
paroles croit ce que ton adversaire . . . li avoit fait entendant, lors dois tu au
commencement de ton conte proumetre que tu vieus dire de ce meismes en quoi li
adversaires se fie plus . . . et faire samblant autresi comme d'une merveille"
(*Trésor,* pp. 341-42).

> Toute bontez en els abonde,
> Ce puet quiconque voudra croire
>
> • • •
>
> Il pueent bien estre preudomme,
> Ce vueil je bien que chascuns croie,
> (vv. 43–44, 57–58)

but don't forget these same friars are down in Rome trying to get a judgment against their benefactors (vv. 59–60).[43]

The appeal to common sense, together with insistence on obvious absurdities, awakens deeply rooted convictions of right and wrong in the poet's hearers. The *reductio ad absurdum* appears frequently when Rutebeuf wishes to attack either the enemy's requests or their actions, by showing how illogical, therefore how wrong, they are. In the *Complainte de Guillaume* the audience's sympathy is won to Guillaume's refusal to forswear himself before the Curia, when the poet links recantation with a series of impossible absurdities:

> Il avroit pais, de ce me vant,
> S'il voloit jurer par couvant
> Que voirs fust fable,
> Et tors fust droiz, et Diex deable,
> Et fors du sens fussent resnable,
> Et noirs fust blanz. (vv. 126–31)

Rutebeuf here again adapts a theme taken from the tradition of general satire[44] to show Guillaume's individual case to be but part

---

43. Similarly, in the *Ordres de Paris,* speaking of the "Filles-Dieu," Rutebeuf says:

> Se vous creez mençonge a voir
> Et la folie por savoir,
> De ce vous cuit je ma partie.
> Je di que Ordres n'est ce mie,
> Ainz est baras et tricherie. (vv. 100–04)

44. See Curtius' section on "The World Upsidedown," *European Literature,* pp. 94–98. Curtius cites examples from satirical works and pamphlets like those written by the Grandimontine monks (see above, p. 80), in which the monks complain that the lay brothers "Pastores sunt et non oves:/ Plaustrum vadit ante boves,/ Plus est corpus quam anima/ et ancilla domina" (Dobiache-Rojdestvensky, *Poésies des goliards,* pp. 151–52). Compare Walther von der Vogelweide's amusing

of a general defense of right, truth, and God's will; any other interpretation would be impossible. Rutebeuf's attack in *Renart le
Bestourné*, "Renart Reversed," is entirely based on such an impossible triumph of wrong over right. In a contemporary piece,
the anonymous *Couronnement Renart*, Renart makes a triumphant
tour of the Near East, after he has been crowned, to spread his
"upside-down" morality throughout the world:

> Renars tout partout fist savoir,
> En Galilee, par tout Pierse,
> Que bleue lainne n'ert pas pierse,
> Ne boueles n'ert mie chars,
> N'avers hom n'ert mie eschars,
> Ne hom couvoitous envïeus,
> Rires, gabers n'estoit pas geus,
> Chapelés ne rert mie aumuche,
> Ne escrins n'estoit mie huche,
> Ne tarbars houche d'autre part. (vv. 2934-43)

A similar theme, which recurs in Rutebeuf's Crusade poetry as
well as in his University pamphlets, is the idea of a "cheap paradise," or "foolish saints."[45] The Mendicants like the Jesuits centuries later, were accused of smoothing the road to Heaven for
their generous donors. The theme is only suggested in the *Complainte de Guillaume:*

> Moult a sainte chose en avoir,
> Quant tel gent le vuelent avoir. (vv. 98-99)

> Paradis est de tel merrien
> C'on ne l'a pas,
> Por Dieu flater, isnel le pas;

---

satire on "manlîchiu wip, wîplîche man,/ pfaflîche ritter, ritterlîche pfaffen"
(*Gedichte*, p. 113).
45. The theme was also used by the masters in their attack on the *Eternal
Gospel* (Faral, *"Le Dit des Règles," Studi Medievali*, Nuova serie, xvi [1943-50],
pp. 197-99).

> Ainz covient maint felon trespas
> Au cors soufferre. (vv. 148–52)

In *Des Règles,* written in the same year of 1259, we find a fuller development. Rutebeuf accuses the friars of fattening themselves at the expense of "bougre parfet" and "userier mal et divers," all the while promising these damned men a false hope of salvation.[46] If, says he, one can buy one's way into Paradise, it would certainly be a good idea to steal (vv. 37–39). He continues:

> S'on a paradis por si pou,
> Je tieng por bareté saint Pou,
> Et si tieng por fol et por nice
> Saint Luc, saint Jaque de Galice
> Qui s'en firent martirier,
> Et saint Pierre crucefier;
> Bien pert qu'il ne furent pas sage
> Se paradis est d'avantage,
> Et cil * si rementi forment   * Saint Paul
> Qui dist que paine ne torment
> Ne sont pas digne de la grace
> Que Diex par sa pitié nous face. (vv. 53–64)

In the *Dit de Sainte Eglise* there is a similar elaboration evoking the austere sacrifices of

> Li saint preudome qu'en musant
> Aloient au bois pourchacent
> Racines en leu de device: * (vv. 31–33)   * riches

How foolish they were to suffer so, says Rutebeuf repeatedly:

> Se l'en puet paradis avoir
> Pour brun abit ou blanc ou noir. (vv. 22–23)

> S'on a Dieu si legierement

---

46. See FB *1,* 269–70, note to vv. 19–64, for the sources of this passage in a letter from Innocent IV, and his bull *Etsi animarum,* as well as *Collectiones.*

Pour large cote et pour pelice. (vv. 35–36)

Se Diex les a pour ce esliz,
Pour po perdi sainz Poz la teste. (vv. 119–20)

The poet's tone is heavily sarcastic, in contrast with the feigned objectivity and open-mindedness of poems like the *Dit d'Hypocrisie* or the open lamentation of the *Complainte de Guillaume*. With sarcasm, Rutebeuf criticizes the language of the friars themselves, whose words conceal their true intentions. He is adroitly flattering his audience's intelligence by expecting them to understand what he means when he says to the prelates:

Il est bien raison et droiture
Vous laissiez la sainte Escriture, (vv. 73–74)

His hearers will not be so easily taken in as the "gent menue," the only ones stupid enough to believe the friars:

L'en lor fet canc'on ve[*ut acroire,*
L'en lor fet croire de ven[*ue*
Une si grant descovenue
Que brebiz blanche est tote noire.
'Gloria laus,' c'est 'gloire loire';
Il nous font une grant estoire
Nes dou manche de la charrue,
Pour coi il n'ont d'autre mimoire.
Dites lor 'c'est de saint Gregoire,'
Quelque chose soit est creüe. (vv. 99–108)

Rutebeuf deliberately places this description of popular misunderstanding of the friars' iniquities and false words in his most sarcastic poem; thus the whole poem is built around the play between words and truth to create suspicion of the fine promises of Heaven promised by the Mendicants.

Rutebeuf seems to use sarcasm more as a polemical weapon than as a strictly didactic tool, for when the saints and martyrs appear

in Rutebeuf's Crusade poetry, they are described in a straightforward way as examples to imitate.[47] Other moralists, however,
use both the shout of protest and the sly insinuation to say that
Paradise must be earned in this world. Compare the direct blast of
a Latin satire against the greed of monks who hope to eat their way
into heaven:

> Sic igitur sperant caelestia regna mereri?
> Non sic impii, non sic![48]

and with the subtle derogation of the well-fed monk implicit in
these verses from the *Testament* attributed to Jean de Meun:

> Mès se vins et viandes, jusques à pance plaine,
> Donnent Diex et santé, la vie est sainte et saine.[49]

The most savage use I know of the theme of a "cheap paradise" in
a polemical work was made by the anonymous continuer of the
Chanson de la Croisade albigeoise, which deserves to be quoted for
its somber, fiery splendor. In a litany for the agonizing suffering of
his southern compatriots, the author pronounces his own epitaph
over Simon of Montfort, leader of the Crusaders who had ravaged
his land, and who died at the siege of Toulouse (1218):

> E ditz e l'epictafi, cel qui·l sab ben legir,
> Qu'el es sans ez es martirs e que deu resperir
> E dins e·l gaug mirable heretar e florir
> E portar la corona e e·l regne sezir.
> Ez ieu ai auzit dire c'aisi·s deu avenir

---

47. In Rutebeuf's *Nouvelle Complainte d'outremer* we read:
   Sovaingne vos que li apostre
   N'orent pas paradix por pou.
   Or vos remembre de saint Pou
   Qui por Deu ot copei la teste:
   Por noiant n'en fait hon pas feste. (vv. 344–48)
For other examples see FB *1,* 271, note to vv. 53–60.
48. *Poésies des goliards,* ed. Dobiache-Rojdestvensky, p. 149. The poem cleverly
alternates a Psalm verse with one of the poet's own invention; his satire is thus
"proved" with biblical texts ("Non sic impii," Psalms 1:4).
49. *Rose,* ed. Méon, *4,* 38.

Si, per homes aucirre ne per sanc espandir
Ni per esperitz perdre ni per mortz cosentir
E per mals cosselhs creire e per focs abrandir
Et per baros destruire e per Paratge aunir
E per las terras toldre e per Orgolh suffrir
E per los mals escendre e pels bes escantir
E per donas aucirre a per efans delir,
Pot hom en aquest segle Jhesu Crist comquerir,
El deu portar corona e e·l cel resplandir! [50]

Fourteen times the "per" resounds, enumerating the crimes of Simon and summoning him to judgment.

POETIC COMPOSITION AND PERSUASION Rutebeuf seems to choose a tone adapted to the central theme of each poem: breathlessly swift narrative for *Renart le Bestourné*, belligerent and declarative for the *Bataille des Vices et des Vertus*, sarcastic to attack the discrepancy between word and intention in the *Dit de Sainte Eglise*. Since shifts in theme lead to a shift in tone and presentation, I cannot entirely agree with Ulrich Leo's "Doppelgedichte" theory. Leo believes that Rutebeuf wrote poem pairs to treat the same theme in different ways. Among the pairs, Leo cites the *Dit de Guillaume* and the *Complainte de Guillaume,* saying, quite correctly, that the former is juristic and didactic in tone, the latter sermon-like and lyric.[51] Although both are about Guillaume's exile, the form varies according to the poet's intent.

In the *Dit de Guillaume* (1257) Rutebeuf carefully constructs an argument to convince his hearers of the justice and logic of a new hearing for Guillaume. The juridic tone of the poem corresponds to Guillaume's repeated requests for the convening of a council to hear him after his exile (FB, *1,* 243; see p. 103). He

50. Ed. Eugène Martin-Chabot, Les Classiques de l'histoire de France au moyen âge, III (Paris, 1961), p. 228, vv. 3–20.
51. *Studien zu Rutebeuf,* pp. 96–97. Leo suggests that Rutebeuf varied his approach to attract the public (p. 98), but later suggests that variations depend on the poet's "mood," a rather hazy critical approach (p. 111).

first raises the legal question of the banishment, saying that Guillaume was exiled "sanz reson" (v. 6)—that is, without due process of law. Who is to blame?

> Mestre Guillaume ont escillié
> Ou li rois ou li apostoles. (vv. 14-15)

If "la pape Alixandre" (v. 23) exiled Guillaume, the Pope has outraged both national sovereignty and legal process, for

> . . . se l'apostoiles de Romme
> Puet escillier d'autrui terre homme,
> Li sires n'a nient en sa terre,
> Qui la verité veut enquerre. (vv. 17-20)

If, however, the King has exiled Guillaume at the Pope's request, Rutebeuf sarcastically says there must be some new code of law in use:

> Més je ne sai comment a non,
> Qu'il n'est en loi ne en canon;
> Car rois ne se doit pas mesfere,
> Por prier c'on li sache fere. (vv. 25-28)

If the King himself, finally, has exiled Guillaume on his own, he has again acted unfairly since he has not heard Guillaume (vv. 29-36). This long series of conditional clauses (seven altogether) weave a tight web of proof for Guillaume's case and show that the poet is interested only in seeing justice done. Logical and clear, Rutebeuf appeals directly to common sense;

> Je le vous moustre a iex voianz;
> Ou droiz est tors, et voirs noianz. (vv. 45-46)

The poet goes on to set the record straight with vivid reminders of the history of the quarrel, the disputes, and the trips to Rome in 1254 and 1256, when

> L'uns l'autre sovent encontra
> Alant et venant a la cort. (vv. 54-55)

After a brief sneer at the Mendicants' abuse of their credit in Rome and at their taste for battle, Rutebeuf reminds his audience of the legality of the Amiable Conciliation and of the King's oath to uphold it:

> Ce fu fiancé a tenir
> Et seëlé por souvenir. (vv. 73–74)

Only after having carefully proved his case step by step, both legally and historically, does Rutebeuf ask the question which should arouse his audience to fight, twice calling on them in the name of right:

> Doit cis escillemenz seoir? *   *be maintained
> Nenil, qui a droit jugeroit
> Qui droiture et s'ame ameroit. (vv. 90–92)

Before enthusiasm can die away, he quickly makes Guillaume's specific proposal known, saying "S'or fesoit li rois une chose . . ." (v. 93). A new series of seven conditional phrases follows in which Rutebeuf suggests that Guillaume asks only permission to return to France long enough to defend himself and, further, to accept whatever judgment is rendered. (vv. 93–108). Only at the end does the poet abandon his impartial tone to throw himself into the fray, thus setting an example for his hearers:

> Endroit de moi vous puis je dire
> Je ne redout pas le martire
> De la mort, d'ou qu'ele me viegne,
> S'ele me vient por tel besoingne. (vv. 117–20)

The *Dit de Guillaume* is not, except for this final leap to the barricades, an effusively fiery indictment of Guillaume's enemies, but rather a legal document recalling precedent and offering a specific proposal. Rutebeuf uses a juridical vocabulary to develop the central theme of justice: "desroi," legal damage; "desraison," iniquity; "pro et contra, requerre, foi, fiance." The word "droit" occurs seven times, "tort" four, and woven through this legal terminology, the words "escille" and "escillement" appear eleven times, insisting on the injustice done to Guillaume. The theme of fair judgment is apposed to that of divine justice four times, at the end of each section of the poem. Stating his subject, Rutebeuf says that God will banish from his kingdom those who unjustly banish men from theirs (vv. 7–8); discussing the legality of Guillaume's exile, Rutebeuf says that God will summon those who did not give a fair hearing on earth to a celestial hearing, just as He did for Abel, whose blood cried out for justice (vv. 37–46). Guillaume's proposal must be heard, "autrement/ Mainte ame ira a dampnement" (vv. 99–100). And when the poet calls for action, he is sustained by his knowledge that God will require an accounting for earthly acts "au jor du grant Juïse" (vv. 113). Justice for Guillaume should be an image of divine justice. Playing on what Marc Bloch called "the obsession of the beyond," so typical of the medieval mentality,[52] Rutebeuf describes Guillaume's hearing by Louis IX and the prelates as a preparation for the great hearing by the King of Kings and his angels in order to awaken an anxious concern for earthly justice which is only the image of God's, whose is infinitely more majestic and fearful.

The tone of the *Complainte de Guillaume* is much more dramatic and violent. The *Dit* convinces without stirring, while emotional and moral appeal are greatly intensified in the *Complainte*. The *Complainte* is not, however, a mere recasting of the same themes into a more emotional mold, as Leo suggested. Circumstances changed, and the poet no longer sought to logically convince but to reanimate support for Guillaume's cause. Rutebeuf excoriates the prelates who have abandoned Guillaume, and blackens the Mendicants where he can. Abandoning his pretense of objectivity, the poet criticizes directly the friars' self-seeking hypocrisy and their

52. *Feudal Society, 1,* trans. L. A. Manyon (Chicago, London, and Toronto, 1961), 86. Roussel contrasts the fear of physical death, characteristic of the late Middle Ages and of poets such as Villon, with the 13th-century preoccupation with salvation ("Notes sur la littérature arrageoise," p. 249). See Johan Huizinga's evocation of the 15th-century fascination with the macabre in "The Vision of Death," *The Waning of the Middle Ages* (trans. F. Hopman, New York, 1956), pp. 138–51.

excessive temporal power in France and Rome. He excoriates the secular clergy who allow Guillaume to languish in exile.

Rutebeuf chooses, in order to touch the hearts as well as the minds of his hearers, the *complainte* form. He writes the lament of *sainte Yglise* as a dramatic monologue, making little reference to the actual events since these were sufficiently familiar, but moving quickly to moral and emotional commentary punctuated with dramatic exclamations such as

> Ha! Fortune, chose legiere,
> Qui oins devant et poins derriere,
>   Comme est marrastre!
> Clergié, comme estes mi fillastre! (vv. 108-11)

The thematic composition is complex, the various grievances being intermingled and repeated, and the lyric tone and disordered structure reflect the distraught state of *sainte Yglise*. The poem seems built on successive waves of feeling following the ululations of the Church, who picks up a new theme with each wail.

The verse form, with alternating short and long lines (the *tercet coué*), seems particularly suitable for the undulating composition and lamenting tone of the *Complainte*.[53] Although the short line frequently completes a sentence or a thought, or provides a moral commentary on the preceding verses, the rhyme pattern aab bbc assures the continuity of movement and forward flow of the poem. The short lines particularly sustain and echo the note of discouragement or sadness stated in the long lines. Bewailing the spineless resistance of the University masters, *sainte Yglise* moans:

53. The *tercet coué* is a strophic form alternating octosyllables with four-syllable lines, usually in triplets, 8 8 4, rhymed aab bbc. Rutebeuf is a master of this strophic form, since nine of the twenty-two poems listed by Naetebus in this form are his (*Die Nicht-lyrischen Strophenformen des Altfranzösischen* [Leipzig, 1891], pp. 185-92; see FB, *1*, 205-08). The strophic form works well in a fast narrative patter, as in Rutebeuf's *Renart le Bestourné*, as well as in the slower *complainte* works. Faral believes it originates in the rhythms of Latin hymns (*Cinquantenaire de l'Ecole des Hautes Etudes* [1921], pp. 263-66), and we shall see in Chap. 4 that liturgical poetic techniques are often adapted to secular satires. See the appreciation of this meter in Leo, "Rutebeuf, persönlicher Ausdruck," pp. 145-46.

> Me vendez, par sainte Marie!
> J'en doi plorer, qui que s'en rie:
> Je n'en puis mais. (vv. 52–54)

The traitorous acts of the friars reduce her to an almost inarticulate cry:

> Li diz est douz et l'uevre dure;
> N'est pas tout or quanc'on voit luire.
> Ahi! Ahi!
> Com sont li mien mort et trahi
> Et por la verité haï
> Sanz jugement! (vv. 20–25)

Communication is here condensed, reduced to the bare essentials. With phrases like "sanz jugement," the poet recalls the entire history of the quarrel; with the proverbs, he squeezes in extensive moral commentary. Paring the message to the bone, he uses the free flowing *complainte* form to expand long echoing phrases of elegiac lyricism whose length is limited only by the poet's powers of invention. Verbs, for example, are repeated to show that *sainte Yglise* has sustained many blows, and to draw out the tone of lamenting suffering:

> Je fui sor ferme pierre assise;
> La pierre esgrume et fent et brise,
> Et je chancele. (vv. 5–7)

> Ce sai je bien: miex ameroit *   * Guillaume
>   Estre enmurez
> Ou desfez ou desfigurez;
> N'il n'ert ja si desmesurez,
>   Que Diex ne veut. (vv. 139–43)

The *complainte* form, although separated from its original function as a funeral poem,[54] never ceases to serve as a vehicle of mourning

---

54. See above, p. 58.

over any lost or desperate cause: Guillaume, the Crusades, Rutebeuf's financial situation. Its dismal vocabulary would always evoke a quick emotional response in a public accustomed to associate doleful feelings with the *complainte* form: "plorer, dolor, me plaing, mat et confus." The hearers would respond readily to its phrases of discouragement: "je n'en puis mais; je n'i voi plus."

This transposition of vocabulary and feelings from the world of the dead to that of the living elevates Rutebeuf's mundane subject matter—the injustice done Guillaume—to the noble level of public disasters like the death of kings and the fall of great cities. His *Complainte de Guillaume* opens on a biblical scale with a translation of Lamentations 1:12, where Jerusalem mourns her afflictions and the triumph of her enemies:

> 'Vous qui alez parmi la voie,
> Arestez vous et chascuns voie
> S'il est dolor tel com la moie,'
> Dist sainte Yglise.

Faral notes that Dante used the same verses in the second sonnet of his *Vita nuova* to bewail the absence of his lady love, and also that the passage was read during the *Tenebrae* of Holy Saturday (FB, *1*, 257–58). Medieval authors typically turned to the Bible for vocabulary, verses, and passages, to affect their hearers and to sustain their flights of rhetoric, and Jeremiah's text was a favorite for laments. An early Latin *planctus* for the death of Lanfranc (d. 1089), Archbishop of Canterbury under William the Conqueror, incorporated the same verse from Lamentations:

> O vos omnes qui transitis, expectate modicum,
> et Lanfrancum mecum flete virum apostolicum,
> ejulando, gemiscendo propter ejus obitum!
> Heü! heü! clamet omnis destituta regio.[55]

---

55. In *Poésies populaires latines du moyen âge,* ed. Du Méril, p. 252. Du Méril includes examples of both the funeral and the satirical *planctus* (pp. 251–84). Pope Innocent IV used Jeremiah's words as the text for a sermon to the First Council of Lyons (1245). In the words of Matthew Paris, the Pope "wholesomely touched

In a polemical vein one lament on the Grandimontine schism, which we have seen earlier, starts with a medley of sad biblical and prophetic themes:

> Respiciat Emanuel,
> qui solus cuncta percipit,
> quomodo patitur Abel,
> et adhunc Caïn desipit;
> Lia ridet, plorat Rachel,
> formosam lippa decipit;
> captivus servit Israël,
> sicut Pharao precipit.[56]

It is by such reference to suffering of biblical proportions that the polemicists, like Rutebeuf, define the scope of the moral calamity implied by their specific subject.

EFFECTIVENESS AND INFLUENCE OF THE UNIVERSITY POLEMIC Rutebeuf's effectiveness as a polemicist cannot be singled out from the whole effect of the campaign led on several fronts by the University masters, since he is nowhere mentioned by name except in his own poems. Certainly the combination of Latin writings and vernacular poems did inflame public opinion against the friars. Matthew Paris, recounting the 1256 trip of the University masters to Rome, says that the Dominicans were, at that time, publicly slandered:

The people ridiculed them, and withheld their accustomed alms, calling them hypocrites, successors of Antichrist, false preachers, flatterers, and evil advisers of kings and princes, despisers and supplanters of ordinary preachers, clandestine intruders into the bedchambers of kings and prevaricators of confessions, men who vagabondized through countries where

---

all his hearers with grief, for their eyes poured forth abundance of tears, and their sighs broke in on his discourses" (*English History*, 2, 68).

56. *Poésies des goliards*, ed. Dobiache-Rodjestvensky, p. 151; see p. 155 n.

168 ८**   THE LANGUAGE OF POLEMICS

they were unknown, and gave encouragement and boldness to
sinners.[57]

We see that the people adopted the insults of the polemicists, and
apparently the citizenry did not restrict itself to mere name-calling.
Louis IX was obliged to post guards around the Dominican convent to prevent arrows from being shot in through their windows.[58]
Humbert of Romans, the Master General of the Dominicans, wrote
in April 1256 of the anguish the friars were enduring. He said that
the University masters had so aroused public opinion against them

> that, by inciting and agitating the masses to rage and raise
> scandal against us, we should not be able to make public the
> apostolic decree [the *Quasi lignum* bull]. . . . Therefore, not
> content with impious decrees—for they had already forbidden
> all scholars to come to our house for any reason, nor could
> they receive us in their houses, and none were to confess to us,
> lavish alms upon us, or attend our preachings and sermons,
> although they protect and observe very diligently everything
> for their own well being—the masters have descended to such
> an abyss of rage and madness that they break out everywhere
> in abusive riots against us; they thus prevent the brothers from
> going about in the city. . . . They have represented the men
> of religion [the friars] as so contemptible, that they are not

57. *English History*, 3, 206 (year 1256). It is difficult to decide whether the
following outburst recorded by Guillaume de Saint-Pathus is an authentic record
of popular opinion or merely an example of humility attributed by Guillaume to
St. Louis. Guillaume, himself a Minorite, recounts that a woman named Sarette
called out to Louis from the stairs of his palace, saying "Fi! fi! Deusses tu estre
roi de France? Mout miex fust que un autre fust roi que tu; car tu es roy tant
seulement des Freres Meneurs et des Freres Preecheurs et des prestres et des clers.
Grant damage est que tu es roy de France, et c'est grant merveille que tu n'es
bouté hors du roiaume." Louis listened to her "diligaument" and answered with
a smile: "Certes, vos dites voir, je ne suis pas digne d'estre roy. Et se il eust
pleu a Nostre Seigneur, ce eust esté miex que un autre eust esté roy que je, qui
miex seust gouverner le roiaume" (*Vie de saint Louis*, ed. H.-François Delaborde
[Paris, 1899], pp. 118–19). Ham notes that a similar sort of outburst appears in
exempla figuring Trajan and a widow, and an old woman and a tyrant (*Renart
le Bestorné*, p. 34).

58. *Chart. Univ.*, *1*, No. 273.

believed anywhere, because the [former] now possess Paris completely; unless God applies a remedy, it seems they will possess all of France everywhere. And if some of them refrain from attacking us bodily, rare is he who holds his tongue from insults and abuses.[59]

Not that the good friar had given up hope! In public he may have preached peace and concord, but to his fellow brethren he sent a clarion call for immediate resistance:

Now, now, the army imitates its commander, the noblest follow the sign of the combatant, and under the flag of faith, may the loyal members follow the leadership of Christ! Now, indeed, is the soldier trained for battle, the athlete tested for warlike blows, and selected for the struggle! Now, in the fiery furnace of tribulation, the dross of our sins is melted out, the virtue of patience is tested, and the merit of glory accumulated! [60]

By the middle of June 1256 the Pope had evidently been able to stop such public agitations, since Humbert wrote: "the grave

59. "Ut contra multitudinis turbatione, furore et scandalo suscitatis, non permittamur mandatum apostolicum publicare . . . Mandatis siquidem impiis non contenti (quibus jam prohibuerant scolaribus universis, quod nullus ex ulla causa ad domum nostram accederet, quod nos non susciperent ab ipsis in domibus propriis accedentes, quod nulli nostrum auderent propria confiteri peccata, quod nobis non presumerent aliquam eleemosinam elargiri, quod nullus apud nos eligeret sepulturam, quod nullus ad predicationes nostras accederet vel sermones que omnia salutis proprie prodigi diligentius custodiunt et observant), in tantum furie et furoris baratrum devenerunt, ut in nos ubique contumeliosis clamoribus irruentes, fratres per civitatem incedere non permittant . . . Ipsos religiosos tam contemptibiles reddiderunt, ut ipsis alicubi non credatur, quod jam ad plenum Parisiis obtinent; et nisi Deus apponat remedium, ubique ut videtur in Francis obtinebunt. Et si plerique eorum ab injuriis corporalibus manum cohibent, rarus tamen vel nullus a contumeliis vel opprobriis continet linguam suam" (ibid., pp. 311–12).

60. "Nunc, nunc igitur imitatur militia principem, sequntur agoniste summi signum, et sub vexillo fidei membra fidelia Christo capiti conformantur. Nunc igitur miles exercitatur ad pugnam et tunsionibus bellicis examinatur athleta, eligitur ad certamen. Nunc in tribulationis fornace succensa peccatorum nostrorum scoria excoquitur, probatur patientae virtus et meritorum gloria cumulatur" (ibid., pp. 312–13).

tribulations of our Paris brethren are now mitigated, thanks be to God." [61]

Bonaventura seemed more touched than Humbert by the possibility that the University masters might have been right. He wrote a letter in 1257 to the superiors of the Franciscan order, enumerating as faults of the friars the very criticisms so often leveled against them by the masters:

Cherchant les causes pour lesquelles la splendeur de notre Ordre s'obscurcit, je trouve une multitude d'affaires pour lesquelles on demande avec avidité de l'argent, et on le reçoit sans précaution, bien que ce soit le plus grand ennemi de notre pauvreté. Je trouve l'oisiveté de quelques-uns de nos frères, qui demeurent dans une sorte d'état de difformité entre la contemplation et l'action; je trouve la vie vagabonde de plusieurs, qui, pour donner du soulagement à leur corps sont à la charge de leurs hôtes et scandalisent au lieu d'édifier; je trouve les demandes importunes qui font craindre aux passants la rencontre de nos Frères comme celle des voleurs; la grandeur et la curiosité des bâtiments qui trouble notre paix, incommode nos amis, et nous expose aux mauvais jugements des hommes; la multiplication des familiarités que notre règle défend, qui causent des soupçons et nuisent à notre réputation . . . l'avidité des sépultures et des testaments qui attire l'indignation du clergé et particulièrement celle des curés . . . Ainsi nous sommes à charge à tout ce monde et nous le serons encore plus si on n'y apporte promptement remède.[62]

If Humbert's letter shows the effectiveness of propaganda in arousing public opinion against the Mendicants, that of Bonaventura

---

61. Ibid., p. 318, No. 279. See also No. 311, pp. 358–59 (May 1257), in which Humbert expresses similar feelings of relief.

62. Cited by Perrod, "Guillaume de Saint-Amour," p. 125. Wyngaert cites a letter of Humbert advising the Dominicans to avoid competing with parish clergy, but one feels caution rather than humility in his words ("Querelles du clergé seculier," pp. 277–78).

shows that many of the blows struck home. There would be little to change except the pronouns for Bonaventura's letter to appear as an attack against the Franciscans.

The only concrete index we have to the effectiveness of poems like Rutebeuf's is the reprisals against them. Not only, as we have seen, did Alexander order vernacular poems against the Mendicants to be burned, but in almost every poem where the friars are mentioned, Rutebeuf includes some reference to fear of speaking the truth or to reprisals against those who resist the Mendicants.[63] Sometimes he says that the friars have succeeded because the prelates and masters do not dare speak the truth about them. Thus, in the *Complainte de Guillaume,*

> . . . Verité a fet son lais;
> Ne l'ose dire ne clers ne lais
>
> . . .
>
> C'on doute plus le cors que l'ame;
>   Et d'autre part
> Nus clers a provende ne part
> N'a dignité que l'en depart,
>   S'il n'est des lor.* (vv. 72–73, 81–85)   * with the friars

Again, in *Du Pharisien,*

> Or n'est més hom qui ne l* 'encline   * to Ypocrisie
>   Ne bien creanz,
> Ainz est bougres et mescreanz.

---

63. In the *Complainte de Constantinople* (1262) we read:
>   Li rois tendra deça concile
>   . . .
>   Et fera nueve remanance *   * building
>   A cels qui font nueve creance,
>   Novel Dieu et nueve Evangile,
>   Et lera semer, par doutance,
>   Ypocrisie sa semance
>   Qui est dame de ceste vile. (vv. 41, 43–48)
See also the *Chanson de Pouille,* vv. 38–40; and *La Nouvelle Complainte d'outremer,* v. 22, as well as st. V of *La Clearison des Ordres.*

> Ele a ja fet toz recreanz
> ses aversaires.[64] (vv. 22–26)

In other poems Rutebeuf portrays himself as writing in spite of ever-present menaces. He starts *Des Règles:*

> Puis qu'il covient verité tere,
> De parler n'ai je més que fere.
> Verité ai dite en mains leus:
> Or est li dires pereilleus
> A cels qui n'aiment verité, (vv. 1–5)

saying, as he did in his *Dit d'Hypocrisie* of his own poetry, and at the end of the *Bataille* of Guillaume's defense in Rome, that truth has powerful enemies.

The above passages, as well as the atmosphere of menace that weighed on the University partisans, indicate the sources of Mendicant strength: they were very powerful in both the Court and the Curia. They controlled laymen by refusing absolution to those who did not name them testamentary executors; they influenced ecclesiastics by menacing condemnation for heresy. The Dominicans had served as papal inquisitors since 1227, as part of a papal effort to encourage orthodoxy and centralization of power in Rome (see above, pp. 97–98). The first papal inquisitor, the Dominican friar Robert le Bougre, had conducted frightening, McCarthy-type investigations during the 1230s,[65] until, as Matthew Paris says, he finally passed "the bonds of moderation and justice; he became elated, powerful, and formidable, involved the good with the bad, and punished the innocent and simpleminded,"[66] and was finally discredited. The threat of being accused of heresy by the Dominicans

---

64. See also the *Dit de Sainte Église,* st. II and vv. 83–84; and the *Bataille,* vv. 115–16, 152, etc.

65. See Haskins, *Medieval Culture,* for complete information on the beginnings of the inquisition in Northern France (pp. 193–244). The Dominicans actually felt their inquisitorial tasks to be a burden; Humbert de Romans listed such work under impedimenta which interfered with the Dominican preaching mission (Bennett, *The Early Dominicans,* p. 129).

66. *English History, 1,* 157.

was evidently a strong deterrent to speaking ill of them in succeeding decades. Rutebeuf tells us that everyone hastens to welcome
the friars,

> Si lor fet cil et joie et feste
> Por ce qu'il se doute d'enqueste.
> (*Bataille*, vv. 167–68)

Was Rutebeuf himself in any personal danger because of his
writings again the Mendicants? He says so, in his *Ordres de Paris:*

> Nus n'en * dit voir c'on ne l'assomme: * of the friars
> Lor haïne n'est pas frivole;
> Je qui redout ma teste fole
> Ne vous di plus, més qu'il sont homme. (vv. 57–60)

Ham wonders why Rutebeuf was not exiled with Guillaume, saying: "surely the poet was too articulate a propagandist to be ignored
as insignificant."[67] Faral notes that *Le Dit d'Hypocrisie* is "la
première en date de ses pièces polémiques où Rutebeuf se nomme,
et, s'il est permis de supposer, la première où il ait osé se nommer"
(FB, *1*, 287). Yet although many texts were burned, the Pope seems
to have taken measures only against influential Church figures who
were at the bottom of the quarrel. Of the four masters who played
a leading role, only Guillaume was exiled and deprived of his
prebends—this, because he refused to retract his statements against
the Mendicants. There is no record of reprisals against nonclerical
writers like Rutebeuf, other than the ban placed on their works.
Although we can perhaps read Rutebeuf's lines as indicating fear
of the considerable political power of the Mendicants,[68] I believe
Rutebeuf includes them to underline the importance of what he
says. Truth-sayers have ever glorified their task by magnifying the

---

67. "Rutebeuf—Pauper and Polemist," p. 232.
68. A fear undiminished through the years; see the verses from Villon below
and Marguerite de Navarre's words on the Franciscans: "Vous feriez mieulx de les
honorer que de les blasmer, dit Saffredent, et de les flatter que de les injurier. Car
ce sont ceulx qui ont puissance de brusler et deshonorer les autres" (*L'Heptaméron,*
ed. Michel François [Paris, 1950], p. 193).

dangers they must overcome. Bourgain cites several examples of twelfth-century preachers who return repeatedly to the age-old moralist's theme that men will suffer for speaking the truth. Raoul Ardent complains eloquently:

Ce que Paul souffrait de la part des Juifs, nous, quoique indignes prédicateurs, nous le souffrons aujourd'hui. Ces chrétiens pervers, parce que nous leur disons non pas ce qui les flatte, mais ce qui est vrai, non pas ce qui leur plaît, mais ce qui est dur, ces chrétiens nous dressent des embûches, nous accablent d'outrages et d'injures. . . . Ils nous haïssent, alors qu'ils devraient nous aimer.[69]

Humbert de Romans, who portrayed the Dominicans struggling to preach in the face of great opposition in Paris, wrote, in the section of his *De eruditione praedicatorum* addressed to the Dominicans, that the greatness of their ministry was in proportion to the dangers they ran:

Brethren, he who joins the Preachers must consider how excellent is that duty, because it is Apostolic: how useful, because it is directly ordered for the saving of souls: how dangerous, because few . . . do the things which duty requires, which is not without great danger, and the greater the danger, the more worthy is the duty.[70]

Technically, the masters won a partial victory, since the Lyons Council of 1274 abolished all Mendicant orders except the Dominicans and Franciscans.[71] Mandonnet observes, however, that the talents of the University masters were consumed by "cette polémique scandaleuse et stérile."[72] The Dominicans did undertake brilliant

69. Translated in *La Chaire française au XIIe siècle*, p. 10 (edited in *Patrologia latina*, CLV).

70. "Fratri, qui transit ad statum Praedicatorum considerandum est quam excellens sit istud officium, quia est Apostolicum: quam utile, quia directe ordinatur ad salutem animarum: quam periculosum, quia pauci . . . faciunt, quae requirit istud officium, quod non est sine magno periculo, & tanto est magis periculosum, quanto est dignius officium" (chap. 14, pp. 461–62).

71. Gratien, *Histoire des Frères Mineurs*, pp. 323–25.

72. *Siger de Brabant et l'averroïsme latin au XIIIe siècle* (Fribourg, 1899), p. cx.

intellectual tasks such as their correction of the Bible, their re-organization of the *Corpus juris*, and their revision of Aristotle. Fermenting, disputatious, the Mendicant masters of Theology at Paris were the intellectual lights of the thirteenth century: Albertus Magnus, Thomas Aquinas, Alexander of Hales, Roger Bacon, *doctores universalis, angelicus, irrefragabilis, mirabilis!* The secular masters offered little to compete with this intellectual revival.[73]

We do find specific traces of the University quarrel in poems about the Mendicants after 1270. Jean de Meun's prestige guaranteed immortality to the polemic, since it is his text which reappears in later works, while Rutebeuf's poems, although preserved in manuscripts, are never referred to by either contemporary or later poets. Durante, in his sonnet sequence *Il Fiore,* of the late thirteenth century, transposed long sections of the *Roman de la Rose* into Italian, including two sonnets on the University polemic from the section about *Faus Semblant.*[74] The author of the second part of the *Roman de Fauvel* (1314) describes *Ypocrisie* as "une dame merveilleuse," who often appears as "Cordelier, puis Cordeliere,/ Puis Jacobin, puis Jacobine." The author refers to the *Roman de la Rose,* "qui en vuelt savoir la glose," for a more profound description of *Faus Semblant* and his followers.[75] Jehan le Fèvre (ca. 1370) translated and abbreviated the long Latin tirade against the Mendicants which Matheolus, the "bigamous" antifeminist, derived from Jean de Meun and included in his *Lamentations* with the words:

> Combien que Mahieu en son livre,
> En ait assés versifié
> Et leurs * meurs diversifié.   * the Mendicant Orders
> Si fist maistre Jehan de Meun;
> Tous les reproucha un et un,
> Ou chapitre de Faulx Semblant.[76]

---

73. Mandonnet, *Siger de Brabant,* pp. lxviii–ix, and David Knowles, *The Evolution of Medieval Thought* (Baltimore, 1962), pp. 222–24.

74. Ed. Ferdinand Castets (Paris, 1881), Nos. XCII and CXIX.

75. Gervais du Bus, *Le Roman de Fauvel,* ed. Arthur Långfors (Paris, 1914–19), vv. 1575–98.

76. *Les Lamentations de Matheolus et le Livre de leesce de Jehan le Fèvre, de*

Arnold Williams says that Chaucer used Guillaume de Saint-Amour's *De periculis* and the *Roman de la Rose* as a source for his attack upon the friars.[77] Chaucer reproached the friars with usurpation of parish duties, begging, and hypocrisy, and drew, in his *General Prologue,* the portrait of Frere Huberd, as arrogant as a "maister or a pope." The friar-hero of the *Summoner's Tale* refuses, with false humility, to let himself be called master:

> 'No maister, sire,' quod he, 'but servitour,
> Thogh I have had in scole that honour.
> God liketh nat that 'Raby' men us calle.'[78]

Finally, when François Villon leaves "grasses souppes jacopines"[79] to the Mendicants, he recalls Matheolus and Jean de Meun with feigned disapproval:

> Maistre Jehan de Mehun s'en moqua
> De leur façon; si fist Mathieu:
> Mais on doit honnorer ce qu'a
> Honnoré l'Eglise de Dieu.
> (*Testament*, CXVIII, 1178-81)

In the next stanza Villon recalls the old theme of fear which we have seen in Rutebeuf; he recalls also the theme of "deeds and words" used against the Mendicants throughout the controversy:

Ressons, 1, ed. A.-G. Van Hamel (Paris, 1892), 92, vv. 1794–99. Matheolus himself refers to a later encounter (ca. 1282) between the Mendicants and secular clergy in which Guillaume de Mâcon, Bishop of Amiens, defended the prelates (*1,* 90–94). Again we see satirical material being reused in new circumstances.

77. "Chaucer and the Friars," *Speculum, 28,* No. 3 (July 1953), 505.

78. *Canterbury Tales,* ed. A. C. Cawley (London and New York, 1962), p. 217, vv. 2185–87. Compare with the Manifesto of the University masters, who quoted Matthew 23:8, "Nolite vocari Rabbi," in an effort to prevent the friars from teaching, on the grounds that perfect evangelical humility forbade them academic honors (*Chart. Univ., 1,* 253, No. 230).

79. Thuasne gives the recipe: "Souppe jacopine de pain tostee, de frommage du meilleur que on pourra trouver, et mettre sur des tosteez, et destramper de boullon de beuf, et mettre dessus de bons pluviers rotis ou de bons chappons." Hardly ascetic! (François Villon, *Œuvres, 2,* ed. Louis Thuasne [Paris, 1923], 311, note to v. 1162).

Si me soubmectz, leur serviteur
En tout ce que puis faire et dire,
A les honnorer de bon cuer
Et obeïr, sans contredire;
L'omme bien fol est d'en mesdire,
Car, soit a part ou en preschier
Ou ailleurs, il ne faut pas dire
Se gens sont pour eux revenchier.
  (*Testament,* CXIX, 1182–89)

We can see by these verses from Villon that the themes and images developed by Rutebeuf and Jean de Meun remained stable, and the same set of criticisms, the same words cast in new verses, reappeared whenever poets wrote against the Mendicants.[80] When Jean de Condé, poet of the Hainaut Court, wrote a fierce poem against the Dominicans, *De l'Ipocresie des Jacobins,*[81] the same old accusations of hypocrisy and greed were used, as was the *tercet coué* so familiar from Rutebeuf. Jean de Condé's subject was Dante's hero, the Emperor Henry VII, who died in Buonconvento (1313); his Dominican confessor, Bernardo de Monte Politiano, was accused of killing him with a poisoned holy wafer. Beyond a necessary allusion to this evil deed (vv. 41–86), *L'Ipocresie des Jacobins* is only an unoriginal rehash of traditional themes, tending toward generalities like:

Tés ordres doit estre haïs
  Qui ainsi oevre.
Lor grans faussetés se descuevre,
Car par paroles et par oevre
  Sont conneü. (vv. 99–102)

80. Most of the anti-Mendicant arguments advanced in the 1250s reappear, for example, in early 15th-century Wyclifite poems such as *Jacke Upland* (1401). The hero of *Jacke Upland,* an attack on the friars for obeying neither English prelates nor the crown, is a legendary figure of popular peasant resistance like the French Jacques Bonhomme. See also the *Reply of Friar Daw Topias* (by John of Walsingham) and *Jacke Upland's Rejoinder* (Wright, *Political Poems,* 2, Introduction, pp. x–xxvii, and pp. 16–114).

81. *Dits, 3,* 181–88, No. LV.

Jean de Condé's *Li Dis des Jacobins et des Fremeneurs* [82] is a more lively piece, being a heated answer to a Mendicant sermon against "menestrez." "D'irour m'en avez eschauffé," says he (v. 280), defending his profession with the edifying examples of David harping before Saul, and the Virgin appearing to the Arras minstrels. [83] He attacks the Mendicants for their sins against their own rule of poverty and abstinence as established by Saints Francis and Dominic, whose virtues he extols, citing the story of Saint Francis, who had himself led around Assisi like a criminal because he had eaten some chicken while he was sick (vv. 178–205). [84]

The *Requeste des Frères Meneurs sur le septième Climent le Quint* [85] is an entertaining satirical commentary on clerical reaction to the seventh book of *Decretals* of Pope Clement V (d. 1314), published by John XXII in 1317. The Pope forbade the secular clergy to hold more than one benefice and imposed severe restrictions on the Mendicants. The anonymous author pretends to sympathize with the seculars, who are reduced to the estate of "bergiers des champs" (v. 28) and who can no longer live from their tonsure and with the Mendicants who, put on a diet of dry bread, will have to rob in order to live. With the verse "Je ne sai qui tant d'ordres fit" (v. 78), the poet introduces a review of all the orders, refurbishing some venerable witticisms for the occasion, such as saying that the Filles-Dieu are "teles que Diex n'a engendrées" (v. 93). [86] In the poet's hostile words against begging friars one recognizes arguments first developed by Guillaume de Saint-Amour against mendicancy:

> Tant est grande l'ypocrisie
> Que l'en ne scet où l'en se fie;

---

82. Ibid., pp. 249–60, No. LXVI.

83. For the Arras miracle, see Henry Guy, *Essai sur la vie et les œuvres littéraires du trouvère Adan de le Hale* (Paris, 1898), pp. xxvi–xxxii.

84. For this anecdote in early biographies of St. Francis, see Moorman's *Sources for the Life of Saint Francis of Assisi* (Manchester, 1940), p. 147. Auerbach cites the story as illustrating Francis' didactic technique, the "graphic, exemplary revelation of a saintly life" (*Mimesis*, p. 147).

85. Rutebeuf, *O.C., 3*, 155–62.

86. Compare with Rutebeuf's *Ordres de Paris*, vv. 97–99: "Diex a non de filles avoir,/ Més je ne poi onques savoir/ Que Diex eüst fame en sa vie."

Car chascuns pense de bouler
Pour toutes ces gens saouler,
Et qui de leurs mains ne labeurent,
Mais par le païs vont & queurent
Et cherchant tous les quarrefours. (vv. 115-21)

The poet attempts to crush the Mendicants with irony: it would be well, he says, if a miracle returned "leur juste possession" (v. 179) to the friars, since they pray so humbly for their worldly goods, "jointes mains & à nus genoulz" (v. 191). In their prayer the Mendicants remind the Pope that the Church is

. . . si foible et si tendre
Qu'au jor d'ui ne se puet deffendre
Des grans lous qui entor li courent, (vv. 220-22)

a sly reference to the damage the poet himself thinks the Mendicants, so often described as wolves in sheep's clothing, have done to the Church.

THE FRIARS IN FICTION Mendicants appear also during the thirteenth and succeeding centuries as heroes or villains in fabliau-type stories. These characterizations may be distinguished from polemical or satirical portrayals of the friars in that the fabliaux do not urge the hearer to self-amendment or to active protest but only to laughter. Jacques de Baisieu's fourteenth-century *Vescie a Prestre* [87] takes, as a point of departure, the well-worn criticism of the Jacobins as avid garnerers of testamentary legacies. Jacques is, however, interested in a good story, well told, of a wily priest who strings along a whole greedy convent of Jacobins with the promise of a beloved "jowel" as legacy. The chagrin of the friars, when they discover that the priest has left them his bladder to keep their pepper in, ends in a hearty guffaw all around:

Et tot chil qui là demorerent
De ris en aise se pamerent

87. Montaiglon and Raynaud, eds., *Fabliaux, 3,* 106-17; and Méon ed., *Nouveau Recueil, 1,* 80-90. See Nykrog, *Fabliaux,* p. 134.

Por la trufe de la vesie
Que li prestes ot tant prisie.

The author himself, who obviously relished his tale, says that the pleasure of narration was his only aim:

Jakes de Baisiw, sans dotance,
La de nex[88] en romant rimée
Por la trufe qu'il a amée.

The Jacobins hardly come off well, but, appearing as greedy simpletons, they are portrayed with malice but not anger. The Dominicans, more politically powerful in the thirteenth century than the Franciscans, thereby come in for more severe attacks in polemical verse. Compare, for example, the ferocity of the stanza against them in Rutebeuf's *Ordres de Paris* with the milder one against the Franciscans who are taxed only with not living up to their ideal. It is their very pretension of extreme austerity which brings the Franciscans under fire in the sexually-oriented fabliau. As Bédier says, the professionally virtuous are more comic, when they sin, than the ordinary mortal.[89] When Franciscans appear in fabliau stories, therefore, they are generally cast, as in Rutebeuf's *Frère Denise,* as hypocritical lechers, whose enforced asceticism is unnatural, therefore dangerous, since it only makes their inner flames the hotter.

88. For "nex," Montaiglon and Raynaud give variant *Tieus,* "Dutch, Low German."
89. *Fabliaux,* p. 334. Not only the sexual desires but the sexual powers of the Franciscans are accentuated in the *Braies du cordelier,* where a woman explains away a strange pair of men's trousers under her bed by saying that they belonged to a Franciscan, and that she hoped that "cele nuit concevroie/ Enfant quant en mon lit auroie/ Les braies d'un Frere menor" (*Montaiglon-Raynaud,* eds., *Fabliaux, 3,* No. 88, p. 285). As Nykrog comments, "Les Franciscains se sont sans doute distingués dans le domaine de Vénus, si de leurs braies mêmes il émane une force qui puisse rendre féconde une femme jusque là stérile" (*Fabliaux,* p. 135). A similar story is told, however, by Jean de Condé about a priest's trousers (*Dits, 2,* 121–25, No. XIV); as Nykrog points out, monks and friars appear in towns and cities after the personnel of the fabliaux are well established and therefore do not appear often or appear in roles which could be equally well filled by a secular priest (*Fabliaux,* pp. 134–35).

Rutebeuf's *Frère Denise* reflects this suspicion of desire cloaked in grey. He includes formulas from his arsenal of propagandistic weapons in his portrayal of Brother Simon, who inveigles naïve Denise into joining his order. The long prologue to his story is an amplification of two proverbs used in his poems against the Mendicants: "Li abis ne fet pas l'ermite" (v. 1) and "Tout n'est pas or c'on voit luire" (v. 15). The story serves as an exemplum to illustrate this brief sermon. The theme of hypocrisy fits naturally enough into the story: Brother Simon *is* a deceitful fellow who preaches an austerity he does not practice. Rutebeuf slips in a few jabs against Franciscans in general, but seems to speak more as a jongleur than as a polemicist, in the tone of Jean de Condé's *Li Dis des Jacobins et des Fremeneurs,* saying:

> Telz genz font bien le siecle pestre
> Qui par dehors samblent bons estre
> Et par dedenz sont tuit porri. . . .
> Un tel Ordre, par saint Denise,
> N'est mie biaus ne bons ne genz.
> Vous desfendez aus bones genz
> Et les dansses et les caroles,
> Vieles, tabours et citoles
> Et deduis de menestrez (vv. 249–51, 256–61)

Although Faral suggests that *Frère Denise* was written at "une période où l'auteur en était encore à mal contenir ses sentiments d'hostilité à l'égard des Ordres mendiants" (FB, 2, 282), Rutebeuf seems rather to be reusing here, as in his polemical verse, ready-made formulas from his bag of poetical and polemical tricks.[90] *Frère Denise* has more in common with fabliaux about lustful priests such as Rutebeuf's own *Sacristain* than with the University polemic.

The friar's garb is treated mostly as a comic peculiarity, as a sort

---

90. Thus a diatribe against "ypocrite papelart" appears somewhat surprisingly in the middle of the *Sacristain et la femme du chevalier,* vv. 403–14, a miracle tale borrowing heavily from fabliau technique (See below, p. 245).

of risible personal defect. The good lady who rescues "Brother" Denise sarcastically calls Simon "sire haus rez" (v. 262), and adds:

> Faus papelars, faus ypocrite,
> Fausse vie menez et orde.
> Qui vous pendroit a vostre corde
> Qui est en tant de lieus noee
> Il avroit fet bone jornee. (vv. 244–48)

Rutebeuf takes advantage of the comic possibilities of a friar-hero to render the seduction scenes in a devout language worthy of Tartuffe. "Je pens," says Brother Simon, "a un sermon,/ Au meillor que je penssaisse onques." Responds Denise, "Or penssez donques!" (vv. 114–16). Indeed, *Frère Denise* seems closer to the jolly fabliau than to the polemical satire, although Nykrog sees in the Rutebeuf of *Frère Denise* a passionate man who attacks under the light surface of his tale, citing in proof the punishment of Simon at the end as "un exemple du vice puni."[91] Yet Simon's sentence is really very light, especially compared to the dreadful end which befalls the priest-lovers of fabliaux like *Connebert* of Gautier le Leu or *Le Prestre et le Leu*.[92] Only too happy to pay up the hundred *livres* required to marry Denise off to a former suitor (who is not informed of her religious career), Simon gets out of the story as fast as he can, and with a sigh of relief that nothing more will be required of him. "Onques n'ot tel joie en sa vie" (v. 281), as when he was so lightly quit of his sin.

The Franciscans are most severely attacked at the time of the Reformation, when they are cited often as examples of religious hypocrisy. Preoccupation with sincere devotion and true evangelical simplicity led Marguerite de Navarre to include 11 tales of cordeliers in her *Heptameron*, one of which is favorable (and that solely in the interests of objectivity). "Il n'y a plus dangereux venyn que celluy qui est dissimullé,"[93] she says, and severely requires that the

91. *Fabliaux*, p. 65; see also p. 169.
92. Montaiglon and Raynaud, eds., *Fabliaux*, 5, 160–70; 6, 51–52.
93. *Heptaméron*, p. 192.

Franciscans be "anges ou plus saiges que les aultres." [94] In this same spirit, scurrilous anti-Franciscan works appeared with such titles as *Les Avantures de la Madona et de François d'Assise . . . Ecrites d'un stile récréatif; et en même temps capable de faire voir le ridicule du Papisme sans aucune controverse.* The enormously popular *Alcoranum nudipedem* by Erasmus Alber was translated into French as *L'Alcoran des cordeliers, tant en Latin qu'en françois. C'est à dire, Recueil des plus notables bourdes & blasphèmes de ceux ont osé comparer Sainct François à Iesus Christ,* criticizing Bartholomew of Pisa's *Liber de conformitate* (1510), which tucked analogies between the lives of Saint Francis and Christ into footnotes.

THE FORTUNE OF HYPOCRISY   What most truly survived the University quarrel was the idea of an allegorical figure incarnating hypocrisy. It is curious to see that vernacular didactic writings of the early thirteenth century tended to be organized around the concept of the vices and virtues, while in the second half of the thirteenth century and in the early fourteenth they are focused on the single idea of deceit disguised as virtue, incarnated in a central figure: *Ypocrisie, Dame Guile,*[95] Renart, Fauvel. The other vices appear only as handmaidens or servants of such central figures. One might say that while Pride and Avarice were fighting it out for first place, Hypocrisy slipped in behind them and took over the whole crime syndicate. Such is the sad outcome of the very strong reform movement of the thirteenth century, which had started off on a wave of hope. The Mendicants epitomized the public desire for a return to old ideals, Crusade fervor burned bright, and vast expectations were centered around figures like Louis IX and Frederick II.

94. Ibid., p. 285.

95. In *Jongleurs et trouvères,* ed. Jubinal, pp. 63–68. The poem is an elaborate example of the theme of allegorical clothing. Dame Guile wears a coif of Falsehood, trimmed with Trickery, a dress of False Greed lined with Fakery, belted with False Notes, buckled with lies, etc. She is represented as omnipotent, as was Rutebeuf's *Dame Ypocrisie:* "Guile est toz partout en toz tans./ Ainz ne fu fame si plentive."

But all these hopes were dashed. The Mendicants failed to reform sinning humanity; pious Louis IX was vanquished by the pagans at Mansourah and died in Tunis; and Frederick died ten years before he was due to accomplish his task as Messiah or Antichrist in the millennium year 1260.

Despair over human failure was expressed in various ways. The impatient, who hoped against hope for a sudden redemption of mankind, for the apocalyptic coming of the Third Age, turned to extremist movements of religious revival such as Joachism or the flagellant sects. The flagellants first appeared in Italy, where tension was most acute, since struggles between the Guelphs and the Ghibellines had added to the miseries of a population ravaged by famine in 1258 and plague in 1259. The flagellants appeared in November of the apocalyptic year of 1260, and their self-punishment represented a last-minute, desperate effort to wrest salvation for mankind from God. Even such a level-headed man as the Franciscan chronicler Salimbene was caught up in the atmosphere of anxious expectancy. Like many others, after losing all hope, he turned to see the world as it is, not as it might be, with a clear, albeit pessimistic, vision. Salimbene wrote: "After the death of the ex-Emperor Frederic, and the passing of the year 1260, then I let that whole doctrine [of Joachim] go; and I am purposed to believe no more than I can see."[96]

The stronger the urge to virtue, to salvation, the darker did man's greed and ambition appear in contrast. It is this expression of what is *seen,* not what is hoped for, which we find in the doleful works of moralists and satirists of the late thirteenth and early fourteenth centuries. Like La Bruyère in the seventeenth century, they saw virtue apparent everywhere, yet existing nowhere, always unauthentic. "Le monde comme il va" is the reign of *Ypocrisie,* is the triumphant ride of Renart, mounted on Fauvel, across a suffering world. "Renardie" is the opposite of "chevalerie," and the world appears upside-down, deception triumphs and virtue founders, and

96. *Chronica,* ed. Holder-Egger, pp. 302–03, trans. Coulton, in *From St. Francis to Dante,* p. 158.

Renart is not merely a fox with an appetite but a devouring beast who has swallowed up all the estates of man. Several traditions converge in the works of the moralists who wrote *Renart le Nouvel, Le Couronnement Renart, Renart le Contrefait, La Queue de Renart*,[97] and *Fauvel*. All use anti-Mendicant satire as developed in the University controversy; all use the more general notion of hypocrisy, incarnated in a ready-made animal figure as the image of deceit. Mendicancy, "renardie," and hypocrisy are henceforth one and the same. In the *Couronnement Renart* [98] (ca. 1251–88) the fox sets out to conquer the world in a half-Dominican, half-Franciscan habit and not only dethrones Noble but triumphantly tours both all of Europe and *outre-mer:* the local pest has become an international menace. In Jacquemars Giélée of Lille's *Renart le Nouvel* (1288) the fox puts on the "gris drap fait d'ypocrisie" (v. 7213) to conquer the last bastions of the clerical world— the Mendicant and Military orders—after winning over "de cest monde bien les .ii. pars/ Des laies gens et du clergié" (vv. 2936–37). The longest fox story, the encyclopedic *Renart le Contrefait*, was written between 1319 and 1342 by a defrocked cleric turned spice-merchant, who included passages both favorable and hostile to the Mendicants.[99] Such inconsistencies are best explained, I believe, if

97. A short estates piece of 24 eight-verse stanzas (Jubinal, ed., *Nouveau Recueil, 2,* 88–95). Contrast with the other late *Renart* works, all of which are extended satires.

98. Ed. Albert Foulet (Princeton and Paris, 1929); like *Renart le Bestourné*, the poem is a political warning to a prince (see FB, *1,* 536–37), and both use the theme of the "hôtel du roi," as does *Renart le Nouvel* of Jacquemars Giélée de Lille (ed. Henri Roussel [Paris, 1961] vv. 2943–54). For a comparison of common satirical themes, see Burchardt's *Beiträge zur Kenntniss der französische Gesellschaft in der zweiten Halfte des XIII. Jahrhunderts, auf Grund der Werke Rutebeufs, des "Roman de la Rose," des "Renart le Nouvel" und des "Couronnement Renart"* (Coburg, 1910); and G. Ward Fenley, "*Faus-Semblant, Fauvel* and *Renart le Contrefait:* A Study in Kinship," *Romanic Review, 23,* No. 4 (October–December 1932), 323–31. See also Flinn's chapters 6–8 on the *Couronnement Renart, Renart le Nouvel,* and *Renart le Contrefait (Le Roman de Renart,* pp. 201–441), and the review article about Flinn's book by André Giacchetti in *Romance Philology, 21,* No. 1 (August 1967), 124–29. However, the continuity of the animal myth reflects less a permanent "malaise de la conscience religieuse" than the basic conservatism of Old French literature.

99. The author has harsh words for the Mendicants at the beginning of his enormous (41,150 verses) poem; he calls them "coquins et demandeurs,/ sont

one realizes that the author is borrowing from a variety of satirical and didactic works and is evidently more interested in accumulating than in ordering his materials. Only the ubiquitous and changeable figure of Renart himself holds the loose narrative together, and the author, like the fox, is not overscrupulous about taking what he needs where he finds it.

Gerard du Bus named an animal figure representing something more than deceitful avidity: the horse Fauvel. The pale figure of the apocalyptic horse of Revelation 7:8 had already appeared in Rutebeuf's *Complainte de Guillaume:*

> Faus Samblant et Morte Color
> Emporte tout: a ci dolor
> Et grant contrere, (vv. 86–88)

and again in the *Roman de la Rose* as an image of *Faus Semblant's* companion, *Astenance Contrainte:*

> El resemblait, la pute lisse,
> Le cheval de l'Apocalisse,
> Qui senefie la gent male,
> D'ypocrisie teinte e pale. (vv. 12,067–70)

Fauvel represents not only hypocrisy but unbridled greed, human passion out of control,

> N'arestei par frain ne par bride,
> Il court par tout et point et ride,
> Par fortune va sans reson
> Et si regne en toute seson.[1] (vv. 295–98)

---

tous mensongniers et flateurs,/ Vont plourant, disant povres sont./ Mauvaises robes, mais souliers ont" (vv. 359–62). Yet in the prose universal history, inserted into the narrative, the author recounts the foundation of the Mendicants, saying: "Sanble que Dieu a la fin du monde ait esleü ces deux lumieres pour enluminer le monde par parolles et par exemples" (*1*, 287, par. 138).

1. *Fauvel*, p. 14. Theophilus' vertiginous fall from grace is cast in a similar image by Gautier de Coincy (vv. 621–702, *Miracles*, ed. Koenig, *1*, 88–93). Theophilus has lost the rein of reason which governs "Nostre cheval, nostre jument/ c'est nostre lasse de charoigne," (vv. 660–61). Thus we see him on "son cheval, col estendu . . . vers enfer droit eslaissiet" (vv. 652–53).

If the animal images of Renart and Fauvel finally replace the more human figure of *Dame Ypocrisie* in the moralists' representation of man, it is because men who have travestied virtue have given up their humanity. They have renounced reason, hope, and salvation, and chosen chaos, evil, and perdition. Bestial stupidity in these works becomes an anti-God which buries the world in darkness instead of light. Man seems, to these authors, to have destroyed the light of God within himself. Rutebeuf, in his *Renart le Bestourné,* desires the extinction of men who have become beasts; he wearily calls for the terrible Ounce, the apocalyptic pard,[2] to bring an end to the world's evils:

> Quar d'un proverbe me sovient
> Que l'en dit: tout pert qui tout tient.
>   C'est a bon droit.
> La chose gist sor tel endroit
> Que chascune beste vodroit
>   Que venist l'Once.
> Se Nobles çopoit a la roinsce,
> De mil n'est pas un qui en gronce:
>   C'est voirs sans faille.
> L'en senesche guerre et bataille:
> Il ne me chaut més que bien n'aille. (vv. 152–62)

The author of *Fauvel* pens a despairing portrait of man who has turned from God to Fauvel, expressing in a moment of intense lyricism the somber depths into which hypocrisy has plunged the world:

> Que Fauvel est du monde sire,
> Que il est par tout honorés
> Et com Dieu en terre aorés.
> Raison a perdu roiauté

2. From Revelation 13:2 and Jeremiah 5:6. See Ham's edition of *Renart le Bestourné,* pp. 28–30; FB, *1,* 544, note to v. 157; and Holbrook, *Dante and the Animal Kingdom,* pp. 88–102. Flinn (*Renart,* pp. 184–85, 308) inexplicably refuses to make any positive identification of the "Ounce," calling its meaning "obscure."

Quant nous voion bestïautei
Sus les hommes si haut assise.
Et resons est au dessous mise.
Einsi l'ordenance devine
Est du tout tornee a ruine:
Nous alon par nuit sans lanterne,
Quant bestïauté nous governe. (vv. 350–60)

POETIC SUCCESS OF THE POLEMICAL POEMS

Rutebeuf's poems on the University controversy are interesting for more than the lively sidelights they throw on a major intellectual controversy of the thirteenth century. One is faced with the question of whether they are good poems, since their primary function seems to be to convey a message, an attitude, or an idea. Where, as with the *Dit de Guillaume,* I believe the poem exists first as communication, the work seems to have been rhymed because such pieces were written in verse then. But when, as in *Du Pharisien,* the *Complainte de Guillaume, Renart le Bestourné,* or parts of *Des Règles, Des Jacobins,* and the others, the poet succeeds in creating living images such as haughty *dame Ypocrisie,* mourning *sainte Yglise,* and Rutebeuf himself in the *Dit d'Hypocrisie,* the poems go beyond the mere transmitting of information, and one is interested in how the poem works and not just what it has to say.

The encounter between poetry and history, which takes place in Rutebeuf's University poems, is perhaps the necessary first step toward our modern conception of poetry as an expression of an individual consciousness. Rutebeuf begins to move away from the closed world of medieval poetry, which seemed to shut out human time, and to move in a topological world of absolute aesthetic or moral experience. He sustains both a concern for formal structure and a desire to express historical human experience; his poetry is both more than mere talking and more than the pure aesthetic experience of the courtly poet. Rutebeuf's poems are filled with human significance; historical being and time mark every line. Yet he continues to work within the means given him by literary tradition because this was the fundamental poetical technique of all medieval poets, and so that he could thus communicate with an audience in comprehensible terms. He sets new political questions within previously established ethical and aesthetic categories or types, again so that what he says would be meaningful to his public.

There is no doubt that Rutebeuf handles expertly the various literary traditions and renews hackneyed themes, images, and rhetorical figures. He directs old forms toward new polemical ends with a sure and professional ease. The University polemic saved Rutebeuf from mere mediocre repetition of satirical and didactic commonplaces by forcing him to combine traditional material and contemporary events. If his *Voie de Paradis* is compared with his *Dit d'Hypocrisie* or his *Du Pharisien* the infusion of controversy seems to make the allegorical figures come alive. *Pitié* in the *Voie* is a pallid cipher compared to the potent and evil figure of Y*pocrisie*.

Some of these poems fail when the hand of intellectual history weighs more heavily than the lighter touch of poetry. It is not only that the close ties between Rutebeuf's poems and their historical circumstances may put off the modern reader, for whom a medieval quarrel between two ecclesiastical factions is a dead issue. Perhaps it is that we feel sometimes that no individual is revealed by the contact with history, but only a faceless group, a party, a faction, or merely a slogan. One can compare these University poems with the Crusade poetry, where the cult of the hero, the human involvement with life, death, and salvation, meant that men appeared clearly, alive although idealized. One cannot and does not seek the autobiographical or passionate self-revelation in the medieval poet, but neither can one accept the total sacrifice of the human to the ideological. The University poems succeed where the poetic image of man is clear; they fail when ideas replace images, when men are effaced by concepts.

CHAPTER FOUR: RHETORICAL PATTERNS IN RUTEBEUF'S POETIC TECHNIQUE

Mais sans mout boin' estude metre
Ne se doit nus om entremetre
De conter ne de fabloier;
Car mal puet sa paine emploier
Se il de tel cose ne traite
C'on die: 'Ceste oeuvre est bien faite.'
Merveilles de Rigomer

The essential elements of Rutebeuf's poetic technique have received much less attention than the historical background of his polemical works, as a glance at the Bibliography will reveal. William Matthews has observed that *genuinely* historical criticism of medieval literature requires "basic studies of medieval literary techniques, tastes, ideas, assumptions, conditions, [and] relationships."[1] Only a very few specific attempts of this sort have been made to come to grips with Rutebeuf's poetic technique and its literary context, partly because of insufficient investigation into literary modes of the thirteenth century, and partly because of an imposition of modern prejudices, tastes, and beliefs in poetic matters. Rutebeuf's art has been misunderstood, even maligned, by many of his editors and critics. Let us proceed, then, with the Schoolmaster Holofernes of *Love's Labour's Lost,* to "smelling out the odoriferous flowers of fancy, the jerks of invention" (IV, 2).

POETIC INDIVIDUALITY AND RHETORIC

We find, to begin with, a good deal of contradiction on the degree of "art," of polished literary technique, to be found in Rutebeuf's poetry. Dehm, taking Rutebeuf's puns on his own name literally, as in the following passage—

> Se Rustebués rudement rime
> Et se rudesce en sa rime a,
> Prenez garde qui la rima.
> Rustebuef, qui rudement oevre,
> Qui rudement fait la rude oevre,

1. Review of R. S. Loomis, *The Development of Arthurian Romance,* in *Speculum,* 39, No. 4 (October 1964), 719.

Qu'assez en sa rudece ment,
Rima la rime rudement . . .
Se Rustebués fet rime rude,
Je n'i part plus, més Rustebués
Est ausi rudes comme uns bués.[2]

—offers the opinion that since the life of the poet was marked by stress, his language was accordingly rough and crude.[3] Now everyone may not agree that a passage like the one above is good art, but it is hardly an uncouth grunt of pure passion. Even Faral's opinions are contradictory, since he says that Rutebeuf shows a "connaissance d'une technique établie bien avant lui" (FB, *1*, 40), yet later says of Rutebeuf's expression that "seulement en quelques rares passages, non sans intention possible de parodie . . . elle rejoint les conventions d'une certaine mode littéraire" (FB, *1*, 59). The wordplay which occurs throughout Rutebeuf's poetry—as puns, equivocal rhymes, or the special rhetorical technique called *annominatio*,[4] exemplified in the preceding quotation—is greeted with almost universal dismay,[5] particularly because the critics think it misplaced humor which undermines the dignity of Rutebeuf's serious poems.[6]

2. *Vie de Sainte Elysabel*, vv. 2156–62, 2166–68. See FB, *1*, 32–33, where five other examples of the same play are cited.

3. *Studien zu Rutebeuf*, p. 62.

4. *Annominatio* consists of repetitions of various forms of a word, words based on the same root, homonyms, or words which are identical except for a letter or two.

5. Faral speaks of "la recherche abusive du jeu de mots" (*Romania*, 70 [1948–49], 324; see also FB, *1*, 40, 59), Clédat speaks of "jeux de mots insipides et obscurs" (*Rutebeuf*, p. 48), which Pesce calls "insupportables" ("Le portrait de Rutebeuf," p. 106, n. 181) and Lucas "fades et puérils" (*Les Poésies personnelles*, p. 74), Legrand d'Aussy joins Dehm in qualifying Rutebeuf as "barbare dans son style" (*Fabliaux*, 2, 236). Albert Junker has made a serious attempt to describe Rutebeuf's use of the stylistic device in his "Über den Gebrauch des Stilmittels der Annominatio bei Rutebeuf," *Zeitschrift für romanische Philologie*, 69, Nos. 5–6 (1953), 323–46. See also Anne-Lise Cohen in her recent "Exploration of Sounds in Rutebeuf's Poetry," *French Review*, 40, No. 5 (April 1967), 658–67; I agree with many of her conclusions.

6. Faral objects to equivocal rhyme as being "contre le bon goût, car elle aboutit en fait au calembour" (FB, *1*, 212). Jubinal persists in seeing Rutebeuf as a sort of 13th-century Voltaire, whose wit is "dans le trait plutôt que dans la pensée. Il ne recule devant aucun jeu de mots, quelque mauvais qu'il soit," and terms annominatio "ce bizarre exercise, peu digne d'un homme de son talent et de sa

It would seem that all consign this aspect of Rutebeuf's poetic technique to that special ledger of Hell of which Raoul de Houdenc speaks in his *Songe d'Enfer*, where "les vies de fols ménestrels" are written up in rhyme "si bel, si bien, si léonime."[7]

In order to understand Rutebeuf's art, we must start by observing that medieval poetry can be broadly defined as technical—that is, that the poets themselves placed a high value on successful manipulation of certain canons or techniques. The joy inherent in poetry expressed so often in the first lines of many medieval poems is not separated from the desire to sing *well*, and good writing verified that the poet's subject was worthy of attention. Even the most severe of moralists, the Renclus de Moiliens, does not separate poetic pleasure from moral intent:

> Dire me plaist et bien doit plaire
> Che dont on prent bon essemplaire.
> Bien sai bons dis est bien plaisans
> A cuer volentiu de bien faire.[8]

Careless or inadequate technique would diminish the dignity of his subject; the moralist, moreover, must please in order to instruct. Craftsmanship finds justification on moral grounds, then, and on practical ones as well. "Biaus chanters trait argent de borce,"[9] and Rutebeuf, a professional who lived by his pen, did not neglect either the moral or the financial value of writing well, as he makes clear in the beginning of a commissioned work, *Le Sacristain et la femme au chevalier:*

valeur." Although Jubinal speaks of "les défauts d'une époque," he does not make any consistent effort to place Rutebeuf within the stylistic traditions of the 13th century ("Etudes nouvelles sur un vieux poète, Rutebeuf," *L'Investigateur*, 4e sér., 4 [May 1864], 155–56).

7. Ed. and trans. Lebesgue, p. 92.

8. *Li Romans de Carité, 1*, ed. A.-G. Van Hamel (Paris, 1885), vv. 1–4. Such phrases are often used as a *topos* in the exordium. See also Jacques de Vitry: "Bonne est la rhétorique qui apprend à parler élégamment et à persuader" (cited by A. Lecoy de la Marche, *Le Treizième Siècle littéraire et scientifique* [Bruges, 1894], pp. 49–50); and John of Garland, who said God did not forbid the use of literary art to glorify his name (*Morale scolarium*, ed. L. J. Paetow, *Two Medieval Satires*, p. 154).

9. Morawski, *Proverbes*, No. 240.

> Ce soit en la beneoite eure
> Que Beneoiz, qui Dieu aeure,
> Me fet fere beneoite oevre!
>
>   . . .
>
> Diex doinst que s'uevre espeneïsse
> En tel maniere que il face
> Chose dont il ait gré et grace!
> Cil qui bien fet bien doit avoir;
> Més cil qui n'a sens ne savoir
> Par qoi il puisse en bien ouvrer
> Si ne doit mie recouvrer
> A avoir garison ne rente. (vv. 1-3, 8-15)

An enormous distance, however, separates us from the medieval idea of what constituted a "biaus chanters." The intervening centuries have given us an entirely different conception of the poet and his art. Phrases like Hugo's "Jetons bas ce vieux plâtrage qui masque la façade de l'art! Il n'y a ni règles, ni modèles," are inconceivable in the Middle Ages. Yet because of such changes in our way of thinking about poetry, we can scarcely now conceive of poetry written within a tradition and not against it, within a tradition that deliberately excludes what Zumthor calls "préoccupations affectives" in favor of technique.[10] It would be a mistake, however, to separate form from content as Faral does,[11] for both are prescribed by literary tradition. Even when the poet chooses a subject from contemporary history, he and his audience understand it through the conventional modes of expression and thought, as we have seen in preceding chapters. The close connections between history and Rutebeuf's poetry, and the apparent, although illusory, relation between his life and his art have obscured the even closer connection

---

10. "Recherches sur les topiques dans la poésie lyrique des XIIe et XIIIe siècles," *Cahiers de Civilisation Médiévale,* Xe–XIIe series, 2, No. 4 (October–December 1959), 409. Zumthor also speaks of the "romantic mythology" of the artist working against or outside of tradition, in which "la variation individuelle apparaissait comme une différence absolue: d'où cet autre mythe, celui de la 'révolution littéraire' " (ibid).

11. FB, *1,* 219.

between the poet and a literary tradition which set him both theme and form. I shall explore further in this chapter what I have already shown in the last—that even contemporary history and politics are rendered in stylized terms taken from preexisting literary traditions. Models existed for treating the things of this world, as well as of the heart and of Heaven.[12]

Recent studies on courtly poetry[13] have clearly outlined the elements used in the courtly lyric, where the poet, working within a very limited, closed system, recombined poetic themes and techniques in various ways. The art of the courtly lyric was something of a poetic specialty, performed by certain poets for an elite and initiated public; it was a codified aesthetic experience occurring within extremely narrow limits. Although rhetorical in their form, the themes of courtly poetry sprang from sources quite unrelated to the traditions from which most of Rutebeuf's poetry derives. One may define his poetry, and the traditions from which it arises, as noncourtly, didactic, and largely nonlyric. Such poetry is much less rigidly limited than the courtly lyric, partly because the subject matter is much more extensive, partly because the vocabulary used is much larger, and partly because the same techniques and themes are used by prose writers and appear in Latin writings as well as in French.

Poetry based on convention is inevitably beset by inner tensions between theme and technique. When the forms are exaggerated, become what Curtius calls "manneristic," we worry that its communicative power may be lost. When we are primarily interested in what the poem is about, we are annoyed by interruptions of what seem like gratuitous poetic ornament. When the theme is derived from contemporary life, the conventional forms may seem ill-adapted to handle it, the conception too confining. Sometimes our uneasiness occurs because we do not understand what the poem is

12. See above, pp. 20–62, on estates, panegyric, and *voie* poems, as well as the chapters on polemical works.

13. In addition to Zumthor's articles on topics above, see also in the Bibliography his *Langue et techniques poétiques à l'époque romane* and the studies by Eugène Vinaver, Robert Guiette, and Roger Dragonetti.

really about, from the medieval point of view, so that, for example, the elegant anaphoristic figure on "Envie" in the *Sacristain* miracle (see below, p. 230) seems to keep us from getting on with the story, whereas it really serves as a moral and psychological explanation of the tale (see FB *1, 208*). We shall see that the medieval poet did not conceive of form as separate from meaning. When he used *ornament*—that is, certain very stylized figures of speech—he followed a pre-set patterned order of words, but the words retained their communicative power. A strict and conventional form was, for the medieval poet, a highly expressive poetic instrument.

To begin with, let us reconsider what constituted poetic individuality in the Middle Ages. It may seem puzzling that there was no search for novelty in theme. We have difficulty distinguishing the work of the individual poet where we find so many conventional forms written in "le style de l'époque," in Bezzola's phrase.[14] We do find admiration for the outstanding success of a predecessor and eagerness to follow in his footsteps. Huon de Meri pays a fine tribute to his masters Raoul de Houdenc and Chrétien de Troyes at the end of his *Tournoiement de l'Antechrist,* portraying them as harvesters of a rich crop of verses:

> Qu'onques bouche de crestien
> Ne dit si bien com il disoient.
> Mès quant qu'il distrent, il prenoient
> Le bel françois trestout à plain,
> Si com il lor venoit à main:
> Qu'après eux n'ont rien guerpi.
> Sé j'ai trové aucun espi
> Après la main as mestriers,
> Je l'ai glané molt volentiers.[15]

Poetic achievement is simply not identified with originality of theme or form, as we can see by the way poets borrowed each other's rhyme

14. See his discussion of poetic creation and individuality in *Le Sens de l'aventure et de l'amour* (Paris, 1947), pp. 82 ff.

15. Ed. P. Tarbé, p. 105.

schemes [16] or casually picked up a work where another had left off, as Jean de Meun added to Guillaume de Lorris.[17] As Brunetto Latini put it, "Matire est semblable a la cire, ki se laisse mener et apeticier et croistre a la volenté du mestre." [18] The poet did not invent his subjects any more than the sculptor the wax or clay for his models; his task was to excel in manipulating, in forming a *matière* which was given, but which was also infinitely malleable. It will become clear that the themes and figures of poetry were studied and learned, and that it was the inimitable touch of the poet, "la main as mestriers," which gave life and beauty to recombinations of inherited materials.

Poets could learn to handle different sorts of traditional materials in various ways. Those who recited fabliaux, mimes, and epics or sang songs probably relied largely on an oral education passed on within jongleur guilds or acquired at special jongleur schools, where they would go, or be sent by their patrons, to renew their repertory.[19] Poets writing within the courtly tradition would learn their

16. See Edw. Järnström, *Recueil de chansons pieuses du XIIIe siècle, 1,* Annales Academiae Scientiarum Fennicae, Ser. B., Vol. 3, No. 1 (Helsinki, 1910), 13–17.

17. Other examples are the *Roman de Fauvel* and the *Chanson de la Croisade albigeoise,* where the second author is an ardent "southerner" diametrically opposed in political opinion to Guillaume de Tudèle. Jehan de la Mote's protestation that he did not plagiarize the Renclus de Moiliens is *most* unusual (even he sounds surprised) and perhaps is a sign of a changing literary concept:

> Pechierres, autrement parlasse . . .
> Si je le Renclus ne doubtasse;
> Mais on diroit: 'Il sieut sa trasse;
> Sour li a prins son fondement.'
> Mais non ai, sachiés vraiement;
> Onques n'oÿ de ses vers cent,
> Mais dire ai oÿ qu'il tout passe
> Et parole si hautement
> C'on ne porroit mieus nullement,
> Tant eüst on temps ou espasse. (*La Voie d'Enfer et de Paradis* [ca. 1340], ed. Sister M. Aquiline Pety [Washington, D.C., 1940], vv. 1465–76).

18. *Trésor,* p. 330.

19. See Gautier, *Les Epopées, 2,* 174–77; and Faral, *Jongleurs,* p. 257 and n. 1. The schools were usually held during Lent when feasts were forbidden and the singers were out of work. *Puys* such as the one in Arras undoubtedly served as schools, as did Courts, where lords and poets alike practiced courtly genres.

techniques within the Courts themselves, as Adenet le Roi tells us, when he pays tribute to his late master, Henri III, Duke of Brabant.

> . . . Cil m'aleva et norri,
> Et me fist mon mestier aprendre;
> Diex l'en vueille guerredon rendre
> Avoec ses sains en Paradis! [20]

But what of the instruction of clerics who became poets in Latin or the vernacular, and of poets like Rutebeuf who did receive the regular students' education in Latin (FB, *1*, 37-42)? Without exception, every literate person, in court, city or monastery, would have been taught the basic elements of rhetoric since grammar, the fundamental subject, included learning the figures of speech and thought, like analogy, etymology, metonymy, allegory, and anaphora.[21] The student would then practice what he learned through explanation and imitation of model authors.[22] Invention, in all the textbooks of the time, is considered far less worthy, certainly more risky, than successful imitation. "Skill ruled by precept," orders Geoffroi de Vinsauf.[23] Rhetoric and poetry, of course, are not identical, but rhetoric did provide the prose writer, the preacher, and the poet with

20. Adenet le Roi, *Cléomadès*, 2, ed. André van Hasselt (Brussels, 1865–66), 290, vv. 18,580–83. Compare with the artistocratic Conon de Bethune's statement that he learned to write from Huon d'Oisy, the chatelain of Cambrai (*Chansons*, ed. A. Wallensköld [Paris, 1921], p. 9, vv. 49–52). See also FB, *1*, 37–42, on Rutebeuf.

21. See Auerbach (*Literary Language*, p. 264), Curtius (*European Literature*, pp. 42–54, 384, 469), and Baldwin (*Medieval Rhetoric*, pp. 195–96).

22. Faral, *Arts poétiques*, pp. 99–103. See also L. J. Paetow, "The Arts Course at Medieval Universities with Special Reference to Grammar and Rhetoric," *The University Studies*, 3, No. 7 (University of Illinois, January 1910).

23. This is the first of Geoffroi's three rules for writers: "Ars, cujus lege regaris;/ Usus, quem serves; meliores, quos imiteris" (*Poetria nova*, vv. 1705–06, ed. Faral, p. 249). Matthieu de Vendôme says that the student should memorize accepted formulas and not interpret in his own fashion that which has already a specific meaning to scholars (*Ars versificatoria*, *1*, 60, ed. Faral, *Arts poétiques*, p. 132). Similarly, Humbert de Romans advises that it is very difficult to invent useful new materials for sermons (*De eruditione praedicatorum*, p. 456), and Gottfried von Strassburg scoffs at his rival Wolfram von Eschenbach, whose words are not "well-laved" and who is incomprehensible because he is an inventor of wild tales and a hired hunter after stories (*Tristan und Isold*, ed. Friedrich Ranke [Berlin, 1930], vv. 4665–66).

the basic tools for writing. Rhetorical techniques can be both superficial and mechanical; but as they were taught, they became the
automatic elements of expression, as natural to the writer as picking
up his pen. The student who had mastered rhetoric was then expected to write poetry, and themes derived from traditional *topoi*
were set as school exercises.[24] The medieval author, then, did not
write with lists of figures and themes in hand; he did not need to,
for they had been ingrained in him with the very process of learning to write. His perception of his subject matter was oriented by
the forms of thought and expression which he had learned. Indeed,
the topics suitable for literature were learned at the same time as
the various ways of expressing them, and new material had to be
related to the traditional topics and forms in order to be expressed
at all.

If one compares Rutebeuf's technique with the descriptive and
prescriptive canons set down in the *Artes versificatoria* of the
twelfth and thirteenth centuries published by Faral, or those in
Brunetto Latini's *Trésor*,[25] one finds abundant evidence that Rutebeuf was schooled in rhetoric, and that this education serves to describe and explain many aspects of his art. The poetic arts say, for
example, that a poem may begin and end "naturally"—that is starting directly with the main subject and following a chronological
order of narration. A poem may also begin and end "artificially"—
that is, begin in the middle of a narrative story, or with a proverb,
exemplum, or general reflection, and end with a proverb or a
prayer.[26] Excluding the *Dit de l'herberie* and *Théopile* as dramatic
works and the *Vie du monde* and the *Neuf Joies* as of doubtful attribution, we find that Rutebeuf starts nine poems with a proverb,
fifteen with a general reflection, three with an example, one with a

---

24. Curtius cites samples of themes and rhetorical exercises set for students and
concludes, "merely from the rhetorical character of medieval poetry, it follows
that, in interpreting a poem, we must ask, not on what 'experience' it was based,
but what theme the poet set himself to treat" (*European Literature*, p. 158).
25. Ed. Francis J. Carmody, Bk. III, pp. 317–90.
26. Faral, *Arts poétiques*, pp. 55–59; Latini, *Trésor*, pp. 327–29, 335–44.

prayer, four with an evocation of nature, and twenty directly with the main subject matter. Better than half, then, have the more elegant "artificial" beginning, and those which start off with a direct entry into the subject matter often have a proverb or maxim placed near the beginning to indicate the importance or general theme of the poem. Five of Rutebeuf's poems end with a proverb, four with a general idea, sixteen with a prayer, and twenty-seven with the subject matter, but again, the theme is usually carried through in such a way as to raise the particular topic to a level of general interest.

Now I have shown that Rutebeuf's polemical verse is characterized by efforts to interpret specific themes as illustrative of general truths, and by the multiplication of as many images, metaphors, comparisons, allegories, examples, and stories as could be usefully brought to bear on his subject, to prove and explain such generalization. These characteristics correspond to the rhetorical concept of *amplificatio*. Amplification, or, as Latini puts it, "comment on puet acroistre son conte en .viii. manieres," means to the medieval rhetorician both the elevation of a subject to its moral dimension, and the variations on a theme through rhetorical ornamentation which develop it in length.[27] The more elevated the subject matter, the more elegant the style. Elegance, moreover, was obtained by the expression of the subject through figural ornament, deemed more important than overall unity of composition.[28]

The theoreticians broke the concept of amplification down into a series of eight procedures (with subdivisions), and it was these procedures which were taught in the schools. We have seen several il-

---

27. Curtius notes that the medieval rhetoricians did not make the classical distinction between *amplificatio*, the moral elevation of a subject, and *dilatio*, its expansion through ornamentation (*European Literature*, pp. 490–92; see Faral, *Arts poétiques*, pp. 61–62).

28. Vinaver observes that "le secret de l'élégance résidait non dans l'unification de la matière mais au contraire dans la multiplication de ses éléments" ("A la recherche d'une poétique médiévale," *Cahiers de Civilisation Médiévale*, 2, No. 1 [1959], 15). See Baldwin's interesting discussion of the subordination of rhetorical figures to the total sweep of composition in Dante and Chaucer (*Medieval Rhetoric*, pp. 280–91).

lustrations in Rutebeuf already, without always giving the technical names. *Interpretatio,* or "aornemens," was to say a single thing with varied words or tones, or to speak about it by means of facts, proofs, sentences, contraries, similarities, examples, or a conclusion; an example is the *interpretatio per litteras* of the *Dit des Cordeliers,* where the value of each letter of the name *Menor* is expounded (see p. 74). *Perifrasis,* or "tourn," appears in expressions of time such as "yver ne estei," meaning a moment's time.[29] Tjaden[30] distinguishes 94 similes and 266 metaphors, examples of *comparatio,* in Rutebeuf. *Apostrophe,* or "clamour," is one of the basic tools of Rutebeuf's polemical and exhortatory verse (see p. 53), as is *prosopopoeia,* or "fainture," the attribution of human qualities to dumb, inanimate objects or abstractions. All of Rutebeuf's talkative allegorical personifications (as well as his *Complainte de Guillaume*) are based on the latter figure. *Oppositio,* or "adoublement," is a development of a subject which proceeds by contrasting opposites, by affirming after negating, and Rutebeuf frequently so opposes descriptive adjectives. Thus he describes *Cortois,* "Qui ne cembloit mie bergier,/ Ainz fu cortois et debonaires,"[31] and *Humilitez,* "la cortoise,/ Qui n'est vilaine ne bufoise/ Més douce, debonere et franche."[32] *Descriptio,* or "demoustrance," was an important element of rhetoric whose essential function was expressly to distribute praise or blame;[33] thus description was very rarely objective, but rather in-

29. *Chanson de Pouille,* vv. 19–20. Rutebeuf uses little periphrase.
30. "Untersuchungen über die Poetik Rutebeufs" (Marburg, 1885). Tjaden's work is a catalogue of similes, metaphors, personifications, etc., divided according to subjects—e.g. clergy, knighthood—by elements of comparison in the animal, vegetable, and mineral kingdoms, and by material and spiritual concepts. His work provides useful cross-references of recurring images, but offers no commentary on how images work within the context of a poem, nor comparisons with contemporary poetry, both essential processes for evaluating Rutebeuf's art. The works of Jordan, Leendertz, Mojsisovics, and Schumacher (see Bibliography) are grammatical studies of Rutebeuf's language and are superseded by the Faral-Bastin edition.
31. *Dit d'Hypocrisie,* vv. 30–31.
32. *Voie de Paradis,* vv. 534–35. The figure can be extended, as in vv. 68–174 of Adam de la Halle's *Jeu de la feuillée,* ed. E. Langlois (Paris, 1951), where Adam contrasts the beauty of his fiancée with the ugliness of his wife.
33. Faral, *Arts poétiques,* p. 76.

tentional, as we have seen in Rutebeuf's descriptions of Crusade heroes, whose eulogies served the overseas cause, and in his attentive and hostile portrayal of the Mendicants. The black sheep of the rhetorical family was *digressio,* or "trespas," and authors often apologize for what they deem excessive departure from their subject, as does Rutebeuf, ending the fancy moral development of his prologue to *La Vie de sainte Elysabel* with the words:

> Por ce qu'a sermoner me grieve,
> Le Prologue briefment achieve,
> Que ma matire ne destruie:
> L'en dit que biau chanter anuie.
> Or m'estuet brief voie tenir,
> A mon propos m'estuet venir.[34] (vv. 191–96)

Any poetry can be described in terms of rhetorical figures. What distinguishes Rutebeuf, and medieval poets in general, is the deliberate adherence to rhetorical techniques and the *density* of ornament, as well as the exploitation of certain tropes in preference to others. The beginning of Rutebeuf's *Du Pharisien* serves both to introduce his theme and to induce in his hearers admiration and wonder for the poet's talent:

> Seignor qui Dieu devez amer
> En cui amor n'a point d'amer
> Qui Jonas garda en la mer
>   Par grant amour
> Les trois jors qu'il i fist demor,
> A vous toz faz je ma clamor
> D'Ypocrisie,

---

34. Similarly, the enumeration of the deeds of *Envie* in the *Voie de Paradis* (vv. 337–60) ends with the verse "ne sai que plus briefment vous die." The proverb "biau chanter anuie" is frequently attested (see FB, *1,* 107, note to v. 194, for references); the idea behind the proverb is that he who carries on verbosely without regard for time or place is *anious,* because he "ne set mesure garder" (variant in *Proverbe au vilain,* ed. Tobler [Leipzig, 1895], p. 166, No. 189), a perhaps welcome testimony that the medieval audience was not infinitely receptive to moralizing and rhetorically stylized verse.

Cousine germaine Heresie,
Qui bien a la terre saisie.
Tant est grant dame
Qu'ele en enfer metra mainte ame;
Maint hom a mis et mainte fame
En sa prison.
Moult l'aime on et moult la prise on;
Ne puet avoir los ne pris hom
S'il ne l'oneure:
Honorez est qu'a li demeure,
Grant honor a, ne garde l'eure;
Sanz honor est qui li cort seure
En brief termine. (vv. 1-20)

The poem begins "artificially"—that is, not directly with the allegorical description of *Ypocrisie,* its central theme, but with an exhortation to the poet's audience. The exhortation presents the moral of Rutebeuf's main subject matter: men should love God, for God's own love offers no bitter rewards, as do the favors of *Ypocrisie,* who sends her followers to eternal damnation. The theme is developed in the exemplum of Jonah which follows. God kept Jonah in his watery prison for three days, but "par grant amour," because he desired Jonah's good. Rutebeuf thus prepares the contrast with *Ypocrisie's* prison (v. 13), which is Hell; she desires to destroy men, not save them.

By the exhortation and the exemplum, Rutebeuf associates his own mission with that of Jonah. His "clamor" is to his own generation of evil men, and recalls Jonah's castigation of Nineveh.[35] The example is ornamented by a five-branch annominatio on the homophones and derivatives of *amer*—love, bitter, and sea." [36] The

35. The verb *clamare* appears 7 times in 58 verses of Job. The story was familiar to vernacular moralists; Hugues de Berzé uses it in vv. 553–619 of his *Bible* as an example of God's omnipotence. See FB, *1,* 250, who date the poem from this exemplum.
36. This was a frequent and traditional figure since the poet could play on the shift in meaning as well as the shift in sound. See *Complainte de Geoffroi de*

"or" sound is repeated in the rhymes of verses 5–6 (for a total of six repetitions in six verses). Then Rutebeuf begins the central description of his poem, the portrait of *Ypocrisie,* who is allegorically personified. The description starts with four interwoven figural developments (vv. 10–20) using annominatio on *ame* ("dame, ame, fame"), on *maint,* thrice repeated in masculine and feminine forms, on *moult,* twice repeated in verse 14, and on *honor,* where sounds are intricately echoed by the verbs ("oneure, honorez est, honor a, honor est"). The description and annominatio are united by the alliterative use of "m," which recurs twenty-two times in the twenty verses (nine times in verses 10–12). To guild the lily, there is an unusual triple equivocal rhyme—"prison, prise on, pris hom."

The poet does not keep up this fantastic rhetorical intensity throughout the poem, but turns, as we have seen, to his central figure. The verbal embroidery of the introductory verses attracts listeners, yet each word illuminated by annominatio is central to the theme: *Dame Ypocrisie's* followers have increased (*maint, moult*) to the extent that she em*pris*ons and dis*honor*s her enemies, and *honor*s her own, whose souls (*ames*) she betrays. The rhetorical flow dwindles to a trickle of rich rhymes, but ends with a final annominatio on *venir,* to predict the coming of the Antichrist:

> Celui qui vient,
> Que par tel gent venir covient;

Sergines (vv. 159–61), *Complainte du comte de Poitiers* (vv. 43–44). For examples outside of Rutebeuf's, see Faral, *Arts poétiques,* pp. 96–97; Gautier de Coinci, *Miracles* (ed. Koenig, *1,* 8). Gottfried von Strassburg, obviously familiar with the French rhetorical tradition, has Tristan reflect on the word "lameir," pronounced by Isolde after they have drunk the philter, and it is through annominatio that they reveal their love in a beautiful passage. "'*Lameir* is what distresses me,' answered Love's falcon, Isolde, 'it is *lameir* that so oppresses me, *lameir* it is that pains me so.' Hearing her say *lameir* so often [Tristan] weighed and examined the meaning of the word most narrowly. He then recalled that *l'ameir* meant 'Love,' *l'ameir* 'bitter,' *la meir* 'the sea': it seemed to have a host of meanings." Avoiding the word "Love," Tristan asked if the sea's tang was the cause of her pain, and finally got "to the bottom of the word and discovered 'Love' inside it. 'Faith, lovely woman,' he whispered, 'so it is with me, *lameir* and you are what distresses me'" (vv. 11,985–12,015, trans. A. T. Hatto, [Middlesex and Baltimore, 1960], pp. 199–200).

Quar il vendra, bien m'en sovient
Par ypocrites. (vv. 112–15)

In spite of the rhetorical elegance of many verses, poems like *Du Pharisien* do not have a polished look about them because of the loose overall structure. Although Rutebeuf wrote about as many poems with as without stanzaic divisions, nothing seems to limit the length of any given poem except the poet's matter and desire to continue. In contrast with the strict limits of volume of the thirteenth-century courtly *chanson*, limits imposed by tradition and by the close connection with a melodic structure and accentuated by the occasional use of refrains and *envois*, Rutebeuf freely multiplies the stanzas or lines of his *dits*. He emphasizes the length of each verse rather than that of the poem by the use of rich or equivocal rhyme and the 8-8-4 pattern of the *tercet coué* in poems like *Du Pharisien*. But although he ornaments and sets off the beginning and end of the poem by annominatio figures, we feel that the body of the poem could have been extended or reduced had the poet so wished.

The first and last of *Du Pharisien* passages remain, moreover, perfectly intelligible in spite of their rich rhetorical ornamentation. Rutebeuf's technique is quite transparent: the figures seem to melt into the meaning of the passage rather than form an opaque packaging. Again, the general impression given by *Du Pharisien,* although it continues with the long allegorical figure already described (above, pp. 140–43), is one not of great artificiality but rather of simplicity and directness. Yet this naturalness, as we shall see in Chapter 5, particularly in the case of Rutebeuf's poems of misfortune, is deceptively artful, and critics have misunderstood these works because they did not adequately recognize the technical elements in such poems.

Certainly such phrases from *Du Pharisien* as "Je qu'en diroie?" (v. 41) or "Or vous vueil dire de son estre" (v. 45) and the final "Or vous ai je tel gent descrites" have a kind of awkward naïveté to them which seems to confer a homespun authenticity incompatible with rhetorical polish. These phrases are, however, the commonest of fillers and are the clumsy mortar cementing together countless verses in Rutebeuf and his contemporaries.

WORDPLAY AND POETIC TOPOI

In this chapter I cannot hope to embrace all the poetic techniques of Rutebeuf, nor even perhaps give an entirely complete feeling for his work. For it is when Rutebeuf seems the most natural that he achieves the most flawless technical perfection; and it is when he seems rigidly rhetorical that he handles rhetoric the most clumsily. For the modern reader, however, the rhetorical side of Rutebeuf's poetic technique creates far greater difficulties than his apparent directness and naturalness. Rutebeuf's poetic style has been correctly described as lively, concrete, and natural (as by FB I, 58); yet many critics have been troubled by rhetorical elements, and particularly by wordplay (see, for example, FB I, 59), whose presence in a great many of Rutebeuf's poems has not yet been explained. It is this rhetorical side that demands sufficient study so that we may read all of any given poem by Rutebeuf with understanding, if not relish, and not dismiss large blocks of Rutebeuf's verse as "hodgepodge." [37]

I have attempted to strike deeply into one particular vein, which appeared unusually rich, and which enables us to better understand at least one very fundamentally misjudged aspect of Rutebeuf, his taste for wordplay. It is evident that the rhetorical figures he preferred are those creating sound patterns,[38] and that he designed his poetry to be heard, not seen. Although there was a considerable literate public by the middle of the thirteenth century, books were very expensive, and difficult to obtain except in university towns.[39]

37. R. Levy's review of Frank's edition of *Théophile, Romanic Review, 41* (April 1950), 131.

38. Auerbach notes that the inverted word order and complex periodic structure of the classical Latin rhetorical phrase were ill suited to French, while rhetorical figures based on sound effects were more easily transposed into French works (*Literary Language*, p. 205).

39. See Henri Pirenne, "L'Instruction des marchands au moyen âge," *Annales d'Histoire Economique et Sociale, 1,* No. 1 (January 15, 1929), 13–28; and Auerbach, *Literary Language*, pp. 280–92.

Literature was therefore generally designed to strike the ear rather than the eye, whether the text was recited by a jongleur in the street or tavern, read to a small courtly circle by a poet, or dictated by a professor to his students.[40] In the following pages I shall attempt to follow one such acoustic figure, annominatio, through the highroads and byways of Latin and vernacular literature. I have chosen annominatio because it is a figure particularly favored by Rutebeuf, who uses it in every sort of poem he wrote, and also because it is a figure characteristic of poetry from the moral-didactic tradition and one which appears both in Latin and vernacular writings. It is a highly stylized figure, whose use reveals general "laws" governing the choice of poetic ornaments for particular genres which apply to all of thirteenth-century French poetry, and which illustrates the relations between author and tradition.

Albert Junker's study of Rutebeuf's use of annominatio provides some useful statistics, but because he limits it almost exclusively to Rutebeuf, his conclusions are in part inaccurate. He first excessively narrows his definition of annominatio by excluding annominatio occurring only on rhymes or obtained through verb inflections.[41]

---

40. Auerbach, *Literary Language*, pp. 204, 291. Poirion shows that "les cours princières, grâce à leurs manuscrits, ont pu . . . connaître avant la fin du Moyen Age ce que le grand public n'obtiendra qu'avec le diffusion des œuvres imprimées: le plaisir de la lecture" (*Le Poète et le prince*, p. 170). See also Faral, *Arts poétiques*, p. 101.

41. "Annominatio," pp. 324–25. We must distinguish between annominatio and equivocal rhymes, which usually extend only through one couplet, although whole works, like Baudouin de Condé's *Dis des trois mors et des trois vifs* (No. XVII, pp. 197 ff.) may use nothing but equivocal couplets. (See partial list of equivocal rhymes in Rutebeuf, in FB, *1*, 212–13, n. 1.) We find an excellent example, however, of annominatio on rhyme words in Rutebeuf's *Disputaison du croisé et du décroisé*, where he uses only verb inflections of the third person singular and plural on words that vary only by a letter or syllable:

> Li mauvais desa *demorront*,
> Que ja nuns boens n'i *demorra;*
> Com vaches en lor liz *morront:*
> Buer iert neiz qui delai *morra.*
> Jamais recovreir ne *porront,*
> Fasse chacuns mieux qu'il *porrat;*
> Lor peresce en la fin *plorront*
> Et, s'il muerent, nuns nes *plorra.* (vv. 209–16)

Even so, the sheer quantity of annominatio in Rutebeuf is enormous; Junker finds 439 examples occurring in 2,360 of the 12,654 total verses of Rutebeuf's poetry, with up to 18 words entering into a single figure.[42] Unfortunately, Junker wrote before the complete edition of Rutebeuf by Edmond Faral and Julia Bastin had appeared with a more accurate dating of the poems than Jubinal gave. Otherwise, he would not have mistakenly asserted that Rutebeuf used annominatio more frequently as he became a more experienced poet. Not only is this a technique learned in school, as part of the rhetorical training,[43] but also Rutebeuf's earliest known poem, the *Dit des Cordeliers,* is riddled with examples.[44]

Junker finds annominatio most frequently used in panegyric poems, fabliaux (in which he includes the *Sacristain* miracle), and saints' lives, and less often in "personal" poetry, satirical and Crusade works, lyric prayers, and *Théophile.*[45] Both these statistics and Junker's conclusions are misleading and even contradictory. First, where the figures occur is as important as how often they occur, as we have seen in *Du Pharisien,* which limits annominatio mostly to the beginning and end of the poem, but uses it densely there. Next, Junker explains his statistics by saying that annominatio appears in those poems in which Rutebeuf felt distant from his subject, and decreases with his personal involvement, in those poems where he expresses "powerful personal feelings";[46] yet when Junker clas-

---

Compare with Nigel Longchamp's dedicatory verses to Honorius, prior of Canterbury, where the rhymes are on different cases of *Nigellus* and *libellus* (cited in Raby, *Secular Latin Poetry,* 2, 99). Annominatio may be distinguished from insistent iteration in that the latter repeats the word without changing either form or meaning, as in "Boens fu au boens confors" (*Complainte du comte de Poitiers,* v. 95), and both from anaphora, in which the same word or phrase is repeated in the same position in the verse or phrase (see vv. 6–10 of his *Des Béguines*), and from alliteration, in which only a letter or syllable is repeated as "Pou prise paradix quant a ce ne se prent" (*Dit de Pouille,* v. 44) or "Piez poudreus et penssee vole" (*Sainte Elysabel,* v. 437).

42. "Annominatio," pp. 324–25.
43. See Faral, *Arts poétiques,* pp. 93–97.
44. Annominatio figures appear on the words *corde, tort, fie, mort, droit, cloche, voie, navre, mire, soi* in the *Dit des Cordeliers.*
45. "Annominatio," p. 326.
46. Ibid., p. 331.

sifies the key words subject to annominatio, he states that they are chosen for their strong affective value for the poet.[47] The true explanation of Rutebeuf's use of annominatio as well as his choice of words lies not within the poet's fiery heart but in his fidelity to well-established literary traditions.

Poets and rhetoricians considered figurative ornaments to be appropriate in and even to create an elevated style, while their absence marked the low style. Such as the rather mechanical understanding of the classical conception of style which we find in the medieval poetic arts.[48] The level of style is mainly related not to the public for whom an author was writing, as Rychner suggested,[49] but to his subject matter; the high style was reserved for writing about people of high social rank or elevated by saintliness, while the common man and comic subjects were to be written about without artifice of rhetoric. Geoffroi de Vinsauf's explicit prescriptions are fairly consistently followed in French as well as in Latin:

> Attamen est quandoque color vitiare colores,
> Exceptis quos sermo capit vulgaris et usus
> Offert communis. Res comica namque recusat
> Arte laboratos sermones: sola requirit
> Plana; quod explanat paucis res ista jocosa
>
>   •   •   •
>
> . . . Sibi consonant undique totum
> Si levis est animus, et res levis, et leve verbum.
> Seria si tractes, sermo sit serius et mens
> Seria, maturus animus maturaque verba,
> Praescriptisque modis et res et verba colora.[50]

47. Ibid., pp. 343–45.

48. Faral, *Arts poétiques*, pp. 86–90.

49. Review of Nykrog's *Fabliaux*, in *Romance Philology*, *12*, No. 3 (February 1959), 337, following Bédier, *Fabliaux*, pp. 371–85. See Nykrog, *Fabliaux*, p. 235 and passim for a revealing survey of the public of courtly works and fabliaux.

50. *Poetria nova*, vv. 1183–87, 1915–19, in Faral, *Arts poétiques*, pp. 255–56. See Nykrog's interesting discussion in *Fabliaux*, pp. 142–44 and 230 ff. Auerbach's article, "Sermo humilis" (in *Literary Language*, pp. 25–66) discusses the altered relation of subject and stylistic level in Christian writings where the humble was incorporated into the sublime.

According to the strictest medieval canons, wordplay such as annominatio belongs to the elevated style, and is a fault not in serious
writing but in comic pieces. It may be, as Bernadine Bujila observes of an annominatio figure on Maria in her edition of the *Vie
de Sainte Marie l'Egyptienne*,[51] that "judged by modern standards,
this display of wit indicates a complete disregard of the respect due
the subject matter and is in singularly bad taste." Yet not only
medieval but even Renaissance poets found wordplay a worthy
ornament to the most serious poems. The *Rhétoriqueurs,* who carried wordplay to extremes that appalled their modern historian,
Henri Guy, did not hesitate to use the most complex annominatio
in sublimely gloomy pieces such as Molinet's funeral lament for
Marie de Bourgogne:

> La fine mort qui tous vivans amasse,
> Thomas et Masse, et Massette et Massin,
> Et tient tout matz ceulx qu'elle contumasse,
> A mis en masse ung fruit dont mieulx j'aymasse
> Que je tumbasse, en musant, du coffin.
> Par son brachin, sa brache et son brach fin,
> A mis a fin la duchesse Marie . . .[52]

Ronsard did not disdain annominatio for the "vers héroïques" of
the prelude to his *Hymne de l'or,* dedicated to his Hellenist master
Jean Dorat:

> Je ferais un grant tort à mes vers et à moi
> Si, en parlant de l'Or, je ne parlais de toi
> Qui as le nom doré, mon Dorat: car cet hymne
> De qui les vers sont d'Or, d'un autre homme n'est digne
> Que de toi, dont le nom, la muse et le parler
> Semblent l'or, que ton fleuve Orence fait couler. (vv. 1–6)

51. P. 88.
52. Henry Guy, *Histoire de la poésie française au XVIe siècle,* Vol. 1: L'Ecole
des rhétoriqueurs (Paris, 1910), p. 93. Guy gives many such examples in his chapter 4, "Les Complications et les jeux rythmiques," pp. 82–101.

Annominatio is both a figure bearing meaning in itself and a highly decorative element which is apt to appear as a formal orna- ment in "presentation" pieces such as the panegyric to Anceau de l'Isle, the *Sacristain* miracle, commissioned by a certain Benoit, or Rutebeuf's *Vie de Sainte Elysabel,* commissioned by Erart de Lézinnes for Queen Isabelle of Navarre (FB 2, 60). The subject of *Sainte Elysabel* is elevated, being a somewhat abridged translation of a Latin *vita* written for the canonization proceedings of Saint Elizabeth of Hungary in 1235. Just as the illuminator adorned the *lettrine,* or capital letter beginning a passage, Rutebeuf designed ornamental moralizing passages to serve as his introduction to the prologue and each of the four parts of Elizabeth's life.[53] He passes from Prologue to *Vie* with wordplay; he adds a rhetorical pause for moral reflection before narrating Elizabeth's death, and a final epilogue on *Rutebeuf* by way of signature and prayer (vv. 2155– 68).[54] These ornamental passages serve as an elegant frame to Elizabeth's story, which is told in a straightforward, natural way. In much the same way, the Marburg reliquary of Saint Elizabeth places simplified repoussé figures within an elaborate, bejeweled setting, ornately executed in complex, intertwining, decorative forms.

53. The comparison with the *lettrine* is still more revealing in that the 13th-century ornaments are "hiératique," in the words of Lecoy de la Marche; that is, their representations are conventional and symbolic in character. Only in the later Middle Ages does the art of miniatures—like medieval art in general—become more naturalistic to appeal to those who were not tutored in the "langue énigmatique des clercs." The first signs of secularization and naturalism appear, according to Lecoy de la Marche, toward the end of Louis IX's reign (*Les Manuscrits et la miniature* [Paris, 1884], pp. 122–25).

54. At one point Rutebeuf glosses over a linguistic incapacity with annominatio. Confronted with the difficulty of translating a list of names of German notables assembled to hear testimony for Elizabeth's canonization, he gives up and says:

> Enquistrent bien icil preudomme
> Dont je les nons pas ne vous nomme
> Et neporquant isnelemant
> Se il ne fussent Alemant
> Les nommaisse, més ce seroit
> Tens perduz, qui les nommeroit.
> Plus tost les nommaisse et ainçois
> Se ce fust langages françois. (vv. 77–84)

Faral describes these ornamental passages as abusively and inter-minably jingly, adding further that their themes are "des lieux communs, sans référence aux particularités qui donnent à l'exemple d'Élisabeth son caractère original" (FB 2, 65). The task of the poet-moralist, however, was not to lose himself in the particularities of one life, but to draw from it the universal lesson. It is the typical, the absolute, which serves as a model to mankind, not the individual and peculiar. Rutebeuf's additions, therefore, are not gratuitous but ornamental indicators of the exemplary value of Elizabeth's life.

The first annominatio figure on *voie*,[55] for example, demonstrates that in the story each will see ("voie") that there is but one way ("voie") to Heaven, that followed by Elizabeth. The annominatio on *cors* and *mort* (vv. 201–07) continues the "sermon" theme that Elizabeth worked miracles after her death because she was in-different to the flesh. The first part of the *Vie,* recounting Eliza-beth's infant piety, starts out with generalizations on belief in God, expressed in annominatio on *croire* (vv. 235–44). The next three parts, describing Elizabeth's good works, her service to God, and her mortification of the flesh, move the poet to amplify through annominatio the key words: *cuer* (vv. 451–57), *servir* (vv. 461–70), *oevre* (vv. 1013–30), and *char* (vv. 1083–96). The importance of the recompense God reserves for those who live such a virtuous life is accentuated in rhetorical developments on *moisson* and *faucille* (vv. 922–33), recalling the parable of the sower, so dear to preachers.[56] Elizabeth's departure from this earth is appropriately illuminated by annominatio on *passe* and *lesse,* as the poem ends with a mixture of *fin* celebrating the end, while admiring the fine heart of the lady and God's in*fin*ite reign (vv. 2179–86).

Rutebeuf's prologue to Part IV is a good illustration of how orna-ment and instruction go hand in hand:

> Esperance d'avoir pardon
> Ou par penitance ou par don

55. Verses 127–42 repeat some form of or word containing *voie* eight times.
56. See below, p. 228.

Fet endurer mainte mesaise
Li endurers fet moult grant aise,
Quar moult legierement endure
Qui eschive paine plus dure.
Ceste dame, qui pou dura,
Penitance dure endura
Por avoir vie pardurable
Avoec le Pere esperitable. (vv. 1393–1402)

Rhetorical amplification here achieves heights of condensation and intensity, illustrating linguistically the close, the necessary relationship between Elizabeth's earthly penitence and her heavenly reward through the variations on *dure:* "endure, difficult, last, everlasting." The passage flows smoothly thanks to the alliterations of p (13 repetitions) and d (12 repetitions). Language is taxed to its extreme limits here, but far from breaking down into meaningless gibberish, each word is packed with as many associations as it can carry, each concept closely tied to its logical consequence through verbal mating. The passage is, of course, extremely solemn in intent and subject; as Gilson said of medieval wordplay in moralizing etymologies, "Ce ne sont des jeux de mots que pour nous; pour eux rien n'est plus sérieux." [57] The process at work here is a deepening of the communicative value of language and an intensified awareness of the necessary relations between cause and effect, expressed verbally. As we shall see below, similarity of words is, to the medieval poet and to the medieval thinker, not happenstance but a sign of a secret relation between ideas. The poet reveals and explores that relation when he joins words together.

It is therefore an error to identify annominatio with *fatrasie* or nonsense as does Zumthor.[58] At its most contrived, Rutebeuf's annominatio is never meaningless. At worst, as in the lament for

---

57. *Les Idées et les lettres*, p. 129, n. 1.
58. Zumthor cites the stanzas of Théophile's repentance as an example of *fatrasie* (*Langue et techniques poétiques*, p. 163); see also Victor le Clerc in *Histoire littéraire*, 23, 508–09.

Anceau de l'Isle, it serves as a rather superficial filler,[59] where the conjuncture of words reveals little of importance, as in the verses:

> Avoec les sainz soit mise *en sele*
> L'ame de mon seignor *Ansel,*
> Car Diex qui ses amis *ensele*
> L'a trové et fin et feel. (vv. 17–20)

The development on *Fortune* of the same poem has a similar triteness, where the student's, not the artist's, hand can be detected. Only the final evocation of a hunt, the favorite pastime of Anceau, bears a trace of life and a breath of the open country:

> Qui remire la bele chace
> Que fere soliiez jadis,
> Les vos brachés entrer en trace,
> Ça cinq, ça set, ça neuf, ça dis. . . . (vv. 49–52)

At its best, annominatio serves to weave a tight web of moral reasoning, as in the verses from *Sainte Elysabel,* or of symbolic relations, as in the annominatio figure on *corde* and *tord* in the *Dit des Cordeliers.*

> [E]n la corde s'entordent cordee a trois cordons;
> A l'acorde s'acordent dont nos descordé sons;
> La descordance acordent des max que recordons;
> En lor lit se detordent por ce que nos tortons. (vv. 16–20)

The Franciscan's triple-knotted cord sash leads Rutebeuf to the idea of the work of concord, of accord between God and man, of man's discordant evil in the world's harmony, and finally to the torturous sufferings the friars endure to redeem man's turning from the path of right. Faral sees in this sort of association by consonance a poetic gimmick, where the appearance of one word sets off a train of similar words (FB *1,* 215). It is true that the appearance of a

---

59. See Junker, "Annominatio," p. 333.

key word—that is, one often subjected to annominatio—will often lead the poet to write a passage of wordplay. But the passages are not without meaning in themselves, and the key word is also a key to the theme of that part of the poem where it appears. *Corde* is entirely relevant to a poem on Cordeliers, whose name reveals their nature and task of redeeming mankind from sin (see above, p. 74). But when, as in the *Complainte du roi de Navarre,* the words "recorde" and "descorde" appear as rhymes (vv. 103–04) but there is no appropriate theme of concord or discord to introduce, the annominatio does not appear. There is, then, a relation between the figure and the theme of the poem.

Annominatio on *corde* appears four more time in Rutebeuf. In *Des Jacobins* (vv. 13–16) the poet contrasts his recollection ("recorder") of the Friars' quarrelsome behavior ("descort") with their fine speeches about accord. Both this theme and the symbolic value of the cord belt are recalled in the stanza on Franciscans in *Les Ordres de Paris* (vv. 61–72), as well as the theme of Mary as "Dame de Misericorde," which appears again in the *Voie de Paradis* (vv. 557–64) and the *Dit de Nostre Dame* (vv. 119–30). The wordplay here turns on Mary's role as the merciful intercessor between God and man, reestablishing harmony in a world cast into discord by Adam and Eve. The *corde* figure is, then, a fitting end to the *Dit de Nostre Dame,* since the poem is a prosopopoeia by Mary, who pleads with Christ to let his lost sheep into Heaven. In the *Voie* Mary lays the foundation of concord for *Humilitez's* house. The passages are far from identical, since the poet reworks his word combinations to the best advantage of his theme. The repetition of a patterned association of words is consequently Rutebeuf's reaffirmation of the truth of basic relationships among men and between men and God, as well as between sign and symbol.

The roots of annominatio lie in literary and theological tradition, for we discover the same figure on *corde* connected with Mary in other authors. In Huon de Meri's *Tournoiement de l'Antechrist* there is but one long example of annominatio, and that one an explanation of the symbolic value of the cord to the bow carried by the "Roi du firmament" into battle against the Antichrist. He appears, majestic, carrying

> . . . l'arc du firmament,
> Qu'encorda d'une doce corde
> La Dame de miséricorde.
> Bon est li arc, qui tel corde a:
> Car la Dame qui l'encorda
> N'eut qu'à son fil nus acordons;
> Que d'une corde à .iii. cordons. . . .[60]

Corde appears a total of 24 times in 19 verses, ending with a reference to "li Amustant de Cordes," the Emir of Cordoba! Obviously the same words and ideas are associated as in Rutebeuf, and annominatio appears here at the holiest moment, when the forces of evil join battle with the forces of good, whose strength is derived from the symbolic value of that very cord. Gautier de Coinci, who opens his miracle narrative *Comment Theophilus vint a penitance* with an annominatio on *port* to express his joy ("deport") in honoring the Virgin, "qui dou ciel est pons et porte" (v. 12), ends with an annominatio on *corde* (vv. 2077–92) to celebrate the Virgin's reestablishment of harmony between Theophilus and God.[61] Watriquet's early fourteenth-century *Confession* ends with a plea for mercy to Christ and the Virgin and 27 annominatio rhymes on *cors/corde*.[62] An anonymous prayer to the Virgin, on the same repentance theme, uses annominatio on *corde* in 7 of its monorhyme alexandrine quatrains.[63]

We have consistently found the themes and images of Rutebeuf's

60. P. 39.
61. Gautier ends each of his miracles with 8–12 lines of moralizing annominatio.
62. *Dits*, pp. 115–16, No. IX.
63. The so-called *Prière Théophilus* (A. Scheler, ed., *Zeitschrift für romanische Philologie*, *1* [1877], 253), written in monorhymed alexandrine quatrains, and in which Mary is invoked as intercessor, has annominatio on *corde* in sts. 60–62 and again on the rhymes of sts. 95–98. See also Tobler, *Vermischte Beiträge*, 2, 252, who cites an example from Deguilleville's *Pélérinage de la vie humaine;* all of this article, by Tobler, "Verblumter Ausdruck und wortspiel in altfranzösischer Rede," is of interest for these traditional techniques of wordplay.

didactic, satirical, and polemical poetry to be related to those of similar Latin literature. And the Latin influence continues even to the choice of rhetorical figures like annominatio. Two excellent studies of Latin hymnody [64] reveal one source of Rutebeuf's usage of annominatio—that is, as verbal wit to reveal meaningful relationships between ideas or events. Walter Ong studies first the hymns of Adam of Saint Victor (fl. ca. 1140), then those of Saint Thomas Aquinas, to show that wit and linguistic conceits are "a normal means of dealing with the mysteries of Christianity" [65] in these authors. They exploit "semantic coincidence" to penetrate "to startling relations in the real order of things." [66] Both Adam and Thomas use wordplay to express the ineffable Christian paradoxes. Adam apposes terms to encompass the concept of Christ's life-bringing death:

> O mors Christi vivifica
> Tu Christo nos unifica;
> Mors morti non obnoxia,
> Do nobis vita premia.[67]

Thomas Aquinas, commissioned to write the office for the newly established Corpus Christi festival (1264), composed his majestic Vespers hymn "Pange, lingua, gloriosi" to express through metaphor and wordplay the mysterious tension inherent in the "unreasonable" concepts of transsubstantiation and incarnation:

> Verbum caro panem verum
> verbo carnem efficit,

64. Ong, "Wit and Mystery," *Speculum*, 22, No. 3 (July 1947), 310–41; and Erich Auerbach, "Dante's Prayer to the Virgin (*Paradiso*, XXXIII) and Earlier Eulogies," *Romance Philology*, 3, No. 1 (August 1949), 1–26.
65. "Wit and Mystery," 323.
66. Ibid., p. 315.
67. Cited by Ong (ibid., p. 313) from *Thesauri hymnologici prosarium*, Pt. II, *1*, ed. C. Blume and H. M. Bannister, 221. On Adam see also F. J. E. Raby, *A History of Christian-Latin Poetry from the Beginnings to the Close of the Middle Ages* (2d ed. Oxford, 1953), pp. 348–63. Compare with the complexities of thought and word in the first chapter of the Gospel of John, with its repetitions of *verbum, lux, tenebrae*.

fitque sanguis Christi merum
et, si sensus deficit,
ad firmandum cor sincerum
sola fides sufficit.[68]

Art and thought are here totally united to reveal the deepest
Christian mysteries in sublime language.

The Latin hymns frequently combine wordplay with metaphors
from the allegorical or typological interpretation of the Old Testament.[69] Indeed, any metaphor is fundamentally the perception of
significant likeness between two objects, just as puns or wordplay
are the revelation of similarities between words or of the different
meanings of one word. The taste for wordplay and metaphor in
the Latin hymns goes far beyond literary technique, to encompass
the whole significance of Christian history. If the metaphors derive
largely from the figural interpretation of the Old Testament, it is
because the theologians no less than the poets felt themselves to be
part of a historical continuity which had started in Old Testament
times. The meaning of the Old Testament had become clear with
Christ's birth, and it was this meaning which they were charged to
reveal. In like manner, their imperfect understanding of the meaning of the New Testament could only be expressed through the complexities of language and wordplay. Their language was an imperfect, therefore complex, expression of the whole single truth of God,
which was not yet revealed to man. Thus Saint Thomas Aquinas
explained the need for sensible images, comparisons, and metaphors,
which are the stuff of poetry and of comprehension of the divine: [70]

68. Cited by Ong, p. 316, from *Hymnographi latini*, 2, ed. G. M. Dreves, Analecta Hymnica Medii Aevi, No. 50 (Leipzig, 1907), 586. Raby discusses the
close relation between Thomas Aquinas' hymns and the scholastic terminology and
doctrinal exposition of dogma in his *Summa theologica* (*Christian-Latin Poetry*,
pp. 402–11).

69. See Auerbach ("Dante's Prayer," pp. 10–11), Raby (*Christian-Latin Poetry*,
pp. 348–75), Baldwin ("Symbolism," *Medieval Rhetoric*, pp. 203–05), and the
bibliography of Tauno F. Mustanoja's edition of *Les Neuf Joies Nostre Dame: A
Poem Attributed to Rutebeuf*, Annales Academiae Scientiarum Fennicae, Ser. B,
LXXIII, No. 4 (Helsinki, 1952, p. 60), for studies on the variety of medieval symbolic and figural themes applying to Virgin.

70. Aquinas distinguished poetry and theology by saying that "the science of

"The mystical sense is engaged with the things signified by the things signified by the words." [71] We feel a yearning for the simplicity of God which appears throughout the intellectual complexities of Aquinas' work:

Though God is wholly simple we must still address him with a multitude of names. Our mind is not able to grasp his essence. We have to start from the things about us, which have diverse perfections though their root and origin in God is one. Because we cannot name objects except in the way we understand them, for words are the signs of concepts, we can name God only from the terms employed elsewhere. . . . Were we to see God in himself we would not call on a multitude of words; our knowledge would be as simple as his nature is simple. We look forward to this in the day of our glory; that in that day there shall be one Lord and his name one. [72]

Adam of Saint Victor calls, therefore, on the *Song of Solomon* for Old Testament prefigurations of the Virgin. The annominatio he uses, the repetitions and progression of words, is like the reappearance of figures in Christianity; Adam is reborn and renewed in Christ; the sensuous beauty of the Shulammite maiden appears again in the Virgin, but purified to a superlative essence, as in the following sequence:

Fontis vitae tu cisterna
Ardens lucens es lucerna;

poetry is about things which because of their deficiency of truth cannot be laid hold of by reason. Hence the reason has to be drawn off to the side by means of certain comparisons. But then, theology is about things which lie beyond reason. Thus the symbolic method is common to both sciences, since neither is, of itself, accommodated to [the human reason]" (from *In sententias Petri Lombardi commentaria,* cited by Ong, "Wit and Mystery," 324). Yet for man the extreme limits of his knowledge seem joined at the point where he ceases to comprehend rationally: "Because philosophy arises from awe a philosopher is bound in his way to be a lover of myths and poetic fables. Poets and philosophers are alike in being big with wonder" (*Commentary,* I *Metaphysics, Lect.* 3, in *Thomas Aquinas, Philosophical Texts,* selected and translated by Thomas Gilby [New York, 1960], pp. 26–27).

71. *Philosophical Texts,* p. 28 (from *Commentary, Galatians,* iv, *lect.* 7).

72. Ibid., pp. 72–73 (from Opusc. XIII, *Compendium theologiae,* 24).

> Per te nobis lux superna
> Suum fudit radium;
> Ardens igne caritatis
> Luce lucens castitatis
> Lucem summae claritatis
> Mundo gignens filium.[73]

The themes and metaphors of the Latin hymns, particularly those dedicated to Mary, were not only stylized but consecrated by theological tradition, and appear virtually unaltered in the vernacular. The characteristic litany structure, which Auerbach studies and which originates in the beautiful enumerations of the *Song of Songs*, reappears again in Rutebeuf's *Ave Maria:*

> Tu es li lis ou Diex repose;
> Tu es rosiers qui porte rose
> Blanche et vermeille.[74] (vv. 115–17)

It is in imitation of the Latin hymns also that Rutebeuf uses wordplay to honor the Virgin, as in the annominatio on *garir* and *chanter* from his song *C'est de Notre Dame:*

73. Auerbach, "Dante's Prayer," p. 15, cited from *The Liturgical Poetry of Adam of St. Victor, 2,* ed. Digby S. Wrangham (London, 1881), 164. Both Auerbach and Ong contrast this figurative and dogmatic style with the emotional directness and lyric affective appeal of the Franciscan hymns such as Thomas Celano's *Dies irae* and Jacopone da Todi's "Stabat mater dolorosa." See Raby, "The Franciscan Poets," *Christian-Latin Poetry,* pp. 415–52.

74. See Raby, *Christian-Latin Poetry,* pp. 365–66; and Auerbach, "Dante's Prayer," pp. 1–10. Compare the Franciscan *Te Deum* verses: "Virgo, virgo, virgo virginum sine exemplo,/ ante partum et in partu et post partum" (cited by Raby, *Christian-Latin Poetry,* p. 375) with Rutebeuf's

> La Vierge Marie:
> Vierge fu norrie,
> Vierge Dieu porta,
> Vierge l'aleta,
> Vierge fu sa vie. (*C'est de Notre Dame,* vv. 41–45)

and the pious song from Järnström's *Chansons pieuses, 1,* 40, No. X:

> Virge porta son enfançon,
> Virge le tint en son geron,
>   . . .
> Virge le vit mort recevoir,
> Et virge en paradis seoir.

Chanson m'estuet chanteir de la meilleur
Qui onques fust ne qui jamais sera;
Li siens douz chanz garit toute doleur:
Bien iert gariz sui ele garira.
Mainte arme a garie.[75] (vv. 1–5)

Such appearance of annominatio in a pious *chanson* is an especially significant mark of the influence of the Latin liturgical
tradition, since vernacular literary convention decreed that authors
of pious songs to the Virgin borrow both their melodic and poetic
forms from the profane courtly lyric.[76] In many cases the editors
of these songs, Edward Järnström and Arthur Långfors, have been
able to identify the model used. The songs are a curious mixture of
profane love themes and traditional symbolism deriving from the
figurative metaphors applied to Mary in the Latin hymns. Number
CXII, "Quant voi la flor novele/ Florir en la praele," [77] for example,
is an imitation of an extremely secular pastourelle, "Quant voi la
flor nouvele/ paroir en la praele," [78] where a thirteen-year old girl,
suffering "des douz maus d'amer," is relieved by a passing gentle-
man, much to her delight. The devout song includes a nine-branch
annominatio on the familiar key-word *corde*.[79] Annominatio is
virtually absent from the profane lyric tradition which derives its
techniques from other poetic sources.[80] Small but important shifts

75. For same theme with annominatio on *cure*, "protection, healing," and *obscure*, "damnable," see Théophile's prayer, vv. 516–21, and *La Mort Rutebeuf*,
st. V.

76. Järnström, *Chansons pieuses*, *1*, 13–15.

77. E. Järnström and A. Långfors, *Chansons pieuses*, *2*, Annales Academiae
Scientiarum Fennicae, Ser. B, XX, No. 4 (Helsinki, 1927), 138–40.

78. Karl Bartsch, *Chrestomathie de l'ancien français* (*VIIIe–XVe siècles*) (12th
ed. New York, 1958), No. 62c.

79. The *corde* annominatio appears also in Järnström-Långfors, *2*, 148, and
Gautier de Coinci's song "Roïne celestre" (ed. Koenig *1*, 35–36, vv. 90–108).
Gautier uses annominatio extensively in his pious songs as well as in his miracles;
his "Amors qui seit bien enchanter" (ed. Koenig, *1*, 24–28) is divided into six
groups of two stanzas, each based on one sound figure.

80. Dragonetti observes that even equivocal rhymes appear only accidentally in
trouvère lyrics: "les rimes riches, grammaticales, léonines, équivoques . . . n'ont
pas particulièrement excité l'imagination des trouvères" (*La Technique poétique*,
p. 421). See A. Jeanroy, *Origines de la poésie lyrique en France au moyen âge*
(3d ed. Paris, 1925), pp. 339 ff.

in vocabulary reveal the influence of the Latin liturgical tradition.
Number CXIV starts off: "Fine amor et bone esperance/ Me fait
un noviau chant chanter," where the model had: "Fine amours
et bone esperance/ Me remaine joie et chanter." [81] The same
annominatio on *chant* appears at the beginning of three other
pious songs [82] as well as in one by Gautier de Coinci, again in
Gautier's nonlyric *Prologue*,[83] and in verse 405 of Théophile's
repentance by Rutebeuf, as well as in *C'est de Notre Dame,* above.
The combination of figures in these pious songs reveals the con-
fluence of two separate technical traditions, each adding its own
forms, themes, and figures.

The Latin hymns cannot be the only source of Rutebeuf's poetic
technique or of the annominatio figure we have chosen to follow,
the more because his work is largely nonlyric,[84] and in this, too,
we see Rutebeuf's separation from the courtly tradition, which is
almost wholly lyric.

Rutebeuf's poetry is an art not only of celebration but of persuasion, as we have seen in his didactic and polemical works. Persuasion, as that good Ciceronian Brunetto Latini tells us, is "li office
. . . selonc ce que Tuilles dist, de parler penseement por faire
croire ce qu'il dist"; [85] it would therefore be appropriate to devotional, moral, and satirical writings like Rutebeuf's as well as to
sermons, which were virtually the only form of oratory in the
thirteenth century.[86] All of these genres seek, in the large sense, to

81. Järnström-Långfors, 2, 142; model listed by Gaston Raynaud, *Bibliographie
des chansonniers français des XIIIe et XIVe siècles*, 2 (Paris, 1884), No. 221.

82. Järnström-Långfors, 2, No. XCI, p. 96; No. XCII, p. 99; and No. XCVI,
p. 105.

83. Ed. Koenig, *1*, 24, vv. 1–2; and 22–23, vv. 65–74.

84. Only four works are qualified as *chansons* (FB, *1*, 211)—that is, could have
been accompanied by music. Bedier specifically excludes Rutebeuf's *Chanson de
Pouille* from his *Chansons de Croisade* (p. xi and n. 1), evidently considering it a
dit in spite of the title.

85. *Trésor*, p. 319. See also Baldwin's reference from Bonaventura, "rhetorica
ad movendum respicit rationem ut motivam . . . ornatum" (*Medieval Rhetoric*,
p. 177, n. 55).

86. See Baldwin, *Medieval Rhetoric*, p. 230. Contrast with the political oratory
of later centuries—for example, the "harangues" recorded by the Burgundian chronicler Georges Chastelain.

convince, and rhetoric serves both didactic prose and didactic poetry alike, as Brunetto Latini states in his "Livre de bone parleure":

La grant partison de tous parliers est en .ii. manieres, une ki est en prose et .i. autre ki est en risme. Mais li ensegnement de rectorique sont commun d'ambes .ii., sauve ce que la voie de prose est large et pleniere, si comme est ore la commune parleure des gens, mais li sentiers de risme est plus estrois et plus fors, si comme celui ki est clos et fermés de murs et de palis, c'est a dire de pois et de nombre et de mesure certaine de quoi on ne puet ne ne doit trespasser.[87]

I have shown in Chapter 1 how often sermon themes and techniques find their way into vernacular poetry; indeed, the *dit* was originally the name given to works expounding theological truths through allegorical interpretations.[88] Latin prose sermons also provided vernacular moralists with examples of rich rhetorical effects, figures of sound, and taught them the "phrasing of certain patterns"[89] of surface decoration which convinces an audience of the fundamental truth of the subject. The preachers received the same education, learned the same techniques as poets who wrote in the didactic manner. Baldwin cites a sermon on the *Magnificat* theme, which is an excellent example of use of word variations and contrasts: "*Magnificat anima mea Dominum.* Magnificat voce, magnificat opere, magnificat affectu. Magnificat laudando, amando, praedicando. Magnificat, laudandi, amandi et magnificandi formam simul et materiam dando. *Magnificat anima mea Dominum:* quia magnifice a magnifico Domino magnifica est."[90] Besides the 11 repetitions of forms of *magnificare,* the preacher subtly varies the cadence of the gerundives: where one expects repetition with a

87. *Tresor,* p. 327. See Harry Caplan, "Classical Rhetoric and the Mediaeval Theory of Preaching" *Classical Philology, 28,* No. 2 (April 1933), 73–96, for the theological environment of rhetoric and a useful bibliography of preaching manuals; and Th.-M. Charland, *Artes praedicandi; Contribution à l'histoire de la rhétorique au moyen âge* (Paris and Ottowa, 1936).
88. Jauss, "Genèse de la poésie allégorique," p. 11.
89. Baldwin, *Medieval Rhetoric,* p. 180.
90. Ibid., p. 256. Baldwin notes that the sermon is doubtfully attributed to St. Bernard (*Patrologia latina,* CLXXXIV, col. 1121).

"praedicandi," one finds progression and resumption of the themes with "magnificandi," while the last "dando" echoes the first gerundive series. Some sermon writers even achieve rhyme within their phrases,[91] although rhetoricians commonly warn against style becoming so ornamental that it is irrelevant to the subject, particularly because, as Latini says, a preacher carried away by his own oratory may not be convincing: "Mais il doit avoir petit de doreure et de jeu et de consonances, por ce que de teus choses naist souvent une suspection comme de chose pensee par grant mestrie, en tel maniere ke li oïeres se doute de toi ne ne croit pas a tes paroles." [92]

There is abundant evidence to show that the rhetorical style was the normal, even the automatic way of writing, from a sampling of the Latin prose outside of sermons. Alexander IV's letter condemning the *De periculis* used opposition, alliteration, and annominatio to attack "libellum quidem non rationabilem, sed reprobabilem, non veritatis, sed mendacii, non eruditionis, sed derogationis, non monentem, sed mordentem." [93] Sound figures like annominatio are used, however, to greater advantage in poetry than prose, since the figure straggles irregularly through a prose sentence, and the pleasure of anticipating the return of a sound is diminished. The ironic play on *generosus* in one of the satirical letters directed by the University masters against Louis IX and Pope Alexander is ineffective because the ear does not expect it: "Generosi sunt principes terre et generosa emicant parentela, qui quanto generosiores sunt, tanto magis rigorem animi sui multorum decet precibus emolliri, quia, sicut dicit Seneca, generosus animus est, qui ad virtutem bene disponitur." [94]

The Latin satirical poets include the wordplay of the didactic

91. On rhyme in sermons see Baldwin, pp. 250–54. Raby, reviewing Gaselee's *Transition from the Late Latin Lyric to the Medieval Love Poem* (*Classical Review*, 46 [1932], 142–43, suggests that rhyme originated in prose, then passed into liturgical verse.

92. *Trésor*, pp. 342–43. Humbert de Romans says that "they who seek adornment are like those who care more for the beauty of the salver in which food is carried than for the food itself" (*De eruditione praedicatorum*, p. 432, trans. Harry Caplan, "Rhetorical Invention in Some Medieval Tractates on Preaching," *Speculum*, 2 [1927], 432). See also Bourgain, *Chaire*, p. 235 and n. 6.

93. *Chart. Univ.*, *1*, 332, No. 288.

94. Ibid., p. 405, No. 357.

and liturgical tradition in their lively verses with devastating effect. Clerics such as Gautier de Châtillon and his school reveal harsh secular truths through verbal coincidences, just as Thomas Aquinas expressed dogmatic mysteries through wordplay. Annominatio on *donum* from an early twelfth-century sermon—"Aspiciamus ergo quod a Deo donatum est nobis, et erga donatorem et donum non simus ingrati" [95]—reappears a century later in Gautier de Châtillon's invective against simony:

> Donum Dei non donatur
> nisi gratis conferatur.[96]

The author of "Utar contra vitia" also plays with the "gift" figure to denounce graft and bribery in Rome:

> Das istis, das aliis, addis dona datis,
> et cum satis dederis, querunt ultra satis.[97]

The satirists, as well as the theologians, reinterpret the Old Testament. Thus David's psalm to God's glory, "night to night proclaims knowledge," becomes a means for Gautier de Châtillon to deplore the greedy ignorance of the cardinals:

> Hi nos docent, sed indocti,
> hi nos docent et nox nocti
> indicat scientam.[98]

While annominatio is extremely frequent in religious and satirical verse it appears only sporadically in other sorts of Latin poems. The extreme stylization of the hymns to the Virgin is, of course, an invitation to parody, which is only effective when the original form is easily identified and well defined. The Goliards prepared enter-

---

95. Hugues de Cluny (d. 1109), sermon on St. Marcel, cited by Bourgain, *Chaire,* p. 228.

96. *Die Gedichte Walters von Chatillon,* ed. Karl Strecker, Vol. 1: *Die Lieder der Handschrift 351 von St. Omer* (Berlin, 1925), p. 46, No. 27.

97. *Carmina burana, 1,* ed. Alfons Hilka and Otto Schumann (Heidelberg, 1930 and 1941), No. 42, I, i, 77.

98. From "Propter Sion non tacebo," *Moralisch-satirische Gedichte . . . ,* ed. Karl Strecker (Heidelberg, 1929), p. 26, No. 2; see Psalms 19:2 (Vulgate 18:3).

taining surprises by using themes and figures from the ultra stereotyped hymnodic writing.[99] The author of "Si linguis angelicis"
gives a new twist to the theme of "flower of flowers":[1]

Vidi florem floridum,	vidi florum florem,
vidi rosam Madii	cunctis pulchriorem,
vidi stellam splendidam,	cunctis clariorem,
per quam ego degeram	lapsus in amorem.

'Ave, formosissima,	gemma pretiosa,
ave, decus virginum,	virgo gloriosa,
ave, lumen luminum,	ave, mundi rosa,
Blanziflor et Helena,	Venus generosa!'

The word "virgin" here is distinctly a figure of speech. Annominatio
can also appear in the Goliardic love lyric as a special technique,
where the sonorous effect is the only concern and no puns are intended. Thus the poet catches the song of the spring bird in this
portrait of a maiden under a green linden tree:

vidi

viridi

Phyllidem sub tilia,

vidi

Phyllidi

quevis arridentia.[2]

---

99. See, for example, the drinking song "Vinum bonum et suave" parodying a
hymn to Virgin, "Verbum bonum et suave," in Lehmann, *Die Parodie im Mittelalter* (1st ed. Munich, 1922), pp. 174–78.

1. *Carmina burana*, ed. Hilka-Schumann, No. 77, I, ii, 53, St. 6, 8. See Raby,
Christian-Latin Poetry (p. 433) for the *flos de flore* image as a symbol for Christ.
This word is the one most frequently subjected to annominatio in Goliardic love
poetry: see *Carmina burana*, Nos. 148, 149, 77, 78, 186; and Raby, *Secular Latin
Poetry*, 2, 250 and 268–69. No. 186 is unusual, being entirely based on annominatio.
In this poem Flora is compared to a flower; the piece ends with the charming
lines: Flos in pictura/ non est flos, immo figura;/ non pingit floris odorem" (I,
ii, 311).

2. *Carmina burana*, No. 84, I, ii, 69.

But annominatio is only one chord in the "scolaris symphonia," [3] which the Latin clerks dedicated to their ladies, and is used discreetly, rarely, and usually for special effects. There is, then, some evidence of contamination between the Latin lyric love poetry and the religious didactic tradition. Yet the two streams can be clearly distinguished, one possible distinction being the characteristic use of figures such as annominatio in liturgical and satirical verse.[4]

French poets make a similar distinction between the techniques proper to the courtly lyric and works written in the didactic tradition. In the latter, annominatio, carrying both verbal and symbolic interest, is one of the most heavily used figures borrowed from Latin. If one chooses examples from poets who wrote both courtly lyrics and moralizing verse, the differentiation of the two traditions becomes very clear on the basis of poetic figures alone. Of the 31 known poems of the Hainaut poet Gontier de Soignies, only one is a moralizing satire, against men who are deaf to virtue and charity, and in that one alone do we find annominatio:

Li xours commence xordement
Xors est li siecles devenus
Et xort en sont toutes les gens, . .
Xors est li siecles et perdus;

* * *

Refrain:
Chanteis, vos ki veneis de cort,
La xorderie por lou xort! [5]

Thus, in turning to a satirical theme, Gontier immediately adopted the conventions peculiar to the didactic tradition, as did the courtly

3. Ibid., No. 65, p. 28.
4. See Raby, "The Origins of the Latin Lyric," where he states that secular lyric poetry seldom imitates liturgical verse (*Secular Latin Poetry*, 2, 322–41, esp. pp. 328, 337).
5. Jeanroy, *Chansons satiriques*, p. 3, No. 2; or Auguste Scheler, *Trouvères belges*, Nouvelle série (Louvain, 1879), p. 39, No. 17, who edits all of Gontier's works (pp. 1–71). Paulin Paris suggests the use of "x" for "s" was in mockery of Blanche of Castille's accent; yet nothing relates Gontier to the French Court, and nothing beyond a complaint that poor knights are no longer generously received at Court (st. IV) could relate this poem to the series on the barons' revolt (*Histoire littéraire, 23,* 604).

poet turned monk, Guiot de Provins. There is no evidence of annominatio in Guiot's lyric works, but some appears in his *Bible,* used
as a satirical weapon rather than as a devotional exercise, as in the
verses against doctors:

> Fisicïen sont apellei,
> sens 'fi' ne sont il pas nommei'
> . . .
> De fi, phisique me defie;
> fous est qui en teil art se fie
> ou il n'ait rien que n'i ait 'fi'—
> dont sui je fous se je m'i fi.[6]
> (vv. 2579–80, 2587–90)

Annominatio appears sporadically in courtly narratives when the
authors borrow themes from preachers and moralists.[7] Chrétien
de Troyes' prologue to *Perceval* which begins:

6. Annominatio appears also as a rather secondary ornament in Huon le Roi;
see, for example, vv. 96–97, 155–57, 171–74, 223–28 of his *Abecés par ekivoche.*
The Provençal poets occasionally adopt annominatio in satirical pieces, as in Guillem
Figueira's *sirventés* against Rome: "Roma enganairitz, cobeitatz vos engana" (v.
15, ed. Raymond Thompson Hill and Thomas Goddard Bergin, *Anthology of the
Provençal Troubadours* [New Haven, 1941], p. 178, No. 121). Jeanroy, observing
that Provençal poets seldom use rich or equivocal rhymes says, "c'est un honneur,
pour les troubadours de la bonne époque, que d'avoir dédaigné ces puérilités"
("Etudes sur l'ancienne poésie provençal," *Neuphilologische milleilungen, 27,* Nos.
5–6 [1926], 157). Verbal complexities in Provençal poetry usually take other forms;
the art of the *trobar clus* of Arnaut Daniel or Raimbaut d'Aurenga is in the rhyme
schemes and use of difficult and new words. See, for example, the famous *sestina* of
Arnault Daniel, "Lo ferm voler qu'el cor m'intra" (Hill-Bergin, *Anthology,* No. 53)
or Raimbaut d'Aurenga's *vers,* "Er resplan la flors enversa" (ibid., No. 34), and
Jeanroy, *Origines* pp. 141–59. Similar complexities in the distribution of words
appear in French works, as in the *Vier retrograde d'amours* of Jean de Condé (*3,*
No. XLVII); see the retrograde verse of John of Garland, cited by Raby (*Christian-
Latin Poetry,* p. 388).
    7. Junker notes correctly that conventions of the courtly novel were quite tight
("Annominatio," p. 325); moreover, they do not derive from the Latin and vernacular moral, didactic, and hymnodic traditions, although some contamination does
occur, perhaps because of the common rhetorical education. Curtius lists some examples of annominatio from courtly narratives ("Neue Dante-Studien," *Romanische
Forschungen, 60* [1947], 273–80, reprinted in his *Gesammelte Aufsätze zur Romanischen Philologie* [Bern and Munich, 1960], pp. 333–38), as does Faral (*Arts
poétiques,* pp. 95–97).

Ki petit semme petit quelt
Et qui auques requellir velt,
En tel liu sa semence espande
Que Diex a cent doubles li rande;
Car en terre qui riens ne valt,
Bone semence seche et faut.
Chrestïens semme et fet semence
D'un romans que il encoumence
Et si le seme en si bon lieu . . .[8] (vv. 1–9)

is exceptional, and is clearly an imitation from didactic texts. Compare with Rutebeuf's verses in Théophile's repentance:

Trop a male semence en semoisons semee
De qui l'ame en sera en enfer sorsemee,[9] (vv. 410–11)

or with Gautier de Coinci's lines against slanderers in *De Sainte Léocade*:

Assez plus tost croist et semence
Qui ne face bone semence
Cil qui langues ont seursemees
Tex semences ont tost semees.
Ou feu d'enfer soient semé
Tuit mesdisant, tuit seursemé.
Por ce me tieng en petit cloistre
Que leur semence n'i puet croistre.[10] (vv. 2122–28)

Here again, familiar moralizing themes come with ready-made figures which the author fashions to fit his particular subject.

One may conclude from all the Latin and French examples of the

8. *Le Roman de Perceval*, ed. William Roach (Geneva-Paris, 1959), compare with the gracious annominatio figure on *fin* which ends Adenet le Roi's *Cléomadès* (vv. 18,595–607).

9. See Rutebeuf, *Sainte Elysabel*, vv. 12–15; *Dit de Pouille*, v. 7; and *Voie de Paradis*, vv. 9–16—where he describes his work with the moralizing sowing image.

10. For examples of the theme in sermons, see Maurice de Sully's homily in French on the parable of the sower (ed. C. A. Robson, pp. 92–94), and Jacques de Vitry's sermon to farmers, vinedressers, and other workmen, in Welter, *L'Exemplum*, App. I, pp. 457–67.

preceding pages that both poets and prose writers in the didactic
tradition worked with various prefabricated [11] literary figures. These
could be transferred easily from poem to poem and from poet to
poet as in the image of the rose and thorn. It appears, for example,
in Adam of Saint Victor's *Sequence for the Nativity of the Virgin
Mary:*

> Salve, verba sacra parens,
> flos de spina, spina carens
> flos, spineti gloria!
> Nos spinetum, nos peccati
> spina sumus cruentati,
> sed tu spinae nescia,[12]

and again, secularized, in Rutebeuf's *Discorde de l'Université et
des Jacobins:* "Rose est bien sor espine assise" (v. 56).[13] The unit
may be an annominatio on *corde* or *semer,* or a development on
Fortune,[14] or an allegorical figure of the vices and virtues.[15] It may
be as small as one rhyme or as big as an overall composition device
like the *voie* theme. The appearance of a key idea produces both
a certain train of thought and calls forth certain linguistic features
of rhyme, vocabulary, or image. The units are most rigid in the
case of verses on the Virgin, where the theological figural tradition
assured continuity in devotion and dogma.

Rutebeuf himself does not always rework such units, but merely
tranfers them bodily from one poem to another, as he did with Saint
Mary the Egyptian's prayer to the Virgin (vv. 261–83), which

11. The word is Faral's (FB, *1*, 59), who criticizes Rutebeuf for following
rhymes rather than ideas to develop his poem. We have seen, rather, that ideas
and figures are inseparable and that Rutebeuf's technique is not exceptional but
typical.

12. *Oxford Book of Medieval Latin Verse,* ed. F. J. E. Raby (new ed. Oxford,
1959), p. 232, No. 163.

13. Guiot de Provins uses the same image to distinguish good doctors from
quacks (*Bible,* vv. 2659–63).

14. See Rutebeuf, *Voie de Paradis,* vv. 174–78, 318; *Anseau de l'Isle,* vv. 25–40,
etc.; and Patch, *The Goddess Fortuna.*

15. See Rutebeuf's *Voie de Paradis* and *Bataille des Vices et des Vertus,* and
Bloomfield, *The Seven Deadly Sins.*

reappears virtually unchanged in the *Sacristain* (vv. 489–506).[16]
Moralizing passages are often of such a general nature that the poet
can fit them in as he needs them; an identical anaphoristic enumeration of the effects of *Envie,* for example, serves both as additional
material for Rutebeuf's description of the sin in his *Voie* (vv. 337–
60) and to describe the Devil's motivation for tempting the sacristan and the knight's wife in the *Sacristain* (vv. 39–62).[17] the
moralizing is so general, in fact, that the same effects are transferred
to the account of *Ire* in the anonymous *Mireour du monde!* [18]

In addition to units derived from rhetorical canons and from
theological writings, medieval poets had at their disposition a large
number of writer's formulas. Some of them date, as Curtius has
traced them, to the earliest known Western literature, like the often
repeated phrase of abbreviation,

> Que vos iroie delaiant
> Ne mes paroles porloignant,[19]

16. See FB, 2, 206–07, also 174–75.

17. See FB, 2, 208–09, where several identical passages in Rutebeuf are discussed.

18. See FB, 1, 352, note to vv. 337–58. As examples of unit borrowing outside
Rutebeuf, see: the passage on woman's flightiness from *Bible Guiot* (vv. 2111–18),
taken from Benoît de Sainte-Maure's *Roman de Troie* (vv. 13,441–48; see Orr's
note, p. 144, in his edition of the *Bible*); the Archpoet's confession which was
imitated frequently (Dobiache-Rojdestvensky, *Poésies des goliards,* p. 58); and a
satirical play on *cardinal* which appears frequently both in Latin and French:
see Gautier de Châtillon's "Propter Sion non tacebo."

> Ita dicunt cardinales,
> ita solent dii carnales. (*Moralisch-satirische Gedichte,* p. 25)

A passage from Gautier de Coinci's *Léocade,*

> En chardonail douceur n'a point,
> Car chardonnaus con chardons point, (vv. 891–92)

continues through 13 lines of annominatio; the *Dit des Mais* has but one extended
annominatio, and that on cardinals:

> Cardonaus si sont dit cardinaus com cardons, . . .
> Mais chardons chardonnaus interpètrent chardons,
> Car il eschardent gens et prenent aus lardons. (Jubinal, ed.,

Nouveau Recueil, 1, 182) See also Tobler (*Vermischte Beiträge, 2,* 261) for an
example from Salimbene, "cardinales-carpinales."

19. Examples in *Complainte du roi de Navarre,* vv. 113–14; *Sainte Elysabel,*
vv. 789–90, 2049–50, 2073–74. See Curtius, *European Literature,* "Brevity as an
Ideal of Style," pp. 487–94, and above, p. 201.

or the formula indicating the author's humility before his subject repeated three times in very similar form in different poems by Rutebeuf:

> Se j'estoie bons escrivains
> Ainz seroie d'escrire vains
> Que je vos eüsse conté
> La tierce part de sa bonté.[20]

Poets also depended heavily on fixed expressions and word sequences such as "Or lera donc Fortune corre," [21] and especially on formulas fixed by rhyme, as in the useful couple *conte*, "count"/ *conte*, "story, tell," which appears everywhere in Rutebeuf and his contemporaries, in verses like:

> Empereor et roi et conte
> Assez plus que je ne vous conte.[22]

Formulas referring to aspects of contemporary culture seem more lively to us, but they undergo a similar stylization and are just as transferable as those from tradition. Rutebeuf, for example, shows a predilection for images taken from weaving.[23] If he wants to describe the approaching Last Judgment:

> Diex soloit tistre et or desvuide:
> Par tens li ert faillie traime (*Plaies*, vv. 4–5)

If he wants to develop the theme of the penniless poet:

> . . . Ci faut traime
> Par lecherie (*Griesche d'hiver*, vv. 89–90)

20. See FB 2, 209; also Rutebeuf's *Voie*, "Si autant de langues come de denz . . ." (v. 876); and Curtius, *European Literature*, "Inexpressibility Topoi," pp. 159–60, and "Affected Modesty," pp. 83–85.

21. *Complainte de Guillaume*, v. 171; *Complainte de Rutebeuf*, v. 134.

22. *Complainte de Geoffroi de Sergines*, vv. 31–32. See *Complainte d'outremer*, vv. 1–2; *Ave Maria Rutebeuf*, vv. 10–11; *Dit de Guillaume*, vv. 95–96; *Voie de Paradis*, vv. 635–36; etc. See outside of Rutebeuf, Baudouin de Conté, *Li Contes d'envie*, vv. 3–4; Jean de Condé's *Avé Maria*, vv. 90–91; *Complainte de Pierre de la Broce*, p. 29, for three examples among many.

23. See FB, *1*, 377, note to vv. 3–5.

The game of chess, enormously popular during the thirteenth century, provided poets with a metaphor to describe any losing situation. Both Rutebeuf and Gautier de Coinci have Théophile describe his fall from honor as a checkmate:

> Bien m'a dit li evesque 'Eschac!'
> Et m'a rendu maté en l'angle;
> (Rutebeuf, *Théophile,* vv. 6–7)

> 'Ha! las! fait il, or sui j'en l'angle,
> Or sui je maz, or sui je pris.'[24]
> (Gautier de Coinci, *Théophilus,* vv. 135–37)

Rutebeuf imagines his struggle with the dice in terms of a chess game where the *griesche* is his opponent;[25] and a chess image serves Jean de Meun to recount Manfred's defeat in Italy.[26]

Such stylization of formulas means that they are no longer exclusively limited to their original cultural context but can be used as idiomatic expressions peculiar to the language of the time, appropriate to an idea, but not characteristic of any one speaker or situation. Critics who have not realized this have sometimes mistaken the value of certain of Rutebeuf's expressions. Grace Frank, for example, has written an interesting article pointing out resemblances between Rutebeuf's *Théophile* and his "personal poetry," suggesting that "an identification of the hero's misfortunes in the play with those experienced by the poet himself might be posited."[27] The likenesses she notes certainly do exist, but they appear, as we shall see in Chapter 5 (p. 271), because the poet is treating similar themes of lament over misfortune or repentance which call

24. See Gautier's prologue to his miracles (I Pr 1, vv. 204–313, ed. Koenig, *1, 12–18*), where in an extremely extended metaphor the Virgin appears as God's "Queen" (*fierce*) and checkmates the Devil.

25. *Griesche d'été,* vv. 14–22; *Dit d'hypocrisie,* vv. 74–75, describes man's trading salvation for material goods as a bad chess move.

26. *Rose,* vv. 6663–6726. For a thorough survey of chess in medieval literature, see H. J. R. Murray, *A History of Chess* (Oxford, 1913), pp. 376 ff. Whole moralizing allegories were constructed around the theme, like the popular works *Les Echecs moralisés* and *Les Echez amoureux.*

27. "Rutebeuf and Théophile," *Romanic Review, 43,* No. 3 (October 1952), 161.

for a certain vocabulary and form of expression. Rutebeuf may cast the theme into either the first or the third person, but the poetic elements or units expressing repentance belong to the theme, not the speaker. Théophile's phrase, "Or est bien ma viele frete" (v. 36), for example, is labeled by Jeanroy as a "métaphore plus naturelle dans la bouche d'un jongleur comme Rutebeuf, que dans celle du clerc Théophile." [28] In fact, the expression means simply, "all is over for me," and is related to another expression, "metre la viele sous le banc," [29] which appears in Latin as well as in French [30] and was even used to describe the death of a pope:

> Mist a Clement, nostre apostoile,
> Sous le banc la mort sa viële.[31]

Still another related expression appears in Gautier de Châtillon's satirical farewell to the world, which starts, "Versus est in luctum/ cythara Waltheri"; [32] this is nothing more than a quote from that oldest of mourners, Job (30:31). Although the dicing terms from *Théophile*—"Bien me seront li dé changié" (v. 122), and "Or t'est il cheü ambes as" (v. 348)—would occur naturally to the author of the *Griesche d'hiver* and *d'été*, they are, nonetheless, as Faral's notes indicate,[33] common expressions for bad luck appearing in the most varying contexts to describe the fortunes of love and war.[34] Other

28. *Le Miracle de Théophile*, trans. A. Jeanroy (Paris and Toulouse, 1932), p. 11. Mario Roques, reviewing Jeanroy's translation, questions this point (*Romania*, 59 [1933], 609).

29. See Grace Frank's edition of *Théophile*, note to v. 36 (p. 27); add to her references the note by Mario Roques in *Romania*, 52 (1926), 199.

30. Robert de Sorbon, commenting on the diminishing numbers of arts students, said, "Certi alii magistri possent bene ponere viellas suas subtus bancum" (*De conscientia et tribus dietis*, ed. F. Chambon [p. 26], cited by Pesce, "Le Portrait de Rutebeuf," p. 155, n. 3). See also Villon, *Testament*, v. 717, in his farewell to love.

31. Death of Clement V (1314) related by Geoffroi de Paris (*Chronique*, vv. 6341–42), cited by Mario Roques in *Romania*, 58 (1932), 85.

32. *Moralisch-satirische Gedichte*, p. 148, No. 17. See the same image in a love poem, *Carmina burana*, No. 105, st. VI (I, ii, 174), and Lehmann, *Die Parodie*, p. 144.

33. FB *1*, 352, note to v. 319; FB, *2*, 192, note to v. 348.

34. See Semrau, *Würfel und Würfelspiel im alten Frankreich*, Beihefte zur *Zeitschrift für Romanische Philologie*, 23 (Halle, 1910), for texts using the metaphors of "snake eyes" (*ambesas*) and loaded dice (*dé changié*), pp. 110–12, 109–113.

stock phrases appropriate to poems of repentance are the image of Mary as healer [35] or the wordplay associated with the commonplace regret of having traded salvation for worldly goods, which produces:

> Molt felonesse rente m'en rendront mi rentier.
>
> (*Théophile*, v. 406)

> De male rente m'a renté
>
> Mes cuers . . . (*Mort Rutebeuf*, vv. 45–46)[36]

There is some evidence during the thirteenth century of a tendency toward overelaboration or mannerism in the handling of traditional figures and themes. If we compare several treatments of an annominatio figure on the name *Maria,* we shall see how the delicate symbolic relations between words may become so distorted and exaggerated that only an empty form really survives. In the early thirteenth-century poets the wordplay is already established but limited in extension. Huon le Roi's *Ave Maria en Roumans*[37] is joyfully playful, uses many equivocal rhymes like "*gracia*-grace i a" (vv. 75–76) or "l'amertume-la mer tume" (vv. 91–92), and includes a discreet play on *Maria:*

> Mere et Marie a droit a non:
>
> A droit a non Mere Marie,
>
> Car mout durement fu marie . . . (vv. 67–69)

35. *Théophile*, vv. 520–21; *La Mort Rutebeuf*, st. V. See p. [23] and Br. Leo Charles Yedlicka, *Expressions of the Linguistic Area of Repentance and Remorse in Old French*, Catholic University Studies in Romance Languages and Literatures, XXVII (Washington, D.C., 1945), pp. 165–66.

36. Compare with the image of the world as a marketplace of salvation, with annominatio on *marchié*, which sets the moral in the *Sacristain*, vv. 17–30.

37. *Œuvres, 1*, 16 ff. The *Ave Maria* is a frequent composition device, deriving from one of the earliest forms of liturgical expression, the tropes or paraphrases and ornamentations added to sacred texts. (See H. P. Ahsmann, *Le Culte de la Sainte Vierge et la littérature française du moyen âge* [Utrecht and Paris, 1930], pp. 12–13.) Naetebus lists at least 21 variants of the *Ave Maria* (*Nicht-lyrischen Strophenformen*). Ilvonen edits an *Ave Maria* parody having political reference to the Hundred Years' War (*Parodies de thèmes pieux dans la poésie française du moyen âge* [Helsinki, 1914] pp 169–73).

Gautier de Coinci does not fail to include the same play as an appropriate end to his medieval "Venus d'Ille" story, *De L'Enfant qui mist l'anel ou doit l'ymage,* where a young student has to keep his promise to marry Mary:

> A Marie se maria.
> Moines et clers qui se marie
> A ma dame sainte Marie
> Mout hautement est mariez,
>
> . . .
>
> Laissons Maros et Marïons,
> Se nos marïons a Marie,
> Qui ses maris ou ciel marie.[38]
> (vv. 184–87, 194–96)

Toward the middle of the century Rutebeuf illuminated the death of Saint Mary the Egyptian, saved from Hell by the Virgin, with a similar annominatio (vv. 1140–46). Faral suggests that he borrowed the figure from Gautier,[39] but we see that it is a common one. The same play occurs again in Rutebeuf's song *C'est de Notre Dame,* whose apparent simplicity is belied by its complex rhetorical effects:

> Quant son doulz non reclainment picheour
> Et il dient son *Ave Maria,*
> N'ont puis doute dou Maufei tricheour
> Qui mout doute le bien qu'en Marie a,
>   Car qui se marie
>   En teile Marie,
>   Boen mariage a:
>   Marions nos la,
>   Si avrons s'aïe. (vv. 19–27)

From these ornamental but comprehensible forms, we pass to the extreme limits of the annominatio on *Maria,* with a work by

38. Ed. Koenig, 2, 204. A similar play occurs in Gautier's song, "Qui que face rotruenge novele," vv. 28–31 (*1,* 30).
39. FB 2, 54, note to vv. 1140–46.

Watriquet de Couvin, minstrel to the Court of Blois during the first third of the fourteenth century. Adopting the *Ave Maria* form, he contrives to end every one of his forty verses with a different form of the base *maria* in lines like the following:

Ave, douz non de	*Maria,*
Marie, en cui Diex	maria.
Gracia plena,	mari as,
Vierge, en Dieu; tu t'i	marias;
Dominus tecum	marié,
Benedicta tu,	Marie. É![40]

The poem is totally focused around the droning repetition of *Maria;* indeed, any other meaning the vocabulary may have is so completely subordinated as to be virtually lost to the hearer. Yet the word may justify such concentration of sound on one point, in a burning adoration of the Virgin which attracts all other thoughts into itself.

Glittering surface play of words may even have a real function within a work. Rutebeuf heightens the mood of his *Miracle de Théophile* at the touching moment of repentance by shifting from the quick-paced octosyllables to monorhymed alexandrine quatrains; and part of the lyric movement of exaltation is created by 15 lines of dense annominatio, with figures on *chant, char, amer, semer, bailli, ors* ("soil"), and *mort* (vv. 405–19).[41] The choice of words is, of course, significant, since Théophile here reaps what he has sown. He recognizes that his soul is in the Devil's grip and that a harsh death awaits him. In addition, the chanting repetitions of words,

---

40. *Dits,* p. 293, No. XXI, vv. 1–6. The same play appears again in the *Rhétoriqueurs* (Guy, *Poésie française au XVIe siècle,* p. 93).

41. Annominatio occurs in the repentance portion of a Latin narrative version of the story of Theophilus, which also uses monorhymed alexandrine quatrains:

> Heu, miser! miseris, inquit, miserior,
> Miser miseria cunctis superior
> . . .
> Adventu judicem crede sub alio
> Cum justo judicans mundum judicio.

(ed. Alfred Weber, *Zeitschrift für romanische Philologie, 1* [1877], 527, 529).

like the anaphoristic constructions in the repentance scene of Gautier de Coinci's *Théophilus* (vv. 731–888), create an effect of incantation which appeals to emotion, not reason. Rutebeuf thus prepares the sacred moment of the actual invocation to the Virgin, where he shifts to 12-line stanzas of hexameters and to the stylized liturgical enumeration of Mary's powers and beauties. The end of Théophile's prayer is marked by a return to the sacred chant, with a double annominatio on the bases *proie* and *voie,* each used with five different meanings:

> Li proieres qui proie
> M'a ja mis en sa proie:
> Pris serai et preez,
> Trop asprement m'asproie.
> Dame, ton chier Filz proie
> Que soie despreez.
> Dame, car leur veez,
> Qui mes mesfez veez,
> Que n'avoie a leur voie.
> Vous qui lasus seez,
> M'ame leur deveez
> Que nus d'aus ne la voie.[42] (vv. 528–39)

The play on *pris-proier* is repeated (vv. 543–57) to provide a transition between this exalted and prayerful pause and the dialogue with the Virgin; and the annominatio on *voie* is repeated (vv. 611–15) in rhetorical remembrance of Théophile's pleading when he later recounts his adventure to the bishop. Rutebeuf thus employs the figure for continuity and transition as well as to raise the level of parts of his play from the conversational to the sublime.

The meaningful and sober wit of the Latin hymns is certainly extremely exaggerated in these passages, and the dangers of excess

---

42. In Jeanroy's translation: "Le pillard qui pilla a déjà de moi fait sa proie; comme une proie je serai pris; fort cruellement il m'est cruel. Dame, prie ton cher Fils que je sois délivré; Dame, défendez-leur, vous qui voyez mes méfaits, de me faire marcher en leur voie. Vous qui êtes assise là-haut, refusez-leur mon âme; qu'aucun d'eux ne la voie" (p. 34).

are evident: the ear may be so intrigued by detail that it can no
longer encompass the meaning of the whole passage. Style can be
reduced to mere decoration "piled on indiscriminately and mean-
inglessly,"[43] where we no longer distinguish variations in a blur of
figures. Baudouin de Condé, contemporary of Rutebeuf and poet in
the court of Flanders, wrote tiresome moralizations on the duties
of knights and vassals. Deprived of imagination and of the gift of
varying his technique, Baudouin casts virtually all of his moralizing in generalizations, unrelieved by the clever allegories, lively
examples, or ethical fervor which bring relief to the didacticism of
better poets. Having learned annominatio figures, he ham-handedly
uses them everywhere and at such length that the meager kernel of
thought is obscured. To say that the life of the flesh is short, he expends 44 verses of extremely dense annominatio and equivocal
rhyme where the word *char* appears 52 times framed in general
statements like:

> Chil ki le mieus la char encarne,
> Mire en soi con mors char descarne,
> Si con d'arier sont descarné
> Tout cil qui fuirent de car né.
> . . .
> Si est uns, cars et escarnie
> De ton mors, il n'est ki carnie
> De ton mors; car ou mors se carnent . . .[44]

43. Curtius defines such art as mannerism, which he sees as a latent possibility
or menace in all rhetorical art (*European Literature*, p. 274; see all of his chapter 15, "Mannerism," which discusses authors from the late Roman empire to the
Spanish baroque). Fourteenth-century Latin authors were influenced by the vernacular rhetorical exaggerations of the thirteenth-century; Matheolus, for example,
includes a long annominatio on *jacob* in his attack on the Mendicants, of which
I cite four lines:
> Verius ergo Jacob quam Jacobus inde potestis
> Dici, quippe quia Jacob, non Jacobus estis
> . . .
> Ut prelatorum Jacob ipsi jus jacobitant,
> Sic curatorum 'chit!' emunt venduntque, maritant.
> (*Lamentations, 1*, 93–94, vv. 1328–29, 1334–35)
44. *Dits, 1*, 147, No. XI, vv. 1–4, 23–25. Compare with Gautier's invective
against *papelarts* in *Léocade*, where *char* occurs 28 times in 13 verses! (vv. 1623–36).

Baudouin's thought is as mediocre as his verse, and his ornaments are annoying rather than revealing. In such incompetent hands rhetoric declines into mere verbal agitation which strikes no spark and illuminates nothing.

Baudouin illustrates also the secularization of moral themes and of the rhetorical figures used to amplify them. He describes in his *Contes dou mantiel* and *dou wardecors*[45] a cloak and a shirt as figures of the duties of the good knight and the loyal vassal. We are far from the ingenious and poetically resonant liturgical figuration of Mary as the burning bush or the inexhaustible fountain. Baudouin's son, Jean de Condé, writing against stingy stewards, turns rhetoric into a household chore in his *Dou villain despensier*,[46] where he repeats the syllable *pen* in each rhyme of the poem's forty verses, in a plodding, mundane work starting:

> Ne sai a coi gentix hons pensse
> Qui vilain carge sa despensse,
> Vilain de cuer, de mal pourpens,
> Car il ne puet veoir despens,
> Ains samble c'on le maine pendre
> Quant il voit son seignour despendre
> Pour faire honour. (vv. 1–7)

Laicization is not necessarily equivalent to despiritualization in poets who transmute Christian fervor and figures into the cult of love, although Baudouin manages to make love dully edifying in his *Contes d'Amours* and *de la Rose*,[47] where he pounds love's darts into tracts with his annominatio and maxims. But Richard de Fournival writes a gracious and light reinterpretation of Christian moralization in his *Bestiaire d'amour*.[48] Jauss has sketched an excellent study of Guillaume de Lorris' innovations in treating the

45. Ibid., No. VI, pp. 80 ff. and No. II, pp. 17 ff. Compare with Raoul de Houdenc's *Roman des eles* (ed. A. Scheler, 1879), which teaches through allegory the duties of the perfect knight and which is imitated from Alanus de Insulis' *De sex alis cherubim*, a didactic treatise on confession and repentance (*Patrologia latina*, CCX, cols, 265 ff.).

46. *Dits, 3,* 241, No. LXIV.

47. Ibid., *1,* IX, 119 ff., and No. X, 133 ff.

48. Ed. C. Hippeau (Paris, 1860).

old *Psychomachia* theme as a representation of the inner psychological movements of the poet-lover and his *Rose*.[49] And Gottfried von Strassburg recreates the sense of liturgical mystery in the prologue to his extraordinary *Tristan*, saying that the lovers' death is the bread of life to us who read their life and death:

> Ir leben, ir tot sint unser brot.
> sus lebet ir leben, sus lebet ir tot.
> sus lebent sie noch und sint doch tot
> und ist ir tot der lebenden brot. (vv. 237–40) [50]

Inspired by Saint Bernard's mystical interpretation of the *Song of Songs*, Gottfried rediscovers the depth of conception plumbed by the theologicans and the powerful expression of passionate and mystical paradox through wordplay. He creates splendid effects within his narrative by using annominatio to express the hesitations of love (see above, n. 36) or the muttering suspicions of King Mark. Repeating *zwivelt* and *arcwan*, "doubt and suspicion," together with the names Tristan and Isolde, Mark pours out his torturous love and sorrow:

> Hier under was ie Marke
> bekumbert harte starke
> mit zweier hande leide:
> in leideten beide
> der zwivel under der arcwan,
> den er hæte und muose han:
> er arcwande genote
> sin herzeliep Isote;
> er zwivelt an Tristande,
>   • • •
> sin vriunt Tristan, sin vröude Isot
> diu zwei waren sin meistiu not:

49. "Genèse de la poésie allégorique," pp. 19–23.
50. *Tristan*, trans. Hatto, Introduction, pp. 14–15. The lovers' cave, where they dwell in banishment, is described with allegorical technique familiar from didactic works like Rutebeuf's *Voie de Paradis* (vv. 16,909 ff.; see Hatto's introduction, p. 15).

si twungen ime herze unde sin.
er arcwande si und in
und zwiveltes ouch beide.[51]
(vv. 13,749–57, 13,761–65)

There is no French author who can equal Gottfried's mastery
of rhetoric as a servant to love. The author of *Partonopeus de Blois*
at the end of the twelfth-century attempted to render love's confusion through annominatio:

> Erranz sui faiz par son sejor
> Et mestornez par son mestor,
> Mestornez par sa mestornee,
> Mesalez par sa mesalee.
> Mes mes mestors, mes mesalers,
> Mes sejors et mes meserrers,
> Toz est a li et toz par li;
> Tot m'avra a force a ami.[52]

Yet there is no mystery here, but only a befuddled lover, and annominatio reveals a state of mind rather than depth of thought. It is
interesting that when Rutebeuf wrote his one extant love scene, in
the *Sacristain et la femme au chevalier,* he adopted his rhetorical
training to narrative purposes. The *Sacristain* is a very elegant
presentation piece, telling how the Virgin saved a pious knight's
wife and virtuous sacristan from the wiles of the Devil. In it

51. Professor W. T. H. Jackson of Columbia University, in a 1964 lecture at
Yale, described a pattern of word motifs in Gottfried's *Tristan* where harmoniously
paired words like *love-heart* and *eyes-ears* are interwoven with disharmonious pairs
like *life-death* in annominatio figures associated with particular characters, much
like Wagner's leitmotivs.

52. Cited by Anthime Fourrier, *Le Courant réaliste dans le roman courtois en
France au moyen âge, 1* (Paris, 1960), 438. A Latin poem on the contradictory
feelings inspired by Venus also makes use of annominatio:

> Que cupit, hanc fugio,
> que fugit, hanc cupio;
> plus renuo debitum
> plus feror in vetitum,
> plus licet illibitum.
> plus licet illicitum.

(*Carmina burana,* No. 71, I ii, 40)

annominatio is used in familiar ornamental and didactic ways: to honor the patron in a figure on his name, *Beneoit* (vv. 1–7); as Rutebeuf's signature (vv. 749–60); and in the moralizing introduction, with play on *marchié,* where the audience is invited to strike a bargain for their souls, not for earthly goods. But annominatio is also used within the narrative to render both the action and the thoughts of the characters. The Devil's brooding envy of the couple and his determination to turn them from paths of righteousness find expression in a complex figure:

> Ces genz moult saintement vivoient.
> Li felon envieus qui voient
> Cels qui vivent de bone vie
> D'els desvoier orent envie.
> De lor enviaus envoierent,
> Soventes foiz i avoierent,
> Tant qu'il les firent desvoier
> De leur voïë et avoier
> A une pereilleuse voie.
> Or est mestiers que Diex les voie. (vv. 155–64)

In this passage Rutebeuf not only sets the moral but provides a "psychological" explanation for the action of his miracle. He strikes a suspenseful note which is maintained until the Virgin comes to the rescue and puts two devils behind bars in place of the couple whom she sends home along with the valuables they stole: "C'onques ne pot apercevoir/ C'on i eüst onques touchié" (vv. 568–69).

Annominatio serves next in the *Sacristain* to represent the magic effects of the Devil's enchantment:

> Anemis si les entama
> Que li amis l'amie ama,
> Et l'amie l'ami amot.
> Li uns ne set de l'autre mot;
> De plus en plus les enchanta.
> Quant cil chantoit *Salve sancta,*

Li *parens* estoit oubliez,
Tant estoit fort desavoiez.[53] (vv. 169–76)

Junker observes that the intoxication of the lovers is reflected in
the language of this passage and in the next figure on *cure,* "worry,
damnable, heal" (vv. 191–204), when the lady struggles against her
guilty passion.[54] Rutebeuf wittily plays, in the verse "li *parens* estoit
oubliez," with the idea that the lovers have not only forgotten
the words to the text [55] but have forgotten their devotion to their
Holy Mother, and the lady her duty to her family. The irresistible
and diabolical attraction which finally draws the two together appears in another passage, where annominatio develops suspense
through repetition: responding to the insistent whisper of the
Devil, the sacristan finally "a li vient:/ Par force venir li covient./
Quant la dame le voit venir . . ." (vv. 253–55). Rutebeuf again uses
annominatio without any interplay of symbolic meaning or moral
overtones to show the guilty haste of the greedy couple, in the
figure on *trousser* (vv. 337–44), when they make off with the church
treasure, and the worried agitation of the convent on discovering
the loss, in the figures on *couvent* and *tresor* (vv. 355–60, 389–93).
Annominatio in these passages clearly serves to sustain a swiftly
moving narrative. They may be contrasted with the static halt for
satire in the figure on *papelart* (vv. 403–14), which may serve to
bridge the time interval between the flight of the couple and the
discovery of the crime, as well as to set the stage for their denuncia-
tion by a gossipy Béguine. But no such rather forced explanation
really justifies what seems here to be a break in the narrative flow,
and the figure itself is an empty invention where verbal difficulty
offers the only interest of verses like:

53. Compare with Gautier de Coinci, who wrote an annominatio figure on *tenter*
and *tornoier* to paint the Devil's temptation, in *Théophile* (vv. 127–31, ed. Koenig,
1, 58).

54. Vv. 191–204. Junker "Annominatio," p. 336) thinks this is straight comedy,
but in the context of the story, the portrayal of the moment of falling from grace
is serious in intent. Contrast with scenes that are truly comic in conception, like
that of the bewildered convent and husband, who think they have been confused
by a "fantosme" (vv. 616–60), and which do not have any wordplay.

55. *Introit* to a mass for the Virgin (FB 2, 219 n.).

> De la loenge du pueple ardent:
> Por ce papelart papelardent.
> Ne vaut rien papelarderie.
> Puis que la papelarde rie
> Jamés n'apapelardirai . . .[56] (vv. 407-11)

The *Sacristain*, then, illustrates Rutebeuf's use of a rhetorical trope at its best in his moralizing and in telling his story, and also at its worst, as in the *papelart* figure, where the unit is mechanically clever and interrupts the intrigue.

The *Sacristain* is interesting, too, because it draws on both the rhetorical and fabliau traditions. The figurative rhetorical elegance, appropriate to a miracle of the Virgin, is enhanced by the anaphoristic construction of the wife's lamenting hesitations, with its alternating "or" and "que":

> Lasse! que porrai devenir!
> Comment me porrai contenir
>
> · · ·
>
> Dirai je lui? Nenil sans doute:
> Or ai je dit que fole gloute,
> Que fame ne doit pas proier.
> Or me puet s'amor asproier,
> Que par moi n'en savra més riens.
> Or sui ausi com li mesriens
> Qui porrist desouz la goutiere;
> Or amerai en tel maniere. (vv. 223-24, 227-34)

The poet uses personifications, of *Nature* (v. 259) and *Renommée* (vv. 415-16, 453-55), and the prayers to the Virgin are stylized in the usual manner (vv. 489-532). However, both characterization and narrative owe much to the fabliau. The portrait of the knight's wife is particularly successful in its use of dialogue to paint her feelings. Her inner struggle in the lament above continues when

56. Gautier de Coinci's diatribe against *papelarts* uses the same play, but in more dilute form and only in a satirical context (*Léocade*, vv. 1147-1698, esp. vv. 1378-84; see FB 2, 225 n.).

the sacristan comes toward her, but it is laughter and desire which she holds back, not a diabolical compulsion to sin, nor an exhalted passion:

> De rire ne se puet tenir.
> Ses cuers li semont bien a dire:
> 'Embrachiez moi, biaus tres douz sire;'
> Més Nature la tient serree.
> Nule des denz n'a desserree. (vv. 256–60)

She is unable to maintain for long her tone of mockery and coquettish indifference (vv. 273–92); and it is she, the eternal Eve, who, once having declared her love, carries their crime still further by proposing that they take all the money. She justifies herself on femininely practical grounds:

> Quar la gent qui va desgarnie
> En estrange leu est honie. (vv. 313–14)

This is woman as the fabliaux portray her: intelligent but not overscrupulous. Her impertinent answers to her baffled husband, who finds his wife beside him in bed again, are in the fabliau tone; "Ma fame ne fust vous onques!" (v. 629), says her husband in violent anger when he thinks he's been made "sire Ernous," patron saint of cuckoldry in the fabliaux[57] (vv. 621–44). For Nykrog only a thin line of edifying intent divides the *Sacristain* miracle from a comic tale,[58] and Morawski briefly notes that most miracles borrow their form and style from profane stories, both fabliaux and epics.[59] Such imitation may be compared to the derivation of the pious song from profane courtly lyrics. Just as the Virgin replaces the lady in the courtly poets' adoration, she shares the power of women in

---

57. See Sire Ernous, the cuckold of *La Dame qui fit trois tours*, and the discourse of *Ami* against marriage in the *Roman de la Rose*, where he describes "la confrairie/ Saint Ernoul, le seigneur des cous/ Don nus ne peut estre rescous/ Qui fame ait . . ." (vv. 9130–33).

58. *Fabliaux*, p. 18.

59. "Mélanges de littérature pieuse," *Romania, 61* (April 1935), 157–61. Morawski further notes (p. 152) that most miracles are written by clerics, friars, or monks, and few by jongleurs like Rutebeuf, whom he cites.

fabliaux, yet is infinitely good; *Eva* becomes *Ave* in the familiar medieval phrase. "Omnia tulit punctum qui miscuit utile dulci," said Jacques de Vitry, from whom Rutebeuf borrowed his *Sacristain* story, recommending humor to awaken men's minds.[60] Although many devout stories are tearfully gloomy, like the *Chevalier au Barizel*,[61] the Virgin's powers are just as efficacious in merry tales, and she saves the insouciant knight's wife as well as weeping Théophile.

Because there has been confusion over the value of wordplay, too often taken as funny, let us briefly see how Rutebeuf uses annominatio in his comic pieces.[62] Theoreticians, as we have seen, formally banned artifice from comic stories about common people; in practice, most fabliaux were written without rhetorical artifice, if not without art.[63] It is possible that the rhetorical style of writing was so ingrained in Rutebeuf that familiar word combinations flowed from his pen, and that he simply did not observe distinctions of style which more cultivated authors would maintain. Such automatic repetition of a verbal unit would explain the sole annominatio figure on *voie*[64] in the *Dame qui fit trois tours autour du moutier*. The figure straddles both narration and dialogue in a scene where the suspicious husband is sidetracked from his rage by paternal pride. The *Dame qui fit trois tours* is by every other standard of technique and conception of character a true fabliau:[65] the lady

60. Prologue to *Sermones vulgares* in *Exempla*, p. xlii n.; Jacques de Vitry is quoting v. 343 of Horace's *De arte poetica*. See Latin text of *Sacristain*, ibid., pp. 117–19, No. CCLXXXII; and FB, 2, 212–13.

61. *Fabliaux*, ed. Barbazan and Méon, *1*, 208 ff.

62. Nykrog corrects Bédier's mistaken assertion that there are no equivocal rhymes in Rutebeuf's fabliaux (Bédier, *Fabliaux*, p. 343; Nykrog, *Fabliaux*, pp. 168–69).

63. Nykrog, *Fabliaux*, pp. 142–44, 230–35. Jean de Condé, who we have seen was very familiar with the rhetorical conventions of the didactic tradition, wrote his five fabliaux without verbal effects other than rich rhymes, and he even admits such negligence as the rhyme of a word with itself in the same meaning (see *Nonette*, vv. 39–40, *Dits, 3*, 272).

64. See the verses quoted from the *Sacristain*, *Théophile*, and also *Griesche d'hiver*, vv. 42–47, for more annominatio on *voie*.

65. FB *2*, 292; and Nykrog, *Fabliaux*, pp. 61, 115.

is a deceitful trifler, her lover a shadowy pawn, her husband a blustering fool given to ferociously grotesque oaths like:

> Voiz, por le sanc et por le foie,
> Por la froissure et por la teste,
> Ele vient d'avoec nostre prestre! (vv. 126–28)

Typical of the fabliau, too, is the little domestic scene where Sire Ernous returns from work "toz moilliez et toz engelez" (v. 55) and finds a wife who, in her haste to rejoin her lover, can hardly wait to cram supper down his throat and get him into bed, but who pretends vast interest in his welfare: [66]

> Ne le vout pas faire veillier
> Por ce n'i ot cinq més ne quatre.
> Aprés mengier, petit esbatre
> Le lessa, bien le vous puis dire.
> Sovent li a dit: 'Biaus douz sire,
> Alez gesir, si ferez bien;
> Veillier grieve sor toute rien
> A homme quant il est lassez:
> Vous avez chevauchié assez.'
> L'aler gesir tant li reprouche,
> Par pou le morsel en la bouche
> Ne fet celui aler gesir,
> Tant a d'eschaper grant desir. (vv. 60–72)

The wife's wheedling tone is in excellent contrast with her acceleration of the action.[67]

The moralizing content is still another way to distinguish between the fabliau and the moral tale. One of the most constant features of fabliaux is the presence of moralizing introductions and

---

66. See Nykrog, *Fabliaux,* "L'Amour et le mariage dans les fabliaux," pp. 176–92, and "La Femme dans les fabliaux," pp. 193–207.

67. In the fabliau *Les Braies au cordelier* an eagerly unfaithful wife wakes her husband up in the middle of the night and convinces him he is late in leaving for market (Montaiglon-Raynaud, eds., *Fabliaux, 3,* No. 88).

proverbial conclusions, which Nykrog explains as the combined influence of school teachings on the way to begin a narrative, of the sermon exemplum, and of the Aesopic fable.[68] The sober moral of the exemplum is not that of the jolly fabliau where the virtues preached are those for getting along in this world, not getting to the next. Both the *Sacristain* miracle and the fabliau of the *Dame qui fit trois tours* end happily, but the latter in the triumph of pleasure without paying. No Christian judgment is imposed on the lady's behavior, in contrast with *Frère Denise,* in which a purely human solution is imposed and the girl's conduct is regularized.[69] The moral of *La Dame,* "Quant fame a fol, s'a son avel," is a simple statement of how the world wags, as is the moral of *Charlot le Juif,* Rutebeuf's warning to those who tinker with a poet's paycheck, which ends "Qui barat quiert, baraz li vient," and the practical advice which ends *Le Testament de l'âne:*

> Rutebués nos dist et enseigne
> Qui deniers porte a sa besoingne
> Ne doit douteir mauvais lyens.[70] (vv. 165–67)

There is no moral imperative, no urgency in the poet's message in these comic tales, but a utilitarian code of conduct and a lesson in living for anyone who cares to take it.

It seems to be that the traditional distinctions of style and subject are occasionally obscured in Rutebeuf's hands, with annominatio turning from a theological and didactic figure to a narrative device and finally to a comic figure in his *Pet au vilain.* There is, for example, one wordplay used in the highly moral *Dit Moniot de Fortune:*

> Fols est qui por Fortune de mal fère s'esforce;
> Tele Fortune faut, n'i a ne foi ne force;

68. Nykrog, pp. 202–03, 248–57; see above, pp. 198–99.
69. Leo observes that there is no inner conversion and no lesson in *Frère Denise* (unless it be a warning to beware of wolves in monk's clothing! "Li abis ne fet pas l'ermite," v. 1); "Rutebeuf: persönlicher Ausdruck und Wirklichkeit," p. 158 n.
70. See Morawski, *Proverbes,* No. 1882: "Qui dan Denier maine a son plait Quanque qu'il commande si est fâit."

Mès Fortune qui homme de bien fère renforce,
Celi ne puet deffère fers, ne fauchons, ne force.[71]

Play on the same word reappears in Rutebeuf's *Pet au vilain* to "ornament" a *vilain's* attempts to relieve himself of a monstrous bellyful of life:

A cest enfort forment s'esforce,
A cest esfort met il sa force;
Tant s'esforce, tant s'esvertue,
Tant se torne, tant se remus . . . (vv. 41–44)

Scatalogical stories such as these are about as low in subject matter and character as one can go, although enormously popular with all classes of society;[72] Rutebeuf insists so heavily on both the vileness of his hero and on the gross details of his story that the humor may come from the utter incongruity of hearing an elegant rhetorical figure in such an unexpected and debased context.[73]

---

71. *Nouveau Recueil,* ed. Jubinal, *1,* 197.

72. The *Pet au vilain* story served again in André de la Vigne's *Farce du munyer* (1496), an entertaining comedy in which an apprentice-devil Berith, much given to swearing, is sent to collect the soul of a miller whose wife beats him and cuckolds him with the priest as he is giving up the ghost. Edited in *Recueil de farces, soties et moralités du quinzième siècle* (Paris, 1876), ed. P. L. Jacob (Paul Lacroix), pp. 233–64. See Paul Meyer's note in *Romania, 7* (1878), 450, on the popularity of *Audigier,* the "épopée scatologique," in Bédier's phrase, which Rutebeuf cites in vv. 174–76.

73. Nykrog cites a similar example from *Esquiriel* (Montaiglon-Raynaud, eds., *Fabliaux, 5,* 102; (*Fabliaux,* p. 154.) Annominatio appears also in a *tour de farce,* "Une Dame de Flandres c'uns chevalier tolli a un autre par force," the tale of a ravished lady who goes to plead her wrongs in Rome; the first 48 verses end with the word *tort,* in lines such as: Or tort, et se destort, or retort, et or tort (v. 18) Barbazan-Méon, eds., *Fabliaux, 3,* 444–45. The piece is a comic bit of antifeminine satire. Although a rare comic device in the thirteenth century, annominatio is used occasionally in fifteenth-century comic theater. Garapon cites a fifteenth-century miracle in which an old whore laments past joys in a 19-branch annomonatio on *coing,* a diverting if indecent variation on a theme familiar from *La Vieille* of *Le Roman de la Rose* and Villon's *Belle Heaulmière* (Garapon, *La Fantaisie verbale,* p. 31; text in Achille Jubinal, *Mystères inédits du XVe siècle, 1* [Paris, 1837], 291–92). Annominatio is also one of the kinds of wordplay in the late medieval *sottie;* see, for example, the extended figure on the key *sot* word *lard* as in "blows" or *pois au lard* (Eugénie Droz, ed., *Recueil Trepperel, 1, Les Sotties* [Paris, 1935], 155.

One confronts another problem of style and tone in Rutebeuf's use of puns, which critics have frequently understood as humorous in intent (see above, p. 191, n. 6). Puns may be distinguished from annominatio in that a pun uses a word once, or at the most twice, and always with two meanings, while annominatio depends upon multiple repetition, in which change of meaning is optional. One of Rutebeuf's puns on *empire*, "empire, to worsen," appears so frequently as to be one of the automatic units of which I have spoken. Rutebeuf uses it three times, and his Voie de Tunes, in which he urges his hearers to take the Cross, is deeply serious in tone.

> Li mauvais demorront, nes couvient pas eslire;
> Et s'il sunt hui mauvais, il seront demain pire;
> De jour en jour iront de roiaume en empire:
> Se nos nes retrouvons, si n'en ferons que rire.[74]
>
> (vv. 129–32)

In Rutebeuf's *Dit de Sainte Eglise* he uses the familiar moral image of the mouth that prays while the heart keeps silent;[75] the poet says that truth is barricaded in her retreat,

> Si ne puet issir dou palais
> Car les denz muevent le trere
> Et li cuers ne s'ose avant trere. (vv. 57–59)

---

74. See also *Paix Rutebeuf*, v. 17; and *Renart le Bestourné*, v. 53. Tobler cites three examples from chronicles, but in which the play is developed as annominatio rather than as a pun (*Vermischte Beiträge*, 2, 256). Other examples appear in *Des Sis Manières de fols*, a moral poem (*Nouveau Recueil*, ed. Jubinal, 2, 70), *Du Jeu de dez*, a work moralizing on dice (ibid., p. 229); and in Baudouin de Condé's *Li Contes du pel*, vv. 17–18, and *Vers de droit*, v. 4 (*Dits, 1, 1* and 245; see p. 379 n.).

75. See FB, *1*, 281, note to v. 58, for other examples in Rutebeuf and from the *Castoiement dou pere;* add also *Bible Guiot* (v. 2111), where the image is directed against faithless women, and the long development in Gautier de Coinci's *Miracle de la nonain* (ed. Koenig, 2, 279–81, vv. 165–208), as well as the *Dit des mais* (Jubinal, ed., *Nouveau Recueil*, *1*, 184) and a sermon of Robert Messier cited by Jubinal (*O.C., 1*, lxix, n. 1).

The pun on *palais,* "palace, palate," [76] serves as a transition between the themes of fortress and prayer; as in the *Voie de Tunes,* the pun is slipped in unobtrusively. Twice again in the *Voie de Tunes* one finds puns: a verse against those who lag in their religious duties reads, "A Dieu servir dou votre iestes vos droit Romain" (v. 112), "true Roman, Roman law," where Rutebeuf alludes to the traditional criticism of Roman avarice; another, referring to France left defenseless during Louis IX's absence, reads, "France est si grace terre, n'estuet pas c'om la larde" (v. 34), "pierce with blows, lard." [77] Authority from the Bible could be cited to dignify the appearance of puns in serious texts,[78] but there are no puns at all in the purely comic pieces of Rutebeuf, his *Testament de l'âne, Dame qui fit trois tours,* and *Pet au vilain,* and only one each in *Charlot le Juif* (v. 127) and *Frère Denise* (v. 174), both in euphemistically obscene passages.[79]

Puns, then, like annominatio, are a verbal artifice little used in medieval comic works. However, a pattern of comic puns does appear with exactly the same jokes in a prose *Herberie* (FB, 2, 268–71), the *Riote du monde,*[80] and *Le Jongleur d'Ely et le roi d'Angleterre.*[81] In these works, it is the dialogue which reveals the puns:

—De quel terre [estes vos]?
—En volez vos faire poz? . . .
—Et ou est la terre?

76. See *O.C.,* 2, 48, "un jeu de mots assez peu digne de la pièce où il se trouve."

77. See also the *Complainte du comte Eudes de Nevers,* "Ne fist mie de sa croix pile" (v. 61), "heads" didn't turn tails before the Crusade—i.e. he didn't try to buy off his Crusade vow; and *Complainte du roi de Navarre,* "Pers auz barons, auz povres peires," v. 65.

78. Gracián called Christ's "Tu es petrus, et super hanc petram aedificabo ecclesiam meum," a "delicadeza sacra" in his baroque work *Agudeza y arte de ingenio* (*Obras completas,* ed. Arturo del Hoyo [Madrid, 1960], p. 387); see Curtius, "Baltasar Gracián" (*European Literature,* pp. 293–301), on rhetorical figures in baroque theory and art.

79. On euphemisims and obscenity in fabliaux, see Nykrog, *Fabliaux,* pp. 209 ff.

80. Cited by Jubinal (*O.C., 3,* 190–91 n.).

81. Montaiglon-Raynaud, eds., *Fabliaux,* 2, pp. 243–44, No. 52.

—Sor l'aive.

—Comment apele l'en l'aive?

—L'en ne l'apele pas, qu'ele vient bien sanz apeler.

This rapid flow of words and dislocation of meaning constitute one technique in the characteristic verbal abundance of the *Herberie* genre which induces a state of admiring euphoria in the spectator.[82] It is not the sense but the flow of words that charms in Rutebeuf's long enumerations of exotic places, stones, herbs, and prescriptions in his *Herberie* although no sentence degenerates into pure nonsense; his mountebank uses both rhythm and rhyme as well as repetition to cast a spell over his hearers:

> et me dist et me conmanda que je preïsse un denier de la monoie qui corroit el païs et en la contree ou je vanroie: a Paris un parisi, a Orliens un orlenois, au Mans un mansois, a Chartres un chartrain, a Londres en Aingleterre un esterlin, pour dou pain, pour dou vin a moi, pour dou fain, pour de l'avainne a mon roncin: car ceil qui auteil sert d'auteil doit vivre. (FB 2, 278)

Special verbal artifice is the prescribed technique for this particular comic genre,[83] and even the contents seem predetermined, since there are many common elements in Rutebeuf's *Herberie,* the prose *Herberie,* and the poem *De La Goute en l'aine:* the wordplay on money, the story of the forging of Judas' thirty pieces of silver, and comic prescriptions. To this base, the prose *Herberie* adds at the beginning some Latin-sounding hocus-pocus, some patter with numbers, and a series of five jokes against women, all to disarm the spectators through laughter and to bewilder them with apparent logic and science. We also find here nonsense religious annominatio

---

82. See Garapon's very interesting remarks (*Fantaisie verbale,* pp. 24–25 and 7–12), in which he contrasts meaningful wordplay with comedy of nonsense and comedy of verbal prodigality; in the two latter, the comic comes from the orgy of words, not from communication.

83. Compare with the mime *La Paix aux Anglais* whose humor is largely founded on verbal confusion in words like *culmandement* ("commandement") or *ma pié* ("mon pied, m'espée"), (Faral, *Mimes français,* pp. 42 ff.).

—"Ge pri a la vraie piteuse, ge di a celi nomeement qui pita as piez de Pitoribus, quant il nasqui de la vrai piteuse" [84]—and a mock battle entirely founded on a string of puns like, "Il me vint et ge li .xxx." Rather than state, finally, that the prose *Herberie* is an imitation of Rutebeuf (FB 2, 267),[85] I believe that all these *Herberies* are examples of a minor comic genre, like the *Jenglerie,* or jongleur's invective against a rival, which we shall see in Chapter 5, since they share so many common elements.[86]

Proverbs are virtually the only verbal unit or patterned grouping of words which appear in every literary genre regardless of stylistic level or subject matter. I was struck by this fact while reading Rutebeuf's *Vie de sainte Elysabel,* where an account of Elizabeth's kindness to a sinner ended with a proverb reeking of the barnyard —"Tant grate chievre que mal gist" (v. 1610)—and earlier where Rutebeuf's comment on the Saint—exiled, widowed, bereft, yet happy to be poor—is, "Qui a bués bee si a bués" (v. 1056). Faral dismisses these proverbs as trivial interpolations, "selon la petite philosophie du poète" (FB 2, 149, 154 nn.). Yet the proverb about the goat, for example, appears in chronicles, courtly narratives, and lyric and satirical works.[87] We have seen how often proverbs are used in Rutebeuf's polemical verse, and that they are a standard

84. On these puns, see Tobler, p. 259, and Faral, *Mimes,* pp. 55–59.
85. Two other corrections to FB annotations of Rutebeuf's *Herberie:* "Trotula" was not in fact a woman doctor (FB 2, 276, n. 2), although Rutebeuf speaks of "ma dame Trote de Salerne, and although women did practice medicine at Salerno (F. Vercauteren, "Les Médecins du VIIIe au XIIIe siècle," *Le Moyen Age,* 57, Nos. 1–2 [1951], 72); the distinction between *La Goute en l'aine* and the *Herberies* cannot be based on the former's verse 7, "Je suis bons mires de Salerne" (FB 2, 267), since Rutebeuf's charlatan is not only "herbier" but says clearly, "Je suis uns mires" (v. 10).
86. See also the comic spiel by *li espiciers* in the *Passion du Palatinus* (ed. Albert Pauphelet [Paris, 1951], *Jeux et Sapience du moyen âge,* pp. 272–73) which is in part a brief *Herberie* incorporated as a prefabricated unit into the play where its vulgar gaiety contrasts oddly with the sad lament of the grieving Maries.
87. Morawski, *Proverbes,* No. 2296; Leroux de Lincy, ed., *Proverbes, 1,* 164, who cites chap. 25 of the *Chronique de Reims; Roman de Renard,* ed. Martin, Br. XVI, v. 300; Huon le Roi's *Descrisson de religions* (see pp. xiii–iv n., giving 9 more references); *Proverbe au vilain,* No. 61, variant (see p. 134 n. with more references); Villon's *Ballade des proverbes,* v. 1; *Erec et Enide* by Chrétien de Troyes, v. 2584.

feature of fabliau "moralizing," as well as of devout stories like Rutebeuf's *Sacristain* (vv. 16, 214) and *Théophile* (v. 334). Indeed, they appear with such frequency that, in spite of their exhaustive annotations, even Faral and Julia Bastin have not identified every proverb in Rutebeuf;[88] even an intellectual like Jean de Meun uses them as freely as the humblest rhymster.[89] According to its context or interpretation, the same proverb can serve a worldly ethic or the most devout aspirations.

One might say that these capsules of wisdom, of commentary on human nature, ideals, and follies, represent a kind of prefabricated thinking similar to the poetic units which are reused by each according to his needs and talents. They are as typical of the medieval desire to glean and retain the best from the past as are the collections of *sententiae,* the anthologies, and *summae* and *miroirs* in which "all knowledge" was garnered. Each generation and each individual reworked what tradition had given them, and their labor of refinement contributed to the perfecting of man, which was to lead to the kingdom of God. The search for the typical, which seems to us to leave many works lifeless and burdened with artifice, was really their search for the ideal and their aspiration to the eternal. What we call a topic (and see as an empty form) was strong language to the medieval author, language rich in possibilities of expression and which could make men think and feel. The topic and the figure survived *because* they had depth of meaning. We have gained since then an acute feeling of individualization, but also of disruptive separation from tradition, and perhaps have lost the sense of the holy that surrounded the words of the medieval language, which somehow bore a divine note that was the author's to sound as best he could.

88. See note [171], for example, or vv. 73–74 of *La Mort Rutebeuf,* a version of Morawski's No. 2151, "Qui tant a fait qu'il ne puet més Bien le doit len lessier en pés."

89. See *Rose,* vv. 6988, 7847–48, 8003–04, 8059–60 for a few samples.

CHAPTER FIVE: THE POET IN HIS POETRY

R epeatedly in the preceding chapters it has been shown that what seemed to some to be expression of personal belief and conviction in Rutebeuf's polemical poetry was actually the reverberation of public debate. It has also been shown that the poet's role in both didactic and polemical works was to express effectively moral and social rather than personal beliefs, in order to influence his public. But does the poet nowhere speak about himself and for himself? Many have thought so, reading the group of works variously called the "personal poems" or, by Edmond Faral and Julia Bastin, "les poèmes de l'infortune." Critics have painted a vivid portrait of a Rutebeuf blowing on his fingers to keep warm while he composed courageous satires, wryly laughing at his own miseries to entertain a crowd in the hope of extracting a few pennies, and finally repenting a life of sin and debauchery at the feet of the Virgin.[1] This is indeed an exciting picture in which the poet appears both endearingly human and admirable in courage and faith.

1. The basic position of Rutebeuf's most recent editors, although somewhat qualified in the *Notices* to the poems of misfortune, is that "pour expliquer ce que Rutebeuf a été dans sa vie . . . l'on a sa confession, qu'il y a lieu de croire sincère et véridique" (FB, *1*, 43; see FB, *1*, 43–45 and 519). Others have uncritically accepted Rutebeuf's poetry as autobiographical. See, for example: Clédat, *Rutebeuf*, pp. 23 ff.; Adolf Kressner, "Rustebuef, ein Dichterleben im Mittelalter" (*Franco-Gallia*, *10*, No. 11 [November 1893], 168); Pesce, "Le Portrait de Rutebeuf," p. 94; Charles H. Post, "The Paradox of Humor and Satire in the Poems of Rutebeuf," *French Review*, *25*, No. 5 (April 1952), 364. Almost all of Lucas' "Etude littéraire" in his edition of Rutebeuf's "personal" poetry is a gloomy extrapolation of Rutebeuf's "autobiography" from his works (*Les Poésies personnelles de Rutebeuf* [Paris, 1938], pp. 55–75). The portrait resulting from these attempts to deduce biography from medieval poetry varies. Cohen calls Rutebeuf the "ancêtre des poètes maudits, préfigure de Villon au XVe et de Verlaine au XIX" (*Poésie en France au moyen âge* [Paris, 1952], p. 70); Lénient is one of several critics who have compared Rutebeuf to Nicolas Gilbert, tlthough the 18th-century poet's misery was legendary in every sense of the word, since he held three pensions at the time of his death (*Satire en France*, p. 55). Dehm thought Rutebeuf had an aristocratic inner nature which forbade him to compromise with a corrupt world (*Studien zu Rutebeuf*, p. 62).

Yet the work of some critics has blurred the outlines of this portrait. As they compared Rutebeuf's personal poetry with other works—with Goliard poems, with vernacular poems on themes of misery, lament, and misfortune—the clearly individualized picture they had of Rutebeuf seemed to dissolve into conventional *topoi* where they thought to find confession. Some have been content to express doubts about Rutebeuf's sincerity without seeking to explore or explain the resemblances of themes and images between Rutebeuf's "personal" poetry and the works of other poets.[2] It is even with reluctance that Ham discovered *topoi* within the "personal" poetry, since for him the appearance of *topoi* in a poem meant that the work was a series of "meaningless clichés" and was therefore valueless.[3] The question of Rutebeuf's appearance in his poetry cannot be reduced, however, to a struggle between sincerity and convention, but involves the medieval idea of self and subjective experience.

THE MEDIEVAL CONCEPT OF SELF AND THE POETIC "I"   The Middle Ages were far from distrusting subjectivity, but understood it mainly as a means of perceiving spiritual truth. The inner consciousness had little value insofar as it was a unique personal experience of life. The relation of the self to others and to God, however, was seen as spiritually profitable. Dreams, for example, were immensely interesting to medieval men when they

2. See, for example, the reviews of Lucas' *Poésies personnelles* by: Julia Bastin, who said, "Il faut faire la part des motifs littéraires" (*Romania, 66*, No. 3 [July 1940], 405); E. Hoepffner, who asks "si l'on n'a pas affaire, au moins en partie, à des thèmes littéraires, à des plaintes conventionnelles, dont la valeur biographique serait nulle ou minime" (*Revue des langues romanes, 68*, Nos. 13–24 [January–December 1938], 225); Jessie Crosland in *Modern Language Review, 35*, No. 1 (January 1940), 102–03. See also "Osservazioni e note sulla lirica di Rutebeuf" by Luciana Cocito, in the *Giornale Italiano di Filologia, 11*, No. 4 (November 28, 1958), 352; and Alfred Foulet's review of FB, in which he asks of the poems of misfortune: "Just how much truth do these doleful tales contain?" (*Speculum, 36*, No. 2 [April 1961], 329). Maurice Delbouille, reviewing FB (*Marche Romane, 10*, No. 4 [Oct.–Dec. 1960] 147–58), also insists that we must distinguish the "acteur" from the poet himself (p. 150).

3. "Rutebeuf, Pauper and Polemist," p. 231.

could be interpreted as signs and prophecies;[4] indeed, dreams were often influential in determining the course of history. Bonaventura recounts that Innocent III, hesitating to approve the new order of Saint Francis, dreamed that he saw the Lateran basilica ready to crumble but held up by a poor man, small and miserably dressed. Recognizing Saint Francis, Innocent gave his approval and benediction to the Minorite order.[5] Innocent's dream, apocryphal or not, expressed the reality of the Church's need to return to spiritual and evangelical concerns. Francis' name appears naturally with the question of subjectivity, since he utterly trusted his inner spirit for guidance in his actions. Each step of his conversion, as related by Bonaventura, was inspired by a dream, a vision, or an irresistible impulse which Francis understood as God moving within him.[6] The inner consciousness was considered, then, a valid approach to divine truth. If allegorized subjective experiences such as Rutebeuf's *Voie* were presented as a "dream," it is because the visionary form gave an extra measure of truth to the work, since dreams were considered divine revelation.[7]

The Middle Ages seem indifferent to the individual, unless he could be seen presenting some exemplary type or expressing a general truth. There were actually very few full medieval autobiographies. That of Guibert, Abbot of Nogent (d. 1124), follows the Augustinian conception of autobiography as the story of a man's striving toward God, of a man's discovery of God's purpose for

4. Matthew Paris reports "for a fact" a dream of Pope Alexander IV, in which Alexander saw his predecessor, Innocent IV, judged and condemned by a divine court, with the words: "Woe to thee! . . . Thou hast disdained, annulled and invalidated the holy decrees, and the benefits conferred by thy holy predecessors, to their injury, wherefore with justice thy acts are adjudged to be annulled" (*English History, 3*, 17–18). A convenient dream from one who himself was about to annul Innocent's bull *Etsi animarum*, which favored the University masters over the Mendicants! Charlemagne's prophetic dreams in the *Chanson de Roland* are, of course, a sign of God's knowledge and guidance of human affairs.

5. *Vie de saint François*, pp. 68–69; See Raby, *Christian-Latin Poetry*, p. 417.

6. *Vie de saint François*, pp. 35–42. See also Lambert, *Franciscan Poverty*, for interesting remarks on the intuitive basis of Francis' "Rule" (pp. 34 ff.).

7. See above, pp. 29, 147–50 and the use of dreams to penetrate into subjective experience in the *Roman de la Rose*, the *Divine Comedy*, and *Piers Plowman*.

himself and of God within him.[8] Much in Guibert recalls Augustine: the experience of sin and the awakening to salvation; the decisive influence of a pious mother whose anxious care for her son's soul is an image of God's concern for man; the relation of the difficulties encountered by a man placed high in the Church hierarchy. Other aspects of Guibert's autobiography, however, show the typical medieval disinterest in the individual himself. We expect to find sustained introspection of the sort appearing in the prayerful first chapter, in which Guibert speaks directly to God just as Augustine did in his *Confessions*. Yet the latter part of his autobiography is mostly a chronicle of miraculous or important events occurring before and during Guibert's lifetime. Our attention is diverted from Guibert himself to the meaning of these pious tales, which show God at work in history, but in which the autobiographer becomes merely a chronicler. The focus of the work shifts from the personal to the historical.

Abélard, extraordinary and controversial, portrays himself and his world in strongly moral terms, since in his *Historia calamitatum* [9] he attributes his calamities to envy of colleagues and to his own lust and pride. The strength of this brief but violent relation of his life's struggles lie in the brutal truthfulness of his descriptions of his motives and acts, in the tensions and antagonisms apparent in every human relation he encountered, and in the underlying sense of a constantly felt presence of physical existence: the untidiness of children; the deep sleep which prevented him from feeling the terrible revenge inflicted by Héloïse's uncle; the sweet repose among the quiet nuns of the Paraclete. Yet Abelard is as exceptional in his autobiographical talent as in his intellectual force, by the depth to which he explores weakness and strength within himself while virtually suspending moral commentary and

8. *Self and Society in Medieval France. The Memoirs.* . . , ed. John F. Benton, trans. C. C. Swinton Bland (New York, 1970). See Georg Misch, *History of Autobiography in Antiquity,* 2, trans. E. W. Dickes (Cambridge, Mass., 1951), 625–92; Misch relates Augustine's *Confessions* to the earlier traditions of autobiography and to such late Latin figures as Boethius.
9. Ed. J. Monfrin (Paris, 1959).

judgment until the very end. He finally invites others to follow his example in enduring persecution for the purification of their souls, words with which he rejoins the commoner level of medieval biography.[10]

Dante's *Divine Comedy* is also a spiritual autobiography, but in which the being-in-time is unimportant, and the being-in-spirit, the quest for perfection, is supreme. Dante's work is filled with human experiences and historical figures, but they are abstracted from any process of temporal change. Immobilized in time, their spiritual essence is revealed to us. Dante's progression toward Heaven is, in terms of human time, the dream of a moment; he gives an account of an instant's perception of the infinite, not a record of experience lived out in time.[11]

Medieval biography, following the concern for inner and spiritual truth, is generally limited to lives of saints or exceptional chiefs of state who can be described as examples for mankind. Joinville, for example, wove together his own experience as *witness* to a holy life with a record of the "saintes paroles et des bons faiz nostre roy saint Looys." [12] Joinville really speaks more as a moralist than a biographer; he wrote his book so that all "qui l'orront, y puissent penre bon exemple, et les exemples mettre à oevre." [13]

When the medieval poet appears in his own poetry, he too makes an effort to draw a general lesson from what he relates about himself. Yet the relation between the poet and what he says of himself in his works is not direct; the poet gives neither an objective self-portrait nor an immediately subjective account of his inner feel-

10. See the excellent study of Abélard's *Historia calamitatum* by Mary M. McLaughlin, "Abélard as Autobiographer: The Motives and Meaning of his 'Story of Calamities,'" *Speculum, 42*, No. 3 (July 1967), 463–88.

11. On the role of personal experience in the *Divine Comedy* and the *Vita nuova*, see Thomas G. Bergin, *Dante* (New York, 1965), pp. 67 ff. and esp. pp. 258–60. See also Auerbach, *Literary Language*, pp. 314–17; and Leo Spitzer, "Note on the Poetic and the Empirical 'I' in Medieval Authors," *Traditio, 4* (1946), 415–22 (see below, p. 260, n. 14).

12. *Vie de saint Louis*, ed. Wailly, p. 2, par. 2.

13. Ibid., p. 10, par. 18. See the valuable discussion of Joinville as moralist by Alfred Foulet, in his "Notes sur la *Vie de saint Louis* de Joinville," *Romania, 58* (October 1932), 551–64.

ings. The self, as we shall see, can only appear after being filtered through the stylization of literary convention. Indeed, I would posit that real information about the poet's own historical life could be incorporated in his poetry only to the extent that it conformed to literary conventions accepted by both poet and public.

I have found a seminal article of Leo Spitzer's, "The Poetic and Empirical 'I' in Medieval Authors," of great help in dealing with the relation between the self that appears in medieval poems and the poet himself. Spitzer starts with the assumption that the medieval public "saw in the poetic "I" a representative of mankind, [and] that it was interested only in this representative role of the poet." [14] The poetic "I" acted both as an individual who transcended the limitations of individuality and as a single consciousness who fixed in words his experience of universal truths. Even when, as with Villon or Dante, there was a degree of concordance between the poetic "I" and the empirical, historical "I," the two sets of facts were not interchangeable; and it was the poetic "I" which revealed important truths of interest to the medieval public.

D. R. Sutherland has further explored the nature of the poetic "I" in an article on Adam de la Halle's appearance in his *Jeu de la feuillée*.[15] Sutherland suggests that the medieval poet created for himself a specific personality which then became his trademark and which reappeared whenever the poet spoke about himself. This process of self-identification may be compared to the choice of a motto or blazon which served to define the essence of an individual life and to guide action.[16] For D. R. Sutherland the

14. Pp. 415–16. Spitzer discusses particularly the poets' adoption of the "ego" in texts they copied. He studies Dante's *Vita nuova* as a "seemingly autobiographical but actually ontological account of the development and course of the feeling of love." In the *Divine Comedy* Spitzer describes the strengthening of Dante's personality as it becomes more truly Christian, until Beatrice appears to replace Virgil as the poet's guide, calling him by name (*Purg.*, XXX, vv. 55–56). Spitzer also studies the Archipreste de Hita, who is both protagonist and image of the potential sinner in his *Libro de buen amor*.

15. "Fact and Fiction in the *Jeu de la Feuillée*," *Romance Philology, 13*, No. 4 (May, 1960), 419–28, esp. pp. 425–28.

16. Poirion describes the aristocratic choice of a blazon or device in the 14th century as a consecration of the self: "C'est un thème affectif, proposé à l'existence, qui rassemble les actions éparses dans la continuité d'une intention première" (*Le Poète et le prince*, p. 63).

invention of a poetic personality, presented as "real," is part of a literary technique "designed to satisfy the taste of thirteenth century audiences for works in which fiction is dressed up as fact."[17]

The identification of a poetic "I" does not mean that the medieval public was not interested in the poet, nor that the poet effaced himself behind his work in the antique anonymity of a "Turoldus." On the contrary, the poet himself occupies an ever more important place in his work in the twelfth and thirteenth centuries. He signs his works,[18] and he steps forth in his prologues to proclaim his talents and the worth of his subject. In the courtly lyric, of course, the poetic "I" entirely filled the poem: the conventional subject of a courtly love poem was the subjective response of a lover to his experience of love, and for the most part the courtly poets chose the first person singular as their form.

Medieval convention further required a tone of convincing verisimilitude in the portrayal of the poetic "I." Even in those works where the poet was most severely limited to a small number of poetic topics, as in the courtly lyric, the poetic "I" had to ring true. If the public felt, for example, that a courtly poet sang not "par amors" but "par esfort" his work was condemned as "deloial"— that is, not conforming to the "laws" governing the theme the poet had set himself or to the rhetorical precept of verisimilitude.[19] The

17. Sutherland cites the Provençal novel *Flamenca,* where real names are used for fictitious characters (p. 428). We may refer also to the 12th-century novelist, Chrétien de Troyes, who places his fantastic adventures within a "realistic" setting by means of, for example, the elaborate descriptions of clothing and armory in *Erec et Enide.* (See Mario Roques' "Index des mots relatifs à la civilisation et aux mœurs," which covers 19 dense pages at the end of his edition of *Erec* [pp. 264–82].) Chrétien's public evidently enjoyed self-portrayal within the ideal world of the chivalric novel.

18. Curtius considers the question of pride of authorship in contrast with conventional anonymity in his "Mention of the Author's Name in Medieval Literature" (*European Literature,* pp. 515–18). See Nykrog's study of fabliaux "signed" by their authors and his conclusions on the circulation of such works (*Fabliaux,* pp. 29–44).

19. Dragonetti, *Technique poétique des trouvères,* pp. 21–30. The convention of verisimilitude, in Dragonetti's words, "se réalise dans la mesure où le trouvère est touché par le sens de la rhétorique dont il use. Nous retrouvons ici un précepte de rhétorique traditionnelle sur l'action de *vraisemblance* du style: est courtoise pour le trouvère et son public, la chanson dont la fiction suggère un sentiment éprouvé de l'amour idéal, inséparable de son expression lyrique" (pp. 29–30).

precept is valid not only for the courtly works but also for moral and didactic works in which authors had to avoid writing so cleverly, yet unconvincingly, that there arose in their hearers, as Brunetto Latini says, "une suspection comme de chose pensée par grant mestrie."[20]

The successful portrayal of a poetic "I" may be compared to an actor playing a part. The actor must be completely convincing in each of his roles: the audience must feel that he not only believes what he says but is what he pretends to be. If the actor's own personality intrudes through the character he plays, the artistic illusion is broken. In the same manner, if the poet's art is more evident than his poetic "I," the public cannot accept the dramatic and poetic tension, the temporary suspension of historical fact, which permits the artistic truth to exist.

If the poet created a believable poetic personality, the medieval audience took his poetic "I" at face value. The public sought the poet *in* the work rather than the man behind the poet. The Provençal *vidas* and *razos,* for example, exploited the public's interest in the apparent "biographical" truth of a poet's works, even when the "biographical" facts were drawn from the body of the poem itself.[21] The *vidas* and *razos* are, indeed, an extension in prose of the conventional verisimilitude maintained in the poem itself.

We have one text which comments on the plausibility of Rutebeuf's own poetic "I." A Dominican, compiling after 1328 an anthology of works to honor the Virgin, wrote 16 verses to introduce the *Mariage Rutebeuf,* which he included as an example of how women make men suffer. Stating that married men always live in discord, the compiler continues:

> Se tu vieus qu'essample te doigne,
> Ruthebeuf trop bien le tesmoigne,
> Qui une fois se maria,

20. *Trésor,* p. 343. See Latini's chapters, "A Conter le Fait voirsemblablement" (p. 355), and "D'Argument voirsamblable" (p. 367); see also above, p. 223.
21. See Guiette, *Questions de littérature,* p. 10, and the *vidas* edited by Boutière and Schutz, *Biographies des troubadours* (Toulouse-Paris, 1950).

Ne sai dist Ave Maria
Ne patenostre ne priere,
Aprés vousist miex estre en biere.
Il de soy mesmes ainsi dist
En un dité que il en fist. (FB, *1, 25*)

The compiler's information about Rutebeuf's "marriage" is taken, of course, from the poem itself: the Dominican accepts Rutebeuf's poetic "I" uncritically, since he is interested in Rutebeuf's tale of matrimonial woe as an example. Any correlation between the poetic matter and the true facts of Rutebeuf's own personal life would have been irrelevant to the Dominican's didactic purpose. Yet the Dominican accepts the truth of what Rutebeuf says in his marriage because the poet's subjective expression was convincing: "Ruthebeuf trop bien le tesmoigne . . . Il de soy mesmes ainsi dist."

I believe the choice of poetic personality, in the broadest sense, is determined by the poetic genre and themes. In the courtly lyric poems of the *trouvères,* for example, the speaker in the poem is either the lover or occasionally the lady. If other figures speak in the poem—a maiden's mother, a jealous husband, the rustic lover of a country lass—they do so only in dialogue, never as the subjective poetic "I." [22] It would not be suitable, however, for a poet to speak as a lover in, for example, a poem about simony. If we approach Rutebeuf's personal poetry by genre and subject, we shall find that many of the apparent inconsistencies or contradictions in his "personality," which have troubled many critics, vanish. [23] Instead, a unique and lifelike portrait of Rutebeuf is seen to be carved out of

22. See Jeanroy, *Origines,* pp. 61–101, on the characters of dramatic courtly lyrics such as the *pastourelle, chanson de mal mariée,* Crusade farewell, etc. See also, on the subjective conventions of the *pastourelle* and the *chanson de toile,* Faral's article in *Romania, 49* (April 1923), 244; and *59* (1946–47), 459; and that of Raymond Joli, "Les Chansons d'histoire," *Romanistisches Jahrbuch, 12* (1961), 51–66.

23. Notably Leo "Persönlicher Ausdruck," p. 140, and Ham, *Renart le Bestorné,* pp. 39–49, where Ham suggests the possibility of "multiple authorship" of the works thought to be Rutebeuf's; Ham's theory is opposed by most critics; see Nykrog, *Fabliaux,* pp. 29–30, and the review of Ham's *Renart* by Faral, in *Romania, 70* (1948), 268–69.

topical matter derived from literary tradition. He established a strong poetic personality within the confines of the appropriate poetic "I" dictated by convention for each poetic genre he chose.

When several poetic personalities appear within one single work, as in Villon's *Testament,* the concept of poetic personalities depending on different genres becomes even more useful. Siciliano has identified the different genres and tones within the *Testament* in a very useful article,[24] but feels the differences within the work exist because different parts were written at various moments in the life of Villon. Siciliano rejects the "ris en pleurs" concept of the poet's nature, feeling Villon laughed when young, wept when old. Yet Siciliano confuses the chronology and nature of the poet with the composition and nature of the poem. The work certainly combines a complex of tones and themes, and the *Testament* was very likely not written all at one sitting nor were all the pieces probably composed at the same period. But the *Testament* is less a "journal poétique" than a work in which the poet chose to represent simultaneously several poetic personalities, to emphasize the play between opposing poetic "I's"—the "amant martyr," the "bon follastre," and the "povre Villon" identified by Siciliano—and these various poetic personalities are enriched by elements borrowed from all Villon saw and did, so that they have an extraordinarily believable density. The resulting rich, complex poetic personality we call "Villon" lent its name to a type who reappears in Rabelais—and in the works of many critics! Compared to Villon, Rutebeuf's poetic "I's", although they differ from poem to poem, are individually rather thin and necessarily one-sided. Yet the process is the same, and the reliance on a poetic personality appropriate to the theme rather than to the man writing the work is a useful key to reading much of medieval literature written in a subjective mode.

Chapters 1–3 describe Rutebeuf's poetic personality in his didactic, moral, and polemical works. He paints himself throughout as a fearless speaker of the truth, frequently completing a verse in which he mentions himself by some formula such as: "Se Rustebués

24. "Sur le *Testament* de François Villon," *Romania,* 65 (January 1939), 39–90.

est voirdisanz,"[25] or "Rustebués dist, qui riens ne çoile."[26] He developed, as we saw, this self-portrait of the righteously outspoken poet most fully in the *Dit d'Hypocrisie,* where he specifically described himself as the redoubtable enemy of hypocrites. Rutebeuf portrays himself as teacher of the truth even in his fabliaux, in such verses as "Rustebués nos dist et enseigne," which introduces the "moral" of his stories.[27] The same poetic personality serves him in his *Disputaison de Charlot et du barbier,* where the poet acts as arbiter in a dispute between two rival jongleurs. The "barber" calls upon Rutebeuf to choose between them, saying:

> . . . se Rustebués
> Qui nous connoist bien a dis anz,
> Voloit dire deus motés nués,
> Més qu'au dire fust voirdisanz
> Ne contre toi ne a mon oés,
> Més par le voir se fust mis anz,
> Je le vueil bien, se tu le veus,
> Que le meillor soit eslisanz. (vv. 81–88)

Here again, of course, it is natural that Rutebeuf appear as a teller of truth, since his decision must be fair.

In *Charlot et le barbier,* however, Rutebeuf adds another individual touch:

> L'autrier un jor jouer aloie
> Devers l'Auçirrois saint Germain

25. *Voie de Paradis,* v. 662; the same expression appears in the *Bataille des Vices contre les Vertus,* v. 38, and in the *Testament* attributed to Jean de Meun, p. 53. See also, "Verité ai dite en mains leus" (*Des Règles,* v. 3).

26. *Complainte d'outremer,* v. 99. Compare, for example, with the didactic "I" of Gautier de Coinci, who portray himself as disinterested:
> Je ne truis pas por avoir pris
> Ne por robes ne por avoir,
> Mais por l'amor la Dame avoir. (*Léocade,* vv. 2322–24)
It is interesting to note also that Gautier scarcely intervenes in the narration of his *Léocade,* but that his didactic self appears in the moralizing satirical interpolations to impose opinion and judgment upon his matter.

27. *Testament de l'âne,* v. 165. See verses 131–32 of *Charlot et la peau de lièvre,* and vv. 169–70 of *La Dame qui fit trois tours.*

Plus matin que je ne soloie,
Qui ne lief pas volentiers main. (vv. 1-4)

The same trait appears in the *Voie de Paradis,* where Rutebeuf says
he has a reputation for sleeping late:

Je, qui n'ai pas non d'estre main
Levez . . . (vv. 70-71)

In both poems the trait is irrelevant to the subject matter [28] and
seems to be Rutebeuf's way of individualizing the poetic "I" he
portrays. It is comparable to his "signature," which uses the familiar
etymology and annominatio on *rude-bués* (see above, p. 190)—a
characteristic wordplay whose substance is dictated by the poet's
name, not by Rutebeuf's opinion of his own technique. However,
even such peculiarities as these are subordinated to the poet's theme:
in Rutebeuf's *Griesche d'hiver,* where his subject required that the
poet seem to have no relief from misery, he said, "Je ne dorm que
le premier somme" (v. 28).

Charlot et le barbier is of interest also because it illustrates a type
of poem in which the poet places himself and his colleagues on the
scene as professional artists, and in which didactic concerns were
absent or secondary. *Charlot et le barbier* is a poem of invective
between rival jongleurs. The two protagonists hurl insults, bearing
on personal traits: [29] Charlot is a Jew, the barber has pimples on

28. Dislike for early rising was a criticism most often leveled at lazy clerics,
especially monks, who were supposed to get up early for Matins (see above,
pp. 47-48). The impudent Goliard's credo, "Cum in orbem universum," establishes
new rules for the *Ordo vagorum* and prohibits Matins as an unhealthy spiritual
exercise:

Ordo noster prohibet matutinas plane:
Sunt quaedam phantasmata que vagantur mane,
Per quae nobis veniunt visiones vanae;
Sic qui tunc surrexerit, non est mentis sane.
(*Carmina burana,* ed. Schmeller, p. 252, No. 193)

29. Compare with Matthieu de Vendôme's attack in his *Arts versificatoria* on a
rival poet, Arnoul de Saint-Evurce, "Rufinus," criticized for having red hair, sign
of a treacherous character (Faral, *Arts poétiques,* p. 2, n. 3, and pp. 109-10). See
also the *jeu-parti* between Thibaut de Champagne and Raoul de Soissons, where
the King of Navarre mocks Raoul's crutch and Raoul Thibaut's "gros ventre farsi"
(No. XLII, *Chansons,* ed. A. Wallensköld [Paris, 1925], pp. 148-50).

his skin. Their competition is not, therefore, on a really professional or mock-professional basis as is that of the *Deus Bourdeors ribaud,* in which the dispute bears on the artistic talents as well as on the personal defects of the combattants.[30] Added to these poems of jongleurs' rivalry are works depicting competition between different sorts of entertainers. In *Des Taboureurs,* for example, a true "menestrel" deplores the success of certain vile peasants who think that because they make a great racket drumming after a day spent in the fields they too are "menestrels."[31] Baudouin de Condé, in his *Contes des hiraus,* appears in a dispute with a "herald" or pursuivant at arms, a new-fangled sort of entertainer who went about the country inventing blazons and preying on the vanity of foolish lords who neglected the good poets at their door.[32]

Another type of poem in which poets appeared "professionally" were works where the poet demanded payment for services rendered or patronage expected. The poet could take a moralizing, reproachful tone, as Rutebeuf did in a brief aside in his *Voie de Tunes,* speaking of Louis IX's sons Philippe and Jean Tristan and of Robert II, Count of Artois, who had just taken the Cross:

Tot soit qu'a moi bien faire soie*nt* tardi*f* et lan*t*,
Si ai je de pitié por eulz le cueur dolant:
Mais ce me reconforte (qu'iroie je celant?)
Qu'en lor venues * vont en paradix volant.   * voyages overseas
(vv. 65–68)

Perhaps Rutebeuf included these verses to show that he was as indifferent to worldly goods, however much deserved, as the three

30. Three poems are edited under the title *Deus Bourdeurs ribauds* in Faral's *Mimes français,* pp. 83–111. Compare also the series of *sirventés* exchanged by the troubadours Sordel and Peire Bremon Ricas Novas (eds. G. Bertoni and A. Jeanroy, *Annales du Midi* [January–April 1916], pp. 269–305), and the Provençal mock letters of recommendation in which poets insult each other cited by Jeanroy, *Troubadours, 1,* 140–42.

31. Jubinal, ed. *Jongleurs et trouvères,* pp. 164–69.

32. No. XII, *Dits, 1,* 153–75. Baudouin's *Contes des hiraus* gives us some taste of the day-to-day life of a wandering poet, since he recounts in dialogue his reception at the hope of a knight in Lorraine. See the remarks of Paulin Paris on heralds in *Histoire littéraire, 23,* 269–72.

young princes who had just taken the Cross. Wit, however, loosened tight purse-strings as fast as a moralizing scowl. Rutebeuf's *De Brichemer*[33] is a gaily sarcastic reproach to a patron whose promised payment was as long in coming as the return of King Arthur from Avalon (v. 16)—a courteous giver, indeed:

> Je nel truis a eschars ne chiche;
> N'a si large jusqu'outre mer,
> Quar de promesse m'a fet riche. (vv. 4–6)

Such epigrammatic revenge in verse, is of course, characteristic of an age in which poets expected to be paid for their verse. Rutebeuf's irony is much like that of Walther von der Vogelweide in his poem against the king who had not paid him a promised pension of thirty marks.

> Der nam ist grôz, der nuz ist aber in solher mâze,
> Daz ich in niht begrîfen mac, gehœren noch gesehen.
>   · · ·
> Nû râte ein ieglich friunt, ob ichz behalte ode ob ichz lâze?[34]

Primas (Hugh d'Orléans), a scholar and virulent satirist of the twelfth century, wrote an entertaining "dialogue" between himself and an unlined cloak, given him by a stingy prelate; "Sed Iacob non Esau sum," says the bald mantle.[35] Compare these poems with Colin Muset's Baedeker of good hostels for poets in "Devers Chastelvilain," in which he celebrates the lord of Chateauvillain for being as quick to give as "uns oitours norrois," and criticizes those of Choiseul, Vignory, and Raynel, who have "mis lor avoir/ En vaiches et en bués" instead of into good verse.[36]

I believe Rutebeuf's *Charlot le Juif et la peau de lièvre* is written

33. For the meaning of *Brichemer,* "trickster," see FB, *1,* 579, and Tobler, *Vermischte Beiträge,* 2, 226.

34. *Gedichte,* p. 35. "The sum is great, but is disbursed in such a measure,/ That it may not be seen, nor heard, nor yet possessed/ . . ./ Advise me, friends, should I renounce or keep this treasure?" (trans. Ian Colvin, *I Saw the World* [London, 1938], p. 91).

35. *Goliard Poets,* ed. Whicher, pp. 80–83.

36. No. XIX, *Chansons,* ed. Joseph Bédier (Paris, 1938), pp. 34–35.

to give a similar warning to those who attempt to pay a poet less
than he deserves:

> Qui menestreil vuet engignier
> Mout en porroit mieulz bargignier. (vv. 1–2)

Charlot et la peau de lièvre is also an excellent example of how
Rutebeuf worked by setting conventional literary material in a
realistic context. His story of how Guillaume, steward to the Count
of Poitiers, killed his horse by chasing a worthless hare is realistically and quickly told. Rutebeuf expands in greater detail the
role of jongleurs at the marriage of Guillaume's cousin, relating
how minstrels came from afar to share the feast and how they
asked for "maitres ou deniers"[37] in payment. Rutebeuf, to give his
tale verisimilitude, adds that he himself was at the wedding:

> Je meïmes, qui i estoie,
> Ne vi piesa si bele faire
> Ne qui autant me peüst plaire,
> Se Diex des ses biens me reparte. (vv. 54–57)

He then recounts the revenge of the jongleur Charlot on his
"maitre," the steward Guillaume, who gave him only the skin of the
hare for which he had killed his horse, saying

> . . . vos cuit teil choze doneir,
> Que que en doie gronsonneir,*   * grumble
> Qui m'a coutei plus de cent souz,
> Se je soie de Dieu assouz. (vv. 85–88)

Charlot, disgruntled, turns the tables by returning the skin, be-
fouled, to Guillaume. The basic idea of scatological revenge appears also in another fabliau, *Jouglet;* in *Jouglet,* however, it is a
minstrel who is victimized by a "vilain" whom he had tried to
trick.[38] Stories of minstrels' capacity for revenge against those who

37. A *maitre* meant a letter written by the host to a friend or relative requesting
that the recipient pay the jongleur for his work. See examples of such letters in
Faral, *Jongleurs,* p. 122, nn. 2, 3.
38. Montaiglon and Raynaud, eds., *Fabliaux, 4,* No. XCVIII; see Nykrog,
Fabliaux, pp. 56 and 131.

do not treat them well appear not only in fabliaux but in exempla.[39]
However, the key to *Charlot,* I believe, is that it is a gloss or
explanation of a proverb: "Bon est le lievre dont cent soulz couste
la pel." [40] Many fabliaux "illustrate" the meaning of proverbs, (see
p. 248), just as *Charlot* proves the truth of the proverb which serves
as conclusion:

> Rutebuez dit, bien m'en sovient:
> Qui barat quiert, baraz li vient. (vv. 131–32)

Clearly, then, no matter how realistic or how convincingly "personal" may seem Rutebeuf's poetry in which he describes himself
or poets like him, the poet's technique remains the same as in his
moral and didactic verse. His material derives from literary tradition, and both the poet and his public sought a convincing and
expert treatment of conventional theme, not an artistic transposition
of historical reality. Realistic elements do enter, but only to support
the plausibility of the poet's development of literary *topoi.* In his
poems of misfortune, therefore, the subject he sets out to treat and
the conventional topics and forms appropriate to the subject must
be defined. His poetic success must be measured not through our
discovery of his inner soul but through our discovery of his poetic
art.

THE POETIC "I" IN POEMS OF REPENTANCE   Since the
individual self was worthy of consideration in its spiritual context,
portrayed either aspiring to God or suffering in a state of sinful
despair and misery, as in the autobiography of Guibert and Dante's
Divine Comedy, the author could cast an experience of sin and
repentance in a didactic mold, portraying himself as Everyman and

39. See Jacques de Vitry, *Exempla,* pp. 28–29, No. LXVII.
40. Morawski, *Proverbes,* No. 284; the proverb is taken from a 15th-century
collection (edited by E. Langlois in the *Bibliothèque de l'Ecole des Chartes,* 60
[1900], No. 117, p. 577). The idea of the hunter who kills his horse to catch a
hare appears in the work of a 13th-century preacher (text cited FB, 2, 257, note
to vv. 19–30). Compare also Olivier's comment on his proud friend Roland: "Pur
un sul levre vait tute jur cornant" (*Chanson de Roland,* ed. Joseph Bédier [Paris,
1960], v. 1780).

discovering in his individual life examples of sins to avoid and virtues to cherish. This is the value of the poetic "I" in Rutebeuf's *Voie de Paradis*, which seems to start out as a personal adventure but ends up as a sermon.

Another genre for representing the spiritual self was the poem of repentance and confession in the form of a prayer, where the author could directly express his longing for God. In such prayers the self is appraised only in terms of sins and failings. These are biographical works in the sense that the introspection includes a backward glance through time along the course of an individual's life; yet facts are entirely subordinated to spiritual considerations, to "the individual's anxious reflection on his moral status."[41] Prayers of sorrow and repentance are a reduction of the Augustinian type of confession, for in Augustine prayer alternated with narrative and thoughtful reflection on the meaning of events. Only the opening of the soul to God's judgment remains in medieval poems of repentance, where salvation is the burning concern. David Kuhn, in his very penetrating analysis of *La Mort Rutebeuf*, emphasizes that only in confession do ordinary words become a sacramental language. Rutebeuf's poetry is thus, like Villon's, assimilated to another, more "legitimate" form of discourse, according to Kuhn.[42]

Rutebeuf wrote four repentance poems: *La Mort Rutebeuf*, ostensibly "personal," and the prayers of regret and repentance in *Sainte Marie l'Egyptienne* (vv. 212–44, 261–332), in *Théophile* (vv. 384–539), and in the *Sacristain* (vv. 488–532). These prayers combine the double elements of a *confessio peccati*, sorrow for sin, and *confessio laudis*, expression of faith in remission of sins, and praise and thanksgiving to God and the Virgin.[43] All use the first person throughout, and no attempt is made to objectify the mind and

---

41. Misch thus describes the early influence of Christian monastic confessional practices, which turned self-analysis into "a method of brooding on sins" (*Autobiography*, 2, 580–81). See all of Misch's chapter, "Religious Self-Portrayal and the Life-Story of the Soul" (ibid., pp. 486–537), particularly the pages on Jeremiah's *Lamentations*, so influential on the subjective and sorrowful tone of the medieval *complainte* (see above, pp. 165–66).

42. *La Poétique de François Villon* (Paris, 1967), pp. 473–80.

43. See Misch, *Autobiography*, 2, 583.

heart through allegory, although the source of sin is represented as
an outward, tempting Devil, salvation as the intervention of the
merciful healing Virgin. The self speaking in all of Rutebeuf's
poems of repentance looks inwardly at his soul, outwardly toward
his life and actions and feels an excruciating sense of unworthiness
and great anxiety over his chances for salvation. The subjective
point of view is maintained throughout *La Mort Rutebeuf*, as in
the other prayers of repentance. Only the final comment on death
is cast in general terms:

> La mort ne lest ne dur ne tendre
> Por avoir que l'en li aport;
> Et quant li cors est mis en cendre,
> Si covient a Dieu reson rendre
> De quanques fist dusqu'a la mort. (vv. 68–72)

La Mort intermingles several themes characteristic of prayers of
repentance: the discovery of the need to repent, and a call to the
heart to shed tears,[44] pray, and serve God. The discovery of the sinful self is set in terms of a sudden awareness of time—time past,
spent in sin, and time future, where salvation or damnation await:
"Tart serai més au repentir" (v. 13).[45] The poet comprehends the
goodness and mercy of God and the Virgin at the same time as

---

44. Compare *La Mort:* "Bien me doit le cuer lermoier" (v. 4), with *Sainte
Marie l'Egyptienne:* "Comment puet cesser plors ne lermes" (v. 231), and
Théophile: "Ja més ne finirai de brere" (v. 561), recalled in *L'Ave Maria Rutebeuf*
(vv. 65–66). See the many examples of tears as a sign of contrition in Yedlicka,
Expressions of the Linguistic Area of Repentance and Remorse in Old French,
pp. 352–76. The similarity and stability of terms of repentance throughout the
Middle Ages is striking; compare *Sainte Marie l'Egyptienne:* [Dieu] ne veut pas
que pechierres muire,/ Ainz convertisse a sa droiture" (vv. 159–60), with the
Testament attributed to Jean de Meun: "Diex qui ne vuelt que muire peschierres,
tant mefface,/ Mais qu'il se convertisse et qu'il vive et bien face" (p. 112),
and finally, with Villon's *Testament:* "Pourtant ne veult pas Dieu ma mort,/
Mais convertisse et vive en bien" (vv. 106–07). See also Jean-Charles Payen,
Le Motif du repentir dans la littérature française médiévale (des origines á 1230)
(Geneva-Paris, 1968), esp. pp. 588 ff. on Rutebeuf.

45. Compare *Théophile:* "En vilté, en ordure,/ En vie trop obscure/ Ai esté
lonc termine" (vv. 516–18), with *Sainte Marie l'Egyptienne:* "Lasse! moi! com
petit daïsme,/ Com fol treü, com fier paiage/ Ai rendu Dieu de mon aage!/
. . ./ Lasse! ja est petiz li termes" (vv. 212–14, 232).

he becomes aware of sin. Indeed, sin appears blacker in contrast with God's infinite goodness. In *La Mort Rutebeuf* the poet imagines his defense before the throne of Judgment, contrasting God's generosity with his own weakness. The poet is both judge and defendant:

> Se je di: "C'est par ignorance,
> Que je ne sai qu'est penitance,"
> Ce ne me puet pas garantir.
>
> Garantir? Las! en quel maniere?
> Ne me fist Diex bonté entiere
> Qui me dona sens et savoir
> Et me fist a sa forme chiere?
> Encor me fist bonté plus chiere,
> Que por moi vout mort recevoir.
> Sens me dona de decevoir
> L'Anemi qui me veut avoir. (*Mort*, vv. 22–32)

God's sacrifices for mankind are seen in very personal terms: it is for the self who speaks in the poem that He died. In stanzas IV-V Rutebeuf insists on his despairing weakness, calling on the Virgin to heal his sick soul, praising her powers, and recalling the example of St. Mary the Egyptian.[46] In stanza III the poet had expressed his fear of Hell:

> La dont nus se puet ravoir
> Por priere ne por avoir:
> N'en voi nul qui reviegne arriere. (vv. 34–36)

46. The reference to St. Mary the Egyptian does not necessarily allow us to deduct that Rutebeuf had already written her life (as suggested in FB, *1*, 577, note to vv. 57–58). Medieval prayers to the Virgin and to God frequently recalled miracles as examples of their power, and Mary Magdalene, Mary the Egyptian, and Theophilus were the three repentant sinners most often mentioned. In Rutebeuf's own *Ave Maria* he cites Theophilus and Mary Magdalene (vv. 37–72 and vv. 106–08). Compare with sts. CCXXXV–VI of the Renclus de Moiliens' *Miserere*, in which all three are mentioned, and with Villon's *Ballade pour prier Nostre Dame:* "Pardonne moy comme a l'Egypcienne,/ Ou comme il feist au clerc Theophilus" (*Testament*, vv. 885–86).

In stanza VI he adds images of death, a familiar spur to repentance and virtuous action in all didactic literature:

> Puis que morir voi foible et fort,
> Comment prendrai en moi confort
> Que de mort me puisse desfendre?
> N'en voi nul, tant ait grant esfort,
> Que des piez n'ost le contrefort,
> Si fet le cors a terre estendre.
> Que puis je, fors la mort atendre? (vv. 61–67)

In this representation of death, however, we do not feel Villon's fascination with physical death, since, rather than sustaining a long description of physical corruption, Rutebeuf turns immediately (vv. 70–72) to the Last Judgment. In contrast with his other poems of repentance, however, he makes no direct appeal to Heaven in *La Mort* except for his final "Diex doinst que ce ne soit trop tart!" (v. 75). The poem ends on a note of suspense: the poet is caught between salvation and damnation, between this world and the next.

La Mort Rutebeuf can be distinguished from Rutebeuf's other repentance poems by the sins cited. In *La Mort* he repents not only of having had a good time without thinking of salvation (vv. 7–8, 37) and of living at others' expense,[47] but of a specifically poetic sin:

> Lessier m'estuet le rimoier,
> Quar je me doi moult esmaier
> Quant tenu l'ai si longuement.
>   · · ·
> J'ai fet rimes et s'ai chanté
> Sor les uns por aus autres plere,
> Dont Anemis m'a enchanté
> Et m'ame mise en orfenté
> Por mener a felon repere. (vv. 1–3, 38–42)

---

47. See Rutebeuf's censure of Mendicants who "engressent les pances/ D'autrui chatels, d'autrui substances" (*Des Règles*, vv. 21–22; see also v. 51, and *Nouvelle Complainte*, v. 281).

Comparison of these verses with repentance poems by other poets reveal that although Rutebeuf did indeed write partisan verse, we are still not reading a directly transposed personal experience of an individual, but a truth which corresponded to a literary type, the "subgenre" of the jongleur's repentance for having sung worldly songs. Rutebeuf includes, then, exactly as much historical truth in *La Mort* as coincided with the literary topics of repentance. The *Droiz au Clerc de Voudai* [48] (mid-thirteenth century; see FB, *1, 41–42*), for example, begins with the poet's statement that he is old:

> De son bordon use la pointe
> Ne n'a mès que la manuele;
> De la pointe orrez la novele:
> Trente-sept anz en s'escuele
> A conversé mingnos et cointe.

Shifting to the first person, the Clerc de Voudai begins his regrets, expressing his desire to repent and his fear of Hell; he continues:

> Je vieng dès ore en grant eage
> Si doi changer mon fol usage.
>
> . . .
>
> Je vous ai mains mos fabloiez,
> Diz et contez et rimoiez;
> Mès or m'en vueil du tout retrère.
> J'ai esté lonc tens desvoiez,
> Or si doi estre toz proiez
> Del mal lessier et du bien fère;
> Quar qui veut à Dame-Dieu plère,
> S'il ne fet l'anemi contrère,
> Il est et fols et desvoiez.

While the Clerc de Voudai simply regrets having written poetry, Rutebeuf specifically repents having written *polemical* works.[49] We

---

48. Jubinal, ed., *Nouveau Recueil, 2,* 132–49.
49. Compare with the repentance of the anonymous author of a life of St. Andrew (cited by Faral, *Jongleurs,* p. 174 n.), that of Thibaut d'Amiens (cited

have seen in Chapter 2 that there were two medieval attitudes toward polemical poetry; yet only a condemnation of propaganda as *médisance* could possibly be suitable for a repentance poem such as Rutebeuf's *Mort.* The only earthly acts a sinner might point to with pride at the moment of confession were acts of devotion to God and the Virgin.[50] Every other worldly deed was condemned as endangering eternal salvation. One might say that Rutebeuf maintained the poetic "I" of his didactic and polemical poetry, but changed his attitude toward it in a way appropriate to the repentance genre.

In the same way, poets who had written courtly lyrics regretted their love songs when they came to write poems of repentance.[51] Walther von der Vogelweide wrote several poems of farewell to this world, using lovely images to compare this life to wind, leaves, grass, dream, and looking glass.[52] Bidding *Frô Welt*[53] farewell, he regrets his love songs, which brought sorrow to his soul:

Lobe ich des lîbes minne, deis der sêle leit:
Si giht, ez sî ein lüge, ich tobe.[54]

---

by Ch.-V. Langlois, *La Vie en France* . . . *d'après les moralistes,* 2, 25 n.) and that of Watriquet in his *Confession* (No. IX, *Dits,* pp. 113–15).

50. See *Sacristain,* vv. 507–09 and 513–16, in which both the sacristan and the knight's wife recall their past service to the Virgin when they implore her help. See also above, p. 271.

51. See the confession of Denis Piram, a late 12th-century courtly poet, who regrets, in the prologue to his *Vie de seint Edmond le Rei,* his "serventeis,/ Chanceunettes, rimes saluz," saying:

Les jurs jolifs de ma joefnesce
S'en vunt; si trei jeo a vielesce,
Si est bien dreit ke me repente;
En altre ovre mettrai m'entente,
Ke mult mieldre est e plus nutable. (vv. 17–21; ed.
Florence L. Ravenel [Philadelphia, 1906], p. 57)

52. *Gedichte,* p. 168. See the haunting refrain of another of Walther's poems, saying that he who covets this earth shall cast heavenly joy away, and expressing yearning for divine bliss: "Swer dirre wünne volget, hât jene dort verlorn,/ iemer mêr ouwê/ . . ./ So wolte ich denne singen wol, und niemer mêr ouwê,/ niemer mer ouwê" (pp. 170–71).

53. See Walther's debate with *Frô Welt,* in which he settles his accounts with her and prepares to die (*Gedichte,* pp. 138–39).

54. Ibid., p. 99.

The authors of the twelfth century offer examples of movingly contrite poems.[55] Pierre de Blois, deploring his "lascivious songs," wrote a poem of repentance "maturiore stylo,"[56] his *Dum iuventus floruit*.[57] Yet in the work of this medieval humanist, we feel that virtue in old age is as much a part of a pattern of life as are the pleasures of youth. Peter's repentance suggests a peaceful resignation to inevitable redemption rather than anxiety over damnation.

> Dum iuventus floruit,
> licuit et libuit
> facere, quod placuit . . .
>
> Etas illa monuit
> docuit, consuluit,
> sic et etas annuit:
> "Nichil est exclusum!"
> omnia cum venia
> contulit ad usum.

There is no sudden awakening of the soul here, but a turning to virtue as natural as the change of season. The stages of man's life

55. History records also examples of noteworthy conversions of poets. The extraordinary vision of Serlo of Wilton which prompted him to withdraw from the world of letters became an exemplum (see Jacques de Vitry, *Exempla*, No. XXXI, p. 12; and Raby, *Christian-Latin Poetry*, pp. 340–41). Folquet de Marseilla's conversion is recorded in his *vida* as is that of Bernart de Ventador (Boutière and Schutz, *Biographies*, pp. 28 and 99), although Folquet turned to religious fanaticism rather than repentance. Dante, who places Folquet in Paradise, says that the troubadour no longer repents in Heaven, since God's plan for him has been completed, just as a poet completes his work:
> Non però qui si pente, ma si ride:
> non della colpa, che a mente non torna,
> ma del valore che ordinò e provvide.
> Qui si rimira ne l'art che adorna
> cotanto effetto, e discernesi il bene
> per che il mondo di sù quel di giù torna. (*Paradiso*, IX, 103–08)
56. Cited by Raby, *Secular Latin Poetry*, 2, 262–63, 323–24. Compare with Guibert who says he was for a time "snared by the wantonness of the sweet words I took from the poets," continuing: "I was carried along to words which were a bit obscene and composed some sort of little compositions, irresponsible and indiscreet, in fact bereft of all decency" (*Memoirs*, p. 87).
57. *Carmina burana*, ed. Hilka and Schumann, No. 30, I, i, 50, St. 1, 3.

are preordained, and there is time for all prodigals to return to God. The tone of the Latin poems of repentance is less mournful, in general, than those of the thirteenth-century vernacular poets; there are fewer tears and no maternal figure of the Virgin to plead for the penitent. Gautier de Châtillon, dying a leper outcast from society, calls directly upon the "auctor pacis et virtutis" in confident hope of salvation:

> Redde michi iam salutem,
> ut per tuam sit virtutem
> in me culpe terminus;
> et confirmer sic in ea,
> ut sit fortitudo mea
> et laus mea dominus.[58]

Other forms of poetical farewell to the world permit poets to incorporate a greater number of local, personal, or historical allusions than the stylized poems of repentance. The last lines of Rutebeuf's *Mort:*

> Por cest siecle qui se depart
> M'en covient partir d'autre part:
> Qui que l'envie, je le lés, (vv. 82–84)

recall, in fact, one such genre, that of the poetic "testament,"[59] as do lines near the end of the *Complainte Rutebeuf,* in which the poet dismisses those friends who have abandoned him in his misery:

> Mi autre ami sont tuit porri:
> Je les envoi a mestre Orri
> Et se li lais.

58. St. 17 of "Dum Galterus egrotaret," No. 18, *Moralisch-satirische Gedichte,* p. 157. See Gautier's "Hactenus inmerito," whose refrain, "Iuventutis levia/redimo per seria," recalls the accents of Pierre de Blois (Raby, ed., *Oxford Book of Medieval Latin Verse,* pp. 293–95, No. 199).

59. See Winthrop H. Rice, *The European Ancestry of Villon's Satirical Testaments,* Syracuse University Monographs, No. 1 (New York, 1941); Rice studies the poetic forms imitating wills and testaments in Latin and vernacular literatures in terms of their legal terminology and satirical and moral intentions.

On en doit bien fere son lais
Et tel gent lessier en relais
    Sans reclamer,
Qu'il n'a en els rien a amer. (vv. 140–46)

Rutebeuf retains little, however, from the poetic testament beyond the word *lais*.[60] In other hands, the testament became a vehicle for moral and satirical commentary on the world, as in the *Testament* attributed to Jean de Meun and, of course, in Villon's masterpiece.[61]

Rutebeuf's editors refer in passing to *La Mort* as a "congé" (FB, *1*, 574). The work is a farewell in the broadest sense, but must be distinguished from the true poetic *congé*, a genre in which poets said goodbye to their friends and patrons. Jean Bodel and Baude Fastoul, also stricken with leprosy,[62] wrote *Congés* in which a solemn tone, appropriate to pilgrims going "dusk'au Grand Val sans revenir,"[63] alternates with merry and tender words for their

60. The editors translate "lais" in v. 143 of the *Complainte* as "abandonner, renoncer"; they translate v. 84 of *La Mort* as "Propose qui voudra de continuer la partie, moi je la quitte" (*envier*, "raise the stakes"; FB, *1*, 578 n.). Robert Guiette translates, "Je le laisse à quiconque il plaît" (*Rutebeuf* [Paris, 1950], p. 24). See the expression "Verité a fet son lais" in the *Complainte de Guillaume* (v. 71) and in the *Dit de sainte Eglise* (v. 52).

61. Grace Frank's suggestion that Villon's *Testament* is not a true document of repentance and contrition fails to take into account the multiplicity of tones which derives from Villon's combination of different genres: the *congé d'amour*, satirical testament, and prayer of repentance, among others ("The Impenitence of François Villon," *Romanic Review*, *37*, No. 3 [October 1946], 225–36). See Siciliano's identification of the different genres in his article on the composition of Villon's *Testament* (*Romania*, *65* [January 1939], 39–90), and above, p. 264.

62. Lepers, too, were John of Garland and Alanus de Insulis (see Dobiache-Rojestvensky, op. cit., pp. 47–48). See Gautier de Châtillon's satirical last look at the world, "Versus est in luctum" (*Carmina burana*, No. 123, ed. Hilka and Schumann, I, ii, 206; see above, p. 233).

63. Baude Fastoul, *Congés*, v. 24, ed. Pierre Ruelle, *Les Congés d'Arras* [Jean Bodel, Baude Fastoul, Adam de la Halle] (Brussels and Paris, 1965). See Guesnon's study in *Mélanges offerts à M. Maurice Wilmotte* (extract, Paris, 1910). See also, in Ruelle's edition, pp. 71–72, where Ruelle defines the formal elements of the *congé*: the Arras setting; the *strophe d'Hélinant*. See also Guesnon's study in *Mélanges offerts à M. Maurice Wilmotte* (extract, Paris, 1910); Charles Foulon, "Les Congés," in *L'Œuvre de Jehan Bodel* (Rennes, 1958), pp. 705–66. Bédier cites another *congé* from Arras by Andrieu Contredit, in *Fabliaux*, p. 375 n.

poet-friends and a grateful or satirical adieu to the rich bourgeois of Arras. Adam de la Halle began his *Congé* on a solemn note of repentance:

> Mais le tans que j'ai perdu plour,
> Las, dont j'ai despendu le fleur
> Au siècle qui m'a amusé. (vv. 7–9)

But his tone abruptly changes with an apostrophic

> Arras, Arras, Vile de plait,
> Et de haïne et de detrait,
> Qui soliés estre si nobile. (vv. 13–15) [64]

Adam's *Congé* is not a work of introspection but a pretext for turning a sharp eye on the society of Arras. The *congé* of the Arras poets was not imitated elsewhere in the thirteenth century and seems to be a literary specialty related to the taste for self-portrayal evident in other thirteenth-century works from Arras which contain an exceptionally large number of topical allusions, in contrast with the poetry of other regions of Northern France.[65] Perhaps the close association of the poets of Arras in their *puy* made for a rather homogeneous style in which conventional didacticism and satire were blended with a generous portion of local color.

Rutebeuf's use of *topoi* rather than personal and historical allusions in his *Mort* in no way diminishes its poetic value. He has fashioned a poignant poem which describes true moods of the human soul; his discovery of sin and his fear of Hell, death, and the Last Judgment lead naturally to his hope for appeal to the Virgin and finally to his prayer that his regret comes not too late.

64. Ed. Ruelle, *Congés*, p. 129.

65. See the texts edited by Jeanroy and Guy, *Chansons et dits artésiens du XIIIe siècle*, and the following studies relating works from Arras to contemporary society: Guy, *La Vie et les œuvres littéraires du trouvère Adan de le Hale*, pp. xii–lvii; Guesnon's review of Jeanroy and Guy's *Chansons satiriques*, extracted from *Moyen Age* (1899); Marie Ungureanu, *La Bourgeoisie naissante: Société et littérature bourgeoises d'Arras aux XII et XIIIe siècles* (Arras, 1955); and the substantial review article of this book by Henri Roussel, "Notes sur la littérature arrageoise du XIIIe siècle," *Revue des Sciences Humaines*, Nouvelle série, Fasc. 87 (July–September 1957), pp. 249–86. See also the article by Sutherland cited above, n. 15.

The historical facts are unimportant, but the feelings of remorse and hope are admirably expressed. The fall and rise of verses such as verses 24–25 of *La Mort* (see above, p. 273), with the repeated "garantir" followed by the sorrowful "las," make Rutebeuf's interior dialogue very touching. He expresses yearning through rhymes on long sounds [66] and through exclamations; emotion rings out in his plea to the Virgin:

> N'est plaie, tant soit anciene,
> Qu'ele ne netoie et escure
>
>   . . .
>
> Si com c'est voirs, si praingne en cure
> Ma lasse d'ame crestiene! (vv. 53–54, 59–60)

The poem appeals to us, perhaps, because the commonplaces of repentance and apprehension of death are set in a subjective form. The anonymous *Debat du cors et de l'ame,* for example, is a vigorous description of the fragility of the weary flesh:

> Cors desloiax, plein de lasté
> Se li drap t'estoient osté
> Dont tu te scés si mettre avant
> Et en véist ta poureté
> Et tote ta fragilité,
> Corroies tu ensi devant? [67]

The *Debat* arouses the intellect, even the imagination, yet does not touch the emotions, as does Rutebeuf's subjective expression of his struggle with a willful heart in *La Mort:*

> . . . Onques ne sot sentir
> Mes fols cuers quels est repentance

66. Of the seven stanzas, only the first, which is declarative rather than contemplative in tone, has rhymes only on short vowels. The fourth and seventh stanzas again recall the poet's past sins and alternate long and short vowels; stanzas II, III, V, and VI expressing regret and meditation on death, have rhymes only on long sounds.

67. Cited in *Histoire littéraire, 23,* 283. See Raby, *Secular Latin Poetry, 2,* 299–303, for similar debates in Latin; and Raby, *Christian-Latin Poetry,* p. 434, for Jacopone da Todi's Lauda XV, a dialogue between soul and body with a typically Franciscan insistence on fleshly decay (see above, p. 219, n. 73).

N'a bien fere lui assentir.

. . .

De male rente m'a renté
Mes cuers ou tant truis de contraire.
(vv. 14–16, 45–46)

Rutebeuf uses a minimum of rhetorical ornament; annominatio, as
in verse 45 above, is never elaborated beyond three or four words,
and then often on the rhymes "cure" and "fort" (vv. 55–59, 61–65).
Much of the poetic ornamentation is related directly to the poetic
"I"; the extended image of Mary as a physician (vv. 43–60) comes
naturally following the poet's expression of spiritual sickness. Even
proverbs appear in the first person singular, as in verses 73–74 (see
above, p. 254, n. 88):

Or ai tant fet que ne puis més,
Si me covient lessier en pés.

The value of a repentance poem was, in fact, in its credible tone
of sincerity; the depths to which repentance stirred the soul and
renewed a troubled heart by cleansing tears was the measure of its
artistic and spiritual truth. Because we recognize a profoundly
human tone in La Mort, it is unimportant whether Rutebeuf speaks
for himself or for all men.

RUTEBEUF IN HIS POEMS OF MISFORTUNE   The poetic
"I" chosen by Rutebeuf for his two Griesche poems and his Mariage,
Complainte, Pauvreté, and Paix is quite a different one from that
of his didactic, satirical, and moral works. The choice of poetic
personality is here once again determined by the intention and
subject of the work. These poems of misfortune were offered to
the public and Rutebeuf's patrons in hopes of payment, as, indeed,
were all of Rutebeuf's works. In the poems of misfortune, however,
the poet's lack of money and his need for help are the central
theme. It would be most inappropriate, therefore, for the poet to
express regret in these poems for receiving money from others, as
he did in La Mort, where he laments:

J'ai toz jors engressié ma pance
D'autrui chatel, d'autrui substance. (vv. 19–20)

Although Rutebeuf uses the same themes in *La Pauvreté,* saying:

J'ai vescu de l'autrui chatei
Que hon m'a creü et prestei:
Or me faut chacuns de creance, (vv. 7–9)

the point of view, the poetic "I" who speaks, is quite a different fellow, who regrets only that "dou sien gardeir est chacuns sages" (v. 18).[68] Nor can the intrepid critic of Mendicants and sluggard knights appear in these poems of misfortune; Rutebeuf the fearless truth-teller, who came out so bravely in the *Dit d'Hypocrisie,* has no place in these works, for, as the proverb says, "Mieiz vaut mentir pur bien avoir que perdre pur dire voir." [69]

Rutebeuf is not, however, "lying" in these poems of misfortune. He simply adopts an appropriate poetic personality, that of the poor fool who has lost everything. "Nis li musars musart me claime," he says at the beginning of his *Mariage* (v. 8). "En recordant ma grant folie/ Qui n'est ne gente ne jolie" begins his

68. Contrast also with yet another view of living at others' expense expressed by Salatin who sympathizes with Théophile's misery:
　　　Molt i a dolor et destrece
　　　Quant l'en chiet en autrui dangier
　　　Por son boivre et por son mengier:
　　　Trop i covient gros mos oïr. (*Théophile,* vv. 64–67)
The theme is thus given various meanings according to context. No one interpretation represents Rutebeuf's "real" opinion of parasitism, and I agree with FB that the theme's appearance in Théophile does not mean that Rutebeuf was inspired by personal experience (FB, II, 181, note to vv. 63–67). To the example cited by FB (ibid.), one should also add Dante, *Paradiso,* Canto XVII: "Tu proverai sì come sa di sale / lo pane altrui, e come è duro calle / lo scendere e 'l salir per l'altrui scale" (vv. 58–60).

69. Morawski, *Proverbes,* No. 1269. The author of the *Dit Chastie-Musart,* however, introduces his satire of women by saying that he is so poor, he need fear no one, and so can speak freely and truthfully (*O.C., 3,* 382–83). This was the advantage Matthew Paris saw in the voluntary poverty of the Minorities, who refuse worldly goods "in order that they may exercise greater freedom, not in soothing down the faults of those in power, but in reprobating and reproaching them with the austerity of censors, for 'Cantabit vacuus coram latrone viator' " (*English History, 3,* 44).

Griesche d'été (vv. 1–2). Faral saw these poems as "requêtes pleurardes et déplaisantes," thinking that the poet showed "une absence d'orgueil regrettable" in exposing his private misery to beg charity.[70] Lucas, who also edited these poems, thought the poet attempted to inspire pity and generosity in his hearers by describing his own misery.[71] Yet, although the poetic "I" *is* pitiable, the poems are largely developments of certain literary *topoi;* and there is every reason to assume that in these "personal" works the poet uses the same technique as in his moral and didactic works; that is, he develops a conventional literary theme with the greatest possible poetic skill. In contrast with the moral and didactic works, however, in which the poetic "I" serves mainly to express general truths, the portrayal of the poetic "I" is the central theme in these poems of misfortune.[72] Moral conclusions may appear, but they are directed toward or derived from the poetic personality depicted in the poems themselves.

I do not believe, then, that Rutebeuf is exhibiting the wounds fate inflicted upon him in his poems of misfortune, but that he is proving his poetic talent. One cannot even say he is begging in these poems. Begging in the Middle Ages was to ask something for nothing (see above, pp. 119–21); Rutebeuf offers his verse for payment. Certainly the poet asks for money in his works, either directly[73] or indirectly; but the poems shame not the poet who wrote them, as Faral has suggested, but only he who is slow to give. Every medieval work moralizing on the virtues of charity

70. *Jongleurs,* p. 152; see FB, *1,* 43–45.

71. *Les Poésies personnelles de Rutebeuf* (Paris, 1938), pp. 60, 62. Rutebeuf does exploit most of "li lieus ki apertient a aquerre pitié [qui] sont .xvi." (Brunetto Latini, *Trésor,* pp. 386–88).

72. In a lecture at Yale University (1964), entitled "Poésie gothique, poésie romane," Paul Zumthor pointed out that in contrast with the affective poetic "I" of the courtly lyric, in which the predominant personal pronoun is "je," Rutebeuf alternates between the subjective "je," which feels, and the objective "me, moi." See below, pp. 305–06. Rutebeuf appears as a subjective suffering consciousness and as a victim of forces outside him.

73. See the *Complainte Rutebeuf* (vv. 137–39, 158–65), *La Pauvreté Rutebeuf,* and *De Brichemer.*

underlines the importance of giving freely;[74] and the author of a poem called the *Honteux Menesterel* describes the ideal relationship between poet and public:

> Se je sai du mestier ouvrer,
> De faire cans & de trouver
> Biaus dis, je croi, sans ma main tendre
> Ne sans rouver, ne trop atendre,
> Me donroit il courtois gentix
> Qui a bien faire est ententix.
>
>   • • •
>
> Or me doinst Dix tel gent trouver
> U je le puisse recouvrer! (vv. 113–18, 125–26) [75]

Rutebeuf, in depicting himself as a poor fool of a jongleur, adopted as his "own" a well-defined conventional character. Jeanroy, editing five poems in which the subject is the "poor fool," calls them examples of "ce que fut la poésie lyrique du nord avant qu'elle eût été transformée par l'influence méridionale." [76] However, these poems cannot be dated with precision, and there is abundant evidence to show that the "poor fool" is a common type who appears

---

74. See, for example, Rutebeuf's *Complainte de Geoffroi de Sergines* (vv. 79–82) and his *Dit d'Aristote* in which he repeats a formulaic maxim:
> Au doneir done en teil meniere
> Que miex vaille la bele chiere
> Que feras, au doneir le don,
> Que li dons: car ce fait preudom. (vv. 63–66)

75. *O.C., 3,* 17. *Honteux* means ashamed to beg what should be freely given. Compare the moral of "Li Camus, qui est nés d'Arras":
> Li rovers * fait rougir la face   * begging
> En rouver a mainte doleur
>
>   • • •
>
> . . . Cil qui done sen avoir
> Doit cent tans plus grant joie avoir
> Que cil ki en reçoit le don. (vv. 58–59, 63–65; Jeanroy and Guy, eds. *Chansons et dits artésiens,* p. 83, No. XX)

76. *Origines de la poésie lyrique,* p. 461. The poems are "Quant je voi yver retorner" (by Colin Muset, No. 14 in his *Chansons*); "Je soloie estre envoisiez," "A definement d'esteit," "Par mainte foiz ai chanté," and "Povre veillece m'asaut" (Nos. XXV–IX, pp. 505–13).

287

in other poems,[77] other languages,[78] and in other forms such as proverbs [79] and sermon exempla (see below, p. 294). There is also a significant coincidence of ideas appearing in Rutebeuf's *Mariage* and the generalizations on the state of the poor man in *Les Plaies du monde:*

> L'en dit que fols qui ne foloie
> Pert sa seson:
> Sui je mariez sanz reson?
> Or n'ai ne borde ne meson.
>
>   · · ·
>
> N'ai pas busche de chesne ensamble;
> Quant g'i sui, si a fou et tramble
>   (*Mariage,* vv. 21–24, 68–70)

> Fols est clamez cil qui n'a rien:
> N'a pas vendu tout son mesrien,
> Ainz en a un fou retenu.
>   (*Plaies du monde,* vv. 23–25)

In both passages Rutebeuf is amplifying proverbial expressions and using wordplay from established literary conventions. The play on *fou* ("fool, beech") of *Les Plaies* is particularly common and even appears as a legend to an illustration in the *Histoire de Fauvain.*[80] In the *Mariage,* however, Rutebeuf illustrates the truth of these commonplaces and proverbs by a particular example whom

77. In addition to those edited by Jeanroy, and Rutebeuf's, see such works as *Le Département des livres* (Méon, ed., *Nouveau Recueil, 1,* 404–06) or *De Niceroles,* the allegorical voyage of a fool to poverty *O.C., 3,* 352–54).

78. See, for example Walther von der Vogelweide's "Ich han min lehen, al die werlt" (*Gedichte,* pp. 37–38), or "La povertà m'ha si disamorato" of Cecco Angiolieri, Dante's contemporary (*Il Canzioniere,* ed. Carlo Steiner [Torino, 1928]. p. 83, No. LXXXI).

79. The proverbial "argent de menestrier" disappears very quickly (Leroux de Lincy, *Proverbes, 2,* 139) and the maxim "Homme ententus aus jongleurs, asseiz tost averroit une femee que on appelle Pauvreté," attributed to Saint Bernard (cited by Pesce, "Le Portrait de Rutebeuf," p. 92, n. 6).

80. Ed. A. Långfors (Paris, 1914), Pl. I. The same pun occurs in the *Roman de la Rose* (vv. 10,242–46); see Tobler, *Vermischte Beiträge, 2,* 220.

he identifies as "himself" and describes in the first person. Here lies, I believe, the true intention and veritable source of these poems of misfortune: in the poet's amplification of proverbial commonplaces. I cannot agree with Leo's theory that the *Mariage* and *Complainte* portray "literary reality" while the *Griesche* poems and Rutebeuf's *Repentance* represent a "real reality." [81] All of these poems are "literary," and any connection with the facts of Rutebeuf's historical existence is truly irrelevant; their connection with a literary tradition, which Rutebeuf illustrated with his poetic technique, is of the utmost importance.

The two *Griesche* poems, the *Mariage*, and the *Complainte*, for example, are based on a conventional explanation of how a fool becomes poor. "Por ce est li fous qu'il face la folie," says the proverb,[82] and the thirteenth century recognized three follies: "Par vin, par fame et par dez Si vient toust homme a povretez." [83] Instead of combining the three, as did the author of *Des Fames, des dez et de la taverne*,[84] and the Archpoet in his *Confessio*,[85] Rutebeuf developed the theme of women separately from the themes of dice and the tavern. Women (or more particularly, "his wife") are nowhere mentioned in the *Griesche* poems on dice; dice and drinking are not cited as causes of his misery in his *Mariage* and *Complainte;* and neither dice nor women are mentioned in his *Povreté* and *Paix*, which are, as we shall see, based on yet another commonplace

---

81. "Rutebeuf: persönlicher Ausdruck," p. 140.

82. Morowski, *Proverbes*, No. 1665. Folly, as we have seen in verse 23 of *Les Plaies*, is equivalent to poverty. See the definition in *Des Sis Manières de fols*: "Homme et fame est bien fol, et je m'i suis pris garde,/ Quant il pert tout le sien . . ." (Jubinal, ed., *Nouveau Recueil*, 2, 68).

83. Morawski, *Proverbes*, No. 1603.

84. Ed. V. Väänänen, *Neophilologische Mitteilungen*, 67, Nos. 5–6 (1946), 104–13.

85. *Gedichte*, pp. 24–29, No. III. The appearance of the theme in Latin (and in the Latin-French jargon of *Des fames, des dez*) make it clear that the triple theme was not popular but a rhetorical topic. The trio appears often. See, for example: *Urbain le courtois*, "Fuez putaine et hasardrie/ Et la taverne ne hauntez mie" (vv. 67–68; ed. P. Meyer, *Romania*, 32 [1903], 68–73); *De Saint Pierre et du jougleor* (vv. 26–27); Barbazan and Méon, eds. *Fabliaux*, 3, 283). In Cecco Angioleri we read "Tre cose solamente mi so' in grado/ . . ./ ciò è la donna, la taverna e 'l dado" (*Canzoniere*, pp. 102–03, No. XCIX).

—the idea that a needy man is deserted by his friends. Rutebeuf's poetic personality, however, remains essentially unchanged throughout the *Griesche* poems, the *Mariage,* and *Complainte:* only the manner of folly varies, as if to chart the various roads to *Niceroles,* "Foolstown." These poems of misfortune, moreover, are laments, appropriate to the poetic personality who speaks in them, and appropriate to the central theme of poverty. The *complainte* form, as we have seen, brings with it a vocabulary of emotional sadness and regret: "me plaing, plor, ce poise moi, je n'en puis més se je m'esmai." The speaker in *complaintes,* furthermore, always uses the first person singular, even when, as in the *Complainte de Guillaume* (see above, pp. 163–67), Rutebeuf wrote a prosopopoeia in the name of *sainte Yglise.*[86]

The mixture of comic and tragic tones in these laments, which many critics have noted, does not come, as Leo thinks, from cracks in a grinning mask.[87] It is rather a result of the poet's choice of poetic personality, which required a mixture of laughter and tears, folly and misery. The fundamental contradiction in tone is complemented by the ironic turn of many verses, as in the "plenty of nothing" which begins the *La Pauvreté:*

> Je ne sai par ou je coumance
> Tant ai de matyere abondance
> Por parleir de ma povretei. (vv. 1–3)

The theme of exemplary suffering is as characteristic of the lament as is its doleful vocabulary.[88] Rutebeuf includes two of the classic

86. Arié Serper has confused the "je" speaking in the *Complainte de Guillaume* with Rutebeuf himself ("L'Influence de Guillaume de Saint-Amour sur Rutebeuf," p. 402); see also Edward B. Ham ("Rutebeuf: Pauper and Polemist," p. 232), who interprets what *sainte Yglise* says as reflecting Rutebeuf's personal sadness.

87. "Rutebeuf: persönlicher Ausdruck," pp. 141–43; see below, p. 301. Leo (pp. 131–32) does point out some of the contradictions in Rutebeuf's account of his misery: in the *Mariage* he says he has no house (v. 24) and that his house is deserted (v. 102); his wife is old and ill, yet in the *Complainte* she has two babies; he is poor, but he has a horse (*Complainte,* v. 54; see Morawski, *Proverbes,* No. 1338: "Ne faut pas dou tout qui a cheval monte").

88. See, for example, the personal laments of the Archpoet, who proclaims himself "Poeta pauperior omnibus poetis" (*Gedichte,* ed. M. Manitius [Munich, 1913],

comparisons which served as the standard for woe in *complaintes:*

> Nis la destruction de Troie
> Ne fu si grant comme est la moie.
> (*Mariage*, vv. 74-75) [89]

> Diex m'a fet compaignon a Job,
> Qu'il m'a tolu a un seul cop
> Quanques j'avoie. (*Complainte*, vv. 20-21)

The lament form required that the speaker's misery be overwhelming and unsurpassed, but the grotesque effect appears because Rutebeuf is treating low subjects—marriage, dice, and money—in the sublime style usually reserved for the death of kings and the fall of great cities.

In addition to the complexity of tone and the contrast between subject and style, Rutebeuf also plays with the ambivalent medieval attitude toward poverty. Poverty appears in his poems of misfortune as a terrible huntress who follows the poet everywhere. When we contrast this cruel harridan with the lovely bride of Saint Francis, *Madonna Povertà,* who promised such celestial rewards to her lovers, we are struck by the distinction made in the Middle Ages between voluntary and involuntary poverty. Voluntary poverty, of course, was a holy, Christ-like state, idealized by moralists who condemned money and avarice as the root of evil (see above, Chapter 1). Involuntary poverty was quite a different matter, being clearly considered the result of misfortune or foolishness.[90] In-

---

p. 35), or Jehan le Fèvre, who, translating the *Lamentations* of Mahieu le Bigame, begins "en sangloutant, en souspirant,/ En gemissant, en empirant" (vv. 111-12) to recount the unsurpassed misery of Mahieu, saying:

> J'ai bien veü l'Apocalipse,
> Ezechiel et Jheremie;
> Mais ne peuent souffire mie
> Contre Mahieu pour bien gemir. (vv. 46-49)

89. See FB, *1,* 549, note to v. 74, on the Latin tradition of deploration of the fall of Troy; see also Raby, *Secular Latin Poetry, 1,* 325-28.

90. Humbert de Romans contrasts "paupertas ribaldica" with the saintly Minorites in *De eruditione praedicatorum,* p. 468. See the estates poem, *Le Dit des planètes* (Jubinal, ed., *Nouveau Recueil, 1,* 380-81):

voluntary poverty not only made the poor man an outcast from society but was a sign of heavenly disfavor.[91]

Both attitudes toward poverty appear in Rutebeuf's *Mariage*. He opens with the double theme of sinful foolishness and martyrdom (vv. 11–20), accentuating both his own action (his foolish marriage to a poor old woman) and the sufferings imposed on him by God. He is both victim and sinner. Rutebeuf finally resolves this contradiction in the last lines, discovering the meaning of his experiences and of his misery by exaggerating them. Plunging into the depths of deprivation, he achieves a paradoxical exaltation and becomes an exemplary figure of saintly austerity:

> L'en se saine parmi la vile
>> De mes merveilles;
> On les doit bien conter aus veilles:
> Il n'i a nules lor pareilles,
>> Ce n'est pas doute.
> Il pert bien que je n'i vi goute;
> Diex n'a nul martir en sa route
>> Qui tant ait fet;
> S'il ont esté por Dieu desfet,
> Rosti, lapidé ou detret,
>> Je n'en dout mie
> Que lor paine fu tost fenie;

Car cil est povre d'esperit
A qui povreté enbelist.
Povres y a d'autre manière,
Qui n'ont de rien povreté chière,
Car moult volentiers s'il pooient
Riches et poissant devendroient; . . .
Les uns sont povres par trop boire,
Les autres par le gieu du dé;
Quant se voient à povreté
Il maugrient saintes et sainz.

91. Both Rutebeuf and his Théophile experience their suffering through poverty as a separation from God. In *Le Mariage* Rutebeuf wistfully moans: "Je cuit que Diex li debonaires/ M'aime de loing" (vv. 54–55); Théophile curses God who "s'est en si haut leu mis/ Por eschiver ses anemis/ C'on n'i puet trere ne lancier" (vv. 27–29).

> Més ce durra toute ma vie
>   Sanz avoir aise.
> Or pri a Dieu que il li plaise
> Ceste dolor, ceste mesaise
>   Et ceste enfance *   * foolishness
> M'atort a vraie penitance
> Si qu'avoir puisse s'acointance. (vv. 120–38)

Whereas the poet said earlier that he was deserted and despised by his friends (vv. 48–52), his figure now inspires awe, terror, and respect in those who cross themselves as they see him. His tale of woes is told as an exemplum around the fire of an evening. He has surpassed all other martyrs by his trials,[92] and his feeling of separation from God has changed to a hope that he may now draw close to the divine presence, as his foolish actions are turned into penitence.

The problem of tone in *Le Mariage* is not easy to resolve in any one single way. The rapid accumulation of verbs of martyrdom— "desfet, rosti, lapidé, detret"—is grotesque, as is the metamorphosis of a miserable wretch into a saintly hero. Certain passages are deliberately ironical, as for example the verses in which Rutebeuf speaks of the spiritual benefits his wife derives from starving during Lent.[93] Yet the final prayer is serious, as is the invocation to God which ends the *Complainte Rutebeuf* (vv. 148–57). I believe one may say that the poet deliberately and insistently plays the tone of serious lament inherent in the form of the *complainte* against his

92. A poem of Cecco Angiolieri uses a similar theme:
> Egli è maggior miracol, com'io vivo,
> cento milia cotanto, al me' parere,
> che non seria veder un olivo,
> che non fosse innestato, menar pere.
> (*Canzioniere*, p. 8, No. XCIV)

Cecco even echo's Rutebeuf's touching "L'esperance de l'endemain/ Ce sont mes festes" (*Mariage*, vv. 114–15) in the same poem: "Ma' che m'aiuta un poco di speranza."

93.   De poisson autant com de cresme
>   Avra ma fame.
> Grant loisir a de sauver s'ame:
> Or geünt * por la douce Dame,   * let her fast
>   Qu'ele a loisir. (vv. 84–88).

grotesque portrait of himself as a poor wretch in order to bring out the contrast. The mixture of tones and the clash between subject and style appear thus as a special poetic technique to be appreciated for its own sake. Moreover, the proverbial attitude attributed to a jongleur is one of just such a contrast: "Tel fois chante li menestriers que c'est de touz li plus courreciés." [94]

Zumthor has described several aspects of a "poétique de contrastes qui constitue l'un des aspects fondamentaux de l'esthétique littéraire médiévale, concluding that toward the end of twelfth-century and during the thirteenth, poets consciously sought and valued contrast of tones and subjects. Zumthor cites, as examples, bilingual texts such as Des fames, des dez, and the pious songs edited by Järnström which use profane love songs as their models; he also includes wordplay and irony as aspects of this poetic of contrasts. [95] The play of contrasts in poetry can only appear when at least two well-defined and separate poetic structures (themes or forms) are joined together; and this sort of technical refinement appears as a consequence of the highly conventional, stylized, and rhetorical nature of medieval poetry in general.

The findings of Ham and Leo in their studies of the Mariage and Complainte may now be seen within the context of such a medieval poetic of contrast. These critics have identified Rutebeuf's treatment of marriage as a parody of the courtly love song. [96] Erich Köhler [97] challenges this view, saying that since marriage is never the principal subject of a courtly poem, there can thus be no "parody," properly speaking. In addition, there is no triangle, no adultery, envisaged in Rutebeuf's poems, but only exhaustion.

94. Morawski, Proverbes, No. 2315, recalling Villon's "Je ris enpleurs."
95. Langue et techniques poétiques, Chap. 2, "L'Ecart rhétorique, and pp. 149–78 of his chapter 3, "Style et registres."
96. Ham, in "Rutebeuf: Pauper and Polemist," relates Le Mariage Rutebeuf rather generally to the mal marié theme (p. 229). Leo, "Rutebeuf: persönlicher Ausdruck," says that Le Mariage is a parody of the Provençal love song, terming Rutebeuf's poem a "grotesk-realistische Ehelied nordischen Charakters" (p. 136). The theme of unhappy marriage, however, is not particular to Northern France (see the Provençal novel Flamenca, for example); moreover, Leo proves that La Mariage is grotesquely unrealistic (see above, p. 288, n. 87).
97. Private communication, 1966.

Marriage, of course, was a "low" topic, unsuited to the "sublime" courtly lyric, in which husbands appear only to be contrasted with lovers.[98]

There are aspects of the *Marriage* and *Complainte,* however, which do reveal some common courtly *topoi.* The *Mariage* begins with a description of winter like those which occasionally replace the joyous lyric spring exordium.[99] Winter is presented as an "anti-spring;" the basic elements of the conventional springtime tableau —leaves and birds—are present, but Rutebeuf describes them in the negative:

> En l'an soissante,
> Qu'arbres n'a foille, oisel ne chante,
> Fis je toute la rien dolante
> Dui de cuer m'aime. (vv. 4-7)

But Rutebeuf is just as wretched as the season, while winter usually serves as a foil to the inner joy felt by the courtly lover. The verses

> Envoyer un homme en Egypte,
> Ceste dolor est plus petite
> Que n'est la moie, (vv. 17-19)

remind us, also by contrast, of courtly attitudes. No suffering, for example, in the courtly Crusade lyric is greater than that of the lovers' farewell. Conon de Béthune expresses profound regret at leaving his lady in the poem "Ahi! Amors, com dure departie":

> Por li m'en vois sospirant en Surie
> Car je ne doi faillir mon Creator.[1]

Rutebeuf, to express his unsurpassed suffering, says that even the Crusades would be preferable to his marriage, just as did the un-happy husband of the *Vallet qui d'aise a malaise se met:* "Or

---

98. See Nykrog, *Fabliaux,* pp. 189–92, for an interesting discussion of marriage as a grotesque, uncourtly institution.
99. See Dragonetti, *Technique poétique,* pp. 176–77.
1. *Chansons,* p. 6, No. IV.

vorrait estre à marier,/ S'en deüst aler outre mer."[2] Yet many elements in these poems by Rutebeuf belong to literary traditions quite distinct from any courtly themes.

The figure of the married and impoverished jongleur is one such highly stylized figure. Rutebeuf says that his house is so barren that he does not dare go home for fear of his wife's reproaches.

> . . . Ma maison est trop deserte
>   Et povre et gaste:
> Sovent n'i a ne pain ne paste.
> Ne me blasmez se ne me haste
>   D'aler arriere,
> Que ja n'i avrai bele chiere:
> L'en n'a pas ma venue chiere
>   Se je n'aporte.
> C'est ce qui plus me desconforte
> Que je n'ose entrer en ma porte
>   A vuide main. (vv. 102–12)

Now the barrenness of the jongleur's house in itself was proverbial, as one can see from the following joke taken from a collection of exempla:

> While a certain jongleur of Mutina was sleeping one night, his wife woke him, because she heard thieves in their house. When the said jongleur heard the thieves going through the house, groping for things to take, he called out to them: "I don't know you, but you're very clever indeed if you can find anything to steal from the house at night, since I can't find anything in it in the daytime.[3]

2. Montaiglon and Raynaud, eds., *Fabliaux*, 2, 170, No. LXIV. It may be true, as Faral proposes, that both Rutebeuf and the "vallet" feared the Crusades because criminals were often sentenced to Crusade service FB, *1*, 423). I believe, however, that both are parodying the painful farewell of the courtly lovers.

3. "Dum quidam joculator de Mutina dormiret, uxor excitavit eum, que senserat noctu latrones in domo. Quos [cum] insensisset dictus joculator ire per domum tentando de rebus ut acciperet, dixit illis: 'Ego nescio vos, eritis bene subtiles si in nocte poteritis aliquid invenire subtrahendum in domo, quia ego de die nihil

Even the image of the reluctant poet, afraid to go home because of his wife's complaints, is equally stereotyped, as several other exempla prove: "Jongleurs, going to their own homes, find them filled with poverty and muttering, because their whole family complains and grumbles about them, and proclaims their defects."[4] The role of the indigent husband is always filled by a jongleur or actor in these exempla; and the wife's role is as stereotyped as that of our modern shrew who waits by the door at night with a rolling pin for her drunken husband to return. The miseries of a poet's marriage, then, are just as conventional as the joys and sorrows of love.

Leo cites Adam de la Halle and Colin Muset as other poets using the "literary motif of the unhappy trouvère marriage."[5] One must distinguish, I believe, the literary motifs of the married cleric from that of the married poet, since each follows a different and typical pattern of development.

Adam de la Halle portrays himself as a cleric throughout his works, but he appears as a *married* cleric only in his satirical comedy, the *Jeu de la feuillée*. Adam does say he has left the "clergie" in his lyric works, but for love, not marriage. He defends love against learning in a *jeu-parti* with Jean Bretel:

> Sire, en servant amours, mout mieus emploi
> Que se je fusse escoliers seulement;
> Et por itant, se l'escole renoi,
> Ch'est por moi emploier plus hautement.
> Et vous dites que j'uevre sotement,
> Qui l'ai eslongie.

---

possum invenire'" (Welter, ed., *Tabula exemplorum*, p. 95). Welter quotes two similar exempla, ibid., p. 65, No. 246, and p. 95.

4. "Joculatores intrantes domos suas, inveniunt eas paupertate et murmure plenas, quia tota familia sua de eis conqueritur et murmurat et defectus suos proclamat" (ibid., p. 95. See also in *La tabula exemplorum*, No. 31, p. 10, and another exemplum, p. 95. See also the proverb, "Il est comme les menestriers, il ne trouve point de pire maison que la sienne" (*Proverbes*, ed. Leroux de Lincy, 2, 139).

5. "Das literarische Motiv der unglücklichen Trovere-Ehe" ("Rutebeuf: persönlicher Ausdruck," p. 136).

Ne doit dire tel folie
Hom qui connoit qu'il aime loiaument.[6]

In the *Jeu de la feuillée,* however, the theme of marriage can appear, because the play is a comedy, therefore "low" in subject. Adam plays on the contrast between his three estates: lover, husband, and student, portraying himself both nostalgically as the courtly lover, before marriage had appeased his desires (v. 174), and ruefully as the cleric trapped in wedlock, who regrets having "por feme ten tans perdu!" (v. 184).[7] Mahieu le Bigame drew another picture of the married cleric in his antifeminine invective, the *Lamentations* (after 1295):[8]

> Perdue, sechée et vergie
> Est libertés de ma clergie.
>
> . . .
>
> Je fu jadis maistre clamés,
> Or suis orendroit bigamés
> Et avalés en bas degré. (vv. 121–22, 133–35)

Both Mahieu and Adam describe themselves as unhappily married in order to introduce satire on women as well as marriage.

Rutebeuf, on the other hand, describes his wife only as an element of his own miseries, not as a preliminary to an invective against marriage or against women. The true theme of Rutebeuf's *Mariage* and *Complainte* is poverty, not marriage; the wife appears as one of the poet's burdens, in accordance with the conventional

6. *Jeu-Parti* XIX, *Œuvres,* p. 179.
7. See above, p. 200, n. 32, on vv. 51–185 of the *Jeu de la feuillée,* in which Adam contrasts the beauty of his fiancée with the ugliness of his wife, thus playing a courtly against a comic *registre.*
8. Mahieu wrote after the Lyons Council of 1274 had condemned the marriages of clerics to widows as bigamous, thus depriving such clerics of their privileges; see Van Hamel's Introduction to the *Lamentations* (2, cxii–xvii). The *Lamentations* are inspired in part by the discourse of *Ami* against marriage in the *Roman de la Rose* (vv. 8456–9999). *Ami* mentions Abelard as a lucky man to have escaped marriage, since he was able to continue studying, "touz siens, touz frans, senz sei lier" (v. 8782). See also the unhappy victims of marriage in fabliaux such as *Do pré tondu* (Montaiglon and Raynaud, eds. *Fabliaux, 4,* No. CIV) and *Du Vallet qui d'aise a malaise se met.*

explanation of how the fool becomes poor. As in the *Jeu de la feuillée*, however, the wife herself is the opposite of the courtly lady. Poor, old, ugly, thin, and dry, she is altogether undesirable:

> Por plus doner de reconfort
> A cels qui me heent de mort
> Tel fame ai prise
> Que nus fors moi n'aime ne prise,
> Et s'estoit povre et entreprise
> Quant je la pris.
> A ci mariage de pris,
> C'or sui povres et entrepris
> Ausi comme ele!
> Et si n'est pas gente ne bele;
> Cinquante anz a en s'escuele,
> S'est maigre et seche:
> N'ai pas paor qu'ele me treche.
> Despuis que fu nez en la greche
> Diex de Marie,
> Ne fu més tele espouserie. (*Mariage,* vv. 26–41)

Rutebeuf's wife is, furthermore, especially comic, since she is portrayed in a loving and even in a potentially sexual role: "Qui de cuer m'aime/. . ./ N'ai pas paor qu'ele me treche" (*Mariage,* vv. 7, 38). The idea of a seductive old woman seemed particularly ludicrous to the medieval mind, for love and desire were seen as appropriate only for the young and the beautiful.[9]

9. The fabliau *La Vieille Truande,* for example, paints a vivid portrait of an old coquette who sees a handsome knight coming down the road; bedaubing herself, she runs to sit by her door:

> Mais ce n'estoit mie bele Aude,
> Ains estoit laide et contrefaite;
> Mais encor s'adoube et afaite
> Por çou k'encore veut siecler.

(Montaiglon and Raynaud, eds., *Fabliaux, 5,* 173)
See also: Jean de Meun's portrait of *La Vieille* (vv. 12,385 ff.) who laughs with embarrassment when *Bel Acueil* gives her a garland (vv. 12,730–39); the *Lamentations* of Mahieu le Bigame, "Vieille savate se veult oindre" (v. 1815, *1,* 94); Conon de Béthune's debate with an overly reluctant belle whose time is past and whose beauty is like Troy after the battle—"Or n'i puet on fors les plaices trover"

Rutebeuf's verses describing his fear of coming home empty-handed have often been compared to those written by Colin Muset in his "Sire cuens, j'ai vielé."[10] Colin Muset asks for his wages, saying:

> Car talent ai, n'en doutez mie,
> De raler a ma mesnie:
> Quant g'i vois boursse desgarnie,
> Ma fame ne me rit mie,
> Ainz me dit: "Sire Engelé,
> En quel terre avez esté,
> Qui n'avez riens conquesté?
>   . . .
> Aval la ville.
> Vez com vostre male plie!
> Ele est bien de vent farsie!
> Honiz soit qui a envie
> D'estre en vostre compaignie!

Thus far the passage is thematically much like Rutebeuf's. But Muset chooses to dramatize his arrival at home; his wife speaks for herself, and Muset intervenes simply as narrator. Rutebeuf included the poet's homecoming as part of his *complainte* and therefore maintained the subjective and emotional tone of the rest of his *Mariage*. Nor does Muset stop with his wife's sarcastic attack. He goes on to portray a contrasting scene of the poet's arrival when he brings money home:

> Quant je vieng a mon ostel
> Et ma fame a regardé
> Derrier moi le sac enflé
> Et je, qui sui bien paré
>   De robe grise,
> Sachiez qu'ele a tost jus mise

(No. X, v. 29, *Chansons*, p. 18); and Morawski, *Proverbes*, No. 2405: "Tout ira bien fors mariage de veille."

10. *Chansons*, pp. 9–10, No. V.

La conoille, sanz faintise:
Ele me rit par franchise,
Ses deus braz au col me plie.

Ma fame va destrousser
Ma male sanz demorer;
Mon garçon va abruver
Mon cheval et conreer;
Ma pucele va tuer
Deus chapons por deporter
  A la jansse alie;
Ma fille m'aporte un pigne
En sa main par cortoisie.
Lors sui de mon ostel sire
A mult grant joie sanz ire
Plus que nuls ne porroit dire.

The differences immediately apparent between Rutebeuf's and
Colin Muset's portrayal of the shrewish wife are significant.
Each poet adapts the theme to the poetic personality he has chosen
as his. Rutebeuf adds the portrait of his wife to his central theme
of poverty, leitmotiv of his poems of misfortune. Colin, on the
other hand, combines the theme with his characteristic *registre,*
that of the "bone vie," [11] appropriate to his chosen poetic personality
of a gay hedonist. Colin Muset's works often end in a merry way:
the image of the poet lying in a green field with his head on
a pretty girl's lap, a good picnic at hand, weaving flower garlands
or playing his *viele* is typical of "la muse Muset." [12] The contrast of

11. Zumthor has defined several *registres* or complexes of themes and motifs
stylized by literary tradition in his *Langue et techniques poétiques* (pp. 123–61). He
defines the *registre* of Colin Muset as that of "la bonne vie," and its motifs as a
welcoming girl, good food, love, and usually music (pp. 156–58). See, for example,
Nos. XIII–XIV of Colin Muset's *Chansons.* Banitt's article, "Le Vocabulaire de
Colin Muset; Rapprochement sémantique avec celui d'un prince-poète Thibaut de
Champagne" (*Romance Philology,* 20, No. 2 [November 1966], 151–67) offers
interesting linguistic observations on the contrast between the vocabulary of Thibaut's
maux d'amour and Colin's *bonne vie,* but mistakenly confuses poetic innovation
with personal experience (esp. p. 152).
12. *Chansons,* No. I, v. 1.

themes he has chosen to make, therefore, is between the comically angry shrew and the joyful pleasures of the good life. Rutebeuf, however, writes an antispring poem, using what might be termed *registres* of the bad life and the unhappy season. The latter themes have as characteristic elements hunger, cold, loneliness, and family burdens.[13] Just as many of Colin Muset's poems show him becoming happier and happier, Rutebeuf's poems of misfortune show the poet going from bad to worse, ever more famished, ever colder, ever more miserable.

Leo has correctly observed that the *Complainte Rutebeuf* is an amplification of the themes first appearing in his *Marriage*,[14] and that there is, in these poems, a mixture of both grotesque comedy and of a gloomy sadness which recalls *La Mort Rutebeuf*. Rutebeuf describes at length the multiplication of his domestic burdens in the *Complainte:*

> Or a d'enfant geü ma fame;
> Mon cheval a brisié la jame
>   A une lice;
> Or veut de l'argent ma norrice,
> Qui m'en destraint et me pelice
>   Por l'enfant pestre,
> Ou il revendra brere en l'estre.
> Cil Damediex qui le fist nestre
>   Li doinst chevance
> Et li envoit sa soustenance
> Et me doinst encore alejance
>   Qu'aidier li puisse,
> Que la povretez ne me nuise
> Et que miex son vivre li truise

13. Contrast Rutebeuf's descriptions of the seasons in his *Mariage* and *Griesche d'hiver* with the motifs of the "registre de la saison joyeuse," defined by Zumthor, whose motifs are good weather, greenery, bird song, joy and comfort (*Langue et techniques poétiques,* p. 158). See also Dragonetti (*Technique poétique,* pp. 176–77) where he emphasizes that a wintry exordium may also serve as foil to the poet's inner joy.
14. "Rutebeuf: persönlicher Ausdruck," p. 132.

Que je ne fais!
Se je m'esmai je n'en puis mais. (vv. 53–68)

Transition from vulgar financial preoccupations to a father's prayer in these verses is not, however, the result of a sudden eruption of "real reality" within a grotesque satire, as Leo believes.[15] The troubles Rutebeuf lists are characteristic of laments over misfortune, and the mixture of tones results from Rutebeuf's combining a sad *complainte* with the portrait of a foolish married poet, again in a way appropriate to the poetic personality of the jongleur, as defined by Brunetto Latini: "Gengleour est celui ke gengle entre les gens a ris et a gieu, et moke soi et sa feme et ses filz et tous autres."[16] Even Rutebeuf's fears that his poverty will be visited upon his children correspond to predictions made for jongleurs in the poem of fortunetelling, the *Geus d'aventures:*

> Petiz fustes-vous mult tingneus,*   * scrofular
> Encor estes ors ménestreus,
> Et si seront tuit votre enfant,
> Quar il lor vient bien de naissant.[17]

In the *Miracle de Théophile* similar ideas appear, but in a consistently sorrowful tone, because the lament over misfortune is placed in the mouth of a tragic sinner:

> Or m'estuet il morir de fain
> Se je n'envoi ma robe au pain.
> Et ma mesnie que fera?
> Ne sai se Diex les pestera.* (vv. 9–12)[18]   * will feed them

---

15. Ibid., pp. 141–43. Leo describes Rutebeuf as carried away by his theme into a directly human and lyric sphere.

16. *Trésor,* p. 204; see also above p. 292.

17. Jubinal, ed., *Jongleurs et trouvères,* pp. 153–54. Several other fortunes in the *Geus* apply to Rutebeuf's poetic "I" in his poems of misfortune: ". . . Si prendrez/ A fame une vielle froncie,/ Qui vous menra mult male vie./ . . ./ En la fin serez vous chétis:/ S'or avez mal vous aurez pis,/ Quar vous irez nus et deschaus,/ Et par les frois et par les chaus./ . . ./ Li geus des tables et des dez/ Vous chaceront à povretez" (ibid., pp. 151–52, 155).

18. See *La Pauvreté,* "Entre chier tens et ma mainie,/ . . ./ Ne m'ont laissié deniers ne gages" (vv. 13, 15), and Grace Frank's article listing similar complaints

The *Complainte Rutebeuf* also amplified several proverbs in subjective form, just as *Charlot et la peau de lièvre* amplified proverbs
in a narrative. The proverbial idea, "Li mal ne sevent seul venir," [19]
which appears in verse 107 of the *Complainte*, is the conclusion to
the recital of domestic woes and is also the central theme to which
Rutebeuf's choice of form contributes. The poet uses a series of
annominatio figures, not to indicate shifts of meaning, but to
accentuate, through iteration, the miseries which crush him.[20] One
of the most touching figures is found in the verses on his faithless
friends: [21]

> Que sont mi ami devenu
> Que j'avoie si pres tenu
>   Et tant amé?
> Je cuit qu'il sont trop cler semé
> Il ne furent pas bien femé,*   * fertilized
>   Si sont failli.
>   . . .
> Je cuit li vens les a osté,[22]
>   L'amor est morte:
> Ce sont ami que vens enporte,
> Et il ventoit devant ma porte
>   Ses enporta,

---

in Rutebeuf's "personal" poetry and in *Théophile*, "Rutebeuf and Théophile," pp.
162–64.

19. See Morawski, *Proverbes*, Nos. 438 and 2454.

20. See *Complainte Rutebeuf*, vv. 16–17. "Et tant a fere/ (Quanques j'ai fet est a
refere), v. 92: "Mi gage sont tuit engagié"; and vv. 81–86:
> . . . Moult me sont changié li ver
> Envers antan:
> Por poi n'afol quant g'i entan.
> Ne m'estuet pas taner en tan,
>   Quar le resveil
> Me tane assez quant je m'esveil.

21. Leo also sees these verses as a direct expression of the poet's personal destiny
("Rutebeuf: persönlicher Ausdruck," p. 143).

22. This is perhaps a reference to the proverb used by Villon in his *Ballade en
vieil langage françoys*, "Autant en emporte ly vens." Siciliano cites four other texts
having an identical verse in his *François Villon et les thèmes poétiques du moyen
âge* (Paris, 1934), p. 261, n. 10.

C'onques nus m'en conforta
Ne du sien riens ne m'aporta.
(vv. 110–15, 120–26)

The four repetitions of *ven* do not seem contrived, but continue naturally the image of his friends as a "crop," already begun in the preceding verses. Because Rutebeuf could not give them money, his friends have drifted off like unfertilized seeds in the ill wind blowing before Rutebeuf's door. His prediction in *Le Mariage* that his door would remain closed after his friends heard the news of his "espouserie" (vv. 41–52, 99–103) has proved the truth of the moral underlying the *Complainte:* "Povre parent nus n'aparente."[23]

The duties of friendship were, of course, a common theme in didactic works. Jean de Meun included a long treatise on friendship in the *Roman de la Rose,* contrasting the true friend with the fickle acquaintance who abandons his companion "si tost con Povretez l'afuble/ De son hisdeus mantel obnuble" (vv. 4795–96).[24] Rutebeuf's *Paix* is closer to this sort of didactic generalization on friendship than are the *Mariage, Complainte,* and *Pauvreté,* which maintain the subjective tone throughout. Rutebeuf preaches the virtues of generosity in *La Paix* as emphatically as he does in his *Dit d'Aristote;* he only interjects his own personal experience at the end to illustrate by his own example that when a man rises in social rank, he forgets his former friends.[25]

Of the many themes recurring in Rutebeuf's own works, similar themes, images, and even expressions appear in poems by his predecessors and contemporaries writing in French, Latin, German, and Italian. One must therefore accept, in my opinion, the basis of

23. *Les Plaies,* v. 14; see the similar proverbs cited by FB, *1,* 378, notes to vv. 13–22; and the *Voie de Paradis,* v. 626; *Dit de Pouille,* v. 50; and *Complainte du roi de Navarre,* v. 83.

24. See *Rose, 2,* ed. Langlois, vv. 4685–4974. See also *Droiz au clerc de Voudai* (Jubinal, ed., *Nouveau Recueil, 2,* 140) or John of Garland's *Morale scolarium* (ed. Paetow, p. 252, v. 622), for two of many other examples of this theme.

25. The same theme recurs in Gautier de Coinci's *Léocade,* vv. 1663–65, and in a guide to good manners, *Urbain le courtois* (ed. P. Meyer, *Romania, 32*).

convention underlying Rutebeuf's "personal" poetry, no matter how well the poet succeeds in making his subject seem convincingly "real." There are, for example, so many poems describing poets losing at dice, that it is surprising that Leo should claim that Rutebeuf based his *Griesche d'hiver* and *Griesche d'été* on a "real experience" of gambling.[26] Throughout these two poems and in his *Ribauds de Grève,* Rutebeuf is working with entirely conventional *topoi.* His portrayal of himself as a shivering, naked figure who has lost his clothes gambling is the archetypal image of every losing dice-player in medieval literature.[27]

Within the conventional framework, however, Rutebeuf's *Griesche* poems are triumphs of his poetic art and high points of the medieval dicing poems, just as the Goliard "In taberna quando sumus" is one of the greatest of all medieval drinking songs.[28]

Rutebeuf constructed his *Griesche* poems around the basic themes of summer and winter.[29] The rather static image of winter of the

26. "Rutebeuf: persönlicher Ausdruck," p. 134. For samples of the abundant French literature of dice and dice players see: Semrau, *Würfel und Würfelspiel im alten Frankreich; du jeu de dez* (Jubinal, ed., *Nouveau Recueil,* 2, 229–234), a moral tale about the devil-inspired invention of dice by a "mauvès senatour" of Rome; the *Crédo au Ribaud* (Ilvonen, ed., *Parodies,* pp. 127–33, No. V). In Latin see "Si quis Deciorum," "Cum in orbem universum," "Tessera blandita," and the parodies of sacred offices, the *Officium lusorum,* and "Ego sum abbas Cucaniensis" (all edited by Schmeller, *Carmina burana,* Nos. 174, 193, 1, 183, 189, and 196; see Raby, *Secular Latin Poetry,* 2, 276–78). For mixed Latin-French dicing poems, see *Des james, des dez* and *De patre Decio* (cited by Zumthor, *Langue et techniques poétiques,* p. 101).

27. See in Rutebeuf's *Griesche d'hiver,* vv. 52–53, 62–63, 82, 85–86, and his *Griesche d'été,* vv. 29–37, 69, 82, 89, 103, 109; a frequent theme, indeed. See also, for example, the *Dit des marchéans,* "par le dé sui desrobes" (Montaiglon and Raynaud, eds., *Fabliaux,* 2, 128), and, in Latin, "Nunc per ludum/ dorsum nudum" (*Carmina burana,* ed. Schmeller, L). FB cites three examples of the single expression "Qui plus en set s'afuble sac" (*Griesche d'été* vv. 23–24; FB, 1, 526–27, note). See also the exemplum "Ribaldus quando vestem amisit, tota die ludit . . . et nudus exire cogitur" (ed. Welter, *Tabula exemplorum,* p. 109) and the sermon on dicing by Robert de Sorbon, cited by Haskins in *Studies in Mediaeval Culture,* p. 58 and n. 6.

28. *Carmina burana,* ed. Schmeller, No. 175.

29. The formulaic expression "par les frois et par les chaus" (*Griesche d'été,* v. 31) often appears as an equivalent for suffering; see: *Roland,* v. 1011, the *Patenostre du vin* (ed. Ilvonen, *Parodies,* p. 71), and Rutebeuf's *Complainte de Geoffroi* (v. 44). Such suffering is often thematically related to losses at dicing; compare the Archpoet's *Confessio,* ". . . cum ludus corpore me dimittat nudo,/

Mariage is set into motion in the *Griesche d'hiver:* the leaves fall, the birds weep, the snowflakes sting like summer flies.

> Diex me fet le tens si a point
> Noire mousche en esté me point,
> En yver blanche.
> Issi sui com l'osiere franche
> Ou com li oisiaus seur la branche:
> En esté chante,
> En yver plor et me gaimante,
> Et me desfuel ausi com l'ente
> Au premier giel. (vv. 32–39)

Winter does not merely inspire the poet's work, as spring did in other lyrics. Rutebeuf explicitly identifies his state with the changes in nature: like the birds and the trees, he is subjected to alternating seasons of joy and sorrow.

The forces which control Rutebeuf have a malevolent will of their own. There is therefore a constant play in Rutebeuf's "personal" poetry between the portrayal of a subjective self which reacts and an objective self which is acted upon by an external world.[30]

Frigidus exterius, mentis estu sudo" (*Gedichte*, p. 26), and *Carmina burana,* ed. Schmeller, No. 174: Per Decium/ supplicium/ suis datur cultoribus,/ quos seviens/ urget hyems/ semper suis temporibus."

30. In like manner the author of *Partonopeus de Blois* contrasts the happy and successful loves of his hero with his own failure to melt the cold heart of his lady love:

> Partenopex a son delit:
> Li parlers de lui molt m'ocit,
> Car il a tot bien de s'amie;
> Je n'en ai rien qui ne m'ocie.
> Il ne la voit, mais a loisir
> La sent, et en fait son plaisir:
> Je voi la moie, et n'en sent rien,
> J'en ai le mal, et il le bien. (Cited by Anthime Fourrier,

Le Courant réaliste dans le roman courtois en France au moyen âge, 1, [Paris, 1960], 429) The author is not so much contrasting "l'histoire véridique de ses propres amours" with that of his fictional hero, as Fourrier suggests, but contrasting two sorts of love narrative, the subjective and the objective, and contrasting two sorts of love, idyllic and unrequited. See also above, p. 284 and n. 72.

The courtly lyric of love usually has no such objective context.
In the *Griesche d'hiver, Povreté* is both the God-given enemy in
the poet and a personified huntress who pursues him:

> Por povreté qui moi aterre,
> Qui de toutes pars me muet guerre
> Contre l'yver.
>
>   . .
>
> Povre sens et povre memoire
> M'a Diex doné, li rois de gloire,
>   Et povre rente,
> Et froit au cul quant bise vente:
> Li vens me vient, li vens m'esvente
>   Et trop sovent
> Plusors foïes sent le vent. (vv. 4–6, 10–16) [31]

This passage, like the following two, is embellished with rhetorical
figures appropriate to the sublime form of the lament, from which
the *Griesche* borrows its sorrowful tone and subjective mode. Yet the
6-branch annominatio on "vent," the repetition of "povre," the alliterative "v," like the play on "aller" and "venir" in verses 49–51,
does not impress us as rhetoric. These poetic figures based on repetition enhance the despairing feelings expressed. But also the subject,
eternal poverty and cold, and the vocabulary, especially in the expression "froit au cul," contrast, as Rutebeuf wished them to, with

31. Compare with the allegorical form of *De Niceroles* (*O.C., 3,* 352–54); the
miserable hero, who lost everything at dice, joins the Mendicant order of *Niceroles*
("Fools"), and travels from *Tramblai* ("Trembling") to *Vile-pointe* ("Hard
Times"), *Froidure, Poverte,* and finally, *Famine.* Compare with the portraits of
Povreté in the *Roman de la Rose,* "nue come vers" (see vv. 441–62 by Guillaume
de Lorris and 10,103–218 by Jean de Meun). Compare also with one of the poems
edited by Jeanroy (*Origines,* No. 27, pp. 507–08), which bears much resemblance
to Rutebeuf's poems of misfortune, since it contains the same themes of winter,
dice, poverty, false friends, and women; the tone and images are strikingly similar
to Rutebeuf's:

> La bixe et li autre vans
> m'i guerroie mout sovent;
>   par darrier et par devant
> me peirt la chair nue;
> or m'i soit Deus aidant,
>   ma joie ai perdue. (st. IV)

the sublime tone and rhetorical figures. The passage does not, therefore, seem elegantly ornamented, in spite of the dense use of rhetorical figures; rather it is one in which rhetoric has achieved its ideal
of convincing verisimilitude. The wind which blows through it is a
real wintry blast, forever chilling. Even in summer the poor wretch
does not seek shade or a cool chamber, since he is always naked and
defenseless against the elements (vv. 80–84). The dice, in turn, are
like creditors who ambush him at every turn:

> Bien le m'ot griesche en covent
> Quanques me livre:
> Bien me paie, bien me delivre,
> Contre le sout me rent la livre
> De grant poverte.
>   .   .   .
> Li dé m'ocient,
> Li dé m'aguetent et espient,
> Li dé m'assaillent et desfient,
> Ce poise moi. (vv. 17–21, 54–57)

The rhetorical repetitions, annominatio, and personifications are
perfectly integrated in the *Griesche d'hiver*. Every generalization
is joined to the poetic self in pounding verses, as in Rutebeuf's interpretation of the proverb, "Tout passera fors que biens faiz": [32]

> Or voi je bien tout va, tout vient;
> Tout venir, tout aler covient,
> Fors que bienfet. (vv. 49–51)

Only at the end does the poet shift to the third person, representing
a beggared gambler trudging across Paris to seek money from his
family and at the "Draperie" and the "Change" (vv. 88–104), before ending on a subjective note of helpless lassitude: "Ainsi vers
moi chascuns s'apaie:/ je n'en puis més." [33]

---

32. Morawski, *Proverbes,* No. 2407, cited by FB, *1,* 523 n.
33. See FB, *1,* 260, note to v. 54, for this expression in Rutebeuf's work.

Rutebeuf's *Dit des ribauds de Grève*[34] seems a distillation of the *Griesche d'hiver*. The poet speaks, yet here only of others. He does not appear himself in a scene which paints a whole way of life in a poem of only a dozen lines:

> Ribaut, or estes vos a point:
> Li aubre despoillent lor branches
> Et vos n'aveiz de robe point,
> Si en avreiz froit a voz hanches.
> Queil* vos fussent or li porpoint   * How precious
> Et li seurquot forrei a manches!
> Vos aleiz en estei si joint
> Et en yver aleiz si cranche!
> Votre soleir n'ont mestier d'oint:
> Vos faites de vos talons planches.
> Les noires mouches vos ont point,
> Or vos repoinderont les blanches.

Every theme and almost every image of the *Dit des ribauds* can be found in the *Griesche d'hiver*. Yet the absence of moralizing generalization and of expressions of lament, and the substitution of the directly challenging "vos" for the poetic "I," give this perfect vignette an entirely different quality than the mournful *Griesche*

34. *Ribaud* meant "vagabond, stevedore, wastrel, rascal," and simply "poor man." Contrast Rutebeuf's portrait with that of Jean de Meun, who uses the *ribauds* to exemplify the ideal of the happy poor man who is content with his lot. One notes anew how one topic may serve different intentions. Jean de Meun describes the life of the *ribauds* in jolly tones:

> Maint ribaut ont les cueurs si bauz,
> Portant sas de charbon en Grieve
> Que la peine riens ne leur grieve,
> S'il en pacience travaillent
>   • • •
> Ne ne prisent tresors treis pipes,
> Ainz despendent en la taverne
> Tout leur gaaing e leur esperne,
> Puis revont porter les fardeaus.
>   • • •
> E vivent si con vivre deivent
> Tuit cil sont riche en abondance
> S'il cuident aveir soufisance.
> (vv. 5048–51, 5054–57, 5062–64)

d'hiver. The poem is exceptional not only with Rutebeuf's work but among thirteenth-century poems, for there is no explanation given for the *ribauds'* poverty and no commentary of hope or despair. Rutebeuf describes only their estate: the *ribauds* have no future or past, but only an eternal present which changes with the seasons.

The summer half of Rutebeuf's *Griesche* diptych is painted with lighter colors. The *griesche* is described as a mighty Amazon, with gamblers as her soldiers:

> De Gresce vient si griez eesche;
> Or est ja Borgoingne briesche.
>   Tant a venu
> De la gent qu'ele a retenu,
> Sont tuit cil de sa route nu
>   Et tuit deschaus;
> Et par les froiz et par les chaus,
> Nés li plus mestres seneschaus
>   N'a robe entiere.
> La griesche est de tel maniere
> Qu'ele veut avoir gent legiere
>   En son servise:
> Une eure en cote, autre en chemise. (vv. 25–36)

Rutebeuf is here parodying a noble epic theme, that of the origin of *chevalerie,* for these verses recall others in the *Complainte de Constantinople:*

> De Gresse vint chevalerie
> Premierement d'ancesserie
> Si vint en France et en Bretaingne. (vv. 121–23) [35]

To complete his description of *la griesche,* he borrows a technique from the didactic allegories (see above, pp. 140–42) and continues by portraying the typical actions of those who follow *la griesche.*

35. See FB, *1,* 428, n., in which similar texts from medieval chronicles are cited in which *griesche* means "dice game" and "Greek."

The tavern scene (vv. 64–89) recalls the boisterous dicing scene of the *Jeu de saint Nicolas*,³⁶ although Rutebeuf narrates rather than dramatizes the frenetic drinking and the heedless squandering of the dice players.

Finally, the scene of the gamblers' departure at dawn provides the one happy ending in Rutebeuf's poems of misfortune. The dice players' follies are set in the past tense, as is their suffering:

> Or faut quaresme,
> Que lor a esté dure et pesme:
> De poisson autant com de cresme
> I ont eü;
> Tout ont joué, tout ont beü. (vv. 93–97) ³⁷

The April warmth stirs the exhausted players into motion again; "viste et prunte et entre" (v. 104), they begin to play again, but in an ascensional movement of joy which ends the poem:

> Lors les verriiez entremetre
> De dez prendre et de dez jus metre:
> Ez vous la joie!
> N'i a si nu qui ne s'esjoie;
> Plus sont seignor que ras sus moie ³⁸
> Tout cel esté.
> Trop ont en grant froidure esté;
> Or lor a Diex un tens presté
> Ou il fet chaut,
> Et d'autre chose ne lor chaut:
> Tuit ont apris aler deschaut. (vv. 106–16)

Rutebeuf himself, in his poetic role of poor fool, withdrew from his *Griesche d'été* after the first 12 verses.³⁹ The somber tones of

---

36. See nine similar tavern scenes cited by Semrau, *Würfel*, pp. 128–59.

37. Compare with the same theme in Rutebeuf's *Mariage* (cited p. 291, n. 93), which has a grimmer note there because he uses the future tense.

38. Leroux de Lincy, ed., *Proverbes, 1,* 199: "Etre dans un endroit comme un rat dans la paille (être à son aise)."

39. Rutebeuf reappears to comment on the truth of what he says in verses 46–48 and 70, in verses such as "J'en sai assez" (v. 48).

his poetic personality did not suit the gaiety of the tavern scene or the warm pleasure of the last verses. He therefore relinquished his poetic "I" as would a poet who had completed one image and turned to another. Only the invisible presence of the artist remained to complete the poem itself.

If I have insisted on the role literary tradition played in determining the subject and even the vocabulary of Rutebeuf's poems of misfortune, it is to prove that our modern critical notions of authenticity, subjectivity, and sincerity cannot apply directly to medieval poetry. One cannot, finally, glean much of any interest from Rutebeuf's "personal" verse about the man, his habits, his tastes, his finances, or his family. Any such move away from the poem to the man is doomed to trail off in a forest of convention and contradiction. Yet the question of the poet's subjective presence within his poem must remain open. With each succeeding generation the poetic form defined here—the subjective lament over misfortune and suffering—widens to allow ever more room for personal history. From Rutebeuf to Deschamps to Villon to Du Bellay, one can see a similarity of themes and metaphors, although the poets' circumstances vary as much as their poetic forms—here a *complainte* or a ballad, there a sonnet. Certainly the role of the author's poetic personality is much greater and more varied in the poetry of the thirteenth century than that allowed him in the didactic, epic, and courtly works of the twelfth. If the poet begins to appear in his poetry ever more prominently, eventually he will appear more directly, just as history and society penetrate into poetry, as we have seen, through a circuitous path of topical satire.

CONCLUSION

*Existe-t-il . . . quelque chose de plus
charmant, de plus fertile et d'une
nature plus positivement excitante
que le lieu commun?*
Baudelaire, Salon de 1859

A t the end of this study of poetic patterns in Rutebeuf it would seem clear that the fundamental elements of his poetry remain the same. Whether he is unfurling the great banner of the Crusades, preaching to ignorant sinners, defending the University against King and Pope, or describing the misery of a poor *ribaud,* Rutebeuf's poetic material is convention, *topoi,* proverbs, and rhetoric; and these, in turn, fashion the poet's perception of his world.

One cannot say that the ideas Rutebeuf expresses are his alone, yet the great fund of moral commonplaces was a treasure in which all shared equally. Such stylized and condensed experiences of generations as compose the common fund of medieval thought were relieved by each generation and renewed by each man. In the words of C. S. Lewis:

> We might equally well call our medieval authors the most unoriginal or the most original of men. They are so unoriginal that they hardly ever attempt to write anything unless someone has written it before. They are so rebelliously and insistently original that they can hardly reproduce a page of any older work without transforming it by their own intensely visual and emotional imagination.[1]

Commonplaces guaranteed comprehension between the poet and public as much as the words the poet used; they also represented for the poet provocative, exciting ideas which he could make his own by the touch of the "main as mestriers." The poet did not feel the distance between his own and others' ideas as we do in our individualistic age, although we have seen how partisanship slipped into Rutebeuf's work under the guise of absolute good and eternal right.

1. *Studies in Medieval and Renaissance Literature,* collected by Walter Hoopes (Cambridge, Eng., 1966), p. 37.

Rutebeuf's poetry has proved to be anchored in its epoch in style, in themes, and in intention. With sufficient initiation, I believe we have been able to approach some works closely without blocking our enjoyment by modern prejudices against "clichés," and that the many comparisons with other poets have revealed Rutebeuf's unique poetic talents: he is not inventive, in our modern sense of the word, yet he renewed traditional themes so that his poetry often appears fresh and, indeed, convincing.

Rutebeuf himself remains an elusive yet beckoning figure who vanishes behind contradictions and convention if we seek auto-biographical confession. Yet although Rutebeuf remains unknown to us, beyond plausible conjectures about the type of life he led, his poetry exists. We perceive him as a poet, at the moment he set words on paper. It is his strength as a poet which stamps his identity on the *dit,* which remained shapeless and mediocre in the hands of his contemporaries. Today Rutebeuf is the one noncourtly French poet before Villon who still stands out in the medieval period.

Finally, it is Rutebeuf as a poet who interests us, not the man behind the work. Whether an author uses his own experience of his historical world to begin his poem, as does the modern poet, or his knowledge of a poetic past, as did the medieval author, every poem is eventually separated from the experience with which it began. Every poet releases his themes from their moorings to the past and to the self, setting them free and giving them life by his art.

BIBLIOGRAPHY

I. COMPLETE EDITIONS OF RUTEBEUF'S WORKS (BY EDITOR)

Faral, Edmond, and Julia Bastin, eds., Œuvres complètes, 2 vols. Paris, 1959–60.
> *Reviews:* Raffaele de Cesare, *Studi Francesi, 5,* No. 1 (January–April 1961), 126–27; Delbouille, Maurice, "En relisant Rutebeuf," *Marche Romane, 10,* No. 4 (October–December 1960), 147–58; Alfred Foulet, *Speculum, 36,* No. 2 (April 1961), 328–32; Edward B. Ham, *Romance Philology, 16,* No. 3 (February 1963), 301–23; Omer Jodogne, *Les Lettres Romanes, 17,* No. 1 (February 1, 1963), 85–88; W. Noomen, *Revue Belge de Philologie et d'Histoire, 40,* No. 3 (1962), 923–25; H. H. Lucas, *French Studies, 15,* No. 2 (April 1961), 157–59; Mario Roques, *Romania, 80,* No. 4 (1959), 549–50 (on Vol. 1), *81,* No. 2 (1960), 288 (on Vol. 2); A. Varvaro, *Studi Francesi, 7,* No. 3 (September–December 1963), 526–27.

Jubinal, Achille, ed., Œuvres complètes de Rutebeuf, trouvère du XIIIe siècle, nouvelle éd. 3 vols. Paris , 1874–75. (1st ed. 2 vols. Paris, 1839.)
> *Reviews:* P. Chabaille, *Journal des Savants* (January 1839), pp. 41–53; (May 1839), pp. 276–88; Paul Meyer, *Romania, 3,* No. 3 (July 1874), 401; Philarète Chasles, *Journal des Débats Politiques et Littéraires* (January 12, 1841), pp. 1–3.

Kressner, A., *Rutebeufs Gedichte,* Wolfenbüttel, 1885.
> *Review:* Anon., *Romania, 15* (1886), 477.

II. PARTIAL EDITIONS OF RUTEBEUF'S WORKS (BY EDITOR)

Arland, Marcel, ed., *Anthologie de la poésie française* (nouvelle éd. Paris, 1947): *De La Griesche d'yver* (pp. 68–71); *La Complainte d'outremer,* (pp. 71–76); *Li Diz des ribaux de greive* (p. 76); *Les .IX. Joies de Nostre Dame,* 4 stanzas (pp. 76–77).

Augsburger, Daniel André, ed., "Rutebeuf et la *Voie de Paradis* dans la littérature française du moyen âge," unpublished dissertation (University of Michigan, 1949; University Microfilms, 1950). Critical edition.

Auguis, Pierre-René, ed., *Les Poètes françois depuis le XIIe siècle jusqu'à Malherbe*. (6 vols. Paris, 1824): *Les Ordres de Paris* (*1*, 308).

Barbazan, Etienne, ed., *Fabliaux et contes des poètes françois des XII, XIII, XIVe & XVes siècles, tirés des meilleurs auteurs* (3 vols. Paris, 1756): *De La Dame qui fist trois tours entour le monstier* (*1*, 48–56); *Dou Pet au vilain* (*1*, 108–12); *Le Testament de l'asne* (*1*, 113–22); *Li Diz de Frere Denise cordelier* (*1*, 122–39); *De Charlot le juif qui chia en la pel dou lievre* (*1*, 140–47).

—— and Dominique Martin Méon, eds., *Fabliaux et contes des poètes françois des XI, XII, XIII, XIV et XVe siècles* (*nouvelle* éd. 4 vols. Paris, 1808): *Des Béguines*, with prose translation and commentary (*1*, 3–38); *Les Ordres de Paris* (2, 293–98); *La Chanson des ordres* (2, 299–301); *De La Dame qui fit trois tours entour le monstier* (*3*, 30–35); *Dou Pet au vilain* (*3*, 67–69); *C'est li testament de l'asne*, (*3*, 70–75); *Li Diz de Freire Denise cordelier* (*3*, 76–86); *De Charlot le Juif qui chia en la pel dou lievre* (*3*, 87–91): *Du Soucretain et de la fame au chevalier* (*4*, 119–43).

Bartsch, Karl, ed., *Chrestomathie de l'ancien français*, revue et corrigée par Léo Weise (12e éd. New York, 1958). Critical edition: No. 75, "Rustebeuf" (pp. 242–46): a. *Le Mariage Rustebeuf*, b. *La Desputoison de Charlot et du barbier*, c. *Miracle de Théophile* (vv. 540–663).

—— and Adolf Horning, eds., *La Langue et la littérature françaises, depuis le IXème siècle jusqu'au XIVème siècle* (Paris, 1887): *La Complainte Rutebeuf* (cols. 443–48), *Li Dis de Jacobins* (cols. 448–50).

Bastin, Julia, and Edmond Faral, *Onze Poèmes de Rutebeuf concernant la croisade* (Paris, 1946). Critical edition.
Reviews: Revue du Moyen Age Latin, 2, (1946), 398–99; Alfred Foulet, *Speculum*, 22, No. 1 (January 1947), 88–89; P. Groult, "Rutebeuf et la Bible," *Les Lettres Romanes*, 1, No. 3 (August 1, 1947), 211–32; E. B. Ham, *Modern Language Notes*,

62, No. 4 (April 1947), 280–83; Albert Henry, *Le Moyen Age,* 53, Nos. 1–2 (1947), 170–71; O. Jodogne, *Les Lettres Romanes, 1,* No. 3 (August 1, 1947), 263–64; F. Lecoy, *Romania, 69,* No. 275 (1946–47), 396–400; Robert Marichal, *Bibliothèque de l'Ecole des Chartes, 106* (1945–46), 383–84; J. Melander, *Studia Neophilologica, 19* (1946–47), 191–93; Lawton P. G. Peckham, *Romanic Review, 38,* No. 3 (October 1947), 253–54; J. Wathelet-Willem, *Revue Belge de Philologie et d'Histoire, 26,* No. 4 (1948), 1102–04.

Brittain, F., ed., *The Medieval Latin and Romance Lyric to A.D. 1300* (Cambridge, 1951) : *La Repentance Rutebeuf* (pp. 224–27).

Bujila, Bernadine A., ed., "Rutebeuf: *La Vie de sainte Marie l'Egyptienne,*" *University of Michigan Contributions in Modern Philology,* No. 12 (June, 1949). Critical edition.

Reviews: Edmond Faral, *Romania, 71* (1950), 119–26; Grace Frank, *Romance Philology, 4* (1950–51), 284–85; Arthur Långfors, *Neuphilologische Mitteilungen, 53,* Nos. 1–4 (April 1952), 118–29; Felix Lecoy, *Le Moyen Age, 56,* Nos. 1–2 (1950), 145–49; C. A. Robson, *Medium Aevum, 20* (1951), 88–91.

Cantera, Angelo, ed. and trans., "A Critical Edition of the *Fabliaux* of Rutebeuf," unpublished doctoral dissertation, University of Michigan, 1960; University Microfilms.

Chabaille, P., ed., *Le Roman du Renart,* Supplément ed. D. M. Méon (Paris, 1835) : *Renart le bestourné* (pp. 31–37).

Clédat, L., ed., *Morceaux choisis des auteurs français du moyen âge* (2e éd. Paris, n.d.) : *Le Mariage Rutebeuf, Le Dit des ribauds de Grève, Le Dit de l'herberie* (pp. 350–61).

Constans, L., ed. *Chréstomathie de l'ancien français (IXe–XVe siècles)* (3e éd. Paris and Leipzig, 1906) : No. XLVIII, *Le Dit de l'erberie,* abridged (pp. 119–20).

Crépet, Eugène, ed., and Louis Moland, ed. and trans., *Les Poètes françaises. Recueil des chefs d'œuvre de la poésie française depuis les origines jusqu'à nos jours* (4 vols. Paris, 1861). Vol. 1: Première période: du XIIe au XVIe siècle; "Rutebeuf" [*notice littéraire*], pp. 249–57; *La Desputizons dou Croisé et dou Descroizié,* with trans., pp. 258–73.

Faral, Edmond, "A propos de l'édition des textes anciens: Le cas du manuscrit unique," in *Recueil de travaux offert à M. Clovis*

Brunel, *1* (2 vols. Paris, 1955), 409–21 (*Dit de Sainte Eglise*).

—— ed., "*Le Dit des Cordeliers* de Rutebeuf," *Romania, 70* (1948–49), 288, 331.

—— ed., *Mimes français du XIIIe siècle* (Paris, 1910): *Dit de l'herberie* (pp. 61–68); Introd. on Rutebeuf, (pp. 55–59).

—— "Pour Le Commentaire de Rutebeuf: *Le Dit des règles*," *Studi Medievali,* Nuova serie, XVI (1943–50), 176–211.

    Review: Jeanne Lods, *Romania, 72,* No. 3 (1951), 407–09.

Frank, Grace, ed., *Le Miracle de Théophile, Miracle du XIIIe siècle* (Paris, 1925; 2d ed. 1949). Critical edition.

    Reviews: Edmond Faral, *Romania, 72* (1951), 199–201; Raphael Levy, *Romanic Review, 41,* No. 2 (April 1950), 130–32; Ruth Whittredge, *Romance Philology, 4* (1950–51), 67–68.

Franklin, Alfred, ed., *Les Rues et les cris de Paris* (Paris, 1874): *Li Diz de l'erberie* (pp. 165–74); *Les Ordres de Paris* (pp. 191–99); *La Chanson des ordres* (pp. 201–04).

Grimm, Jakob, ed., *Reinhart Fuchs* (Berlin, 1834): *Renart le Bestourné* (pp. 443–44).

Groult, P., and V. Edmond, eds., *Anthologie de la littérature française du moyen âge des origines à la fin du XIIIe siècle* (2 vols. Gembloux, 1942). Vol. 1 (textes): "Rutebeuf," pp. 187–94; *Le Dit des béguines,* pp. 187–88; *Le Dit des ribauds de Grève,* p. 189; *La Pauvreté Rutebeuf,* pp. 190–99; *La Repentance Rutebeuf,* pp. 192–94; *Miracle de Théophile,* pp. 216–20, vv. 424–43, 492–503, 528–97. Vol. 2 (Notes): pp. 49–52, 58–59.

Ham, Edward B., ed. *Renart le Bestorné,* in *University of Michigan Contributions in Modern Philology,* No. 9 (April 1947). Critical edition.

    Reviews: Alfred Ewert, *Medium Aevum, 17* (1948), 54–55; Edmond Faral, *Romania, 70,* No. 278 (1948), 257–69; Percival B. Fay, *Romance Philology, 1,* No. 2 (November 1947), 163–66; Robert V. Merrill, *American Oxonian, 35* (1948), 124–25; A. W. Reed, *Modern Language Review, 43,* No. 2 (April 1948), 247–48; Winthrop H. Rice, *Symposium,* No. 1 (May 1948), 126–27.

Henry, Albert, ed., *Chrestomathie de la littérature en ancien français* (2 vols. Berne, 1953). Vol. 1 (textes): No. 136, *Complainte de Constantinople,* pp. 245–48; No. 135, *Griesche d'hiver*, pp. 244-45; No. 149, Prose part of *Dit de l'herberie*, pp. 278-80; No. 146, *Miracle de Théophile* (vv. 384-601), 264-68.

Jeanroy, A., ed. *Chansons satiriques et bachiques du XIIIe siècle* Paris, 1921): *La Chanson des ordres* (pp. 13-16); notes and variants (pp. 92-93).

Johnston, R. C., and D. D. R. Owen, *Fabliaux* (Oxford, 1957): *Testament de l'âne* (pp. 39-43).
    Review: Jean Rychner, *Romance Philology, 12*, No. 3 (February 1959), 340-42.

Jubinal, Achille, ed., *Le Miracle de Théophile*, Paris, 1838.
    Review: L.C. [name not known], *Journal des Savants* (January 1838), p. 57.

———— *La Complainte d'outremer et celle de Constantinople*, Paris, 1834.

Langlois, Ernest, and Gaston Paris, eds. and trans., *Chrestomathie du moyen âge* (13e éd. Paris, n.d.): *Le Dit des béguines* (pp. 265-66).

Legrand d'Aussy, Pierre-Jean-Baptiste, *Fabliaux ou contes; fables et romans du XIIe et du XIIIe siècle* (5 vols. Paris, 1829; 1st ed. 4 vols. 1779). Vol. 2: Résumé, *Miracle de Théophile*, pp. 180-84; trans. of *Dispute du Croisé et du Décroisé*, pp. 211-21; résumé, *Voie de Paradis*, pp. 226-39; abbreviated trans. of *De La Femme qui fit trois fois le tour des murs de l'église;* abbreviated trans. of *Indigestion du vilain*, pp. 352-354. Vol. 3: abbreviated trans. of *Charlot le juif*, pp. 90-92; abbreviated trans. of *Le Testament de l'âne*, 105-16; Vol. 4: résumé, *Frère Denise*, pp. 380-84. Vol. 5: résumé, *Sacristain et la femme au chevalier*, pp. 83-84.

Lucas, H. H., ed., *Poèmes concernant l'Université de Paris* (Paris, 1952). Critical edition. Poems: *Li Diz de l'Universitei de Paris; La Descorde de l'Université et des Jacobins; Li Diz de maistre Guillaume de Saint Amour; La Complainte de maistre Guillaume de Saint Amour; Des Règles; La Bataille des Vices contre les Vertus.*
    Reviews: Edmond Faral, *Romania, 74* (1953), 109-20; Grace Frank, *Modern Language Notes, 69*, No. 2 (February 1954), 151-52; F. W. A. George, *Medium Aevum, 23*, No. 2 (1954), Edward B. Ham, *Romance Philology, 11*, No. 1 (August 1957),

88–96; Urban T. Holmes, Jr., *Speculum, 28,* No. 2 (April 1953), 415; Omer Jodogne, *Les Lettres Romanes, 8,* No. 4 (November 1, 1954), 460; J. Orr, *Modern Language Review, 48,* No. 3 (July 1953), 368.

———— *Les Poésies personnelles de Rutebeuf* (Paris, 1938). Critical edition: *Mariage Rutebeuf; Complainte Rutebeuf; Prière Rutebeuf; Griesche d'yver; Griesche d'este; Povreté Rutebeuf; Repentance Rutebeuf.*

 Reviews: Julia Bastin, *Romania, 66,* No. 3 (July 1940), 398–407; Jessie Crosland, *Modern Language Review, 35,* No. 1 (January 1940), 102–03; E. Hoepffner, *Revue des Langues Romanes, 68,* Nos. 13–24 (January–December 1938), 224–28.

Méon, Dominique, ed., *Nouveau Recueil de fabliaux et contes inédits des poètes français des XIIe, XIIIe, XIVe et XVe siècles* 2 vols. Paris, 1823): *Li Diz de l'erberie (1,* 185–91).

Monmerqué, L.-J.-N., and Francisque Michel, eds. and trans., *Théâtre français au moyen âge* (Paris, 1885; 1st ed. Paris, 1839): *Miracle de Théophile,* with translation (pp. 139–56).

 Review: Charles Magnin, *Journal des Savants* (August 1846), pp. 449–65.

Montaiglon, Anatole de, and Gaston Raynaud, *Recueil général et complet des fabliaux* (6 vols. Paris, 1872–90). Critical edition. Vol. 3: No. 68, *Le Pet au vilain,* pp. 103–05; No. 79, *De La Dame qui fit .iii. tors entor le moustier,* pp. 192–98; No. 82, *Le Testament de l'asne,* pp. 215–21; No. 83, *De Charlot de juif qui chia en la pel dou lievre,* pp. 222–26; No. 87, *De Frere Denise,* pp. 263–74.

Mustanoja, Tauno, *"Les Neuf Joies Nostre Dame;* A poem attributed to Rutebeuf," *Annales Academiae Scientiarum Fennicae,* Ser. B, *73,* No. 4, Helsinki, 1952.

 Reviews: Jean Frappier, *Romance Philology, 10,* No. 1 (August 1956), 66–70; F. W. A. George, *Medium Aevum, 23,* No. 2 (1954), 102–04; Urban T. Holmes, Jr., *Speculum, 28,* No. 2 (April 1953), 410–11; Y. Lefèvre, *Le Moyen Age, 62,* No. 3 (1956), 372–73; C. E. Pickford, *Modern Language Review, 48,* No. 4 (October 1953), 499.

Omont, Henri, ed., *Fabliaux, dits et contes en vers français du XIIIe siècle.* Fac-simile du manuscrit français 837 de la Bibliothèque Nationale. (Paris, 1932). Includes Rutebeuf's poems from MS A.

Oulmont, Charles, ed., *La Poésie française du Moyen Age; XIe–XVe siècles* (Paris, 1913): *La Complainte Rutebeuf* (pp. 302–08).

Paris, Gaston, and Ernest Langlois, eds. and trans., *Chrestomathie du Moyen Age* (13th ed. Paris, n.d.: *Li Diz des beguines,* with translation (pp. 265–66).

Pauphilet, Albert, ed., *Jeux et sapience du moyen âge* (Paris, 1941): *Le Miracle de Théophile* (pp. 135–56); *Le Dit de l'herberie* pp. 201–07).

—— Régine Pernoud and A.-M. Schmidt, eds., *Poètes et romanciers du Moyen Age,* Paris, 1963. "Rutebeuf," pp. 925–51: *Mariage Rutebeuf, Complainte Rutebeuf, Prière Rutebeuf, Griesche d'yver, Griesche d'été, Povreté Rutebeuf, Repentance Rutebeuf, Complainte d'outremer, Chanson de Pouille, Le Dit de Brichemer, Le Dit des ribauds de Gréve.*

Spaziani, Marcello, ed., *Antica lírica francese* (Modena, 1954): *La Povretei Rutebeuf* (pp. 123–25); *Le Repentance Rustebeuf* (pp. 126–29).

Studer, Paul, and E. G. R. Waters, eds., *Historical French Reader. Medieval Period* (Oxford, 1924): No. 29, a. *De La Descorde de l'Université et des Jacobins;* b. *La Complainte Rutebeuf;* No. 30, *Le Miracle de Théophile* (vv. 144–374).

Tiby, Paul, ed., and Achille Jubinal, ed. and trans., "*La Dispute du croisé et du non-croisé.* Pièce du trouvère Rutebeuf (XIIIe siecle). Documents historiques originaux, XIV," *Bulletin de la Société de l'Histoire de France,* 2e partie, *1* (1834), 53–66.

Toynbee, Paget, *Specimens of Old French (IX–XV Centuries)* (Oxford, 1892): *Complainte de Constantinople* (pp. 202–08).

Voretzsch, Karl, ed., *Altfranzösisches Lesebuch zur Erläuterung der altfranzösischen Literaturgeschichte* (Halle, 1921): *C'est de Nostre Dame* (pp. 102–03); *Li Testamenz de l'asne* (pp. 110–12).

Wagner, Robert Léon, *Textes d'étude d'ancien et moyen français* (Lille and Genève, 1949). Critical edition: *La Griesche d'yver,* vv. 1–39 (pp. 107–09).

III. TRANSLATIONS OF WORKS BY RUTEBEUF

Bogaert, J., and P. Passeron, ed. and trans., *Les Lettres françaises. Moyen Age* (Paris, 1954): *La Povretei Rutebeuf*, partial (pp. 170–71); *Miracle de Théophile*, vv. 256–87, vv. 384–527 (partial), vv. 540–93 (partial).

Cohen, Gustave, ed. and trans., *Anthologie de la littérature française du moyen âge* (Paris, 1946): *Miracle de Théophile*, vv. 230–56, 384–87, 404–07, 428–31, 1st stanza of Théophile's prayer, (pp. 105–09); *Dit de l'herberie*, partial trans. (pp. 120–24); *La Griesche d'hiver*, partial trans. (pp. 126–27); *La Complainte Rutebeuf*, partial trans. (pp. 128–29).

———— trans., *Le Miracle de Théophile, miracle du XIIIe siècle*, Paris, 1934, 1948.

———— trans., "Nos Pages anthologiques. Rutebeuf: L'Ancêtre des poetes maudits," *Les Nouvelles Littéraires*, No. 7 (January 18, 1936). Reprinted in *Relais de Fontaine*, 1946. Complete and partial translations: *Le Mariage Rutebeuf; Le Dit de l'herberie* (complete); *La Griesche d'hiver; La Pauvreté Rutebeuf; La Complainte Rutebeuf; La Morte Rutebeuf.*

———— trans., in *Université* (February 15, 1936): *Disputaison du Croisé et du Décroise* (pp. 11–12); (April 15, 1936), *La Complainte Rutebeuf* (pp. 7–8).

Douhet, Jules, Comte de, trans., *Le Miracle de Théophile, Dictionnaire des mystères, 43: Nouvelle Encyclopédie théologique*, ed. J.-P. Migne (Paris, 1854), cols. 933–42.

Flores, Angel, ed., *An Anthology of Medieval Lyrics* (New York, 1962): *La Pauvreté Rutebeuf; La Repentance Rutebeuf; La Disputaison de Charlot et du barbier; La Chanson de Notre Dame* (pp. 140–47).

Gassies des Brulies, G., trans., *Anthologie du théâtre français du moyen âge* (Paris, 1927): *Le Miracle de Théophile* (pp. 74–85); *Le Dit de l'herberie* (pp. 86–90).

Glomeau, M. A., trans., *Rutebeuf. La Vie de sainte Marie l'Egyptienne, suivi de La Légende de sainte Marie l'Egyptienne, par Jacques de Voragine*, Paris, 1935.

Gourmont, Rémy de, trans., *Trois Légendes du moyen âge* (Paris, 1919): *Miracle de Théophile* (pp. 87–122).

Greene, Henry Copley, *Théophile. A Miracle Play* (Boston, 1898). A modern rendering of *Miracle of Théophile*, partially based on Rutebeuf's version. Reprinted in H. C. Greene, *Pontius Pilate, St. Ronan of Brittany and Theophile. Three Plays in Verse*, New York, 1903.

Gsteiger, Manfred, trans., *Das Mirakelspiel von Theophilus*, St. Galten, 1955.

Guiette, Robert, trans., *"Le Mariage Rutebeuf" et autres poèmes* (Paris, 1950): partially modernized text of *Le Mariage Rutebeuf, Le Dit des ribauds de Grève, La Pauvreté Rutebeuf, La Complainte Rutebeuf, La Repentance Rutebeuf*.

Hellman, Robert, and Richard O'Gorman, trans., *Fabliaux. Ribald Tales from the Old French*, with notes and afterward (New York, 1965): *Brother Denise* (pp. 135–41).

Jeanroy, A., trans., *Le Miracle de Théophile*, Paris and Toulouse, 1932.

  Review: Mario Roques, *Romania, 59*, No. 4 (October 1933), 609.

——— trans., *Le théâtre religieux en France du XIe au XIIIe siècles* (Paris, 1924): *Miracle de Théophile* (partial trans.).

Klint, A. H., ed. and trans., *Le Miracle de Théophile*, Upsal, 1869.

Nogaret, François Félix, *Contes en vers* (5th ed. Paris, 1810): *Testament de l'âne*.

Palfrey, Thomas R., and William C. Holbrook, eds. and trans., *Medieval French Literature; Representative Selections in Modernized Versions* (New York and London, 1934): *Le Mariage de Rutebeuf* (partial); *Le Dit des ribauds de Greve* (pp. 153–56).

Pariser, Anton, ed. and trans., *Die Frühzeit der französischen Lyrik. Gedichte aus fünf Jahrhunderten* (Vienna, 1961): *C'est de la povreté Rutebeuf* (pp. 18–21).

Pauphilet, Albert, trans., *Contes du jongleur* (Paris, 1932): *Le Testament de l'âne* (pp. 21–29).

Pernoud, Régine, ed. and trans., *La poésie médievale française.* (Paris, 1947): Partial translation of: *Le Mariage Rutebeuf; La Complainte Rutebeuf; La Grièche d'hiver*, pp. 121–31.

Teissier, Maurice, ed. and trans., *Chansons de geste, contes, chroniques.* (Paris, 1947): *Le Dit de l'herberie* (partial), pp. 201–03; *Le Miracle de Théophile* (partial), pp. 250–53.

Woledge, Brian, ed. and trans., *The Penguin Book of French Verse.* Vol. 1: *To the Fifteenth Century* (Middlesex and Baltimore, 1961): *La Complainte d'Outremer,* pp. 165–67 (partial); *La Complainte Rutebeuf,* pp. 168–71.

IV. WORKS ON RUTEBEUF

Bastin, Julia, "Quelques propos de Rutebeuf sur le roi Louis IX," *Bulletin de l'Académie Royale de Langue et de Littérature Française, 38,* No. 1 (1960), 5–14.

Bienert, Oswald, *Le Tableau de son temps que nous donne le trouvère Rutebeuf* (Dresden, 1885).

Burchardt, Albert, *Beiträge zur Kenntniss der französische Gesellschaft in der zweiten Hälfte des XIII. Jahrhunderts auf Grund der Werke Rutebeuf, des "Roman de la Rose," des "Renart le Nouvel" und des "Couronnement Renart."* Coburg, 1910.

Chabaille, P., "Rutebeuf," in *Nouvelle Biographie générale,* Gen. ed. M. le Dr. Hoefer, *42,* cols. 929–32 (Paris, 1866).

Clédat, L., *Rutebeuf,* ("Les Grands Écrivains Français") (Paris, 1910).

    Review: Jules Lemaître, *Journal des Débats Politiques et Littéraires* (July 1891), 1–2; Stengel, E., *Zeitschrift für französische Sprache und Litteratur 13,* No. 2 (Leipzig, 1891), 153–57.

Cocito, Luciana, "Osservazioni e note sulla lirica di Rutebeuf," *Giornale Italiano de Filologia, 11,* No. 4 (November 1958), 347–57.

Cohen, Anne-Lise, "Exploration of Sounds in Rutebeuf's Poetry," *French Review, 40,* No. 4 (April 1967), 658–67.

Cohen, Gustave, "Rutebeuf, l'ancêtre des poètes maudits," *Etudes Classiques, 21,* No. 1 (January 1953), 3–18.

———— "Littérature. Les chefs-d'œuvre animés au souffle de la jeunesse. La plus ancienne pièce de notre théâtre en France, *Le Miracle de Théophile,*" *Conferencia, 31,* No. 2 (January 1937), 83–93.

Cohen, Gustave, *Rutebeuf*. *"Le Miracle de Théophile." Miracle du XIIIe siècle;* explication par . . . (Paris: Centre de Documentation Universitaire, 1933).

——— "Le Théâtre en Sorbonne," *Université* (February 15, 1936), 13-14.

Dehm, Christian, *Studien zu Rutebeuf*. (Würzburg, 1935.)

Denkinger, Tiberius, "Die Bettelorden in der französischen didaktischen Literatur des 13. Jahrhunderts, besonders bei Rutebeuf und im *Roman de la Rose*," *Franziskanische Studien* (1915), pp. 63-109; pp. 286-313. Tübingen, reprinted Munster i. Westf., 1915.

Faral, Edmond, "Le Dit d'Aristote," *Neophilologus, 31,* No. 3 (July 1947), 100-03.

——— "Quelques Remarques sur *Le Miracle de Théophile* de Rutebeuf," *Romania, 72* (1951), 182-201.

——— "Trois Remarques sur *La Vie sainte Elysabel* de Rutebeuf," *Studi Medievali,* Nuova serie, *17,* No. 1 (June 30, 1951), 93-103.

Feger, Gerhard, *Rutebeufs Kritik au den Zuständen seiner Zeit,* Freiburg-in-Baden, 1920.

Flinn, John, *Le "Roman de Renart" dans la littérature française et dans les littératures étrangères au moyen âge,* Toronto, 1963. Ch. V. *"Renart le Bestourné,"* pp. 174-200. *Review:* André Giacchetti, *Romance Philology, 21,* No. 1 (August 1967), 124-29.

Frank, Grace, "Rutebeuf and Théophile," *The Romanic Review, 43,* No. 3 (October 1952), 161-65.

Frappier, Jean, *La Poésie lyrique française aux XIIe et XIIIe siècles: Les auteurs et les genres,* Paris, n.d. "Rutebeuf," pp. 220-31.

Friesland, Carl, "Die Quelle zu Rutebeufs Leben der Heiligen Elisabeth," *Zeitschrift für Romanische Philologie, 19* (1895), 375-82.

Ham, Edward Billings, *Rutebeuf and Louis IX,* Chapel Hill, 1962. *Review:* Arié Serper, *Romance Philology, 18,* No. 3 (February 1965), 371-74.

——— "Rutebeuf" in *Dictionnaire des lettres françaises: Le Moyen Age, 4* (Paris, 1965), 664-65.

—— "Rutebeuf and the Tunis Crusade," *Romance Philology, 9,* No. 2 (November 1955), 133–38.

—— "A Rutebeuf Crux," *Romance Philology, 3,* Nos. 2 and 3 (November 1949–February 1950), 168–72.

—— "The Rutebeuf Guide for Salescraft," *Studies in Philology, 47,* No. 1 (January 1950), 20–34.

—— "Rutebeuf—Pauper and Polemist," *Romance Philology, 11,* No. 3 (February 1958), 226–39.

—— "Two patrons of Rutebeuf," *Romance Notes, 3,* No. 2 (1962), 1–6.

Henry, Albert, "Rutebeuf et Troyes en Champagne," *Travaux de Linguistique et de Littérature publiés par le Centre de Philologie et de littérature romanes de l'Université de Strasbourg, 2,* No. 1 (1964), 205–06.

Houville, Gérard d', "Spectacles: Festival Rutebeuf," *Revue des Deux Mondes,* 8e période, *31* (February 1936), 683–86.

Jeandet, Yette, "Théâtre et Université," *La Revue des Jeunes,* Nos. 7–8 (July–August 1936), 79–85.

Jordan, Ludwig, *Metrik und Sprache Rutebeufs,* Göttingen, 1888.

Jubinal, Achille, "Etudes nouvelles sur un vieux poète. Rutebeuf," *L'Investigateur, 4,* 4e série (May 1864), 145–58.

Junker, Albert, "Über den Gebrauch des Stilmittels der Annominatio bei Rutebeuf," *Zeitschrift für Romanische Philologie, 69,* Nos. 5–6 (1953), 323–46.

Keins, Pablo. "Politische Satire und 'poésie personelle' bei Rutebeuf," *Zeitschrift für Französische Sprache und Literatur, 74,* No. 3 (October 1964), 241–62.

—— "Rutebeuf und Villon, Ein Vergleich," *Die Neueren Sprachen,* No. 3 (1963), 130–35.

—— "Rutebeuf y Villon. Estudio comparativo," *Revista de la Universidad de Buenos Aires,* Quinta época, *5,* No. 3 (July–Sept. 1960), 359–66.

—— "Rutebeufs Weltanschauung im Spiegel seiner Zeit," *Zeitschrift für Romanische Philologie, 53,* Nos. 5–6 (1933), 569–75.

Kressner, A., *Rustebeuf, ein französischer Dichter des XIII Jahrhunderts* (Cassel, 1894). Reprint of his articles in *Franco-Gallia:* "Rustebeuf, ein Dichterleben im Mittelalter," in *10,* No. 11 (November 1893), 165–70; "Rustebeuf als Satirendichter," in *11*, No. 2 (February 1894), 17–23; "Rustebeuf als Fableldichter und Dramatiker," in *11*, Nos. 8–9 (August–September 1894), 113–21.

Långfors, Arthur, "A Propos de Rutebeuf: Les Cerfs de la forêt de Bierre ou de Fontainebleau," *Neuphilologische Mitteilungen, 49,* Nos. 1–2 (1948), 49–53.

Lafeuille, Germaine. *Rutebeuf,* Paris, 1966.

Lanson, Gustave, "Rutebeuf," in *Histoire illustrée de la littérature française, 1, Le Moyen Age* (Paris and London, 1923), 86–90.

Lecoy, Félix, "Sur un passage difficile de Rutebeuf; *Chanson des Ordres,* vv. 49–50," *Romania, 85,* Nos. 2–3 (1964), 368–72.

Leendertz, P., Jr., "De Strophen van Rutebeuf," *Neophilologus, 4,* No. 3 (1919), 202–11.

Le Grand d'Aussy, Pierre-Jean-Baptiste, *Notices et extraits des manuscrits de la Bibliothèque Nationale et autres bibliothèques publiés par l'Institut National de France, 5* (Paris, An VII: 1798). *Notices: Renart le Bestourné* (pp. 328–29); *Bataille des Vices contre les Vertus, Chanson des Ordres, De Brichemer* (pp. 404–14).

Leo, Ulrich, "Rutebeuf: persönlicher Ausdruck und Wirklichkeit," *Saggi e richerche in memoria di Ettore Li Gotti, 2* (Palermo, 1962), 126–62.

———— *Studien zu Rutebeuf. Entwicklungsgeschichte und Form des Renart le Bestourné und der ethisch-politischen Dichtungen Rutebeufs,* Halle, 1922.

    Review: Heinrich Gelzer, *Archiv für das Studium der neueren Sprachen und Literaturen, 146* (1923), 266–68; Emil Winkler, *Die Neueren Sprachen, 32* (1924), 101–02.

Mojsisovics, Edgar von, *Metrik und Sprache Rustebeufs,* Heidelberg, 1906.

Monnard, Charles, "La Satire française au treizième siècle et Rutebeuf," *Bibliothèque Universelle de Genève,* Nouvelle Série, *42* (1842), 21–45.

Morawski, Joseph, "Quelques sources méconnues du *Roman de Renart le Contrefait* [Rutebeuf, Brunetto Latini, Alart de Cambrai]," *Zeitschrift für romanische philologie, 49* (1929), 536–44.

Paris, Paulin, "Rutebeuf," *Histoire littéraire de la France, 20* (Paris, 1842), 719–83.

Pesce, L.-G., "Le Portrait de Rutebeuf," *Revue de l'Université d'Ottawa, 28,* No. 1 (January–March 1958), 55–118.

Post, Charles H., "The Paradox of Humor and Satire in the Poems of Rutebeuf," *French Review, 25,* No. 5 (April 1952), 363–68.

Reed, Joselyne, *"Le Miracle de Théophile* de Rutebeuf," *Bulletin des jeunes romanistes, 11–12* (Strasbourg, 1965), 34–55.

Regalado, Nancy Freeman, "Two Poets of the Medieval City: Rutebeuf and Villon," *Yale French Studies, 32* (1964), 12–21.

Schumacher, Ernst, *Zur Syntax Rustebeufs,* Kiel, 1886.

Sclafert, Clément, "Un Jongleur de Notre-Dame," *Etudes, 181* (October–December 1924), 554–80.

Sepet, Marius, "Un Drame religieux du moyen âge, *Le Miracle de Théophile," Revue Historique et Archéologique du Maine, 35* (1894), 26–54.

    Review: Henri Strohmayer, *Romania, 23* (1894), 601–06.

Serper, Arie, "La Foi profonde de Rutebeuf," *Revue de l'Université d'Ottawa, 33,* No. 3 (July–September 1963), 337–41.

—— "L'Influence de Guillaume de Saint-Amour sur Rutebeuf," *Romance Philology, 17,* No. 2 (November 1963), 391–403.

—— *"Renart le Bestourné,* poème allégorique," *Romance Philology, 20,* No. 4 (May 1967), 439–55.

—— "Le Roi saint Louis et le poète Rutebeuf," *Romance Notes, 9,* No. 1 (1967), 134–40.

—— "Rutebeuf, poète satirique," unpublished doctoral dissertation (University of Paris), Paris, 1961.

Tjaden, Heinrich Peter, *Untersuchungen über die Poetik Rutebeufs,* Marburg, 1885.

V. MEDIEVAL WORKS

Abélard, Peter, *Historia Calamitatum; The Story of my Misfortunes; An Autobiography,* trans. Henry Adams Bellows, Saint Paul, 1922.

Adam de la Halle, *Canchons und Partures des altfranzösischen trouvère Adan de le Hale le bochu d'Aras,* ed. Rudolf Berger. Vol. 1: *Canchons,* Halle, 1900.

—— *Le Jeu de la feuillée,* ed. Ernest Langlois, 2d rev. ed. Paris, 1951.

Adam de la Halle, *Œuvres complètes.* (*Poésies et musique*), ed. E. de Coussemaker, Paris, 1872.

Adenet le Roi, *Li Roumans de Berte aus grans piés,* ed. Aug. Scheler, Brussels, 1874.

────── *Li Roumans de Cléomadès,* ed. André van Hasselt, 2 vols. Brussels, 1865–66.

Aegidius Assisiensis, *The Golden Sayings of the Blessed Brother Giles of Assisi,* ed. and trans. Fr. Paschal Robinson, Philadelphia, 1907.

Alanus de Insulis, *Summa de arte praedicatoria* (cols. 109–98), *Sermones octo* (cols. 198–222), *Sermones alii* (cols. 221–28), and *Opusculum de sex alis cherubim* (cols. 265 ff.), in J.-P. Migne, ed., *Patrologia latina,* CXX, Paris, 1855.

Alfonso El Sabio, *Las Siete Partidas,* ed. Gregorio Lopez, 5 vols. Paris, 1851.

Angiolieri, Cecco, *Il Canzoniere,* ed. Carlo Steiner, Turin, 1928.

Anonymous:

Die Apokalypse des Golias, ed. Karl Strecker, Leipzig, 1928.

Aucassin et Nicolette, ed. Mario Roques, 2d rev. ed. Paris, 1929.

La Bataille d'Enfer et de Paradis (*Arras contre Paris*); *poème inédit du XIIIe siècle,* ed. A. Guesnon (Paris, 1909). Extract from *Bulletin de la Société de l'Histoire de Paris et de l'Ile-de-France, 36* (1909), 45–57.

La Chanson de la croisade albigeoise, ed. Eugène Martin Chabot, 3 vols. Paris, 1931–61.

La Chanson de Roland, ed. and trans. Joseph Bédier, Paris, 1960.

La Complainte et le Jeu de Pierre de la Broce, chambellan de Philippe-le-Hardi, qui fut pendu le 30 juin 1278, ed. Achille Jubinal (Paris, 1835). Reedited by F. Schneegans, *Romania, 58* (1932), 520–50.

"*Complainte sur la bataille de Poitiers,*" ed. Ch. de Beaurepaire, in *Bibliothèque de l'Ecole des Chartes,* 3d ser., 2 (January–February 1851), 257–63.

Le Couronnement de Renard. Poème du treizième siècle, ed. Alfred Foulet, Princeton and Paris, 1929.

Courtois d'Arras. Jeu du XIIIe siècle, ed. Edmond Faral, Paris, 1961.

De Babione; Poème comique du XIIe siècle, ed. Edmond Faral, Paris, 1948.

Del Tumbeor Nostre Dame; Altfranzösische Marienlegende (um 1200), ed. Erhard Lommatzsch and Max Leopold Wagner, Berlin, 1920.

"Des Fames, des dez et de la taverne: Poème satirique du XIIIe siècle mêlant français et latin," ed. Veikko Väänänen in *Neuphilologische Mitteilungen, 67,* Nos. 5–6 (1946), 104–13.

"Le Dit de Dame Jouenne. Version inédite du fabliau du *Pré Tondu,"* ed. Arthur Långfors, in *Romania, 65* (January 1918–19), 99–107.

"Dou Pape, dou roy et des monnaies," ed. and trans. P. Chabaille, in *Bulletin de la Société de l'Histoire de France,* 2e partie, Documents, 2 (1835), 221–24.

Le Garçon et l'aveugle, jeu du XIIIe siècle, ed. Mario Roques, 2d ed. Paris, 1921.

Gesta romanorum [attributed to Pierre Bercheure], trans. Charles Swan, Preface by Thomas Wright, 2 vols. London, 1871.

The Life of Saint Dominic in Old French Verse, ed. Warren Francis Manning, Cambridge, Mass., 1944.

Le Mireour du monde, ed. Félix Chavannes, Lausanne, 1846.

La Résurrection du Sauveur, ed. and trans. Achille Jubinal, Paris, 1834.

"Richeut, Old French Poem of the Twelfth Century, with Introduction, Notes and Glossary," ed. I. C. Lecomte, in *Romanic Review, 4,* No. 3 (July–September 1913), 261–305.

Li Roman de Bauduin de Sebourc, IIIe roy de Jherusalem; poème du XIVe siècle, ed. L. N. Boca, 2 vols. Valenciennes, 1841.

Le Roman de Fauvel [attributed to Gervais du Bus], ed. Arthur Långfors, Paris, 1914–19.

Le Roman de Renart, ed. Ernest Martin, 3 vols. Strasbourg and Paris, 1887. Other editions: ed. Mario Rogues, 5 vols. Paris, 1948–60; ed. Dominique Méon, 5 vols. Paris, 1926, Supplément ed. P. Chabaille, Paris, 1835; trans. L. Robert-Busquet, Paris, 1935.

Le Roman de Renart le contrefait, eds. Gaston Raynaud and Henri Lemaître, 2 vols. Paris, 1914.

Un Sermon en vers, ed. Achille Jubinal, Paris, 1834.

La Tabula exemplorum secundum ordinem alphabeti. Recueil

d'exempla compilé en France à la fin du XIIIe siècle, ed. J.-Th. Welter, Paris and Toulouse, 1926.

"Le *Tournoiement d'Enfer:* Poéme allégorique et satirique, tiré du manuscrit français 1807 de la Bibliothèque Nationale," ed. A. Långfors, in *Romania, 44* (January–October 1916–17), 511–58.

Li Vers de le mort, ed. Carl Auguste Windahl, Lund, 1887.

"Vida de Maria Egipcia," ed. J. Cornu, in *Romania, 11* (1882), 366–81.

La vie de Lazarillo de Tormes, ed. Marcel Bataillon, trans. A. Morel-Fatio, Paris, 1958.

Des. xxiii. *Manières de vilains, pièce du XIIIe siècle,* eds. Achille Jubinal and Eloi Johanneau, Paris, 1834.

Archipoeta, *Die Gedichte des Archipoeta,* ed. Max Manitius, Munich, 1913.

Aspin, Isabel, S. T., ed., *Anglo-Norman Political Songs,* Oxford, 1953.

Augustine, Saint, *The Confessions,* trans. F. J. Sheed, New York, 1943.

—— *Obras* (texto bilingüe). Vol. 2: *Las Confesiones,* ed. P. Angel Custodio Vega, 3d ed. Madrid, 1955.

Baker, A. T., *"Vie de sainte Marie l'Egyptienne,"* *Revue des Langues Romanes, 59,* Nos. 3–6 (May 1916–December 1917), 145–401.

Bartholomew of Pisa, *L'Alcoran des cordeliers, 2,* trans. by Conrad Badius from the German ed. by Erasmus Alberus, nouvelle éd., 2 vols. Amsterdam, 1734.

Baudouin de Condé and Jean de Condé, *Dits et contes,* ed. Aug. Scheler, 3 vols. Brussels, 1886–67.

Bédier, Joseph and Pierre Aubrey, eds., *Les Chansons de croisade,* Paris, 1909.

Bernhard, B., "Recherches sur l'histoire de la corporation des ménétriers ou joueurs d'instruments de la ville de Paris," *Bibliothèque de l'Ecole des Chartes, 3* (1841–42), 377–404.

Berry, André, ed. and trans., *Anthologie de la poésie occitane,* Paris, 1961.

Bertoni, G., and A. Jeanroy, eds., "Un Duel poétique au XIIIe siècle. Les sirventés échangés entre Sordel et Peire Bremon

Ricas Novas," *Annales du Midi, 28* (January–April 1916), 269–305.

Biblia Sacra mixta Vulgatam Clementinam, eds. Albert Colunga and Lorentio Turrado, 3d ed. Madrid, 1959.

Bierbaum, Max, *Bettelorden und Weltgeistlichkeit au der Universität Paris. Texte und Untersuchungen zum literarischen Armuts—und Exemptionsstreit des 13. Jahrhunderts, 1255–1272,* Münster-in-Westf., 1920.

Bodel, Jean, "Les *Congés,"* ed. Raynaud Gaston, in *Romania, 9* (April 1880), 216–47.

—— *Le Jeu de saint Nicolas,* ed. Alfred Jeanroy, Paris, 1958.

Boethius, *The Consolation of Philosophy,* trans. H. R. James, London, 1897.

Bonaventura, Saint, *Obras* (edición bilingüe), eds. Frs. León Amoros, Bernardo Aperribay, Miguel Oromi, 2d ed. 6 vols. Madrid, 1955.

—— *Vie de saint François d'Assise,* trans. R. P. Damien Vorreux, Paris, 1951.

Boutière, Jean and A.-H. Schutz, eds., *Biographies des troubadours,* Toulouse and Paris, 1964.

Bozon, Nicolas, *Les Proverbes de bon enseignement,* ed. A. Chr. Thom, Lund, 1921.

—— *Seven More Poems,* ed. Sister M. Amelia Klenke, OP, New York and Louvain, 1951.

Carmody, Francis J., trans., *Physiologus: The Very Ancient Book of Beasts, Plants and Stones, Translated from Greek and other Languages,* San Francisco, 1953.

Chabaneau, Camille, ed., *Les Biographies des troubadours en langue provençale* (extract from *Histoire générale de Languedoc, 10,* ed. Privat), Toulouse, 1885.

Chaucer, Geoffrey, *Canterbury Tales,* ed. A. C. Cawley, London and New York, 1962.

Chrétien de Troyes, *Cligés,* ed. Wendelin Foerster, 3d ed. Halle, 1910.

—— *Eric et Enide,* ed. Mario Roques, Paris, 1955.

—— *Le Roman de Perceval,* ed. William Roach, Geneva and Paris, 1959.

Colin Muset, *Les Chansons,* ed. Joseph Bédier, Paris, 1912.

Conon de Béthune, *Les Chansons,* ed. Axel Wallensköld, Paris, 1921.

—— *Chansons,* with a biography by Axel Wallensköld (Helsingfors, 1891). Critical edition.

Couci, Le Châtelain de, *Chansons,* ed. Alain Lerond, Publications de la Faculté des Lettres et Sciences Humaines de Rennes, 7, Paris, 1964.

Crapelet, Georges Adrien, ed., *Proverbes et dictons populaires, avec les dits du mercier et des marchands et les criéries de Paris, aux XIIIe et XIVe siècles,* Paris, 1831.

Dahnk, Emile, *L'Hérésie de Fauvel,* Leipzig, 1935.

Dante Aligheri, *The Divine Comedy,* ed. and trans. Thomas G. Bergin, New York, 1955

—— *La Vita nuova,* ed. Natalino Salpegno, Florence, 1931.

Dasent, George Webbe, ed., *"Theophilus" in Icelandic, Low German and Other Foreign Tongues from MSS in the Royal Library, Stockholm,* London, 1845.

Denifle, Henri, and Emile Châtelain, *Chartularium Universitatis Parisiensis,* Paris, 1889.

Denis, Piramus, *La Vie seint Edmund le Rei. An Anglo-Norman Poem of the Twelfth Century,* ed. Florence Leftwich Ravenel, Philadelphia, 1906.

Deschamps, Eustache, *Poésies morales et historiques,* ed. G.-A. Crapelet, Paris, 1832.

Dinaux, Arthur, *Les Trouvères,* 4 vols. Paris, 1837–63.

Dobiache-Rojdestvensky, Olga, ed. and trans., *Les Poésies des goliards,* Paris, 1931.

Dreves, Guido Maria, and Clemens Blume, eds., *Analectica Hymnica Medii Aevi,* Leipzig, 1886–1922.

Droz, Eugénie, ed., "Fragment d'un miracle de Théophile," *Bulletin de la Société des Historiens du Théâtre,* 2, Nos. 1–2 (January–March 1934), 15–21.

—— *Le Recueil Trepperel, 1, Les Sotties* (Paris, 1935), 2, with H. Lewicka, *Les Farces* (Geneva, 1961).

Du Méril, Edélestand, ed., *Poésies populaires latines antérieures au douzième siècle,* Paris, 1843.

—— *Poésies populaires latines du moyen âge,* Paris, 1847.

Durante, *Il Fiore: Poème italien du XIIIe siècle en ccxxxii sonnets, imité du "Roman de la Rose,"* ed. Ferdinand Castets, Paris, 1881.

Etienne de Bourbon, *Anecdotes historiques, légendes, et apologues tirés du recueil inédit d'Etienne de Bourbon,* ed. A. Lecoy de la Marche, Paris, 1877.

Eudes, Archbishop of Rouen, *The Register,* trans. Sydney M. Brown, ed. Jeremiah F. O'Sullivan, New York and London, 1964.

Fagniez, Gustave, ed., *Documents relatifs à l'histoire de l'industrie et du commerce en France,* 2 vols. Paris, 1898–1900.

—— "Les Ménétriers parisiens," *Bulletin de la Société de l'Histoire de Paris et de l'Ile-de-France,* 2 (1875), 103–04.

Faral, Edmond, ed., *Les Arts poétiques du XIIe et du XIIIe siècle,* Paris, 1923.

Review: W. B. Sedgwick, "Notes and Emendations on Faral's *Les Arts poétiques du XIIe et du XIIIe siècle,*" *Speculum,* 2 (1927), 331–43.

Gace Brulé, *Les Chansons,* ed. Gédéon Busken Huet, Paris, 1902.

Gautier de Châtillon, *Die Gedichte Walters von Chatillon,* ed. Karl Strecker. Vol. 1: *Die Lieder der Handschrift 351 von St. Omer,* Berlin, 1925.

—— *Moralisch-satirische Gedichte Walters von Chatillon aus deutschen, englischen, französischen und italienischen Handschriften,* ed. Karl Strecker, Heidelberg, 1929.

Gautier de Coincy, *De Sainte Léocade au tans que Sainz Hydlefons estoit arcevesques de Tholete cui Nostre Dame donna l'aube de prelaz,* ed. Eva Vilamo-Pentti, Helsinki, 1950.

—— *Etudes sur les "Miracles Nostre Dame" de Gautier de Coinci,* ed. Arlette P. Ducrot-Granderye (*Annales Academiae Scientiarum Fennicae,* Series B, 25, No. 2), Helsinki, 1932.

—— *Les Miracles de Nostre Dame,* ed. V. Frédéric Koenig, 3 vols. Paris and Geneva, 1955–66.

—— *Miracles . . . extraits du manuscrit de l'Ermitage,* ed. Arthur Långfors (*Annales Academiae Scientiarium Fennicae,* Ser. B, 34, No. 2), Helsinki, 1937.

Gennrich, Friedrich, ed., *Altfranzösische Lieder,* Vol. 1, Halle, 1953; Vol. 2, Tübingen, 1956.

Giélée, Jacquemars, *Renart le nouvel,* ed. Henri Roussel, Paris, 1961.

Giraldus Cambrensis, *The Autobiography,* ed. and trans. Harold Edgeworth Butler, London, 1937.

Gottfried von Strassburg, *Tristan and Isolde,* ed. Friedrich Ranke, Berlin, 1930.

—— *Tristan with the Tristan of Thomas,* trans. A. T. Hatto, Middlesex and Baltimore, 1960.

Guibert of Nogent, Self and Society in Medieval France. The Memoirs of . . . , trans. C. C. Swinton Bland, rev. ed. John F. Benton, New York, 1970.

Guichard de Beaulieu, *Le Sermon,* Paris, 1834.

Guillaume IX, *Les Chansons,* ed. A. Jeanroy, Paris, 1913.

Guillaume de Lorris and Jean de Meun, *Le Roman de la Rose,* ed. M. Méon, 4 vols. Paris, 1814; ed. Ernest Langlois, 5 vols. Paris, 1914–24; ed. Félix Lecoy, 2 vols. (through v. 16, 698), Paris, 1965–66.

Guillaume de Nangis, *Chronique latine de G. de N. de 1113 à 1300 avec les continuations de cette chronique de 1300 à 1368,* ed. H. Géraud, 2d ed. 2 vols. Paris, 1843.

—— *Vie et vertus de Saint Louis,* ed. René de Lespinasse, Paris, 1877.

Guillaume de Saint-Amour, *Liber de Antichristo et ejus ministris* . . . , in *Veterum scriptorum et monumentorum* . . . , eds. E. Martène and U. Durand (Paris, 1733), cols. 1271–1446.

—— *Magistri Guillielmi de Sancto Amore opera omnia quae reperiri potuerunt,* Constance, 1632.

—— "Les *Responsiones* de Guillaume de Saint-Amour," ed. Edmond Faral, *Archives d'Histoire Doctrinale et Littéraire du Moyen Age, 18* (1950–51), 337–94.

Guillaume de Saint-Pathus (confesseur de la reine Marguerite), *Vie de saint Louis,* ed. H. François Delaborde, Paris, 1899.

Guillaume le Clerc de Normandie, *Le Besant de Dieu,* ed. Ernst Martin, Halle, 1869.

—— *Le Bestiaire,* ed. Robert Reinsch, Leipzig, 1892.

Guiot de Provins, *Les Œuvres,* ed. John Orr, Manchester, 1915.

Hilka, Alfons, ed., "Altfranzösische Mystik und Beginentum," *Zeitschrift für Romanische Philologie, 47* (1927), 121–70.

—— and Otto Schumann, eds., *Carmina burana* (2 vols.) Heidelberg, 1930, 1941). Vol. 1: Text; Vol. 2: Commentary.

Hill, Raymond Thompson, and Thomas Goddard Bergin, eds., *Anthology of the Provençal Troubadours,* New Haven, 1941.

Hocsem, Jean de, *La Chronique,* ed. Godefroid Kurth, Brussels, 1927.

Houx, Jean Le, *Vaux-de-Vire d'Olivier Basselin et de Jean Le Houx,* Ed. A. Asselin, L. Dubois, Pluquet, Julien Travers, et Charles Nodier; nouvelle éd. revue, publiée par P. L. Jacob [pseud. Paul Lacroix], Paris, 1858.

Hoveden, Roger de, *Chronica,* ed. William Stubbs, 4 vols. London, 1868–71.

——— *The Annals,* trans. Henry T. Riley, 2 vols. London, 1853.

Hue Archevesque, *Les Dits de Hue Archevesque, trouvère normand du XIIIe siècle,* ed. A. Héron, Rouen, 1885.

Hugues de Berzé, *La "Bible" au Seigneur de Berzé,* ed. Félix Lecoy, Paris, 1938.

Humbert de Romans, *De eruditione praedicatorum,* in *Maxima bibliotheca veterum patrum et antiquorum scriptorum, 25,* ed. Margarina de la Bigne (27 vols. Lyons, 1677), 421–567.

Huon de Meri, *Le Tournoiement de l'Antechrist,* ed. P. Tarbé, Reims, 1851.

Huon le Roi de Cambrai, *Œuvres, 1,* ed. A. Långfors, Paris, 1913.
    Review: A. Guesnon, *Moyen Age,* 2e série, *19* (January–June 1915), 58–77.

Ilvonen, Eero, ed., *Parodies de thèmes pieux dans la poésie française du moyen âge. Pater—Credo—Ave Maria—Laetabundus,* Helsinki, 1914.
    Review: Arthur Långfors, *Romania, 44* (July–October 1915), 280–83.

Jacob, P. L. [pseud. Paul Lacroix], ed., *Recueil de farces, soties et moralités du quinziéme siècle,* Paris, 1876.

Jacques de Vitry, *Die exempla aus den "Sermones feriales et communes,"* ed. Joseph Greven, Heidelberg, 1914.

——— *The Exempla or Illustrative Stories from the "Sermones Vulgares,"* ed. Thomas Frederick Crane, London, 1890.

Järnström, Edward, ed., *Recueil de chansons pieuses du XIIIe siècle. I. (Annales Academiae Scientiarum Fennicae,* Ser. B, *3,* No. 10), Helsinki, 1910.

——— and Arthur Långfors, eds., *Recueil da chansons pieuses du*

XIIIe siècle. II. (Annales Academiae Scientiarum Fennicae, Ser. B, *20,* No. 4), Helsinki, 1927.

Jeanroy, Alfred, ed., *Jongleurs et troubadours gascons des XIIe et XIIIe siècles,* Paris, 1923.

―――― et Henri Guy, *Chansons et dits artésiens du XIIIe siècle,* Bordeaux, Marseille, Montpellier, Paris, and Toulouse, 1898. *Review:* A. Guesnon, "La Satire à Arras au XIIIe siècle," *Moyen Age* (1899–1900).

――――and Arthur Långfors, eds., *Chansons satiriques et bachiques du XIIIe siècle,* Paris, 1921.

Jehan de le Mote, *La Voie d'Enfer et de Paradis,* ed. Sister M. Aquiline Pety, Washington, D.C., 1940.

Jehan le Teinturer d'Arras, *Le Mariage des sept arts,* ed. Arthur Långfors, Paris, 1923.

Joachim de Flore, *L'Evangile éternel,* with a biography by Emmanuel Aegerter, 2 vols. Paris, 1928.

Jodogne, O., "Fragment d'un pamphlet contre les frères mendiants," in *Mélanges de linguistique et de littérature romanes offerts à Mario Roques, 1* (4 vols. Paris, 1951), 129–38.

John de Garlande, *The Dictionarius* in *A Volume of Vocabularies, 1,* ed. Thomas Wright (2d ed. 2 vols. Liverpool, 1882), 120–38.

Joinville, Jean, Sire de, *Histoire de saint Louis, Credo, et Lettre à Louis X,* ed. Natalis de Wailly, 2d ed. Paris, 1874.

Jubinal, Achille, ed., *Jongleurs et trouvères, ou choix de saluts, épîtres, rêveries et autres pièces légères des XIIIe et XIVe siècles,* Paris, 1835.

―――― ed., *Nouveau Recueil de contes, dits, fabliaux et autres pièces inédites des XIIIe, XIVe et XVe siècles,* 2 vols. Paris, 1839.

Kjellman, Hilding, ed., "Une Version anglo-normande inédite du *Miracle de S. Théophile,*" *Studier i Modern Spraakvetenskap, 5* (Uppsala, 1914), 183–227.

Langland, William, *The Book Concerning Piers the Plowman,* ed. and trans. Donald and Rachel Attwater, London and New York, 1957.

Langlois, Ch.-V, ed., *Formulaires de lettres du XIIe du XIIIe et du XIVe siècles,* Paris, 1896.

―――― ed. and trans., *La Vie en France au moyen âge de la fin du*

XIIe au milieu du XIVe siècle (4 vols. Paris, 1925–28). Vol.
1: *D'après les romans mondains du temps;* Vol. 2: *D'après
Les Moralistes du temps;* Vol. 3: *La Connaissance de la nature
et du monde;* Vol. 4: *La Vie spirituelle, enseignements,
méditations et controverses.*

Langlois, Ernest, ed., "Anciens Proverbes français," *Bibliothèque
de l'Ecole des Chartes,* 60 (1899), 569–601.

Lapa, Manuel Rodrigues, ed., *Cantigas d'escarnho e de mal dizer,*
Coimbra, 1965.

Latini, Brunetto, *Li Livres dou tresor,* ed. Francis J. Carmody,
Berkeley and Los Angeles, 1948.

Laurent d'Orléans, *The Book of Vices and Virtues,* A Fourteenth
Century Translation of the *Somme le Roi* of Lorens d'Orleans.
Ed. W. Nelson Frances, London, 1942.

Lecoy de la Marche, A., trans., *L'Esprit de nos aïeux. Anecdotes et
bons mots tirés des manuscrits du XIIIe siècle,* Paris, n.d.

Leroux de Lincy, ed., "Chansons historiques des XIIIe, XIVe et
XVe siècles," *Bibliothèque de l'Ecole des Chartes, 1,* No. 4
(March–April 1840), 359–88.

——— *Recueil de chants historiques français depuis le XIIe jusqu'au
XVIIIe siècle.* Vol. 1: *Première série. XIIe, XIIIe, XIVe et
XVe siècles,* 2 vols. Paris, 1841.

——— and L. M. Tisserand, eds., *Paris et ses historiens aux XIVe
et XVe siècles,* Paris, 1867.

Marguerite de Navarre, *L'Heptaméron,* ed. Michel François,
nouvelle éd. Paris, 1950.

Mary, André, ed. and trans., *Anthologie poétique française. Moyen
Age,* 2 vols. Paris, 1967. ("Rutebeuf," *1,* 407–25).

Matheolus (Mahieu le Bigame), *"Les Lamentations de Matheolus"
et le "Livre de leesce" de Jehan le Fèvre, de Ressons,* ed. A.-G.
Van Hamel, 2 vols. Paris, 1892–1905.

Maurice of Sully, *Maurice of Sully and the Medieval Vernacular
Homily,* ed. C. A. Robson, Oxford, 1952.

Méon, Dominique Martin, ed., *Nouveau Recueil de fabliaux et
contes inédits des poètes français des XIIe, XIIIe, XIVe, et XVe
siècles,* 2 vols. Paris, 1823.

Meyer, P. ed., "Les Manuscrits français de Cambridge," *Romania,
32* (1903), 18–120.

Momigliano, Attilio, ed. Vol. 1: *Antologia della letteratura italiana.*

Dalle Origini alla Fine del Quattrocento, 9th rev. ed. Milan and Messina, 1959.

Montluc, Comte de Cramail, *La Comédie des proverbes,* nouvelle éd. Paris, 1665.

Morawski, J. "Mélanges de littérature pieuse," *Romania, 61* (April 1935), 145–209; (July 1935), 316–50; *64* (October 1938), 454–88; *65* (July 1939), 327–58; *66* (October 1940–41), 505–29.

—— *Proverbes français antérieurs au XVe siècle,* Paris, 1925.

Munro, Dana Carleton, ed. and trans., *The Medieval Student,* in *Translations and Reprints from the Original Sources of European History, 2,* No. 3, rev. ed. Philadelphia, 1903.

—— *Monastic Tales of the XIIIth Century,* in *Translations and Reprints from the Original Sources of European History, 2,* No. 4, Philadelphia, 1895.

Nigellus Wireker, *The Book of Daun Burnel the Ass,* trans. with an Introd. and Notes by Graydon W. Regenos, Austin, Texas, 1959. Also trans. by J. H. Mozley under the title *A Mirror for Fools,* Oxford, 1961.

—— *Speculum stultorum,* eds. John H. Mozley and Robert R. Raymo, Berkeley and Los Angeles, 1960.

Nivard of Ghent, *Ysengrimus,* ed. Ernst Voigt, Halle, 1884.

Otto, Frid. Guil., *Commentarii critici in codices bibliothecae academicae gissensis graecos et latinos philologicos et medii aevi historicos ac geographicos,* Gissae, 1842.

Paetow, Louis John, ed. and trans., *Two Medieval Satires on the University of Paris: "La Bataille des vii ars" of Henri d'Andeli and the "Morale scholarium" of John of Garland,* Berkeley, 1927.
  Review: Alfred Jeanroy, *Romania, 44* (July–October 1915), 278–79.

Pannier, Léopold, ed., *Les Lapidaires français du moyen âge des XIIe, XIIIe et XIVe siècles,* Introd. G. Paris, Paris, 1882.

Paris, Matthew, *Chronica majora,* ed. H. R. Luard, 7 vols. London, 1872–83.

—— *English History. From the Year 1235 to 1273,* trans. J. A. Giles, 3 vols. London, 1853.

Paris, Paulin, ed., *Le Romancero françois: Histoire de quelques trouvères et choix de leurs chansons,* Paris, 1833.

Pauphilet, Albert and Edmond Pognon, eds., *Historiens et chroniqueurs du Moyen Age: Robert de Clari, Villehardouin, Joinville, Froissart, Commynes,* Paris, 1952.

Petry, Ray C., ed., *No Uncertain Sound: Sermons That Shaped the Pulpit Tradition,* Philadelphia, 1948.

Pflaum, H., ed., "Poems of Religious Disputations in the Middle Ages (with a Hitherto Unknown Text in Old French [*La Desputoison du juyf et du crestien*])," *Tarbiz,* 2, No. 4 (July 1931), 443–76.

Philippe de Thaün, *Le Bestiaire,* ed. Emmanuel Walberg, Lund and Paris, 1900.

Pierre de Blois, *Opera omnia,* in J.-P. Migne, ed., *Patrologia latina,* CCVII, Paris, 1855.

Prudentius, *Works,* with an English trans. by H. J. Thomson, 2 vols. Cambridge, Mass., and London, 1949.

Raby, F. J. E., ed., *The Oxford Book of Medieval Latin Verse,* new ed. Oxford, 1959.

Raoul de Houdenc, *Le Songe d'Enfer suivi de La Voie de Paradis,* ed. and Introd. Philéas Lebesgue, Paris, 1908.

Raynouard, François Juste Marie, ed., *Choix des poésies originales des troubadours,* 6 vols. Paris, 1816–21.

Renclus de Moiliens, *Li Romans de Carité et Miserere, poèmes de la fin du XIIe siècle,* Ed. A.-G. Van Hamel, 2 vols. Paris, 1885.

Ritter, Eugène, ed., *Poésies des XIVe et XVe siècles,* Geneva, Basle, Lyons, 1880.

Ruelle, Pierre, ed., *Les Congés d'Arras* (Jean Bodel, Baude Fastoul, Adam de la Halle), Brussels and Paris, 1965.

Salimbene de Adam, *Cronica,* ed. Oswald Holder-Egger, Hanover and Leipzig, 1905–13.

Scheler, Aug., ed., *"Li Priere Theophilus,"* Zeitschrift für Romanische Philologie, 1 (1877), 247–58.
   Review: Gaston Paris, *Romania,* 6 (1877), 627.

———— *Trouvères belges de XIIe au XIV siècle: Chansons d'amour, jeux-partis, pastourelles, dits et fabliaux par Quenes de Bethune, Henri III, duc de Brabant, Gillebert de Berneville, Mathieu de Gand, Jacques de Baisieux, Gauthier le Long,* etc., Brussels, 1876.

———— *Trouvères belges (nouvelle série): Chansons d'amour, jeux-partis, pastourelles, satires, dits et fabliaux par Gonthier de*

Soignies, Jacques de Cisoing, Carasaus, Jehan Fremaus, Laurent Wagon, Raoul de Houdenc, etc., Louvain, 1879.

Stone, Louise W., ed., "Fragments d'une *Vie de saint François d'Assise* en vers anglo-normands," extract from *Archivum Franciscanum Historicum, 31,* Fascs. I–II, Florence, 1938.

Symonds, J. A., trans., *Wine, Women and Song: Medieval Latin Student Songs,* London and Boston, 1884.

Thibaut de Champagne, roi de Navarre, *Les Chansons,* ed. A. Wallensköld, Paris, 1925.

Thomas Aquinas, Saint, *Philosophical Texts,* selected and trans. Thomas Gilby, New York, 1960.

Tilander, Gunnar, ed., *Les Livres du Roy Modus et de la Royne Ratio,* 2 vols. Paris, 1932.

Tobler, Adolph, ed., *Li Proverbe au vilain,* Leipzig, 1895.

Villon, François, *Œuvres,* ed. Louis Thuasne (3 vols. Paris, 1923); ed. Auguste Longnon, revue par Lucien Foulet (4th ed. Paris, 1932).

Waddell, Helen, ed., *Medieval Latin Lyrics,* London, 1929.

Walther von der Vogelweide, *Die Gedichte,* ed. Carl V. Kraus, Berlin and Leipzig, 1936.

—— *"I Saw the World"; Sixty Poems,* trans. Ian G. Colvin, London, 1938.

—— *Poems,* ed. and trans. Edwin H. Zeydel and Bayard Quincy Morgan, Ithaca, New York, 1952.

Watriquet de Couvin, *Dits,* ed. Aug. Scheler, Brussels, 1868.

Weber, Alfred, ed., "Zwei ungedruckte Versionen der Theophilussage," *Zeitschrift für Romanische Philologie, 1* (1877), 521–40.

Whicher, George F., ed. and trans., *The Goliard Poets. Medieval Latin Songs and Satires,* Cambridge, Mass., 1949.

White, T. H., ed., *The Bestiary: A Book of Beasts, Being a Translation from a Latin Bestiary of the Twelfth Century,* New York, 1960.

Wright, Thomas, ed., *Anecdota literaria,* London and Paris, 1844.

—— *The Anglo-Latin Satirical Poets and Epigrammatists of the Twelfth Century,* 2 vols. London, 1872.

—— *The Latin Poems Commonly Attributed to Walter Mapes,* London, 1841.

——— *Political Poems and Songs Relating to English History Composed during the Period from the Accession of Edward III to that of Richard III*, 2 vols. London, 1859.
——— *A Selection of Latin Stories from the Manuscripts of the Thirteenth and Fourteenth Centuries*, London, 1842–43.

VI. STUDIES OF MEDIEVAL LITERATURE; HISTORY AND REFERENCE WORKS

Ahsmann, H.-P., *Le Culte de la Sainte Vierge et la littérature française du moyen âge* (Utrecht and Paris, 1930). "Rutebeuf," pp. 118–24.
Allen, Philip Schuyler, *Medieval Latin Lyrics*, Chicago, 1931.
——— *The Romanesque Lyric. Studies in its Background and Development from Petronius to the Cambridge Songs, 50–1050*, with renderings into English verse by Howard Mumford Jones, Chapel Hill, 1928.
Alter, Jean V., *Les Origines de la satire anti-bourgeoise en France; Moyen Age-XVIe siècle*, Geneva, 1966.
Ancelet-Hustache, Jeanne, *Sainte Elizabeth de Hongrie*, Paris, 1946.
Anglade, Joseph, *Grammaire élémentaire de l'ancien français*, Paris, 1958.
Apel, Willi, R. W. Linker, and U. T. Holmes, *French Secular Music of the Late 14th Century*, Cambridge, Mass., 1950.
Arnould, E. J., *Le Manuel des péchés: Etude de littérature religieuse anglo-normande (XIIIe siècle)*, Paris, 1940.
Auerbach, Erich, "Dante's Prayer to the Virgin (*Paradiso*, XXXIII) and Earlier Eulogies," *Romance Philology, 3*, No. 1 (August 1949), 1–26.
——— *Literary Language and Its Public in Late Latin Antiquity and in the Middle Ages*, trans. Ralph Manheim, New York, 1965.
——— *Mimesis. The Representation of Reality in Western Literature*, New York, 1957.
Austin, H. D., "Dante and the Mineral Kingdom," *Romance Philology, 4* (1950–51), 79–153.
Baldwin, Charles Sears, *Medieval Rhetoric and Poetic (to 1400) Interpreted from Representative Works*, Gloucester, Mass., 1959.

Banitt, M., "Le Vocabulaire de Colin Muset; Rapprochement sémantique avec celui d'un prince-poète Thibaut de Champagne," *Romance Philology*, *20*, No. 2 (November 1966), 151–67.

Baron, Hans, "Franciscan Poverty and Civic Wealth as Factors in the Rise of Humanistic Thought," *Speculum*, *13*, No. 1 (January 1938), 1–37.

Barreau, Jules Louis, *Description de la Cathédrale, des vitraux de Bourges et des autres monuments de la ville*, 2e éd. Chateauroux, 1885.

Baudrillart, le Cardinal, et al, *Dictionnaire d'histoire et de géographie ecclésiastiques*, 15 vols. Paris, 1912–64.

Bédier, Joseph, *Les Fabliaux: Etudes de littérature populaire et d'histoire littéraire du moyen âge*, 4th ed. Paris, 1925. "Rutebeuf," pp. 399–418.

—— and Paul Hazard, eds., *Histoire de la littérature française illustrée*. Vol. 1: E. Faral, *Le Moyen Age*, Paris, 1923; 2d ed. 1948.

Bégule, Lucien, *Monographie de la Cathédrale de Lyon*, Lyon, 1880.

Beichner, Paul E., "The Allegorical Interpretation of Medieval Literature," *PMLA*, *82*, No. 1 (March 1967), 33–38.

Bennett, Ralph F., *The Early Dominicans*, Cambridge, Eng., 1937.

Benton, John F., "The Court of Champagne as a Literary Center," *Speculum*, *36*, No. 4 (October 1961), 551–91.

Bergin, Thomas G., *Dante*, New York, 1965.

Bezzola, Reto R., "Guillaume IX et les origines de l'amour courtois," *Romania*, *66* (April 1940), 145–237.

—— *Les Origines et la formation de la littérature courtoise* (500–1200), three parts in 4 vols., Bibliothèque de l'Ecole des Hautes Etudes, Paris, 1944–67.

—— *Le Sens de l'aventure et de l'amour*: *Chrétien de Troyes*, Paris, 1947.

Bligny, Bernard, "Les Premiers Chartreux et la pauvreté," *Le Moyen Age*, *57*, Nos. 1–2 (1951), 27–60.

Bloch, Marc, *Feudal Society*, trans. L. A. Manyon, Chicago, London and Toronto, 1961.

—— *La France sous les derniers Capétiens*, *1223–1328*, Paris, 1958.

Bloomfield, Morton W., *The Seven Deadly Sins. An Introduction to the History of a Religious Concept* (with special reference to medieval English literature), East Lansing, Michigan, 1952.

Blum, A., "L'Esprit satirique dans un recueil de 'Dicts Moraux' accompagnés de dessins du XVIe siècle," *Mélanges offerts à M. Emile Picot*, 2 (2 vols. Paris, 1913), 431–46.

Bonneau, l'Abbé, "Description des verrières de la Cathédrale d'Auxerre," *Bulletin de la Societé des Sciences Historiques et Naturelles de l'Yonne*, 39 (1885), 296–348.

Bossuat, Robert, "Coup d'oeil sur la littérature didactique," *L'Esprit Créateur*, 2, No. 3 (Fall 1962), 101–06.

—— *Manuel bibliographique de la littérature française du moyen âge*, Melun, 1951; Supplément (1949–53), with Jacques Monfrin, Paris, 1955; 2d Supplément (1954–60), Paris, 1955–61.

—— *Le Moyen Age* (Paris, n.d.), "Rutebeuf," pp. 98–102.

—— *Le Roman de Renard*, Paris, 1957.

Boulay, C. E. Du, *Historia Universitatis Parisiensis*, 6 vols. Paris, 1666.

Bourgain, L., *La Chaire française au XIIe siècle d'après les manuscrits*, Paris, 1879.

—— "Les Sermons latins rimés au moyen âge," *Mémoires de la Société Nationale d'Agriculture, Sciences et Arts d'Angers*, Nouvelle période, 22 (1880), 215–31.

Brosnahan, Leger, "Wace's Use of Proverbs," *Speculum*, 39, No. 3 (July 1964), 444–73.

Cabeen, D. C., ed., *A Critical Bibliography of French Literature*. Vol. 1: *The Medieval Period*, ed. Urban T. Holmes, Jr., Syracuse, 1947.

Cahier, Charles, *Caractéristiques des saints dans l'art populaire*, 2 vols., Paris, 1867.

Callebaut, Fr. André, OFM, "La Deuxième Croisade de S. Louis et les Franciscains," *La France Franciscaine*, 1 (1922), 282–88.

Calvert, Jean, and Marcel Gruppi, *Le Bestiaire de la littérature française*, Paris, n.d.

Campbell, Gerard J., S.J., "Clerical Immunities in France during the Reign of Philip III," *Speculum*, 39, No. 3 (July 1964), 404–24.

Caplan, Harry, "Classical Rhetoric and the Medieval Theory of

Preaching," *Classical Philology, 28,* No. 2 (April 1933), 73–96.

—— "The Four Senses of Scriptural Interpretation and the Medieval Theory of Preaching," *Speculum, 4,* No. 3 (July 1929), 283–90.

—— "Rhetorical Invention in Some Medieval Tractates on Preaching," *Speculum, 2* (1927), 284–95.

Charland, Th.-M., O.P., *Artes praedicandi: Contribution à l'histoire de la rhétorique au moyen âge,* Paris and Ottawa, 1936.

Chatelain, E., "Notes sur quelques tavernes fréquentés par l'Universite de Paris aux XIVe et XVe siècles," *Bulletin de la Société de l'Histoire de Paris et de l'Ile-de-France, 25* (1898), 87–109.

Cirlot, Juan Eduardo, *A Dictionary of Symbols,* trans. Jack Sage, London, 1962.

Citron, Pierre, *La Poésie de Paris dans la littérature française de Rousseau à Baudelaire,* 2 vols. Paris, 1961.

Clédat, Léon, *La Poésie lyrique et satirique en France au moyen âge* (Paris, 1893), "Rutebeuf," pp. 195–219.

—— *Le Théâtre en France au moyen âge* (Paris, 1896), "Rutebeuf," pp. 73–77.

Clément, S., and A. Guitard, *Vitraux de Bourges; Vitraux du XIIIe siècle de la Cathédrale de Bourges,* Bourges, 1900.

Cohen, Gustave, "Experiences Théophiliennes," *Mercure de France, 273* (February 1937), 453–77.

—— *La Grande Clarté du moyen âge,* New York, 1943.

—— *Histoire de la mise en scène dans le théâtre religieux français du moyen âge,* nouvelle éd. Paris, 1951.

—— *La Poésie en France au moyen âge,* Paris, 1952.

—— *Le Théâtre comique au moyen âge* (Paris, n.d.), pp. 115–120, on *Dit de l'herberie.*

—— *Le Théâtre en France au moyen âge: Le Théâtre religieux* (Paris, 1948), pp. 99–101, on *Dit de l'herberie.*

—— *Le Théâtre en France au moyen âge: Le Théâtre religieux* (Paris, 1948), pp. 30–32, on *Miracle de Théophile.*

Cohn, Norman, *The Pursuit of the Millennium; Revolutionary Messianism in Medieval and Reformation Europe and Its Bearing on Modern Totalitarian Movements,* 2d ed. New York, 1961.

Colby, Alice M., *The Portrait in Twelfth-Century French Litera-*

ture: An Example of the Stylistic Originality of Chrétien de Troyes, Geneva, 1965.

Collingwood, R. G., *The Idea of History*, New York, 1956.

Copleston, Frederick C., *Medieval Philosophy*, New York, 1961.

Coppin, Joseph Léon, *Amour et mariage dans la littérature française du Nord au Moyen-Age*, Paris, 1961.

Cornelius, Roberta D., *The Figurative Castle. A Study in the Medieval Allegory of the Edifice with Especial Reference to Religious Writings*, Bryn Mawr, 1930.

Coulton, C. G., *From St. Francis to Dante: Translations from the Chronicle of the Franciscan Salimbene (1221-1288)*, 2d ed. London, 1907.

Craig, Barbara, "Didactic Elements in Medieval French Serious Drama," *L'Esprit Créateur*. 2, No. 3 (Fall 1962), 142-48.

Creizenach, Wilhelm, *Geschichte des neueren Dramas*. Vol. *1: Mittelalter und Frührenaissance* (Halle, 1911), pp. 140-42, on *Miracle de Théophile*.

Curtius, Ernst Robert, *European Literature and the Latin Middle Ages*, trans. Willard R. Trask, New York, 1953.

—— "Neue Dante-Studien," *Romanische Forschungen, 60* (1947), 237-89. Reprinted in *Gesammelte Aufsätze zur Romanischen Philologie*, Bern and Munich, 1960.

Damon, Phillip W., "Style and Meaning in the Medieval Latin Nature Lyric," *Speculum, 28*, No. 3 (July 1953), 516-20.

Daniel, E. Randolph, "A Re-examination of the Origins of Franciscan Joachitism," *Speculum, 43*, No. 4 (October 1968), 671-76.

Daunou, Pierre Claude, *Discours sur l'état des lettres au XIIIe siècle*, nouvelle éd. Paris, n.d.

De Bruyne, E., *Etudes d'esthétique médiéval*, 3 vols. Bruges, 1946.

Delalande, Jean, *Les Extraordinaires Croisades d'enfants et de pastoureaux au moyen âge*, Paris, 1962.

Delaporte, Yves, and Etienne Houver, *Les Vitraux de la Cathédrale de Chartres*, 3 vols. Chartres, 1926.

Des Granges, C.-M., *De Scenico soliloquio (Gallice: Monologue dramatique) in nostro medii aevi theatro*, Paris, 1897.

Deutsch, Babette, *Poetry Handbook; A Dictionary of Terms*, 2d ed. New York, 1962.

Dobiache-Rojdestvensky, Olga, *La Vie paroissale en France au XIIIe siècle d'après les actes épiscopaux*, Paris, 1911.

Dragonetti, Roger, *La Technique poétique des trouvères dans la chanson courtoise. Contribution à l'étude de la rhétorique médiévale*, Bruges, 1960.
Reviews: Robert Bossuat, *Revue Belge de Philologie et d'Histoire, 41*, No. 2 (1963), 541–43; Paul Zumthor, *Romania, 82*, No. 3 (1961), 418–22.

Du Bellay, Joachim, *La Défense et illustration de la langue française suivi du projet de l'œuvre intitulé "De La Précellence du langage françois" par Henri Estienne*, ed. Louis Humbert, Paris, n.d.

Edwards, W., *A Medieval Scrap-Heap*, London, 1930.

Fabre, Adolphe, *Les Clercs du palais: Recherches historiques sur les Bazoches des parlements & les sociétés dramatiques des Bazoches & des Enfants-sans-Souci*, 12th ed. Lyon, 1875.

Faillon, Etienne Michel, *Monuments inédits sur l'apostolat de Sainte Marie-Madeleine en Provence*, 2 vols. Paris, 1848.

Faligan, Ernest, "Des Formes iconographiques de la légende de Théophile," *Revue des Traditions Populaires, 5*, No. 1 (January 15, 1890), 1–14.

Faral, Edmond, "Les Chansons de toile ou chansons d'histoire," *Romania, 69*, No. 276 (1946–47), 433–62.

—— "Le Conte de *Richeut;* ses rapports avec la tradition latine et quelques traits de son influence," *Bibliothèque de l'Ecole des Hautes Etudes, 230* (1921), 253–70.

—— *Les Jongleurs en France au moyen âge* (Paris, 1910), chap. 8, "Un Type de jongleur: Rutebeuf," pp. 159–66.

—— "La Pastourelle," *Romania, 49* (April 1923), 204–59.

—— *Petite Grammaire de l'ancien français*, Paris, 1941.

—— "Le Procès d'Enguerran IV de Couci," *Revue Historique de Droit Français et Etranger*, 4e série, 26, Nos. 3–4 (1948), 213–58.

—— "Le *Roman de la Rose* et la pensée française au XIIIe siècle," *Revue des Deux Mondes* (September 15, 1926), pp. 430–57.

—— *La Vie quotidienne au temps de saint Louis*, Paris, 1938.

Fauchet, Claude, *Les Œuvres*, Paris, 1610.

—— *Recueil de l'origine de la langue et poesie françoise, ryme et romans. Plus les noms et sommaire des œuvres de cxxvii. poetes François, vivans avant l'an m.ccc.* (Paris, 1581). Bk. II, "Rutebeuf," pp. 160–63. (Bk. I, reedited by Janet G. Espener-Scott, Paris, 1938.)

Fenley, G. Ward, "Faus-Semblant, Fauvel, and Renart le Contrefait: A Study in Kinship," *Romanic Review, 23* (October–December 1932), 323–31.

Ferguson, George, *Signs and Symbols in Christian Art,* New York, 1959.

Foucher, Jean-Pierre, *La Littérature latine du moyen âge,* Paris, 1963.

Foulet, Alfred, "Notes sur la *Vie de saint Louis* de Joinville," *Romania, 58* (October 1932), 551–64.

Foulet, Lucien, *Petite Syntaxe de l'ancien français,* 3d ed., Paris, 1967.

—— *Le Roman de Renard,* Paris, 1914.

   Review: G. Huet, *Moyen Age, 19* (January–June 1915), 87–91.

—— "Villon et la scolastique," *Romania, 65* (1939), 457–477.

Foulon, Charles, *L'Œuvre de Jehan Bodel,* Rennes, 1958.

Fourquin, Guy, "La Population de la région parisienne aux environs de 1328," *Le Moyen Age, 62,* Nos. 1–2 (1956), 63–91.

Fourrier, Anthime, *Le Courant réaliste dans le roman courtois en France au moyen âge.* Vol. 1: *Les Débuts,* Paris, 1960.

   Review: J. Frappier, *Romania, 82,* No. 4 (1961), 536–50.

Frank, Grace, "The Impenitence of François Villon," *Romanic Review, 37,* No. 3 (October 1946), 225–36.

—— *The Medieval French Drama* (Oxford, 1954), chap. 11, *"Le Miracle de Théophile* and *Le Dit de l'herberie,"* pp. 106–13.

Frappier, Jean, *Le Théâtre profane en France au moyen âge, XIIIe et XIVe siècles,* Paris, 1961.

Freymond, Emile, *Jongleurs und Menestrels,* Halle, 1883.

Friedländer, Max J., *Landscape, Portrait, Still-Life: Their Origin and Development,* New York, 1963.

Garapon, Robert, *La Fantasie verbale et le comique dans le théâtre français du moyen âge à la fin du XVIIIe siècle,* Paris, 1957.

Gautier, Léon, *Les Epopées françaises. Etudes sur les origines et l'histoire de la littérature nationale*, 2d ed. 4 vols. Paris, 1878–92.

Gilson, Etienne, *Les Idées et les lettres*, Paris, 1932.

Glorieux, l'abbé Polémon, "Le *Contra Impugnantes* de S. Thomas: Ses sources—son plan," *Mélanges Mandonnet: Etudes d'histoire littéraire et doctrinale du moyen âge, 1* (2 vols. Paris, 1930), 51–81.

—— *Répertoire des maîtres en théologie de Paris au XIIIe siècle*, 2 vols. Paris, 1933.

Godefroy, Frédéric, *Dictionnaire de l'ancien langue française et de tous ses dialectes du IXe au XVe siècle*, 10 vols. Paris, 1937–38.

—— *Lexique de l'ancien française*, Paris, 1901.

Gracián, Baltasar, *Obras completas*, ed. Arturo del Hoyo, Madrid, 1960.

Grandsaignes d'Hauterive, R., *Dictionnaire d'ancien français; moyen âge et renaissance*, Paris, 1947.

Gratien, P., *Histoire de la foundation et de l'évolution des frères mineurs au 13e siècle*, Paris and Gembloux, 1928.

Gross, Charles, "The Political Influence of the University of Paris in the Middle Ages," *American Historical Review, 6*, No. 3 (April 1901), 440–45.

Guesnon, A., "Adam de la Halle et le *Jeu de la feuillée*," *Le Moyen Age*, 2e série, *19* (January–June 1916), 173–233.

—— *Les "Congés" de Baude Fastoul, trouvère artésien*, Paris, 1910. Extract from *Mélanges offerts à M. Maurice Wilmotte*, Brussels, 1910.

Guiette, Robert, *Questions de littérature*, Gand, 1960.
  Review: Daniel Poirion, *Revue Belge de Philologie et d'Histoire, 41*, No. 2 (1963), 537–40.

Gunn, Alan M. F., *The Mirror of Love. A Reinterpretation of "The Romance of the Rose,"* Lubbock, Texas, 1952.

Guy, Henri, *Essai sur la vie et les œuvres du trouvère Adan de le Hale*, Paris, 1898.

—— *Histoire de la poésie française au XVIe siècle*. Vol. *1:* *L'Ecole des rhétoriqueurs*, Paris, 1910.

Hård af Segerstad, Kerstin, *Quelques Commentaires sur la plus ancienne chanson d'états française, "Le Livre des manières" d'Etienne de Fougères*, Uppsala, 1906.

Haessner, Max, *Die Goliardendichtung und die Satire im 13. Jahrhundert in England,* Leipzig, 1905.

Halpern, Louis, "Les Débuts de l'Université de Paris," *Studi Medievali,* Nuova serie, 2, No. 1 (April 1929), 134–39.

Hamann, Richard, and Heinrich Kohlhaussen, *Der Schrein der heiligen Elisabeth zu Marburg,* Marburg, n.d.

Harvey, Howard Graham, *The Theatre of the Basoche. The Contribution of the Law Societies to French Medieval Comedy,* Cambridge, Mass., 1941.

Haskins, Charles H., *The Renaissance of the Twelfth Century,* Cambridge, Mass., 1928

—— *The Rise of the Universities,* New York, 1923.

—— *Studies in Mediaeval Culture,* Oxford, 1929.

d'Haucourt, Geneviève, *La Vie au moyen âge,* Paris, 1952.

Heaton, Herbert, *Economic History of Europe,* rev. ed. New York, 1948.

Henri, Albert, "Introduction stylistique au *Jeu de saint Nicolas,*" *Romania,* 82, No. 1 (1961), 200–39.

Henriot, Emile, *Neuf Siècles de littérature française des origines à nos jours,* Paris, 1958.

Herkless, John, *Francis and Dominic and the Mendicant Orders,* New York, 1901.

Hilka, Alfons, "Altfranzösische Mystik und Beginentum," *Zeitschrift für Romanische Philologie,* 47 (1927), 121–70.

Histoire littéraire de la France (Ouvrage commencé par des religieux bénédictins de la congrégation de Saint-Maur et continué par des membres de l'Institut [Académie Royale des Inscriptions et Belle-Lettres]) (Paris). Vol. 6 (1824); Vol. 19, Louis Petit-Radel, "Guillaume de Saint-Amour," pp. 197–215 (1838); Vol. 22 (1852); Vol. 23 (1856).

Holzknecht, Karl Julius, *Literary Patronage in the Middle Ages,* Philadelphia, 1923.

Hopper, V. H., *Medieval Number Symbolism,* New York, 1938.

Howland, Arthur C., *Ordeals, Compurgation, Excommunication and Interdict,* rev. ed. Philadelphia, 1901.

Hughes, Philip, *The Church in Crisis. A History of the General Councils, 325–1870.* New York, 1961.

Huizinga, Johan, *Homo Ludens: A Study of the Play-Element in Culture,* Boston, 1960.

—— *The Waning of the Middle Ages; A Study of the Forms of Life, Thought and Art in France and the Netherlands in the XIVth and XVth Centuries,* trans. F. Hopman, New York, 1956.

Jauss, Hans Robert, *Genèse de la poésie allégorique française au moyen âge (de 1180 à 1240), (Chapitre échantillon), Probekapitel aus Band 6: Die didaktische, allegorische, und satirische Literatur. Grundriss der romanischen Literaturen des Mittelalters,* Hans Robert Jauss, Erich Köhler, Jean Frappier, Martín de Riquer, and Aurelio Roncaglia, gen. eds. Heidelberg, 1962.

Jeanroy, A., *Bibliographie sommaire des chansonniers français du moyen âge (Manuscrits et éditions),* Paris, 1918.

—— "Etudes sur l'ancienne poésie provençale, I," *Neuphilologische Mitteilungen,* 27, Nos. 5–6 (1926), 129–64.

—— *"Ne garder l'eure,* histoire d'une locution," *Romania,* 44, No. 175–6 (January–October 1916–17), 586–94.

—— *La Poésie lyrique des troubadours,* 2 vols., Toulouse and Paris, 1934.

—— *Origines de la poésie lyrique en France au moyen âge,* 3d ed. Paris, 1925.

Joly, Raymond, "Les Chansons d'histoire," *Romanistisches Jahrbuch,* 12 (1961), 51–66.

Katzenellenbogen, Adolf, *Allegories of the Virtues and Vices in Medieval Art from Early Christian Times to the Thirteenth Century,* trans. Alan J. P. Crick, New York, 1964. (Original ed. London, 1939.)

Ker, W. P., *Epic and Romance. Essays on Medieval Literature.* 2d ed. New York, 1957. (Reprint of 1908 ed.; 1st ed., 1896.)

Kilgour, Raymond Lincoln, *The Decline of Chivalry as Shown in the French Literature of the Late Middle Ages,* Cambridge, Mass., 1937.

Knowles, David, *The Evolution of Medieval Thought,* Baltimore, 1962.

—— *The Monastic Order in England (940–1216),* 2d ed. Cambridge, 1963.

Knox, Winifred E., *The Court of a Saint*, London, 1909.

Koehler, Erich, "Observations historiques et sociologiques sur la poésie des troubadours," *Cahiers de Civilisation Médiévale, 7,* No. 1 (January–March 1964), 27–51.

—— *Trobadorlyrik und höfischer Roman; Aufsätze zur französischen und provenzalischen Literatur des Mittelalters,* Berlin, 1962.

Kohane, Henry and Renée, "L'Enigme du nom de Cligès," *Romania, 82,* No. 1 (1961), 113–21.

Kölbing, Eugen, *Beiträge zur vergleichenden Geschichte der Romantischen Poesie und Prosa des Mittelalters,* Breslau, 1876.

—— "Die jüngere englische fassung der Theophilussage, mit einer einleitung zum ersten male herausgegeben," *Englische Studien, 1* (1877), 16–57.

Kuhn, David, *La Poétique de François Villon*, Paris, 1967.

Långfors, Arthur, "Etienne de Fougères et Gautier de Coinci," *Neuphilologische Mitteilung, 46,* Nos. 5–6 (1945), 113–22.

—— and Paul Meyer, *Les Incipit des poèmes français antérieurs au XVIe siècle,* Paris, 1918.

Lambert, M. D., *Franciscan Poverty. The Doctrine of the Absolute Poverty of Christ and the Apostles in the Franciscan Order, 1210–1323,* London, 1961.

Landry, B., "Les Idées morales du XIIe siècle: Les Ecrivains en latin; satiristes et fabulistes: Gautier Map, Nigel Wireker, Jean de Hauville, Pierre Alphonse Nivaro," *Revue des Cours et Conferences, 40,* No. 13 (June 15 1939), 423–48.

Langlois, Ch.-V., *Le Règne de Philippe III le Hardi,* Paris, 1887.

Langlois, Ernest, "Notes sur le *Jeu de la feuillée* d'Adam de Bossu," *Romania, 32* (1903), 384–93.

—— *Origines et sources du "Roman de la Rose,"* Paris, 1890.

—— *Table des noms propres de toute nature compris dans les chansons de geste imprimées,* Paris, 1904.

Lecoy, F., "Notes de lexicographie française," *Romania, 70,* No. 3 (1948–49), 332–54.

Lecoy de la Marche, A., *La Chaire française au moyen âge spécialement au XIIIe siècle d'après les manuscrits contemporains,* Paris, 1886.

—— *Les Manuscrits et la miniature,* Paris, 1884.

Lecoy de la Marche, A., "La Prédication de la croisade au treizième siècle," *Revue des Questions Historiques, 48* (July 1, 1890), 5–28.

—— *Le Treizième Siècle littéraire et scientifique,* Bruges, 1894.

Le Gentil, Pierre, *La Littérature française du moyen âge,* Paris, 1963.

Lehmann, P., *Die Parodie im Mittelalter,* Stuttgart, 1963.

Le Nain de Tillemont, Louis Sebastian, *Vie de saint Louis,* ed. J. de Gaulle, 6 vols. Paris, 1851.

Lenient, C. *Le Satire en France au moyen âge* (3e éd. Paris, 1883), "Ruteboeuf," pp. 52–66.

Lewis, C. S., *The Allegory of Love; A Study in Medieval Tradition,* New York, 1958. (Reprint of 1936 ed.)

—— *The Discarded Image; An Introduction to Medieval and Renaissance Literature,* Cambridge (England), 1967.

—— *Studies in Medieval and Renaissance Literature,* ed. Walter Hooper, Cambridge (England), 1966.

Lintilhac, Eugène, *Histoire générale du théâtre en France.* Vol. 1: *Le Théâtre sérieux du moyen âge* (Paris, [1904]), pp. 174–84, on *Miracle de Théophile.*

Lote, Georges, *Histoire du vers francais,* 3 vols., Paris, 1949–55.

Lottin, Odon, *Psychologie et morale au XIIe et XIIIe siècles.* Vol. 6: *Problèmes d'histoire littéraire,* Gembloux, 1960.

Löwith, Karl, *Meaning in History,* Chicago, 1949.

Lundgren, Hjalmar, *Studier öfver Theophiluslegendes Romanska Varianter,* Uppsala, 1913.

Mâle, Emile, *L'Art religieux du XIIe siècle en France,* 3d ed., Paris, 1928.

—— "Les Chapiteaux romans du musée de Toulouse et l'école toulousaine du XIIe siècle," *Revue Archéologique,* 3e série, *20* (July–December 1892), 28–35.

—— *The Gothic Image. Religious Art in France of the Thirteenth Century,* trans. Dora Nussey (from the 3d French ed., originally published 1913), New York, 1958.

Mandonnet, Pierre, "De L'Incorporation des Dominicains dans l'ancienne Université de Paris, 1229–1231," *Revue Thomiste, 4,* No. 2 (May 1896), 133–70.

—— *Siger de Brabant et l'averroïsme latin au XIIIe siècle: Etude critique et documents inédits,* Fribourg, 1899.

Mayer, Gilbert, *Lexique des œuvres d'Adam de la Halle,* Paris, 1940.

McDonnell, Ernest W., *The Beguines and Beghards in Medieval Culture with Special Emphasis on the Belgian Scene* (New Brunswick, N.J., 1954), "The Protest of Rutebeuf," pp. 465–73.

McKeon, Peter R., "The Status of the University of Paris as *Parens Scientiarum:* An Episode in the Development of Its Autonomy," *Speculum, 39,* No. 4 (October 1964), 651–75.

McLaughlin, Mary, "Abelard as Autobiographer: The Motives and Meaning of his 'Story of Calamities,'" *Speculum, 42,* No. 3 (July 1967), 463–88.

Menéndez Pidal, R., *Poesía juglaresca y orígenes de las literaturas románicas. Problema de historia literaria y cultural,* 6th ed. Madrid, 1957.

    Review: Félix Lecoy, *Romania, 80,* No. 3 (1959), 419–23.

Meyer, Paul, "Le Couplet de deux vers," *Romania, 23* (1894), 1–35.

—— "Les Manuscrits des sermons français de Maurice de Sully," *Romania, 23* (1894), 177–91

—— "Manuscrits français de Cambridge," *Romania, 15* (1886), 236–57.

—— "Manuscrits médicaux en français," *Romania, 44* (1915–17), 160–214.

—— "Notice du MS. 10925–304 de la Bibliothèque Royale de Belgique," *Romania, 30* (1901), 295–316.

—— "Notice et extraits du MS. 8336 de la Bibliothèque de Sir Thomas Philipps à Cheltenham," *Romania, 13* (1884), 511–12.

—— "Périodiques," *Romania, 9* (1880), 154–70.

Micha, A., "Raoul de Houdenc, est-il l'auteur du *Songe de Paradis* et de la *Vengeance Raguidel?*" *Romania, 68,* No. 3 (1944–45), 316–60.

Michelet, Jules, *Histoire de France, 2,* 17 vols., Paris, 1833.

Sister Miriam Joseph, C.S.C., *Shakespeare's Use of the Arts of Language,* New York, 1947.

Misch, Georg, *History of Autobiography of Antiquity,* trans. E. W. Dickes, 2 vols., Cambridge (Mass.), 1951.

—— *Geschichte der Autobiographie; Das Mittelalter,* 2 vols., Frankfurt, 1955–59.

Moll, Ruth, *The Three Estates in Medieval and Renaissance Literature*, New York, 1933.

Moorman, John R. H., *The Sources for the Life of S. Francis of Assisi*, Manchester, 1940.

Munro, Dana Carleton, ed., *Selections from the Laws of Charles the Great*, Philadelphia, 1900.

Murray, H. J. R. *A History of Chess*, Oxford, 1913.

Naetebus, Gotthold, *Die nicht-lyrischen Strophenformen des Altfranzösischen*, Leipzig, 1891.

Neff, Théodore Lee, *La Satire des femmes dans la poésie lyrique française du moyen âge*, Paris, 1900.

Nichols, Stephen G., Jr., "Discourse in Froissart's *Chroniques*," *Speculum, 39*, No. 2 (April 1964), 279–87.

Noomen, Willen, "Passages narratifs dans les drames médiévaux français: Essai d'interprétation," *Revue Belge de Philologie et d'Histoire, 36*, No. 3 (1958), 761–85.

Nykrog, Per, *Les Fabliaux: Etude d'histoire littéraire et de stylistique médiévale*, Copenhagen, 1957.

   Review: Jean Rychner, *Romance Philology, 12*, No. 3 (February 1959), 336–39.

Oldenbourg, Zoé, *Les Croisades*, Paris, 1965.

Ong, Walter J., "Wit and Mystery: A Revaluation in Medieval Latin Hymnody," *Speculum, 22*, No. 3 (July 1947), 310–41.

Opie, Iona and Peter, *The Oxford Dictionary of Nursery Rhymes*, Oxford, 1951.

Owst, G. R., *Literature and Pulpit in Medieval England*, Cambridge, 1933.

Paetow, Louis John, "The Arts Course at Medieval Universities with Special Reference to Grammar and Rhetoric," *The University Studies, 3*, No. 7 (University of Illinois, January 1910).

Palfrey, Thomas R., Joseph G. Fucilla, and William C. Holbrook, *A Bibliographical Guide to the Romance Languages and Literatures*, 3d ed. Evanston, Ill., 1947.

Panofsky, Erwin, *Gothic Architecture and Scholasticism*, New York, 1951.

Pasquier, Estienne, *Les Recherches de la France*, Paris, 1617.

Patch, Howard R., "Characters in Medieval Literature," *Modern Language Notes, 40*, No. 1 (January 1925), 1–14.

—— *The Goddess Fortuna in Medieval Literature,* Cambridge, Mass., 1927.

Pauphilet, Albert, *Le Moyen Age,* Paris, 1937.

Payen, Jean-Charles, *Le Motif du repentir dans la littérature française médiévale (des origines à 1230),* Geneva and Paris, 1968.

Pernoud, Régine, *Histoire de la bourgeoisie en France; des origines aux temps modernes,* Paris, 1960.

Perrod, Maurice, "Etude sur la vie et sur les œuvres de Guillaume de Saint-Amour, Docteur en théologie de l'Université de Paris, Chanoine de Beauvais et de Mâcon (1202–1272)," *Mémoires de la Société d'Emulation du Jura,* 7e série, 2 (Lons-le-Saunier, 1902), 61–252.

Petersen Dyggve, Holger, "Personnages historiques figurant dans la poésie lyrique française des XIIe et XIIIe siècles," *Neuphilologische Mitteilungen, 30* (1929), 177–214; *31* (1930), 1–62, 84–90; *36* (1935), 1–29, 65–91; *37* (1936), 257–83; *39* (1938), 386 ff.; *41* (1940), 12–29, 46–60, 118 ff.; *42* (1941), 155–83; *43* (1942), 7 ff., 62–100, 121–41; *44* (1943), 55–97, 194 ff.; *45* (1944), 11–35, 61–91, 111–27, 161–85; *46* (1945), 21–55, 77–93, 123–53; *55* (1949), 144–74.

Petit de Julleville, L., gen. ed., *Histoire de la langue et de la littérature française des origines à 1900.* Vol 2: *Des Origines à 1500,* Paris, 1909.

Pfander, Homer G., *The Popular Sermon of the Medieval Friar in England,* New York, 1937.

Picot, Emile, "Le Monologue dramatique dans *l'ancien théatre français,*" *Romania, 15* (1886), 358–422; *16* (1887), 438–542; *17* (1888), 207–75. *Dit de l'herberie* in *16* (1887), 492–95.

Pirenne, Henri, *Histoire économique et sociale du moyen âge,* Rev. ed., Paris, 1963.

    Reviews: Alfred Foulet, *Romanic Review, 59,* No. 2 (April 1968), 123–26; Pierre Le Gentil, *Romania, 87,* No. 352 (1968), 548–57.

—— "L'Instruction des marchands au moyen âge," *Annales d'histoire économique et sociale, 1,* No. 1 (January 15, 1929), 13–28.

Pirenne, Henri, *Medieval Cities,* trans. Frank D. Halsey, Garden City, N.Y., n.d. (1st ed. Princeton, 1925.)

Plenzat, Karl, *Die Theophiluslegende in den Dichtungen des Mittelalters,* Berlin, 1926.

Poëte, Marcel, *Une Vie de cité: Paris,* 3 vols. Paris, 1924.

Poirion, Daniel, *Le Poète et le prince; L'Evolution du lyrisme courtois de Guillaume de Machaut à Charles d'Orléans,* Paris, 1965.

Pope, M. K., *From Latin to Modern French with Especial Consideration of Anglo-Norman Phonology and Morphology,* rev. ed. Manchester, 1952.

Porter, Lambert C., *La Fatrasie et le fatras. Essai sur la poésie irrationnelle en France au moyen âge,* Geneva and Paris, 1960.

—— "Brunetto Latini et les Moralistes," *L'Esprit Créateur, 2,* No. 3 (Fall, 1962), 119–25.

Powicke, F. M., and C. R. Cheney, *Councils and Synods with other Documents Relating to the English Church, 2,* 2 vols. Oxford, 1964.

Raby, F. J. E., *A History of Christian-Latin Poetry from the Beginnings to the Close of the Middle Ages,* 2d ed. Oxford, 1953.

——*A History of Secular Latin Poetry in the Middle Ages* 2d ed. 2 vols. Oxford, 1957.

Ramé, Alfred, "Explication du bas relief de Souillac, La Légende de Théophile," *Gazette Archéologique, 10* (1885), 225–32.

Rashdall, Hastings, *The Universities of Europe in the Middle Ages,* 3 vols. Oxford, 1895.

Raymond, Gaston, *Bibliographie des chansonniers français des XIIIe et XIVe siècles,* 2 vols. Paris, 1884.

Raymond, Marcel, *Le Jeu retrouvé,* Montreal, 1943.

Remy, Paul, "La Lèpre; thème littéraire au moyen âge: Commentaire d'un passage du roman provençal de *Jaufré,*" *Le Moyen Age, 52* (1946), 195–242.

Rice, Winthrop Huntington, *The European Ancestry of Villon's Satirical Testaments,* New York, 1941.

Roquefort-Flaméricourt, Jean Baptiste Bonaventure de, *De L'Etat de la poésie françoise dans les XIIe et XIIIe siècles,* Paris, 1815.

Roques, Maria, "La Vielle sous le banc: Mélanges," *Romania, 58* (1932), 83–85.

—— Review of *La Comtesse d'Anjou*, ed. Bruno Schumacher and Ewald Zubke, in *Romania*, 52 (1926), 196–99.

Roussel, Henri, "Notes sur la littérature arrageoise du XIIIe siècle," *Revue des Sciences Humaines*, Nouvelle série, Fasc. 87 (July–September 1957), 249–86. [Review of Marie Ungureanu, *La Bourgeoisie naissante: Société et littérature bourgeoises d'Arras au XIIe et XIIIe siècle* (Arras, 1955).]

Runciman, Steven, *A History of the Crusades*, 3 vols. Cambridge, Eng., 1951–54.

—— *The Sicilian Vespers. A History of the Mediterranean World in the Later Thirteenth Century*, Baltimore, 1960.

Rychner, Jean, *Contribution à l'étude des fabliaux: Variantes, remaniements, dégradations*, 2 vols. Neuchâtel, 1960.

Sapegno, Natalino, *Disegno storico della letteratura italiana ad uso delle scuole medie superiori*, Florence, 1948.

Saulnier, Verdun L. *La Littérature française du moyen âge*, Paris, 1943.

Sayous, Ed., *La France de saint Louis d'après la poésie nationale*, Paris, 1866. Cites Rutebeuf extensively.

Scheler, Max, *Ressentiment*, ed. Lewis A. Coser, trans. William W. Holdheim, New York, 1961.

Schrade, Leo, "Political Compositions in French Music," *Annales Musicologiques: Moyen Age et Renaissance, 1* (Paris, 1953), 9–63.

Scudder, Vida Dutton, *The Franciscan Adventure: A Study in the First Hundred Years of the Order of St. Francis of Assisi*, London and New York, 1931.

Seesholtz, Anna, *Saint Elizabeth*, New York, 1948.

Semrau, Franz, *Würfel und Würfelspiel im alten Frankereich*, Halle, 1910.

Sepet, Marius, *Le Drame religieux au moyen âge*, 4th ed. Paris, 1908.

Siciliano, Italo, *François Villon et les thèmes poétiques du moyen âge*, Paris, 1934.

—— "Sur le *Testament* de François Villon," *Romania*, 65 (January 1939), 39–90.

Silverstein, Theodore, "Allegory and Literary Form," *PMLA*, 82, No. 1 (March 1967), 28–32.

Spencer, Theodore, "Chaucer's Hell: A Study in Mediæval Convention," *Speculum*, 2 (1927), 177–200.

Spitzer, Leo, "Etude ahistorique d'un texte: *Ballade des dames du temps jadis*," *Modern Language Quarterly, 1*, No. 1 (March, 1940), 7–22.

—— "Joinville Etymologiste (*preu home-preudome*)," *Modern Language Notes, 62*, No. 8 (December 1947), 505–14.

—— *Linguistica e historia literaria*, Madrid, 1955.

—— "Note on the Poetic and the Empirical 'I' in Medieval Authors," *Traditio, 4* (1946), 415–22.

—— "Two Dante Notes: I. An Autobiographical Incident in *Inferno* XIX; II. *Libicocco*," *Romanic Review, 34*, No. 3 (October 1943), 248–62.

Strohm, Paul, "Guillaume as Narrator and Lover in the *Roman de la Rose*," *Romanic Review, 59*, No. 1 (February 1968), 3–9.

Sutherland, D. R., "Fact and Fiction in the *Jeu de la feuillée*," *Romance Philology, 13*, No. 4 (May 1960), 419–28. [Review of Alfred Adler, *Sens et composition du "Jeu de la feuillée*," Ann Arbor, Michigan, 1956.]

Taylor, Henry Osborn, *The Mediæval Mind*, 2 vols. Cambridge, Mass., 1949.

Thouzellier, Christine, "La Place du *De periculis* de Guillaume de St. Amour dans les polémiques universitaires du XIIIe siècle," *Revue Historique, 156*, No. 310 (September–October 1927), 69–83.

Throop, Palmer A., "Criticism of Papal Crusade Policy in Old French and Provençal," *Speculum, 13*, No. 4 (October 1938), 379–412. [Preliminary version of chap. 2 of his *Criticism of the Crusades*.]

—— *Criticism of the Crusade. A Study of Public Opinion and Crusade Propaganda*, Amsterdam, 1940.

   Review: John R. La Monte, *Speculum, 16*, No. 2 (April 1941), 262–65.

Tillyard, Eustice M. W., and C. S. Lewis, *The Personal Heresy: A Controversy*, London, New York, Toronto, 1939.

Tobler, Adolf, "Exegetisches. 'Plus a paroles au plain pot/De vin qu'an un mui de cervoise,'" *Zeitschrift für Romanische Philologie, 4* (1880), 80–85.

—— *Vermischte Beiträge zur französischen Grammatik,* 5 vols. Leipzig, 1906.

—— and Erhard Lommatzsch, *Altfranzösisches Wörterbuch,* 7 vols. Berlin, 1925–69.

Vercanteren, F., "Les Médecins du VIIIe au XIIIe siècle," *Le Moyen Age,* 57, Nos. 1–2 (1951), 61–92.

Verrier, Jean, *La Cathédrale de Bourges et ses vitraux,* Paris, 1942.

Verrier, P. *Le Vers français, formes primitives, développement, diffusion,* Paris, 1931–32.

Vinaver, Eugene, "A la recherche d'une poétique médievale," *Cahiers de Civilisation Médievale,* 2, No. 1 (January–March 1959), 1–16.

Waddell, Helen, *The Wandering Scholars; The Life and Art of the Lyric Poets of the Latin Middle Ages,* New York, 1961.

Weinberg, Julius R., *A Short History of Medieval Philosophy,* Princeton, 1964.

Welter, J.-Th., *L'Exemplum dans la littérature religieuse et didactique du moyen âge,* Paris and Toulouse, 1927.

Wentzlaff-Eggebert, F. W., *Kreuzzugsdichtung des Mittelalters. Studien zu ihrer geschichtlichen u. dichterischen Wirklichkeit,* Berlin, 1960.

   Review: G. Muraille, *Les Lettres Romanes,* 16, No. 4 (1962), 368–72.

Weston, Jessie L., *From Ritual to Romance,* New York, 1957.

Williams, Arnold, "Chaucer and the Friars," *Speculum, 28,* No. 3 (July 1953), 499–513.

Wood, Mary Morton, *The Spirit of Protest in Old French Literature* (New York, 1917), chap. 3, "The Defense of Guillaume de Saint Amour [Rutebeuf and Jean de Meun]," pp. 115–33.

Wyngaert, P. Anastase Van den, "Querelles du clergé séculier et des Ordres Mendiants à l'Université de Paris au XIIIe siècle," *La France Franciscaine,* 5 (1922), 257–81, 369–97; 6 (1923), 47–70.

Yedlicka, Leo Charles, *Expressions of the Linguistic Area of Repentance and Remorse in Old French,* Washington, D.C., 1945.

Young, Karl, *The Drama of the Medieval Church,* 2 vols. Oxford, 1933.

Yunck, John Adam, *The Lineage of Lady Meed. The Develop-

ment of Mediæval Venality Satire, Notre Dame, Ind., 1963.

—— *Nummus, Munera, and Lady Mede: The Development of a Medieval Satirical Theme,* New York, 1956.

Zumthor, Paul, *Histoire littéraire de la France médiévale (Xe–XIVe siècles),* Paris, 1954.

—— *Langue et techniques poétiques à l'époque romane (XIe–XIIIe siècles),* Paris, 1963.

—— "Recherches sur les topiques dans la poésie lyrique des XIIe et XIIIe siècles," *Cahiers de Civilization Médievale,* 2, No. 4 (October–December 1959), 409-27.

INDEX

(Extended discussions are indicated by italicized page numbers.)